Maya® Studio Projects

Maya® Studio Projects

TEXTURING AND LIGHTING

LEE LANIER

Wiley Publishing, Inc.

Acquisitions Editor: Mariann Barsolo
Development Editor: Kim Wimpsett
Technical Editor: Campbell Strong
Production Editor: Liz Britten
Copy Editor: Sharon Wilkey
Editorial Manager: Pete Gaughan
Production Manager: Tim Tate
Vice President and Executive Group Publisher: Richard Swadley
Vice President and Publisher: Neil Edde
Media Assistant Project Manager: Jenny Swisher
Media Associate Producer: Josh Frank
Media Quality Assurance: Shawn Patrick
Book Designer: Caryl Gorska, Maureen Forys, Happenstance Type-O-Rama
Compositor: JAmes D. Kramer, Happenstance Type-O-Rama
Proofreader: WordOne, New York
Indexer: Ted Laux
Project Coordinator, Cover: Katie Crocker
Cover Designer: Ryan Sneed
Cover Image: Lee Lanier

Published simultaneously in Canada

ISBN: 978-0-470-90327-8

For general information on our other products and services or to obtain technical support, please contact our Customer Care Department within the U.S. at (877) 762-2974, outside the U.S. at (317) 572-3993 or fax (317) 572-4002.

Wiley also publishes its books in a variety of electronic formats. Some content that appears in print may not be available in electronic books.

Library of Congress Cataloging-in-Publication Data

Lanier, Lee, 1966-

Maya studio projects. Texturing and lighting / Lee Lanier.

p. cm.

ISBN: 978-0-470-90327-8 (pbk.)

ISBN: 978-1-118-09148-7 (ebk)

ISBN: 978-1-118-09147-0 (ebk)

ISBN: 978-1-118-09146-3 (ebk)

1. Computer animation. 2. Maya (Computer file) 3. Texture (Art) 4. Three-dimensional display systems. I. Title.

TR897.7.L374 2011

006.6'96--dc22

2011008891

10 9 8 7 6 5 4 3 2 1

Dear Reader,

Thank you for choosing *Maya Studio Projects: Texturing and Lighting*. This book is part of a family of premium-quality Sybex books, all of which are written by outstanding authors who combine practical experience with a gift for teaching.

Sybex was founded in 1976. More than 30 years later, we're still committed to producing consistently exceptional books. With each of our titles, we're working hard to set a new standard for the industry. From the paper we print on, to the authors we work with, our goal is to bring you the best books available.

I hope you see all that reflected in these pages. I'd be very interested to hear your comments and get your feedback on how we're doing. Feel free to let me know what you think about this or any other Sybex book by sending me an email at `nedde@wiley.com`. If you think you've found a technical error in this book, please visit `http://sybex.custhelp.com`. Customer feedback is critical to our efforts at Sybex.

Best regards,

Neil Edde
Vice President and Publisher
Sybex, an Imprint of Wiley

Acknowledgments

Special thanks to all the enthusiastic animators who've purchased my books over the years, the fine editorial and production staff at John Wiley & Sons, and my lovely wife, Anita, who knows the value of always learning something new.

About the Author

Lee Lanier is a 3D animator, digital compositor, and director. His films have played in more than 200 museums, galleries, and film festivals worldwide. Before directing the shorts *Millennium Bug*, *Mirror*, *Day Off the Dead*, *Weapons of Mass Destruction*, *13 Ways to Die at Home*, and *Blood Roulette*, he served as a senior animator in the lighting and modeling departments at PDI/DreamWorks on *Antz* and *Shrek*. He created digital visual effects for such films as *Mortal Kombat* while at Buena Vista Visual Effects at Walt Disney Studios. He is the author of *Professional Digital Compositing*, *Advanced Maya Texturing and Lighting*, and *Maya Professional Tips and Techniques*, all from Sybex. You can view his work at `BeezleBugBit.com`.

CONTENTS AT A GLANCE

Contents

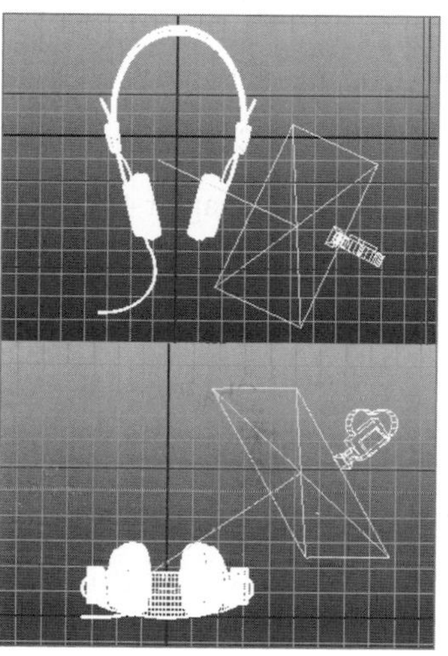

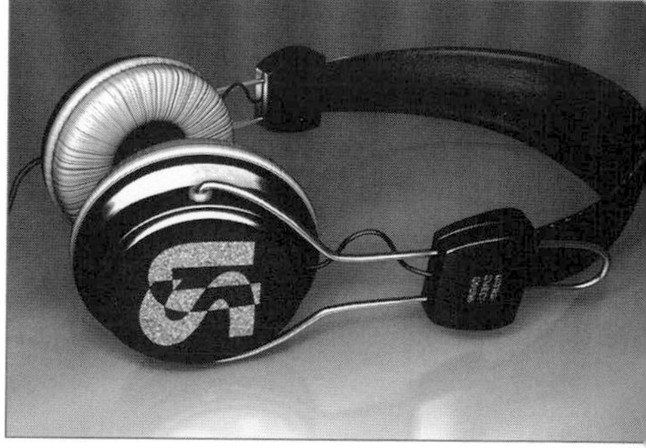

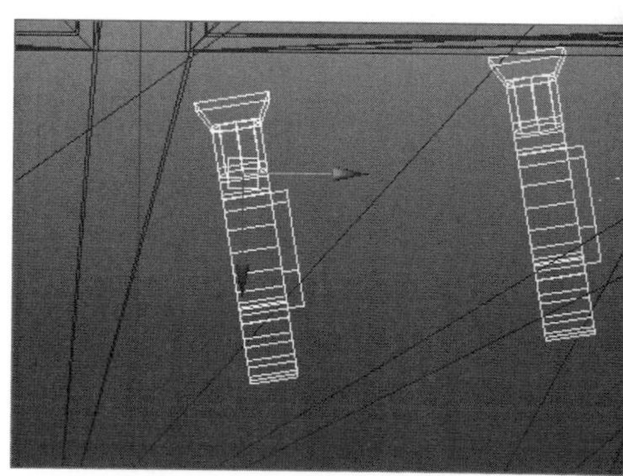

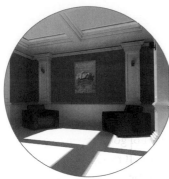

Introduction

"Half of good lighting is good texturing, and half of good texturing is good lighting" is my favorite sage advice to new animators. It's difficult to separate the two areas of computer animation. Texturing—the re-creation of specific surface qualities through the application of shaders, procedural textures, and bitmap textures—is dependent on an understanding of light and how it interacts with various real-world materials. Lighting, the act of placing and adjusting virtual lights in a 3D environment, becomes a difficult and possibly pointless exercise if no appropriately textured surfaces exist. Conversely, even a beautiful texturing job can be ruined by poor lighting.

Although large animation studios separate the texturing and lighting into two distinct departments, it pays to have a firm understanding of both areas. Hence, this book covers the most important texturing and lighting techniques available in Maya. Whereas other books (some of which I have written) concentrate heavily on theory, this one presents the material through four step-by-step tutorials.

Who Should Buy This Book

Maya Studio Projects: Texturing and Lighting is written for beginning- to intermediate-level Maya users who want to refine their lighting and texturing skills. Although the projects in this book require a basic knowledge of the Maya user interface, it's possible to light and texture successfully with little prior experience.

How This Book Is Structured

Maya Studio Projects: Texturing and Lighting contains four step-by-step tutorial projects. Each project is split into two chapters:

Chapters 1 and 2: Texturing and Lighting a Product

Chapters 3 and 4: Texturing and Lighting a Character

Chapters 5 and 6: Texturing and Lighting a Vehicle

Chapters 7 and 8: Texturing and Lighting an Environment

The first half of each project guides you through critical steps necessary for an initial high-quality render. The second half of each project builds upon the first half by applying advanced tools and techniques. Note that the complexity and difficulty of the projects increase with each chapter; thus, I recommend you follow the existing chapter order.

A Note on Rendering and UV Manipulation

Rendering is a critical part of lighting. As such, rendering is appropriately covered throughout this book. For example, information concerning render setting attributes, render layer management, and batch rendering is included. In the professional arena, rendering is generally the responsibility of the lighter.

On the other hand, UV mapping and manipulation is covered in a limited manner. Texturing and lighting departments usually receive models with a finished UV texture space. That is, the modelers are responsible for UV map creation and fine-tuning. Hence, the source files provided for the projects in this book contain geometry with ready-to-texture UV texture spaces.

Maya and Photoshop Versions

The projects and supporting examples in *Maya Studio Projects: Texturing and Lighting* were created with Maya 2011 and tested with Maya 2012 on a Windows-based PC. All the scene files included on the accompanying DVD are saved as `.ma` files and can be opened with pre-2011 versions of Maya (choose File → Open Scene → ❒ and select the Ignore Version check box). Differences in workflow between recent versions of the software are noted in the text.

Because texturing is an integral part of this book, it will be necessary to use a digital paint or image manipulation program to prepare bitmap textures. Step-by-step instructions for the use of Adobe Photoshop CS4 are included. Other image manipulation programs, such as GIMP or Corel Painter, can be used with equal success; however, the tool and menu names will vary.

Hardware Requirements

Thanks to the rapid advancement of technology, most mid-priced PCs will run Maya and Photoshop with few problems (at least where the book's tutorial projects are concerned). That said, it's recommended that you use a Maya-certified graphics card to avoid interface and view panel drawing errors. For a list of recommended cards, visit `www.autodesk.com/maya`. This book, for example, was written on a laptop running Vista 64-bit with 4 GB of RAM, a 2.2 GHz dual-core processor, and an NVIDIA-based graphics card.

The Companion DVD

You will find all the files for completing the tutorials and understanding concepts in this book in the ProjectFiles directory on the companion DVD. In addition, color versions of the chapter figures are located in the ColorFigures folder.

The project files are located in the following directory structure:

ProjectFiles\Project*n*\: Maya scene files

ProjectFiles\Project*n*\Textures\: Bitmap textures

ProjectFiles\Project*n*\Reference\: Maya scene files and bitmap textures that serve as reference but are not mandatory for the success of each tutorial

When opening sample Maya scene files, you can avoid missing bitmap textures by first choosing File → Project → Set and browsing for the ProjectFiles/Project*n* folder, where *n* is the project number. Follow this step whether the folder remains at its original location on the DVD or is located on a drive after the DVD contents have been copied. You can also reload missing bitmap textures through the Hypershade window; techniques for accomplishing this are discussed in Chapter 1.

Naming Conventions

The projects in *Maya Studio Projects: Texturing and Lighting* use common conventions for three-button mouse operation. Here are a few examples:

LMB: Click the left mouse button.

MMB+drag: Hold the middle mouse button while dragging.

RMB+click: Click right mouse button and release.

Shift+click: Press the Shift key and the left mouse button to make multiple selections.

When referring to different areas and functions of Maya, I have used the terminology employed by the software's own help files. Whenever there is a deviation in terminology (usually for the sake of clarity), I've included a note to explain the change.

How to Contact the Author

Feel free to contact me at light@BeezleBugBit.com. If you're a fan of short films, visit www.DamShortFilm.org. For errata and other information concerning this book, go to www.sybex.com/go/msptexturelight.

Texturing and Lighting a Product, Part 1

In this chapter and Chapter 2, "Texturing and Lighting a Product, Part 2," you will texture and light a pair of headphones. This chapter, which contains part 1 of the project, will guide you through the following steps:

- **Reviewing the scene file**
- **Assigning materials**
- **Creating lights and shadows**
- **Applying textures**
- **Raytracing reflections**

In addition, important lighting and texturing theory is included as follows:

- **Material types and critical attributes**
- **Hypershade functionality**
- **Lighting techniques and Maya light types**
- **Procedural textures**
- **Scanline and raytraced rendering**

Although many tutorials would treat a pair of headphones as a traditional still life, this project approaches the scene as if selling a product. In the realm of business, a *product* is a good or service that fulfills the need of a particular market. A product is often a physical object a seller offers a potential buyer. Hence, the goal of texturing and lighting a product is to present it aesthetically so that a buyer might desire it. This requires a unique approach to texturing and lighting.

Project: Reviewing the Scene File

Before starting the texturing process, review the scene file and its contents. Open the `headphones-start.ma` scene file from the `ProjectFiles/Project1` folder on the DVD. The scene hierarchy, surface UV texture space, camera setup, and unique light box geometry should all be examined before proceeding further.

Checking the Hierarchy and UVs

The headphones model is constructed from 16 polygon surfaces. The surface nodes are grouped together as a single hierarchy (see Figure 1.1). You can view the hierarchy through the Hypergraph (Window → Hypergraph: Hierarchy) or the Outliner (Window → Outliner). You can select group or surface nodes through the Hypergraph and the Outliner. Technically speaking, a *node* is a construct that holds specific information and any actions associated with that information. In Maya, a node may be a surface, a light, a camera, a material, and so on.

All the polygon surfaces carry a completed UV texture space. That is, each surface's UV points are arranged in such a fashion that the texturing may begin immediately. The UV points are laid out as a single shell or as multiple shells surrounded by empty UV texture space (see Figure 1.2). You can examine the UV texture space of a surface by selecting the surface and choosing Window → UV Texture Editor. Approaches for examining and utilizing the UV points and shells are discussed in the section "Creating Custom Bitmaps" later in this chapter. Technically speaking, *UV texture space* refers to a coordinate system that relates pixels of a texture map to positions on a surface. UV points represent the location of a polygon's vertices within a UV texture space.

If polygon faces overlap within the UV texture space, they share the same section of an assigned texture. Hence, the majority of surfaces in the headphones scene possess a UV layout that avoids overlapping faces. The few faces that are allowed to overlap are for small, unseen parts of the model. For an example of such overlapping, see the section "Creating Custom Bitmaps" later in this chapter.

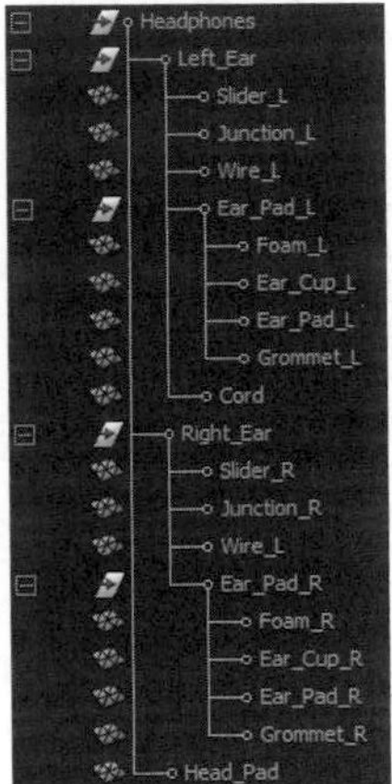

Figure 1.1

(Left) Hypergraph view of the headphones hierarchy. (Right) Outliner view of the same hierarchy. Group nodes are indicated by the white trapezoid symbols.

Working with Multiple Cameras

The headphones scene file contains two perspective cameras: persp and Render. By default, the persp camera is included in every Maya scene file. You can use the persp camera to examine different parts of the model. The Render camera, on the other hand, is positioned and animated for the final render and should not be moved. To switch between persp and Render in any view panel, choose Panels → Perspective → *camera name* from the view panel menu.

Note that the Render camera has the Resolution Gate option activated. The Resolution Gate appears in the view panel workspace as a green box with a grayed-out outer area (see

Figure 1.3). The box indicates the outer edge of the render; surfaces outside the box will not render. To toggle the Resolution Gate on or off for any camera, choose View → Camera Settings → Resolution Gate from the view panel menu.

To manipulate the persp camera, select the persp node in the Hypergraph or Outliner and use the standard transform tools. You can also interactively move the camera with the Alt key and mouse buttons in a perspective view panel.

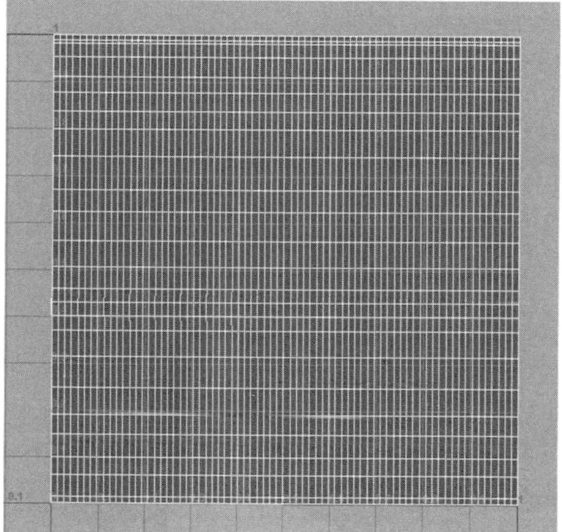

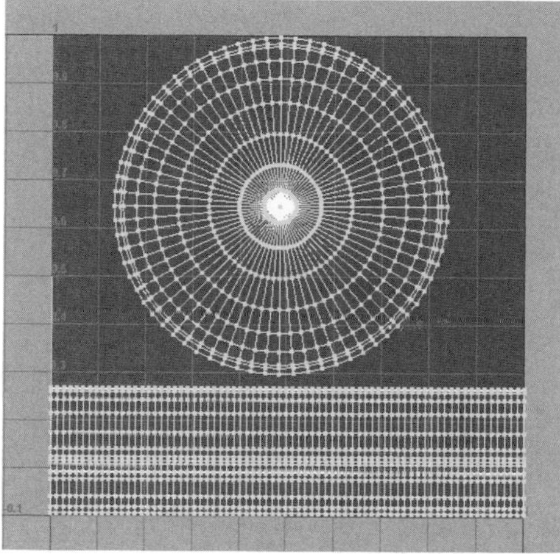

Figure 1.2

(Left) The UV Texture Editor view of the Ear_Pad_R surface. A single UV shell occupies the entire UV texture space. The dark gray area represents the 0-to-1 UV range, whereby a texture is tiled one time. (Right) The UV Texture Editor view of the Ear_Cup_R surface. Two UV shells fill a portion of the UV texture space. In this case, UV points are selected and appear as green dots in Maya.

The render resolution of the scene file is set to 640×360, which is one-half the size of HD 720 (1280×720). This is suitable for test renders. We will raise the resolution to 1280×720 toward the end of this chapter. In addition, the anti-aliasing render quality will be switched from low quality to high quality.

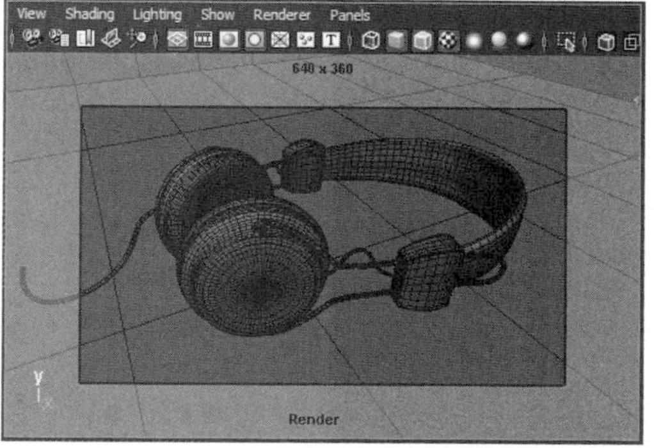

Figure 1.3

Render camera view. Grayed-out areas outside the box of the Resolution Gate do not render.

Examining the Light_Box Geometry

The headphones are surrounded by a large cube named *Light_Box*. Real-world *light boxes* (or light tents) are small structures covered with fabric or other translucent material that diffuses incoming light (see Figure 1.4). Because the diffused light arrives from a multitude of directions, the subject is evenly lit and does not produce harsh shadows. As such, product photographers and videographers often employ light boxes. As an added bonus, light boxes allow for the creation of a "seamless background," in which there is no obvious horizon line.

In this chapter, you'll use the Light_Box cube to create large specular highlights and reflections in the plastic and metal of the headphones. In Chapter 2, you'll have the chance to illuminate the scene by using the Light_Box cube's material attributes and the Final Gathering rendering option.

Figure 1.4
(Top) The Light_Box cube. (Bottom) A real-world light box

Material Types and Critical Attributes

Materials, sometimes referred to as *shaders*, are small programs that determine the surface qualities of the geometry they are assigned to. In common terms, surfaces are described as rough, smooth, shiny, dull, and so on. A material uses a shading model, which is a mathematical algorithm that simulates the interaction of light with a surface.

Working with Lambert, Blinn, Phong, Phong E, and Anisotropic Materials

The Lambert material is considered a "parent" material in Maya. That is, four other Maya materials (Blinn, Phong, Phong E, and Anisotropic) inherit common attributes from the corresponding Lambert node (see Figure 1.5).

The shared attributes include the following:

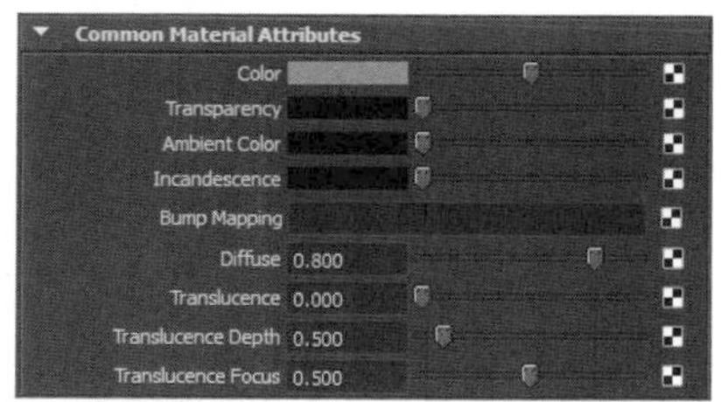

Figure 1.5

Attributes shared by Lambert, Blinn, Phong, Phong E, and Anisotropic materials

Color Color determines its namesake. You can enter specific red, green, and blue values by clicking the color swatch and updating the Color Chooser window. For more information on the Color Chooser window, see the "Adjusting Colors and Transparency" section later in this chapter.

Transparency Much like Color, Transparency uses a color swatch. By default, Transparency employs a scalar (grayscale) range in which black is opaque and white is transparent. However, you are free to choose any color value through the Color Chooser window.

Ambient Color Ambient Color represents diffuse reflections arriving from all other surfaces in a scene, as well as reflections from participating media (particles suspended in air, such as dust, smoke, or water vapor). To simplify the rendering process, the diffuse reflections are assumed to be arriving from all points in the scene with equal intensities. In practical terms, ambient color is the color of a surface when it receives no direct light. A high Ambient Color value will reduce the contrast of an assigned surface.

Incandescence Incandescence creates the illusion that the surface is emitting light. The color value of the Incandescence attribute is added to the color value of the Color attribute, thus making the material appear brighter. (You can use the Incandescence attribute to contribute light to a scene when using the mental ray renderer and the Final Gathering option; this is demonstrated in Chapter 2.)

Bump Mapping At the point of render, bump maps perturb surface normals along the core of a surface (the central section facing the camera). They do not, however, affect the surface's silhouette edge. For example, in Figure 1.6, a primitive sphere is assigned to a bump-mapped material. While the core of the sphere appears craggy, the sphere's silhouette edge remains perfectly smooth. Nevertheless, the bump effect can often sell the idea that a surface is rough. When the Bump Mapping attribute is mapped, middle-gray values (0.5, 0.5, 0.5 on a 0 to 1.0 RGB scale) have no effect. Higher values cause peaks, and lower values cause valleys to form. For a demonstration of the bump effect, see the section "Procedurally Mapping Bumps" later in this chapter.

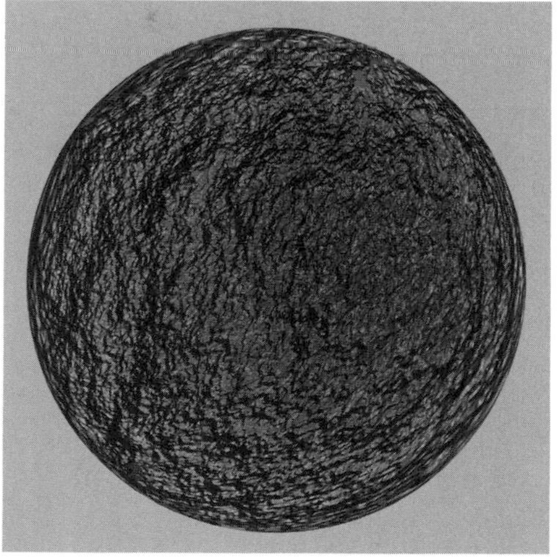

Figure 1.6

A bump-mapped sphere renders with a craggy core and a smooth silhouette edge.

Diffuse The term *diffuse* refers to that which is widely spread and not concentrated. Hence, a real-world diffuse surface appears matte-like and does not create highlights or specular "hot spots." This is because of the presence of myriad surface imperfections that scatter light in a random fashion. For example, paper and cardboard are diffuse surfaces. In Maya, the Diffuse attribute controls the degree to which light rays are reflected in all directions. A high Diffuse value produces a bright surface. A low Diffuse value causes light rays to be absorbed and thereby makes the surface dark.

Translucence, Translucence Depth, Translucence Focus The Translucence attribute, in conjunction with Translucence Depth and Translucence Focus, simulates the diffuse penetration of light into a solid surface. In the real world, you can see the effect when holding a flashlight to the palm of your hand. Translucence naturally occurs with hair, wax, fur, paper, leaves, and human flesh. The Translucence attribute is discussed further in Chapter 4, "Texturing and Lighting a Character, Part 2."

Adding Specularity

The Lambert material does not possess specularity. *Specularity* is the consistent reflection of light in one direction that creates a "hot spot" on a surface. In CG programs, specularity is emulated by creating a specular highlight. In Maya, specular highlights are controlled through a material's Specular Shading section (see Figure 1.7).

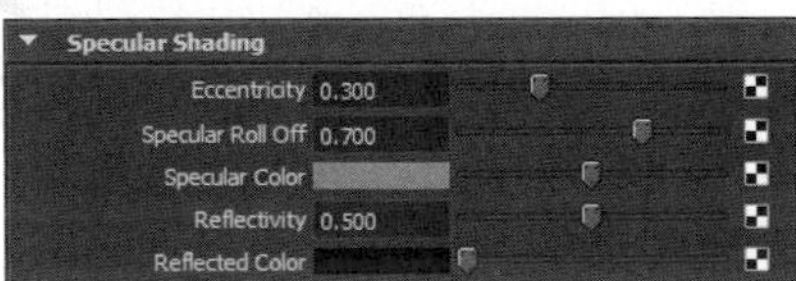

Figure 1.7
The Specular Shading section of a Blinn material

The Specular Shading section is carried by Phong, Phong E, Blinn, and Anisotropic materials. All four materials share the following specular highlight attributes:

Specular Color Specular Color sets the color of the specular highlight.

Reflectivity Reflectivity controls the intensity of raytraced reflections and reflections simulated with the Reflected Color attribute. By default, the Maya Software renderer does not raytrace. For an introduction to raytracing, see the "Project: Raytracing Reflections" section later in this chapter.

Reflected Color If the Reflected Color attribute is set to any color other than black or is mapped, a simulated reflection is applied directly to the assigned surface. Reflected Color does not require raytracing to function. The Reflected Color attribute is demonstrated in Chapter 5, "Texturing and Lighting a Vehicle, Part 1."

Whereas the Blinn material controls the specular highlight size with the Eccentricity attribute, Phong uses the Cosine Power attribute, and Phong E uses the Roughness and Highlight Size attributes. The Anisotropic material controls the size, shape, and rotation of its specular highlight with the Angle, Spread X, Spread Y, and Roughness attributes. The Anisotropic highlight can assume circular, vertical, or horizontal patterns (see Figure 1.8).

Technically speaking, an anisotropic surface is one that reflects light unevenly; in such a case, the unevenness is dependent on direction. Real-world anisotropic surfaces possess parallel channels, grooves, fibers, or tube-like structures. Human hair, brushed metal, and choppy water therefore fit the anisotropic category. If a surface creates specular highlights that are elongated and perpendicular to the channels/grooves/fibers/tubes, it is anisotropic.

Keep in mind that 3D specular highlights are an artificial construct. Real-world specular highlights are actually reflections of intense light sources, such as a day sky or a bright lamp.

The intensity of the Maya specular highlight is controlled by the Specular Roll Off (Blinn), Whiteness (Phong E), and Fresnel Index (Anisotropic). With the Phong material, you can adjust the specular intensity by changing the Specular Color.

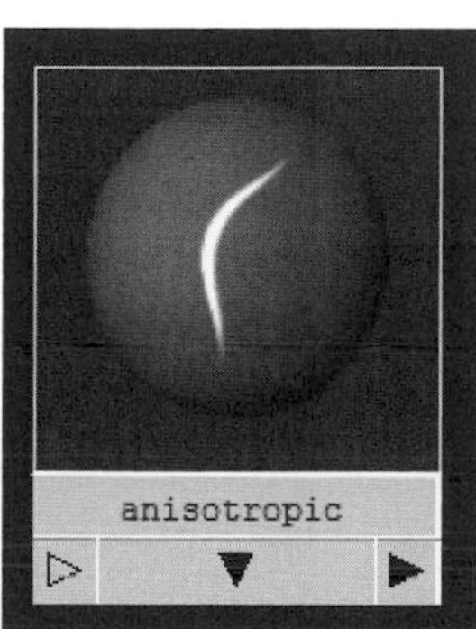

Figure 1.8

(Left) Nonspherical highlight of Anisotropic material. (Middle) Anisotropic highlight on human hair. (Right) Anisotropic reflection on choppy water

Using Specialized Materials

In addition to Lambert, Blinn, Phong, Phong E, and Anisotropic, Maya offers several specialized materials. These are available in the Maya section of the Hypershade Create tab. In addition, a large number of mental ray materials are included in the mental ray section. Although the mental ray renderer can render either Maya or mental ray materials, the Maya Software renderer can render only Maya materials. Nevertheless, while texturing and lighting the headphones, we'll work solely with Maya materials. Information on mental ray materials is included in Chapter 7, "Texturing and Lighting an Environment, Part 1." Of the specialized Maya materials, Surface Shader, Use Background, and Layered Shader are perhaps the most useful. Descriptions of each follow:

Surface Shader The Surface Shader material is a "pass-through" node. It carries no shading properties and does not take into account any lights or shadows. A surface assigned to a Surface Shader material will appear self-illuminated. Hence, the material is appropriate for any surface that needs to retain a maximum intensity regardless of the scene's lighting. For example, a half-sphere assigned to a Surface Shader with a sky photo mapped to its Color attribute does not need to be lit. As a working example, a Surface Shader material will be assigned to the Light_Box geometry later in this chapter.

Use Background The Use Background material picks up the color of the camera's Background Color attribute (which is black by default) or an image plane attached to the camera. If you assign Use Background to surfaces that are receiving shadows, the shadows are trapped in an alpha channel and the RGB channels remain black. This offers a handy means to render shadows as a separate render pass. For a demonstration of the Use Background material and render passes, see Chapter 6, "Texturing and Lighting a Vehicle, Part 2." For a demonstration of image plane use, see Chapter 5.

Layered Shader The Layered Shader material allows you to combine two or more materials. For a demonstration, see Chapter 7.

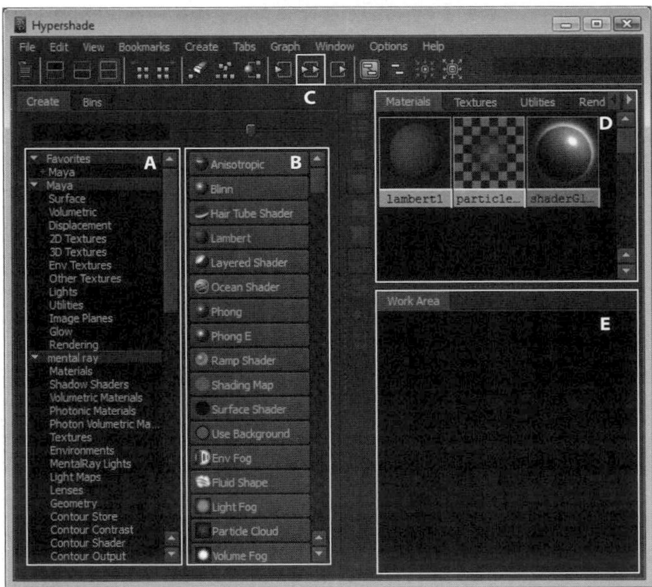

Figure 1.9

The Maya 2011 and 2012 Hypershade window with (A) Create tab rollout column, which includes the Favorites, Maya, mental ray, and Autodesk Materials (2012) sections, (B) node list column, which is filtered by selections within the Create tab rollout column, (C) Input And Output Connections button, (D) node tabs, and (E) work area

Hypershade Functionality

Maya 2011 introduced a newly designed Hypershade window (Window → Rendering Editors → Hypershade). Nevertheless, the window's tabs, menus, and work areas remain virtually identical to earlier versions of the software. In addition, Maya 2012 uses the same Hypershade layout as Maya 2011. Figure 1.9 illustrates the key areas of the window.

In Maya 2011 and 2012, the Create tab is broken into two halves: a rollout column and a node list column. The rollout column filters what appears in the node list column. For example, if you click the word *Surface* under the word *Maya*, the node list column shows only standard Maya materials.

Creating a New Material

To create a new material, click one of the material icons in the Create tab. The new material is added to the Materials tab. To access the material's attributes in the Attribute Editor, click the material icon in the Materials tab (if the Attribute Editor is closed, double-click the material icon). To rename the material, update the name cell at the top of the material's Attribute Editor tab.

Assigning a Material

To assign a material to a surface, select the surface, RMB+click the material icon in the Hypershade window, and choose Assign Material To Selection from the marking menu. You can also MMB+drag the material icon and drop it on top of a surface in a view panel; however, this method is less precise and is prone to incorrect surface assignment.

When selecting a surface, it's generally best to make your selections through the Hypergraph: Hierarchy or Outliner windows. If you select surfaces through a view panel, do so while the Select By Object Type button is activated on the Status Line (see Figure 1.10). If the Select By Hierarchy And Combinations button is activated instead, you may inadvertently select a group node. If a material is assigned to a group node, all the group node's children automatically inherit the same material.

Figure 1.10

Selection buttons on the Status Line include the (A) Select By Hierarchy And Combinations button, (B) Select By Object Type button, (C) Select By Component Type button, and (D) object type/component type option buttons.

Exploring Shading Networks

Any material you create is part of a larger shading network composed of multiple nodes. The nodes are represented as square icons in the Hypershade node tabs and work area. Some nodes are provided automatically and are necessary for basic rendering. Others arrive as you add texture maps.

To view a shading network, go to the Materials tab of the Hypershade, RMB+click a material icon, and choose Graph Network from the marking menu. The network is revealed in the work area (see Figure 1.11). Initially, several nodes are hidden. To see the entire network, select the visible nodes in the work area and click the Input And Output Connections button (see Figure 1.9 earlier in this chapter). It may be necessary to select all the visible nodes and click the button several times. Within the work area, you can delete node connections or add new ones. For more information, see Chapters 5 and 6.

You can change the view within the work area by using the camera controls (Alt key and mouse buttons). If the work area becomes cluttered, you can clear it by choosing Graph → Clear Graph from the Hypershade menu.

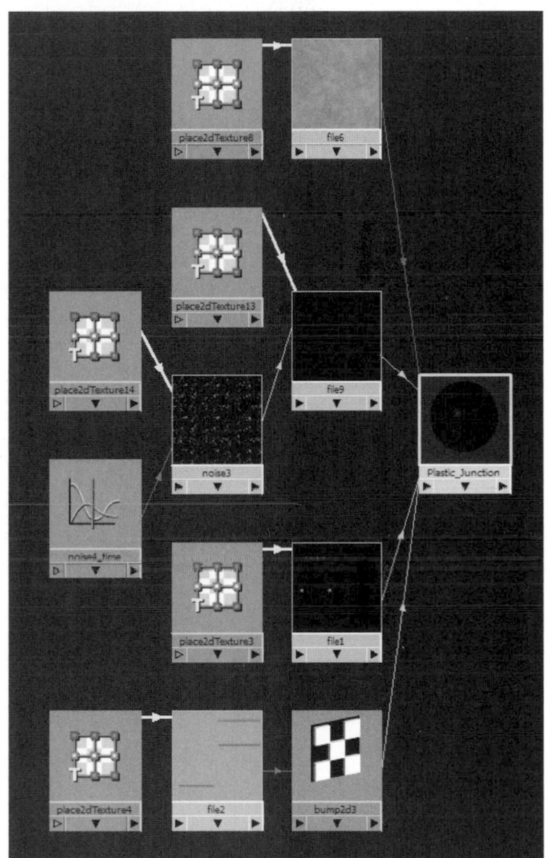

Figure 1.11

A shading network revealed in the Hypershade work area

Project: Assigning Materials

After examining the scene file, the first important step to texturing and lighting is the creation of new materials and their assignment to surfaces. As such, you must decide what types of materials to create. In addition, you must determine whether surfaces will share assignments. After material assignments have been made, you can adjust the materials' Color and Transparency attributes.

Choosing Material Types

Generally, it's best to match the Maya material type to the real-world material the surface is emulating. For example, if a material needs a specular highlight, a Lambert material is inappropriate and a Blinn is suitable. As such, Table 1.1 lists each of the surfaces found in the headphones scene file, the real-world material it will try to emulate, and the recommended Maya material type.

Table 1.1
Recommended material types

SURFACE NAME	REAL-WORLD MATERIAL	RECOMMENDED MAYA MATERIAL
Slider	Chromed metal	Phong
Junction	Black plastic	Blinn
Wire	Black rubber	Blinn
Foam	Gray cell foam	Lambert
Ear_Cup	Black plastic	Blinn
Ear_Pad	Thin, bunched white leather	Blinn
Grommet	Semitransparent yellow plastic	Blinn
Head_Pad	Plastic stamped to simulate leather	Blinn
Light_Box (wall)	Translucent white fabric	Surface Shader

You can take one of two approaches to determine the total number of materials needed for a scene:

- Create a new material for each surface. For example, assign the Foam_L surface to a Foam_L_Color material and assign the Foam_R surface to a Foam_R_Color material. This allows each surface's material to be adjusted separately. However, the Hypershade may become difficult to manage if a scene is complex and contains numerous surfaces.
- Assign a single material to every surface that shares the same look. For example, create a single Foam material and assign it to both the Foam_L and Foam_R surfaces. This simplifies the contents of Hypershade but limits flexibility when adjusting attributes.

Either of these approaches is suitable for this project. Should one approach prove limiting, you can delete materials, reassign materials, or create new materials at any time. To delete a material, simply select its icon in the Hypershade Materials tab and press the Delete key. If a material is deleted, any surface assigned to it will not render until it is assigned to one of the other surviving materials. Note that newly created primitives, NURBS, and polygon surfaces are automatically assigned to the Lambert1 material. Although you can edit Lambert1, you cannot delete it. You can assign a surface to a new or different material at any time.

Assigning Multiple Materials to One Surface

When you assign a polygon surface to a material, all the polygon faces are assigned to the same material. However, if you select individual faces before assigning, the surface can be assigned multiple materials. For example, with the Light_Box geometry, it would be preferable to assign the floor to one material and the walls and ceiling to a second material. To do so, follow these steps:

1. In the Hypershade, create a new Blinn material and Surface Shader material.
2. In a view panel, RMB+click the Light_Box geometry and choose Face from the marking menu. Shift+click all the polygon faces along the floor. If you accidentally select

an incorrect face, deselect it by Ctrl+clicking. After all the floor faces are selected, return to the Hypershade window, RMB+click the new Blinn material, and choose Assign Material To Selection from the marking menu.

3. In a view panel, select the entire Light_Box. This deselects the floor faces and selects the remaining faces. Return to the Hypershade and assign the selected faces to the new Surface Shader material.

Organizing the Hypershade

As you work with the Hypershade, it's important to keep the resulting contents organized. The easiest way to achieve this is to name the materials clearly. For example, name each material after the real-world substance it's supposed to replicate. Thus, *Chrome* and *Foam* are useful names. You can also include the name of the surface a material is assigned to. For example, you might use *Plastic_Junction* or *Leather_Ear_Pad*. Avoid generic names that may become confusing in the long run. For example, it might not be clear which surfaces are assigned to *Plastic1*, *Plastic2*, and *Plastic3*. One trick is to imagine that your scene will be handed off to another animator; if the materials are named clearly, the animator will have no problem navigating the Hypershade and determining how the materials are assigned. For example, Figure 1.12 shows materials created for the headphones scene file.

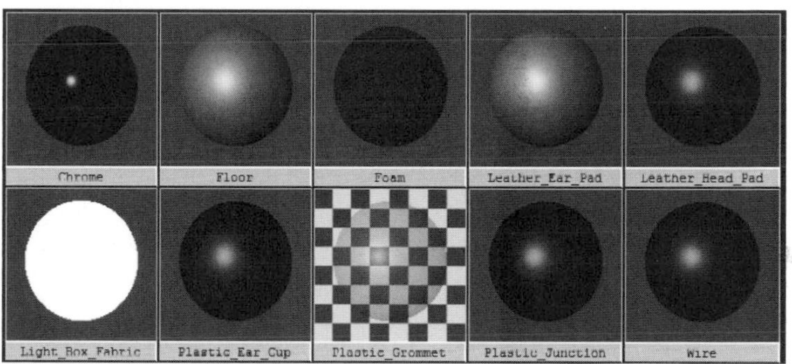

Figure 1.12

Materials created for the headphones scene. Each material is assigned to surfaces that share the same look. For example, the Wire material is assigned to the Wire_L, Wire_R, and Cord surfaces. Note that the material names are easy to interpret. A sample Maya file is saved as `headphones-step1.ma` in the `ProjectFiles/Project1` folder on the DVD. For a color version of the figure, see the color insert.

Adjusting Colors and Transparency

After you've assigned materials to all the surfaces in the scene, adjust the Color attribute for each material. Match the colors listed in Table 1.1 earlier in this chapter as well as those illustrated in Figure 1.12. To access the Color Chooser, click the Color attribute's color swatch. With the Color Chooser, you can select a color by LMB+dragging the color wheel handles or the R/G/B (red/green/blue) sliders. You can also enter values into the R/G/B number cells. By default, the color scale runs from 0 to 1.0 for each color channel. You can switch from the RGB color model to an HSV (hue/saturation/value) one by changing the lower-right menu. After you move your mouse off the Color Chooser panel, it closes and the selected color is placed in the swatch.

The Transparency attribute, on the other hand, should be left set to 0 (black) unless a surface calls for the namesake quality. Of all the surfaces included in the headphones scene file, the grommets alone should be a semitransparent plastic. As such, set the corresponding material's Transparency color swatch to a medium gray.

Lighting Techniques and Maya Light Types

Successful lighting in animation depends on a wealth of techniques developed for cinematography and still photography. This necessitates an understanding of Maya light types and the equivalent real-world lights they emulate.

Understanding Product Lighting

As mentioned earlier in this chapter, light boxes (light tents) are useful for evenly lighting products that fit within their structure. However, the Light_Box geometry included in the headphones scene cannot provide illumination at this point (although it will contribute to specular highlights and reflections). We will activate the illumination capability of the Light_Box in Chapter 2 by using mental ray and Final Gathering. In the meantime, we will use other real-world lighting techniques.

Figure 1.13

(Top) A model is lit by two lights placed on either side of the camera. The left light carries a soft box. Bounced light from the white walls works as a back light. (Bottom Left) The result of similar lighting on a face. (Bottom Right) The result of similar lighting on a product (in this case, a restaurant meal)

Because the goal of this project is to light the headphones aesthetically, we can copy lighting approaches applied by glamour photography and music video videography. One common technique of such media requires the addition of a strong, diffuse key light or lights placed beside or close to the camera. A single light might take the form of a fluorescent ring that circles the camera. Alternatively, two equally intense lights might be placed on either side of the camera and softened by translucent "soft boxes" or diffusion material (see Figure 1.13). Such lights may also be bounced off reflective cards or purpose-built reflective umbrellas. By aligning the lights with the camera, visible shadows are minimized. For a human, this results in the reduction of noticeable wrinkles and similar flaws. For a product, this ensures that the parts of the product are clearly seen; that is, no part is made obscure by darkness. On a psychological level, a brightly lit subject with few shadows often produces a positive reaction. Conversely, a poorly lit subject with deep, dark shadows is associated with gloomy or disturbing subject matter such as film noir or horror.

When a light is referred to as diffuse, its light rays diverge and overlap in such a way as to produce soft-edged shadows. A focused light, on the other hand, creates parallel rays of light that create hard-edged shadows. Diffuse lights are often referred to as soft. Focused lights are often referred to as hard.

Adding Lights to a Scene

When adding lights in Maya, it's generally best to create one at a time. That is, each light should be satisfactorily positioned and adjusted before additional lights are created. As such, it pays to follow the lighting conventions used for cinematic and photographic lighting: Each light is assigned a specific task that ultimately determines its position and intensity. The tasks are generally broken down into the following:

Key A key light is the most intense light in the scene. The key light's source is generally identifiable (the sun, a lamp, and so on). The key light usually produces the strongest shadow in the scene. If two light sources are equally intense, as is the case with the glamour photography in Figure 1.13, they both may be considered key lights.

Fill A fill light is a secondary light that is less intense than the key. This light "fills in" the dark areas of a subject and the shadows produced by the key. Fill lights often represent light from a key that has bounced off a surface, such as a wall.

Rim A rim light is an intense light source that arrives from the back of a subject so that it strikes the subject along the edge. Rim lights, when used in photography and cinematography, are also known as *back lights* or *hair lights*. When a rim light is used to fill in the dark side of a person's face, it is known as a *kicker*.

Figure 1.14 is included as an example of lighting in Maya that adds a key, fill, and rim light.

The color and shadow quality of each light is determined by the real-world light source it's attempting to replicate. For example, if a Maya directional light is acting as a midday sun, it should arrive from a high angle, create hard-edged shadows, and carry a color that is slightly blue. (Light replication is discussed in more detail throughout the remaining chapters of this book.)

Understanding Maya Light Types

Maya provides six basic light types (see Figure 1.15). This chapter and Chapter 2 use an area light and volume light, and the remaining lights are utilized throughout the remaining chapters.

The key qualities of each light type follow:

Directional The directional light creates parallel rays. As such, the light has direction but not position. Hence, the position of the light icon will not affect the light quality. Directional lights are suitable for emulating the sun or other light sources that are a great distance from the subject.

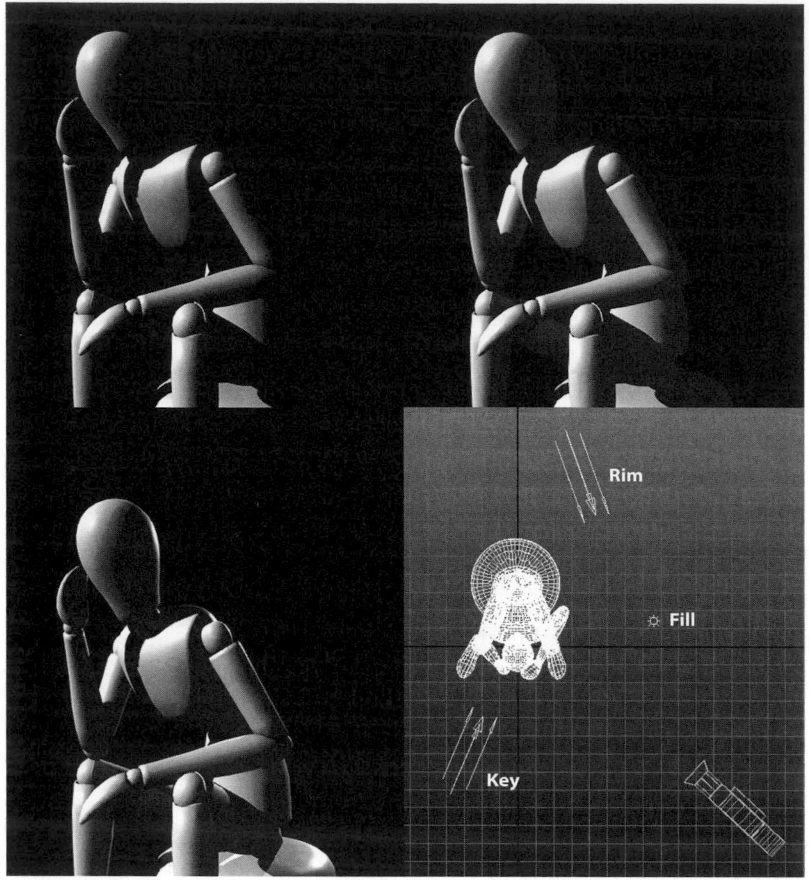

Figure 1.14

(Top Left) Mannequin lit by a key light. (Top Right) Mannequin lit by key and fill. (Bottom Left) Mannequin lit by key, fill, and rim. (Bottom Right) Positions of all three lights as seen in a Top view panel. The three lighting scenarios are included as `key.ma`, `key_fill.ma`, and `key_fill_rim.ma` in the `ProjectFiles/Project1/Reference` folder on the DVD.

Point The point light produces omnidirectional rays originating from the light icon. Point lights are similar to lightbulbs or other sources that have a small, physically spherical shape.

Spot The Maya spot light re-creates a spotlight found on a stage or motion picture set. Thanks to its conical shape, the spot light produces naturally divergent rays. In general, the light can emulate artificial sources that are close to the subject. Because of the spot light's cone, it has an identifiable falloff from 100 percent to 0 percent intensity. The size of the cone is controlled by the Cone Angle attribute. The softness of the cone edge is set by the Penumbra attribute, which is 0 by default. Note that the scale of the spot light icon does not affect its light quality.

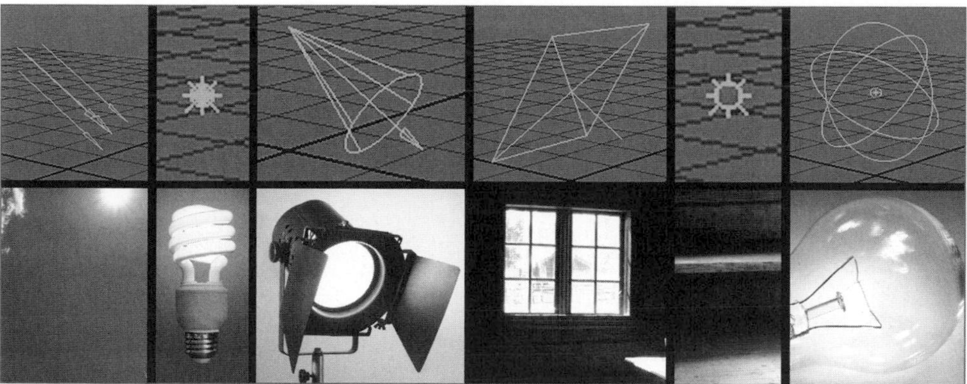

Figure 1.15

(Top Row) Maya light types. (Bottom Row) The corresponding real-world lighting scenarios emulated by Maya lights. From Left to Right: A directional light re-creates the parallel rays of an unobstructed sun; a point light acts like a lightbulb with omnidirectional rays originating from a specific point; a spot light simulates the divergent rays of a real-world spotlight from film and stage; an area light duplicates light arriving from a rectangular plane, such as a window; an ambient light acts like bounced light (in this case, window light bounced off a floor); a volume light functions as a point light, but the illuminated surfaces must be placed within the light's volume shape.

Area The area light possesses a rectangular icon and can be scaled in either the X or Y direction. Hence, area lights can emulate a source that is transmitted through a plane with a fixed size. For example, an area light might re-create sunlight arriving through a window or a bank of lightbulbs placed behind a rectangular marquee. Area lights are the most physically accurate of the basic Maya light types. As such, the light intensity is affected by the distance and angle of the light icon in relation to lit surfaces. Although an area light is represented by a rectangular icon, it actually functions as an array of point lights. This array causes the area light to be fairly soft. Nevertheless, area lights operate in one direction; this is indicated by the small "pointer" extending from the light icon's center.

Ambient The ambient light is extremely soft and produces little, if any, variation in intensity. By default, the light is a mixture of omnidirectional and directional rays. The light's Ambient Shade attribute controls this mixture. If Ambient Shade is lowered from the default 0.45 to 0, the light becomes equally intense at all points within a scene; this leads to a flat, "toon" look. If Ambient Shade is raised to 1.0, the light radiates from the light icon and is identical to a point light. Ambient lights are suitable as fill and are usually inappropriate as a key.

Volume The volume light acts as a point light but is contained within the volume of the light's icon. You can scale the icon to any size. By default, the icon is spherical, but you can change it to a cylinder or cone through the light's Light Shape attribute. By default, the light's intensity tapers from the icon center to the icon edge. The rapidity of this taper is controlled by the Color Range and Penumbra gradients. For a surface to be lit by a volume light, it must rest within the interior of the light icon. For a demonstration of the volume light's unusual functionality, see Chapter 2.

Project: Creating Lights and Shadows

After you've adjusted the material Color and Transparency attributes, you can begin lighting. Although Maya provides a default light when no light nodes are present, the light quality is not driven by any particular light source. Hence, the default light is not suitable for judging assigned materials or added textures.

Setting the Key Light

Although you have a fairly wide selection of light types in Maya, we will use an area light to serve as the key for the headphones scene. The soft quality of the area light makes it suitable for product lighting. Use the following steps to create and place the light:

1. Choose Create → Lights → Area Light. The new area light is placed at 0, 0, 0. Select the light and interactively scale it so that it's 10, 10, 20 units in X, Y, Z. For greater precision, you can enter values into the Channel Box. Rename the light **Key**. You can enter a new name through the top cell of the Channel Box while the light is selected.

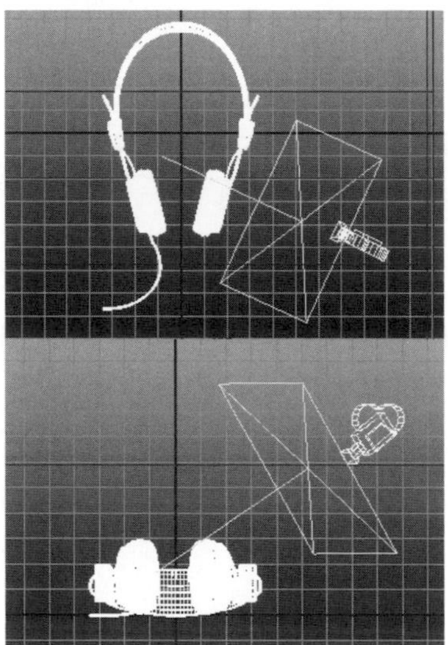

Figure 1.16
Scaled and positioned area light that will serve as the key, as seen from the Top and Front view panels

2. Position and rotate the light so that it is in front of and slightly higher than the Render camera icon (see Figure 1.16). The light should point in the same direction as the Render camera. The direction the area light is pointing is indicated by the "pointer" extending from the light's center. Note that the Render camera is animated and moves in a short arc around the headphones. Use the Timeline controls to see where the camera starts and stops.
3. Render a test. To do so, choose Window → Rendering Editors → Render View and choose Render → Render → Render from the Render View menu. At this point, the render settings are set to low quality. We will raise the quality after we add shadows.

Fine-Tuning Material Attributes

After you've set the key light, you can begin to fine-tune additional material attributes. First, examine the overall brightness of the surfaces in the render. If the surfaces are consistently too bright or too dark, adjust the Key light's brightness. To do so, open the light's Attribute Editor tab (with the light selected, press Ctrl+A) and change the Intensity attribute value. If individual surfaces are too bright or too dark, adjust the corresponding material's Diffuse attribute. Lower Diffuse values produce darker surfaces. If necessary, further adjust each material's Color attribute. For example, in Figure 1.17, the Key light's intensity is set to 0.4, while several materials have had their Diffuse and Color values lowered.

Figure 1.17

Headphones lit with an area light serving as a key. The Diffuse and Color attributes of several materials are adjusted. A sample file is saved as `headphones-step2.ma` on the DVD.

As you adjust the materials, render out additional tests in the Render View window. To save time, render out only the region of interest. You can define a region by LMB+dragging in the Render View render area to form a red region box. After releasing the mouse, click the Render Region button.

Aside from the Color and Diffuse attributes, it's important to adjust attributes controlling specular highlights. For example, the render shown in Figure 1.17 features black plastic parts with intense specular highlights. The highlights reduce the overall contrast for the plastic surfaces and thus make them appear milky. In particular, the Ear_Cup geometry carries large areas that verge on pure white. To defeat the overly intense specular highlights, adjust the Eccentricity, Specular Roll Off, and Specular Color attributes. Reducing Eccentricity creates a smaller highlight. Lower Specular Roll Off and/or Specular Color values reduce the highlight intensity. For the Ear_Cup geometry, the following settings work well (assuming the Key light's Intensity is set to 0.4):

Color: Dark gray (RGB values 0.02, 0.02, 0.02)

Diffuse: 0.3

Eccentricity: 0.15

Specular Roll Off: 0.3

Specular Color: Medium gray (the default value)

Each material may require its own unique set of specular settings (see Figure 1.18). Note that you can change the Specular Color to a nonwhite color. For example, the headphone's grommets are a semitransparent plastic. By setting the corresponding material's Specular Color to a yellow-gold, the highlight becomes more subtle.

Figure 1.18
Eccentricity, Specular Roll Off, and Specular Color attributes of materials are adjusted. A sample file is saved as `headphones-step3.ma` **on the DVD. For a color version of the figure, see the color insert.**

While adjusting the specular quality of each material, check each of the Reflectivity attributes. For any material that need not be reflective, set the Reflectivity attribute to 0. When raytracing is activated later in this chapter, any material with a nonzero Reflectivity value will automatically reflect within the scene.

Adding Depth Map Shadows

After the Key light is in place, you can create shadows. Follow these steps:

1. With the Key light's Attribute Editor tab open, expand the Shadows section. Select the Use Depth Map Shadows check box.
2. Render a test. The shadow edge will appear jagged. This is partially because of the low-quality render settings. Choose Window → Rendering Editors → Render Settings. In the Maya Software tab of the Render Settings window, change the Quality menu to Production Quality.
3. Render a test. The overall quality of the render is improved. However, the shadow remains jagged. To remedy this, you can raise the light's Resolution value. For example, in Figure 1.19, the Resolution is set to 2048.

The higher the Resolution value, the smoother the depth map shadow edge will appear. However, Resolution alone will not affect the hardness or softness of the shadow edge. You can soften the shadow by adjusting the Filter Size attribute. When adjusting the Resolution and Filter Size, you can use the following rules of thumb:

- For a hard-edged shadow, choose a *high* Resolution value and a *low* Filter Size value.
- For a soft-edged shadow, choose a *low* Resolution value and a *high* Filter Size value.

The Filter Size attribute blurs the shadow equally along its edge. The Resolution attribute determines the pixel size of a depth map bitmap written to disc. The bitmap is the view of the shadowing light written as a Z-depth buffer. With a Z-depth buffer, the distance from the light is encoded in various shades of gray; surfaces close to the light receive higher values, and surfaces far from the light receive lower values.

If there is only one light in a scene, the shadow renders black. You can add a fill light to brighten the shadow. However, the fill light will also brighten the unshadowed area of the surface. An alternative solution is to adjust the light's Shadow Color attribute. For example, in Figure 1.20, Shadow Color is set to a light blue. In this case, Filter Size is set to 32.

Figure 1.19

(Left) Detail of depth map shadow with default 512 Resolution. (Right) Improved shadow with 2048 Resolution. A sample file is saved as `headphones-step4.ma` **on the DVD.**

2D and 3D Procedural Textures

Maya provides a number of textures that are procedural. A *procedural texture* is one that is mathematically generated through a predefined algorithm. Procedural textures are resolution independent and do not have defined edges or borders. The textures fall into two categories: 2D and 3D.

2D procedural textures create a pattern in two dimensions: U (left/right) and V (down/up). These textures include Bulge, Checker, Cloth, Fractal, Grid, Mountain, Noise, Ramp, and Water. When you map a 2D texture to the attribute of a material, two nodes are created and connected to the material node. The first node is the texture node, which carries the attributes that determine the quality of the texture. Because several procedural textures are based on fractal noise patterns, a number of attributes are shared. The second added node is a 2d Placement utility node (see Figure 1.21). This node controls the UV tiling of the texture. If the node's Repeat UV attribute is set to 1, 1, the texture appears one time across the surface in the U and V directions. Additionally, the 2d Placement utility node offers attributes to offset, mirror, or rotate the procedural pattern.

Figure 1.20

Filter Size is set to 32, and Shadow Color is set to a light blue. A sample file is saved as `headphones-step5.ma` **on the DVD.**

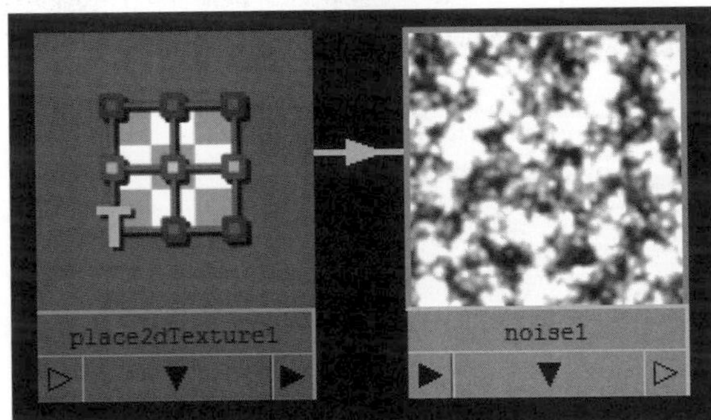

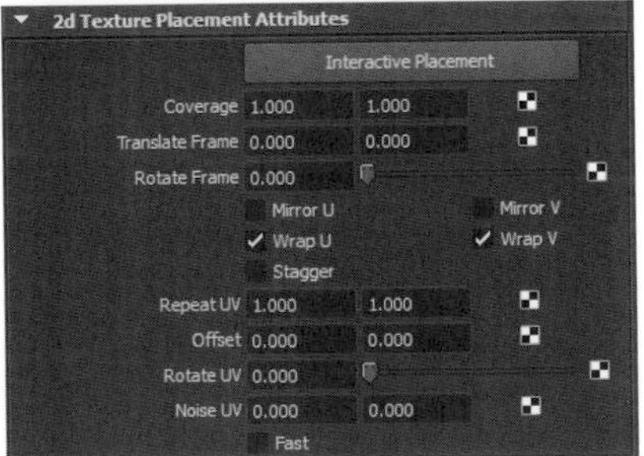

Figure 1.21

(Top) A 2d Placement utility node, automatically named place2dTexture1, connected to a Noise texture node. (Bottom) The utility's UV tiling attributes

Note that two naming conventions are applied to any given node in Maya: a "nice" name and a "long" name. A nice name includes spaces and features capitalization. A long name carries no spaces and sometimes features a different word order. For example, 2d Placement is a nice name while place2dTexture is a long name. Nevertheless, 2d Placement and place2dTexture refer to the same node. The Hypershade work area uses the long naming convention to label the node icons. The Hypershade Create tab node list, however, uses the nice naming comvention.

In contrast to procedural textures, several 2D textures are based on bitmaps imported by the user; these include File, Movie, and PSD File. When mapped to an attribute, a bitmap-based 2D texture is connected to its own 2d Placement utility node.

When a 3D procedural texture is mapped to an attribute, a 3d Placement utility node is connected to the shading network. The node is visible in each view panel as a green placement box (see Figure 1.22). By default, the box is placed at 0, 0, 0 and is 2×2×2 units in size. The utility determines the color of each assigned surface point by locating the point's position within or relative to the placement box. This process is analogous to a surface dipped into a square bucket of swirled paint or a surface chiseled from a solid cube of veined stone. Hence, the scale, translation, and rotation of the placement box affects the way in which the texture appears across the assigned surface. If the surface is transformed relative to the box or deforms over time, the texture will change. To avoid such a change, it may be necessary to parent the 3d Placement node to the surface. More drastically, you can convert 3D textures to 2D textures through the Convert To File Texture tool. 3D textures include Brownian, Cloud, Crater, Granite, Leather, Marble, Rock, Snow, Solid Fractal, Stucco, Volume Noise, and Wood.

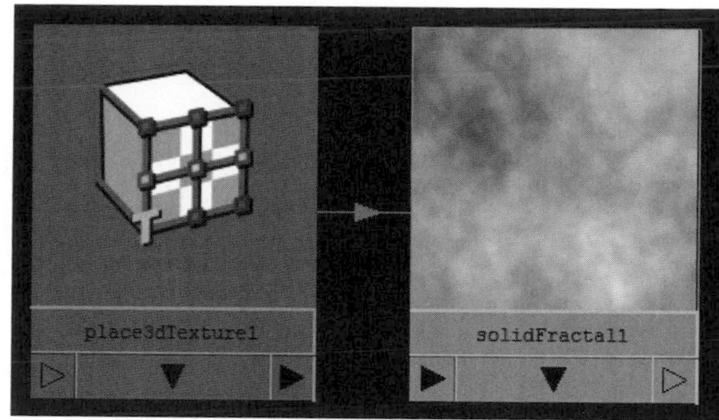

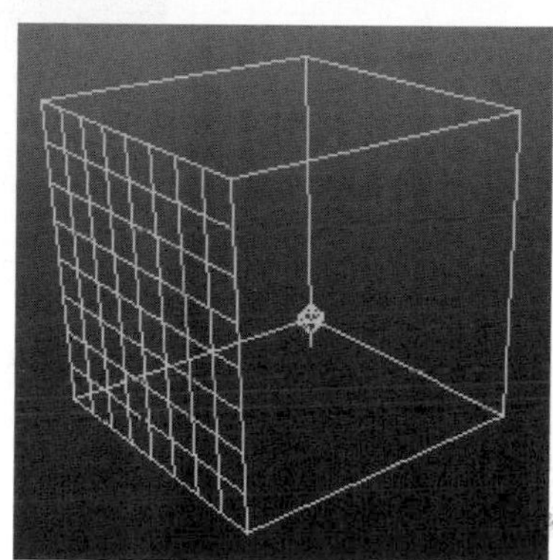

Figure 1.22

(Top) A 3d Placement utility node, automatically named place3dTexture1, connected to a Solid Fractal texture node. (Bottom) The corresponding placement box displayed in a view panel

Project: Applying Textures

After basic material attributes are adjusted under the Key light, you can begin adding textures. Both procedural textures and custom bitmap textures will lend the render greater complexity.

Because textures will add fine detail to the various surfaces, it's necessary to increase the render resolution to accurately gauge the result. Open the Render Settings window and change the Presets menu, in the Image Size section, to HD 720.

Procedurally Mapping Bumps

At the present stage of this project, the surfaces of the headphones appear perfectly smooth. To defeat this perfection, you can map Bump Mapping attributes with various procedural textures. For example, to add a leather-like bump to the Head_ Pad geometry, follow these steps:

1. Open the Hypershade window and click the material assigned to the Head_Pad surface. (The material is named Leather_Head_Pad in the included sample scene files.) In the material's Attribute Editor tab, click the Bump Mapping attribute's checkered Map button.
2. In the Create Render Node window, click the Leather texture icon. To simplify the node list column, click the phrase *3D Textures* under the word *Maya* in the rollout column. After the Leather texture is selected, three nodes are added to the material's shading network: a Leather node, a Bump 3d node, and a 3d Placement node. (To view the network, follow the instructions listed in the "Exploring Shading Networks" section earlier in this chapter.)
3. Render out a test. A leather-like bump appears across the Head_Pad surface (see Figure 1.23). At this point, the leather pattern is small and too deep. To reduce the bump depth, open the Attribute Editor tab for the Bump 3d node. Change the Bump Depth attribute to 0.3. Render a test.

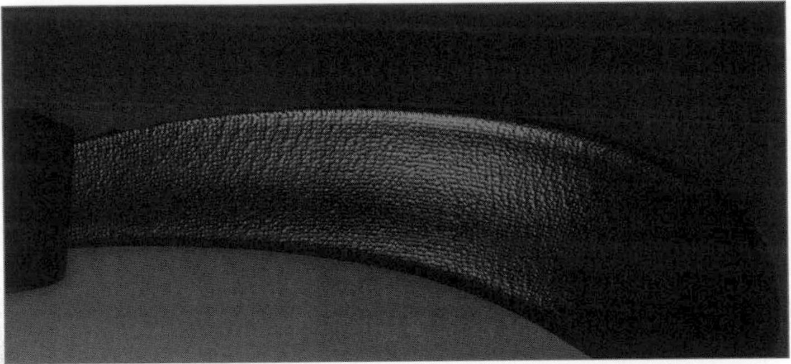

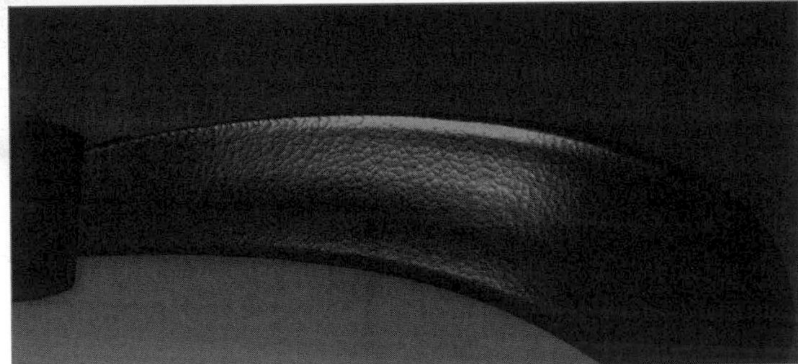

Figure 1.23

(Top) Detail of render after addition of the Leather texture as a bump map. (Bottom) Render after the adjustment of the Bump 3d and Leather node attributes. A sample file is saved as `headphones-step6.ma` on the DVD.

4. Open the new Leather node's Attribute Editor tab. Reduce the Cell Size to 0.8 to enlarge the overall size of the pattern. Despite this adjustment, vertical lines appear across the surface. This is because of the regularity of the leather cells. To defeat this, change the Leather's Randomness attribute to 1.0 (see Figure 1.23).

Although the addition of the Leather bump map increases the realism of the head pad, it does not create the illusion that the pad was constructed out of multiple pieces. To create the illusion that the edges of the pad are stitched, you can apply a Grid texture as a bump map with the following steps:

1. Select the Head_Pad surface and choose Window → UV Texture Editor. Note how the surface is split into multiple UV shells (see Figure 1.24). The top shell contains the polygons sitting on the top of the pad. The middle shell contains the polygons sitting on the bottom of the pad. The bottom shell, which takes the form of a square, includes all the polygon faces along the forward and back edges of the pad. To see which polygon faces a shell includes, RMB+click in the UV Texture Editor and choose Face from the marking menu. Proceed to select faces in the UV Texture Editor by either LMB+clicking individual faces or LMB+dragging a selection box around multiple faces. The selected faces are highlighted in the view panels. Note that each of the edge faces shares exactly the same UV texture space. This means that every edge face will receive the same exact part of the texture assigned to the surface.

2. Open the Hypershade. Create a new Blinn material. Name the new Blinn **Leather_Pad_Edge** or something equally appropriate. Return to the UV Texture Editor. Clear the face selection by clicking on an empty area of the UV space. LMB+drag a selection box around the bottom square shell. All the edge faces are selected. Return to the Hypershade. RMB+click the new Blinn node and choose Assign Material To Selection. Although the pad's UV texture space contains the faces for the entire pad, only the selected edge faces are assigned to the new Blinn. The old material's assignments of the remainder of the pad are not changed.

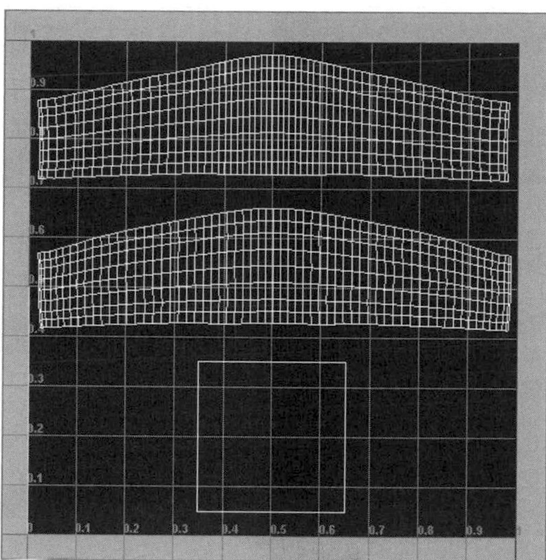

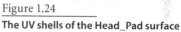

Figure 1.24
The UV shells of the Head_Pad surface

3. Open the new Blinn node's Attribute Editor tab. Change the attributes to match the material assigned to the remainder of the pad. (The included sample scene files use the Leather_Head_Pad material.) Click the checkered Map button beside the Bump Mapping attribute. In the Create Render Node window, click the Grid texture icon. Grid, Bump 2d, and 2d Placement nodes are added to the Blinn's shading network. Render a test. Small divots appear along the pad edges (see Figure 1.25).

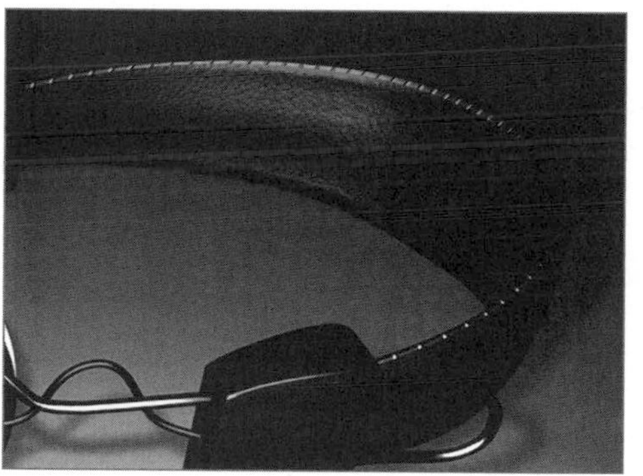

Figure 1.25
(Left) Detail of render after addition of the Grid texture as a bump map. (Right) Render after the adjustment of the 2d Placement and Blinn node attributes. A sample file is saved as `headphones-step7.ma` on the DVD.

4. To refine the bump pattern, open the new 2d Placement node's Attribute Editor tab. Change the Rotate UV attribute to 45. This creates diagonal grid lines. Open the Grid node's Attribute Editor tab. Change UV Width to 0.3, 0.3. This thickens the grid lines so they will become more visible. To further exaggerate the bump, readjust the Blinn node's attributes. For example, the render on the right side of Figure 1.25 sets Diffuse to 0.2, Eccentricity to 0.16, and Specular Roll Off to 0.4. Render a test. An impression of stitching is created.

The Foam surface, which represents the material covering the headphone's built-in speakers, can also benefit from a bump-mapped noise. To add such a bump, follow these steps:

1. In the Hypershade, select the material assigned to the Foam_L and Foam_R surfaces. (The included sample scene files use the Foam material.) Open the material's Attribute Editor tab and click the checkered Map button beside the Bump Mapping attribute. In the Create Render Node window, click the Noise texture icon. Render a test. Blobbish pits appear on the Foam surfaces (see Figure 1.26).

Figure 1.26

(Left) Detail of render after addition of the Noise texture as a bump map. (Right) Render after the adjustment of the 2d Placement, Bump 2d, and material node attributes. A sample file is saved as `headphones-step8.ma` **on the DVD.**

2. To make the surfaces appear as if they are made of closed-cell foam that possesses tiny, bubble-like air pockets, adjust the 2d Placement node connected to the new Noise texture node. Change the Repeat UV attribute to 10, 10 to create smaller "cells." To further randomize the noise pattern, select the Stagger check box. To reduce the depth of the bump, change the Bump 2d node's Depth attribute to 0.5. Last, fine-tune the Color and Diffuse attributes of the material assigned to Foam surfaces. Figure 1.26, for example, has Color set to dark gray (0.19, 0.19, 0.19 in RGB) and Diffuse set to 0.36.

Creating Custom Bitmaps

Although procedural textures are suitable for creating semirandom patterns, they cannot re-create specific designs or features. Hence, the addition of printed logos for the headphones requires the creation of custom bitmaps.

To create a custom bitmap, it will be necessary to export the UV texture space of a targeted surface from Maya and bring it into a digital paint program. For example, to create a bitmap texture for a headphone junction (the plastic part between the chrome slider and the head pad), you can use Adobe Photoshop with the following steps:

1. In Maya, select the Junction_R geometry as a surface and choose Window → UV Texture Editor. From the editor's menu, choose Polygons → UV Snapshot. The UV Snapshot window opens, allowing you to export the UV texture space as a bitmap (see Figure 1.27). Use the File Name browse button to choose a file name and directory location. Change the Size X and Size Y attribute values to an appropriate resolution.

In this case, it's best to choose a resolution that will match the desired resolution of the final texture. For example, 1024×1024 is appropriate for a small piece of geometry when rendering at HD 720. Change the Image Format menu to a format that's supported by a digital paint program (such as Photoshop). For example, JPEG is a commonly used format that produces sufficient quality for the texture-painting process. (If you choose an image format that supports alpha, such as Targa or TIFF, the UV information will be written to an alpha channel.) Click the OK button. The UV texture space is written out with the name and location defined by the File Name attribute.

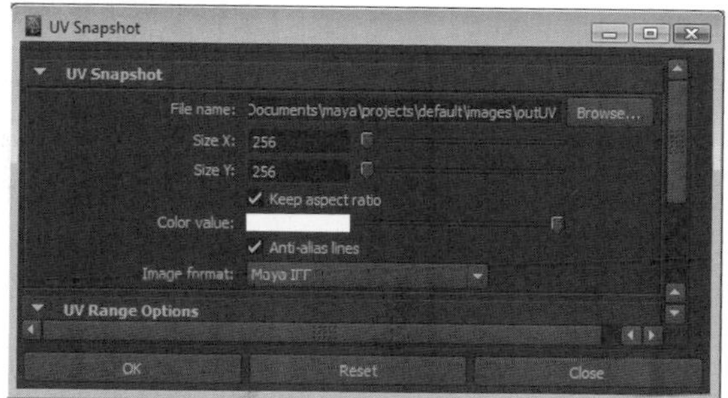

Figure 1.27

The UV Snapshot window

2. Launch Photoshop. Open the UV snapshot file you just wrote out. The UV texture space appears with the UV shells laid out in white over a black background (see Figure 1.28). By default, only the 0 to 1.0 UV space is included. U runs left to right, and V runs down to up with 0, 0 at the bottom-left corner. (If UV shells or UV points fall outside the 0 to 1.0 area, they receive a repeated part of the texture.) Note that the tubes running through the center of the Junction_R surface overlap the surface sides. Overlapping faces share the same part of any assigned texture. For this reason, you usually want to avoid such overlap. However, in this situation, the overlap is unimportant because the walls of the tubes are not seen by the rendering camera.

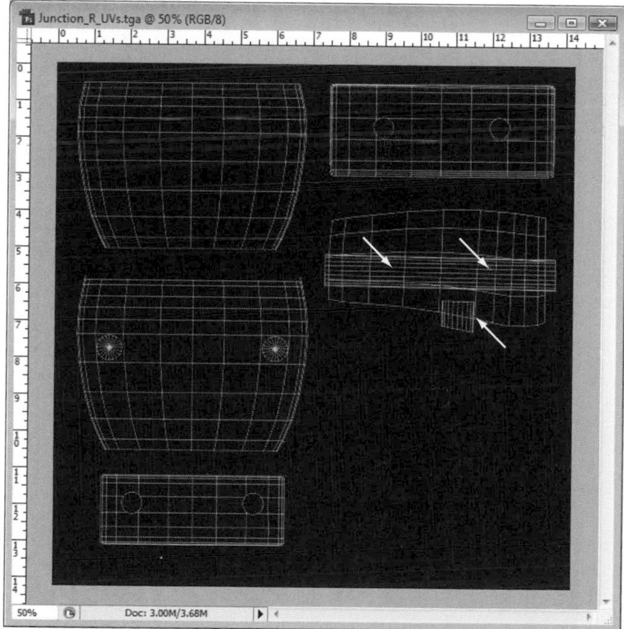

Figure 1.28

A UV snapshot of the Junction_R surface as seen in Photoshop. The arrows point to several areas where polygon faces overlap in the UV texture space.

3. In Photoshop, double-click the Background layer in the Layers panel. The New Layer window opens. Enter a new name, such as **UV Snapshot**, into the Name field, and click OK. This converts the locked Background layer into a layer that you can reposition in the layer stack. Choose Layer → New → Layer. Double-click the new layer to open the New Layer window. Enter a new name, such as **Texture**, into the Name field, and click OK. LMB+drag the UV Snapshot layer to the top of the layer stack. Change the UV Snapshot layer's blending mode menu from Normal to Screen. The Screen blending mode allows the white lines of the snapshot to appear over the lower texture layer. An example PSD file with this setup is included

as `UV_setup.psd` in the `ProjectFiles/Project1/Reference` folder on the DVD. Proceed to paint on the lower texture layer. Note that the general color of the texture does not need to be pure black. Even though the junction is composed of black plastic, you can add subtle scratches, smudges, or slight color variations (see Figure 1.29).

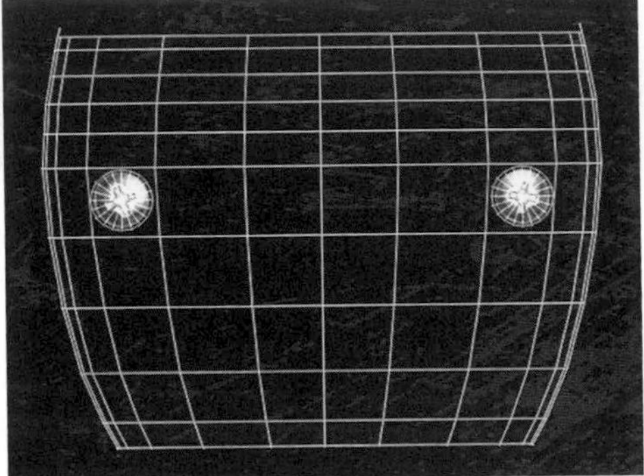

Figure 1.29

(Left) Detail of color variation added to the black representing the plastic. The contrast is exaggerated for print. The actual texture variation is more subtle. (Right) Photo of screw head pasted twice into texture, as seen in Photoshop. A finished texture is included as `Junction_Color.tga` in the `ProjectFiles/Project1/Textures` folder on the DVD.

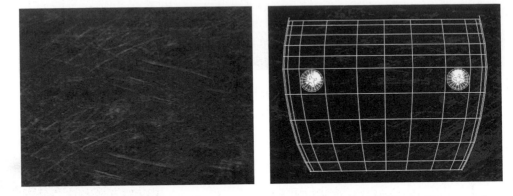

4. To add additional realism, feel free to cut and paste from photo bitmaps. For example, the junction geometry includes two cylindrical holes that represent the locations of screws. Instead of painting screw heads by hand, cut and paste from a photo bitmap of a screw (you can take the photo yourself or find one through a stock photo or 3D texture website). To cut and paste, choose File → Open and retrieve the photo bitmap. Switch to the opened photo bitmap by clicking on the top bar of its window. Using the Lasso tool, draw a selection marquee around the screw head. Choose Edit → Copy. Switch back to the texture you started with. Choose Edit → Paste. Press Ctrl+T to reveal the transformation handle. Interactively scale, position, and rotate the pasted screw head into location over a screw hole indicated by the UV snapshot (see Figure 1.29).
5. To create a specific logo on the side of the junction, you can use Photoshop's Type tool or cut and paste from a bitmap that already carries text. You can leave the text a solid color. On the other hand, you can add color variation to make the text appear more complex. For example, to give the sense that the printed logo uses metallic flake paint, you can use masking tools to cut a noisy layer into a text-like shape (see Figure 1.30). To do so, create a new layer and add white text. Again, you can use the Type tool or cut and paste from a bitmap that already carries text. Create a new layer and paint a pattern that emulates gold flake paint. If this is too difficult to paint, cut and paste from a photo that has a similar noisy pattern (for example, glitter or sand). If the photo's colors are incorrect, choose Image → Adjustments → Color Balance and fine-tune the red, green, and blue mixture. After the gold flake paint layer is completed, switch back to the text layer by clicking on the corresponding layer name in the Layers panel. Using the Magic Wand tool, click within the white area of one letter. Choose Select → Similar. This selects all the white text. Choose Select → Inverse. Return to the gold flake paint layer. Choose Edit → Cut. The gold flake paint is cut out in the shape of the text.

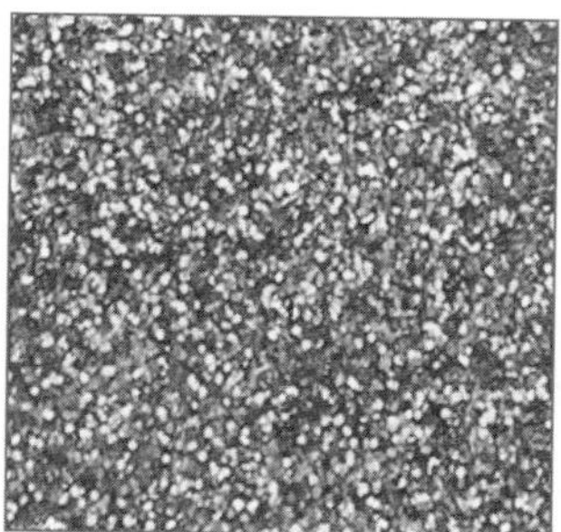

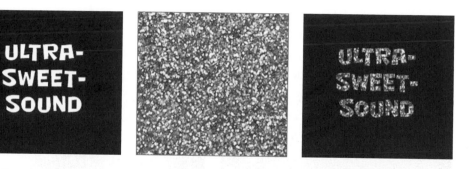

Figure 1.30

(Left) White text over black (Middle) Bitmap photo of gold glitter. (Right) Photo cut out in the shape of the letters with the application of the Magic Wand, selection, and cut tools. A finished texture is included as `Junction_Color.tga` in the `ProjectFiles/Project1/Textures` folder on the DVD.

6. When you've finished painting the various layers, choose Layer → Flatten Image. Choose File → Save and select a Maya-compatible file format. Targa or TIFF are both high-quality formats. When choosing a filename, strive for clarity. For example, name the file **Junction_Color**. Return to Maya. Open the Hypershade, select the material assigned to the Junction_R surface, and open its Attribute Editor tab. Click the Color checkered Map button. In the Create Render Node window, click the File texture icon. File and 2d Placement nodes are added to the shading network. Open the new File node's Attribute Editor tab. Click the Image Name attribute's Browse button and retrieve the texture you wrote out from Photoshop. If the Junction_L surface is assigned to a separate material, repeat this process with that material. Render a test. The screw heads and logo should appear in the correct locations (see Figure 1.31).

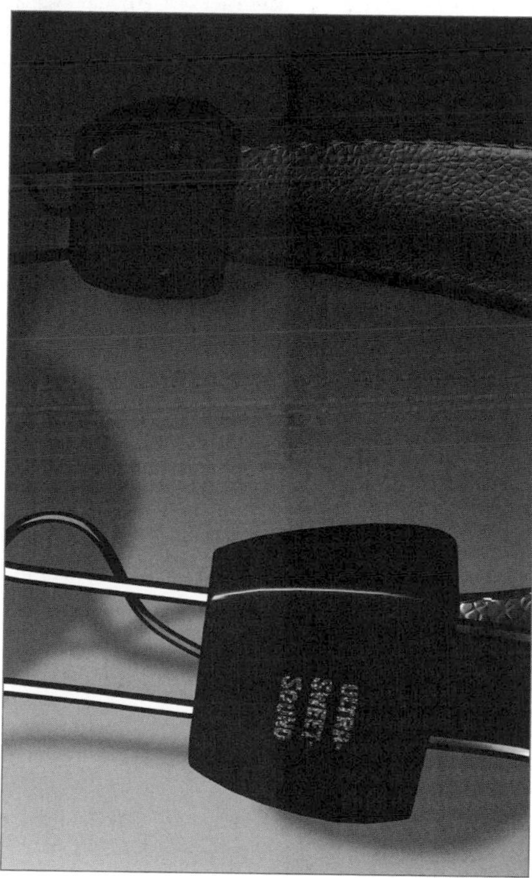

Figure 1.31

Custom bitmap texture applied to Junction material (as seen on frame 36). For a color version of the figure, see the color insert.

It's important to remember that Maya does not store bitmap textures in its scene file. That is, when you save an `.mb` or `.ma` Maya scene file, the bitmap textures are left in their original location and in their original state; the file simply records the location of the texture as a line of text. Therefore, it's best to save the textures in a logical and accessible location. For example, if the scene files are saved to `C:/ProjectFiles/Project1`, save the bitmap textures to `C:/ProjectFiles/Project1/Textures`. If you open a scene file and discover that a File texture is missing or otherwise renders black, you will need to reload it. To do so, open the File texture node's Attribute Editor tab and click the Reload button below the Image Name attribute. If Reload fails, use the Image Name Browse button to relocate the texture file.

When opening Chapter 1 sample scene files, you can avoid missing bitmap textures by first choosing File → Project → Set and browsing for the `Project1` folder whether the folder remains at its original location on the DVD or is located on a drive after the DVD contents have been copied.

When creating custom bitmaps, you're not limited to color. For example, you can create the illusion that the plastic junction is composed of two halves with a central groove by painting a new texture and mapping it to the Bump Mapping attribute of the associated material. The groove requires a black line on the texture while the unaffected areas are filled with 50 percent gray (see Figure 1.32).

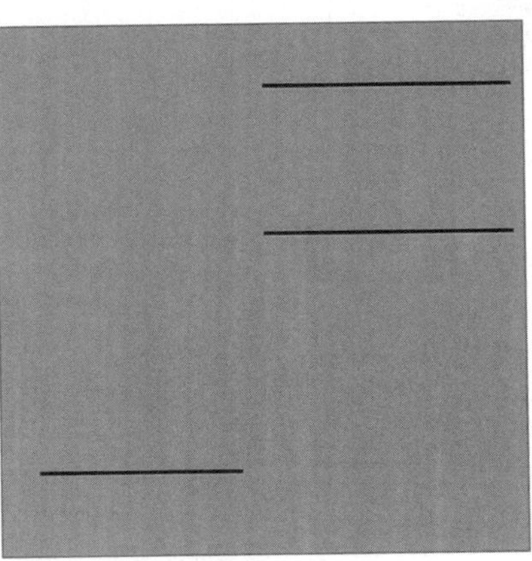

Figure 1.32
(Left) Custom bump texture. (Right) Junction rendered with a bumped groove along the side. A sample file is saved as `headphones-step9.ma`**. A finished texture is included as** `Junction_Bump.tga` **in the** `Project Files/Project1/Textures` **folder on the DVD.**

When painting the bump map texture, it may be difficult to determine where the groove should be positioned in relation to the UV snapshot. To make this process easier, you can follow these steps:

1. In a Maya view panel, RMB+click the Junction_L or Junction_R surface and choose Face from the marking menu. Proceed to Shift+click the faces that would make a suitable location for the groove.
2. Open the UV Texture Editor. The selected faces will be isolated. Make a note of the face locations within the UV texture space. If need be, you can switch back and forth between Maya and Photoshop while painting the texture.
3. Even though the anti-aliasing quality has been set to high, you may notice that small details appear soft. In part, this is because of the automatic activation of the Use Multi Pixel Filter attribute. Multi-pixel filtering averages the pixels within a render as a post-process. This helps prevent anti-aliasing issues such as stair-stepping. Unless the render is destined for video output, however, the filtering can make the render excessively blurry. You can turn off the filtering by deselecting the Use Multi Pixel Filter check box in the Maya Software tab of the Render Settings window.

Other parts of the headphones model can benefit from custom bitmaps mapped to Color attributes. For example, the plastic ear cups are a suitable location for a large logo (see Figure 1.33). To create such a bitmap, you can follow steps similar to those listed at the beginning of this section.

Figure 1.33

(Left) Custom color texture. (Right) Ear cup rendered with logo. A sample file is saved as `headphones-step10.ma`**. A finished texture is included as** `Ear_Cup_Color.tga` **in the** `ProjectFiles/Project1/Textures` **folder on the DVD.**

The headphone ear pads can also benefit from a custom bump texture. The Pad_L and Pad_R surfaces utilize the full UV texture space with a single UV shell for each surface. Because each polygonal surface is doughnut-shaped, there is a seam where the left and right sides of the UV texture space meet in 3D space. You can locate this seam by RMB+clicking in the UV Texture Editor, choosing Face from the marking menu, and Shift+clicking all the faces that form a vertical column on the far left or far right side. The corresponding faces are highlighted in the view panels (see Figure 1.34).

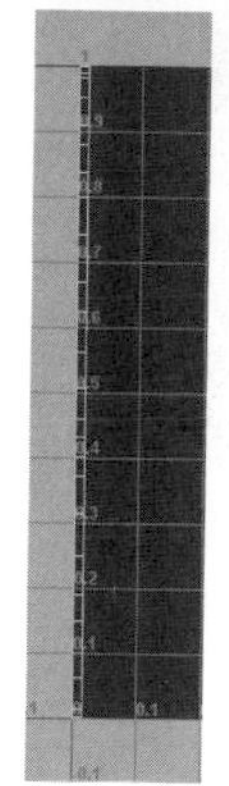

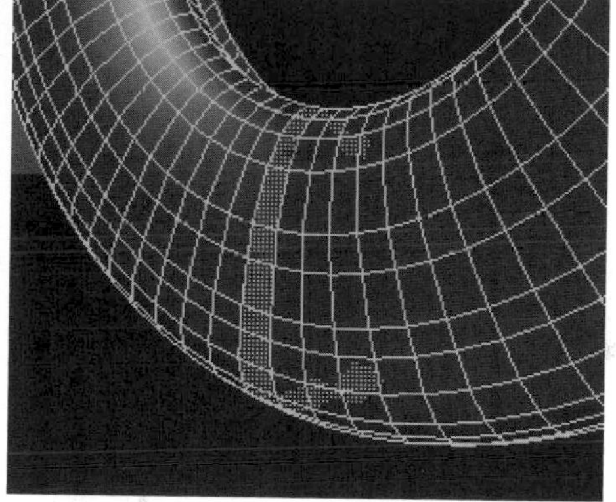

Figure 1.34

(Left) Leftmost column of faces of the Pad_L surface are selected in the UV Texture Editor. (Right) Corresponding faces are highlighted orange in the persp view panel. This indicates the seam where the left and right sides of the UV texture space meet.

Real-world headphone ear pads are often bunched leather that creates numerous parallel grooves. Because the UV shell for the pad geometry is square, such bunches must be painted as vertical black, gray, and white streaks, as shown in Figure 1.35. (When it comes to bump maps, 50 percent gray leaves the surface unaffected, while high values create ridges and low values create grooves.) You can create such streaks in Photoshop by manually using the Brush tool or cutting and pasting from a photo that contains similar vertical features. As a bonus, you can add horizontal white dashes to replicate stitching that occurs near the pad edge. For example, Figure 1.35 illustrates a completed texture. Note that a texture need not be perfectly square to function. In fact, with the pad geometry, it's easier to fit in a sufficient number of vertical lines when the texture has a greater number of pixels in the U direction than in the V direction. After the texture is mapped to the Bump Mapping attribute of the appropriate material, it's necessary to adjust the Bump 2d node's Bump Depth and the material's Diffuse and specular attributes. For Figure 1.35, the following settings are used:

Bump Depth: –0.2 (a negative value inverts the bump result)

Diffuse: 0.4

Eccentricity: 0.2

Specular Roll Off: 0.2

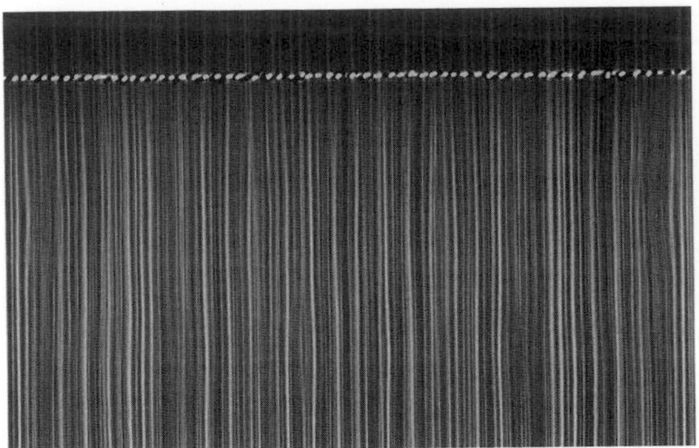

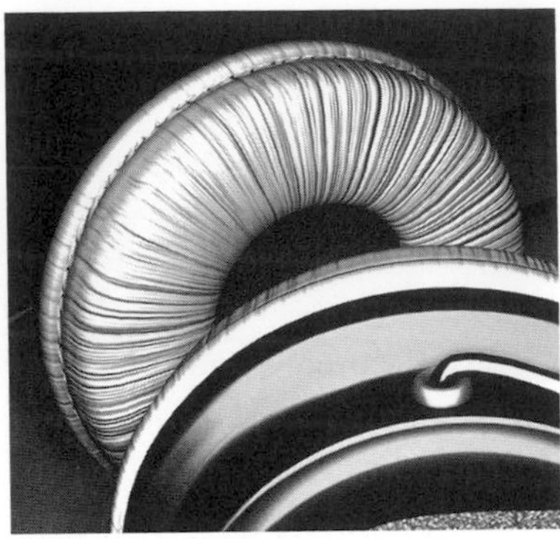

Figure 1.35
(Left) A custom bump texture with vertical lines to replicate bunched leather and short horizontal dashes to re-create stitching. The texture is included as `Ear_Pad_Bump.tga` **in the** `ProjectFiles/Project1/Textures` **folder on the DVD. (Right) Detail of render after the addition of the bump texture. A sample file is saved as** `headphones-step11.ma`.

Another material attribute that benefits from custom bitmaps is the Specular Roll Off. By mapping the Specular Roll Off, you can create the illusion that the surface is scratched, smudged, or slightly imperfect. In this situation, it is not necessary to make a specific map for a specific piece of geometry. Instead, you can create a "generic" bitmap that can be mapped to multiple materials and hence multiple surfaces. For example, you can map a low-contrast, grayscale, noisy bitmap to the Specular Roll Off attributes of the materials assigned to the Junction_L, Junction_R, Cup_L, Cup_R, Grommet_L, and Grommet_R surfaces (see Figure 1.36). If the pattern found within the bitmap appears too similar between surfaces, you can offset each instance by adjusting the Offset UV or Rotate UV attributes of the connected 2d Placement nodes. If a surface is relatively small, such as Grommet_L or Grommet_R, you can use a portion of the texture by reducing the Repeat UV values below 1, 1. Note that the Eccentricity and Specular Color attributes will require adjustment after Specular Roll Off is switched from a solid color to a mapped file. In addition to adjusting the Eccentricity and Specular Color to affect the size and intensity of a highlight, you can lighten or darken the generic specularity texture within Maya. To darken the texture, lower the texture node's Color Gain attribute value. To lighten the texture, raise the texture node's Color Offset value. Color Gain and Color Offset are located in the texture node's Color Balance section. If you raise the Color Offset while lowering the Color Gain, you reduce the contrast found within the texture.

Figure 1.36
(Left) Generic Specular Roll Off texture. The texture is included as `Generic_Spec.tga` **in the** `ProjectFiles/Project1/Textures` **folder on the DVD. (Right) The result of the texture mapped to the ear cups and grommets. A sample file is saved as** `headphones-step12.ma`.

To create a generic noise pattern, you can combine photos of real-world surfaces. Rusty metal, stucco, dirty concrete, and similar surfaces often contain interesting patterns. In fact, if you layer several different photos in Photoshop and adjust each layer's Opacity, you can generate a more complex result. For example, if you stack three different rusty metal photos and reduce each layer's Opacity, an interesting pattern forms (see Figure 1.37). To convert the result to grayscale, choose Layer → Flatten Image and Image → Adjustments → Desaturate. To adjust the overall contrast, apply Image → Adjustments → Brightness/Contrast or Image → Adjustments → Curves.

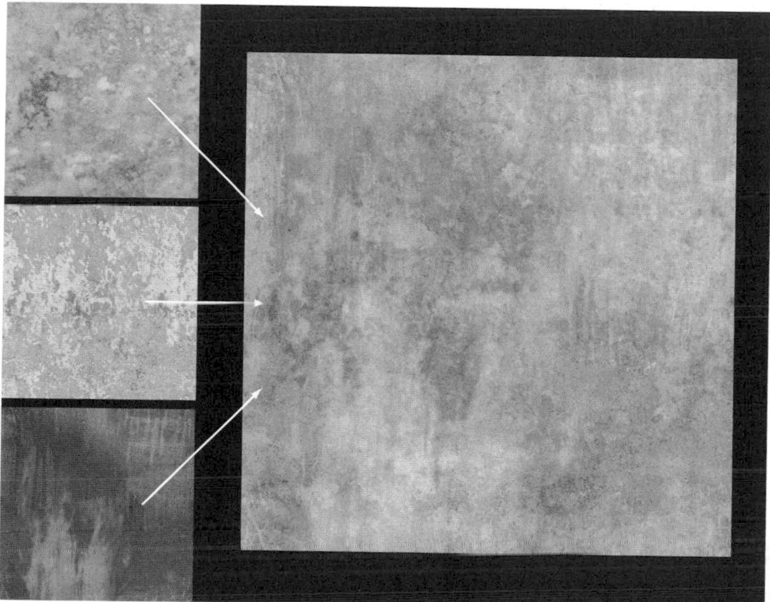

Figure 1.37
Three photo bitmaps of rusty metal are placed on three different layers in Photoshop. The top and middle layers are given reduced Opacity values, leading to a more complex result after the layers are flattened and desaturated.

Scanline and Raytraced Rendering

By default, the Maya Software renderer operates in a scanline mode. The scanline process operates with these basic steps:

- Surfaces visible to the rendering camera are noted. Occlusion of one surface by another is taken into account.
- Polygon faces of the visible surfaces are projected into 2D screen space. The faces are processed in scanline order. A *scanline* is a row of pixels within a render. (Technically speaking, a *pixel* is a sample point that carries an x, y coordinate and a color value; for an image to be stored in a digital system, it must be broken down into a discrete number of pixels.) Hence, a 1280×720 render has 720 scanlines (with each scanline possessing 1280 pixels).

- The final color of each pixel within a scanline is based on the material qualities of the polygon face found within the pixel. In addition, the surface's relationship to lights and cast shadows is taken into account.
- To optimize memory usage, the scanline approach is often broken into tiles. The size of any given tile is based on the number and complexity of surfaces found with a particular area of the camera's view. For example, when you render with Maya Software in the Render View window, the bottom-center section of the view is the first to appear.

In contrast, the raytracing process fires off a virtual ray from the camera eye through each pixel of the view plane. Essentially, the view plane is a 2D grid that's perpendicular to the axis of the camera lens (that is, the grid is coplanar to the virtual film back). The grid possesses the same dimensions as the pixel size of the chosen render resolution. The first surface a ray hits determines the pixel color. That is, the material qualities of the surface are used in the shading calculation of the pixel. If the surface is reflective or refractive, additional rays are created at the surface intersection point. One ray represents the reflection, and one ray represents the refraction. These rays continue until they intersect another surface. Additional reflection and/or refraction rays are born at the new intersection point if the associated material is reflective or refractive. To prevent an infinite number of rays from being born, limits are placed on the total number of permitted rays. Refraction differs from reflection in that a refractive ray travels *through* a surface. Real-world refractive materials, such as glass or water, are perceived as transparent or semitransparent.

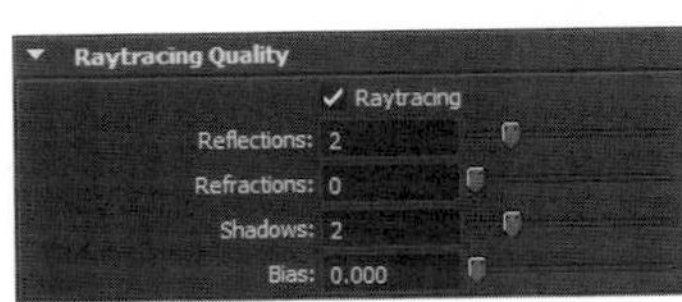

Figure 1.38

The Raytracing Quality section of the Maya Software tab in the Render Settings window

With Maya Software, raytracing is activated via the Raytracing check box found within the Raytracing Quality section of the Maya Software tab of the Render Settings window (see Figure 1.38). The number of times an initial ray is allowed to reflect or refract is controlled by the Reflections and Refractions attributes. For example, if Reflections is set to 3, a ray is allowed to create three additional reflection rays. Along those lines, any reflective surface is allowed to reflect any ray that hits it so long as that ray has been previously reflected *two* times or less. Additionally, you can control the number of raytraced shadows that appear in recursive reflections or retractions by setting the Shadows attribute. If Shadows is set to 2, the render creates one recursive raytraced shadow in any reflection or refraction. If Shadows is set to 1.0, standard shadows appear but no raytraced shadows appear within reflections or refractions. In contrast, depth map shadows appear in all reflections and refractions and are unaffected by the Shadows attribute. For more information on raytraced shadows, see Chapter 2.

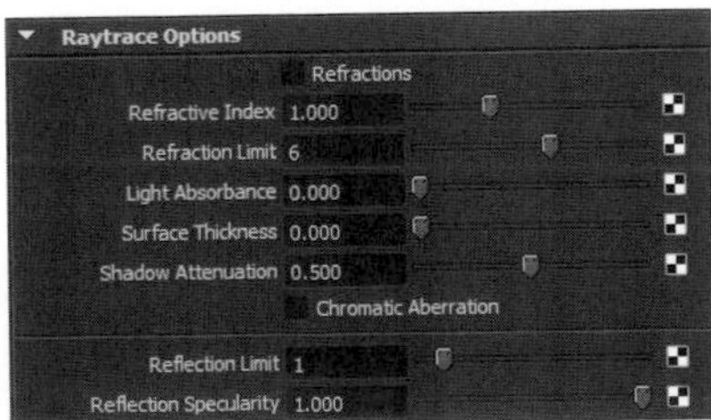

Figure 1.39

The Raytrace Options section of a Blinn material

Blinn, Phong, Phong E, and Anisotropic materials possess a Raytrace Options section (see Figure 1.39).

A list of the most critical attributes and their functionality follows:

Refractions Activates refractivity for the surface assigned to the material. For the refractivity to be visible, the material's Transparency attribute must be set above 0.

Refractive Index Determines the degree of refractivity present. If set to the default 1.0, no refraction occurs. In the real world, a refractive index is a number that indicates the change in the speed of light when the light ray crosses the boundary between two materials. For example, water has a refractive index of 1.33, which means light slows by 25 percent. The actual equation is (speed of light in vacuum)/(speed of light in water) or 1.0/0.75, which equals 1.33. The change in speed affects the perceived angle of the light rays, which causes refracted surfaces to appear bent. For example, a straw placed in a glass of water appears bent below the water line. Lists of real-world materials and their refractive indexes are easily found on the Internet.

Refraction Limit and Reflection Limit Are local material overrides for the Reflections and Refractions attributes found in the Render Settings window. The lower value between matching attributes determines the number of reflective or refractive rays that the surface assigned to the material is permitted to generate. For example, if Reflection Limit is set to 1, the assigned surface is allowed to reflect any ray that hits it so long as that ray has not been reflected previously. If Reflection Limit is set to 4, an assigned surface is allowed to reflect any ray that hits it so long as that ray has been reflected previously *three* times or less. If refractions and/or reflections are missing from a surface when it renders, yet the Reflections and Refractions attributes in the Render Settings window have high values, raise the Refraction Limit and/or Reflection Limit values.

Project: Raytracing Reflections

Thus far, no surface in the headphones scene is creating reflections. To create reflections, you must select the Raytracing check box in the Maya Software tab of the Render Settings window. After Raytracing is activated, all surfaces are potentially reflective. To alter this behavior, you must adjust the Reflectivity attribute of each material in the scene. If you prefer that a surface does not reflect, change the Reflectivity attribute of its assigned material to 0. To increase the strength of a surface's reflection, raise the Reflectivity value of its assigned material; you can exceed the default limit of 1.0 by entering a higher value into the number cell. Because reflectivity is also affected by Specular Roll Off and Specular Color, those attributes may require adjustment. Table 1.2 lists the recommended reflective surfaces and the corresponding Specular Color and Reflectivity settings (the Specular Roll Off attributes were mapped in the section "Creating Custom Bitmaps" earlier in this chapter).

Project: Accentuating the Logos

In Chapter 1, you added logos to the ear cups and adjusters of the headphones. The logo color was made to look like metallic paint by adding a graininess that varied from dark to light values. In a real-world situation, such metallic paint would sparkle when the camera view changes. This is because of the metal flakes within the paint resting at different angles relative to the plastic surface, which thereby causes the specular reflections to suddenly appear and disappear. You can re-create such a sparkle by mapping the material's Incandescence and animating a Noise texture.

To begin this phase of the tutorial, open the scene file you created for the last step of Chapter 1. A completed sample file is saved as `headphones-step13.ma` in the `ProjectFiles/Project1` folder on the DVD. Note that the sample scene files included for Chapters 1 and 2 assume that the bitmap textures are located within the `Textures` folder of the `ProjectFiles/Project1` project directory. Before opening a sample scene file, choose File → Project → Set and browse for the Project1 folder whether the folder remains at its original location on the DVD or is located on a drive after the DVD contents have been copied.

Mapping the Incandescence

To affect the logos without unduly changing the look of the plastic, you will need to create bitmap masks. You can use the following steps to create and apply a mask for the logo appearing on the side of the ear cup geometry:

1. Using Photoshop or a similar program, create a bitmap that features a white logo over black. The logo should be positioned so it lines up perfectly with the corresponding color bitmap (see Figure 2.1). For example, with the Chapter 1 sample scene files, the Plastic_Ear_Cup material is assigned to the ear cup surface; `Ear_Cup_Color.tga` is mapped to the Plastic_Ear_Cup material's Color attribute.

Figure 2.1

(Left) Color bitmap used for the ear cup surface. (Right) Black-and-white bitmap created to mask the logo. Sample textures are included as `Ear_Cup_Color.tga` **and** `Ear_Cup_Logo_Mask.tga` **in the** `ProjectFiles/Project1/Textures` **folder on the DVD.**

2. Open the Hypershade. Open the Attribute Editor tab for the material assigned to the ear cup surface. Click the Incandescence attribute's checkered Map button. In the Create Render Node window, click the File texture icon. With the new File texture node's Attribute Editor tab open, browse for the newly created black-and-white mask bitmap.

3. Render a test. The logo appears pure white. This is because of the high Incandescence values provided by the bitmap. You can reduce the intensity by lowering the Color Gain value of the File node. Color Gain serves as a multiplier.

For example, a Color Gain value of 0.5 reduces the values within the loaded bitmap by 50 percent. You can find the Color Gain attribute in the Color Balance section of the File node's Attribute Editor tab.

You can map the Color Gain attribute with a Noise texture and therefore force the Incandescence to take on a grainy pattern. To do so, follow these steps:

1. Click the checkered Map button beside Color Gain. In the Create Render Node window, click the Noise texture icon. Render a test. Wherever the Noise texture is dark, the Incandescence is reduced. Figure 2.2 illustrates the resulting shading network.
2. At this point, there is little variation in the Incandescence (see Figure 2.3). Open the place2dTexture node connected to the Noise node. You can reveal the node by RMB+clicking the associated material and choosing Graph Network from the marking menu. In the Attribute Editor, change Repeat UV to 8, 8. This shrinks the size of the noise pattern relative to the UV texture space.
3. Render a test. The Incandescence, although more varied, remains too intense. To give the pattern greater contrast, return to the Noise node's Attribute Editor tab. Set Amplitude to 0.15, Ratio to 0, Density to 0.2, and Spottyness to 1.0 (see Figure 2.4). As a final touch, increase the Noise node's Color Gain to 2.0. To do so, click the color swatch cell to open the Color Chooser window. Change the lower-right menu to HSV and enter **2.0** in the V (value) cell. Increasing the Color Gain to a value above the default 1.0 exaggerates the bright portions of the incandescence.

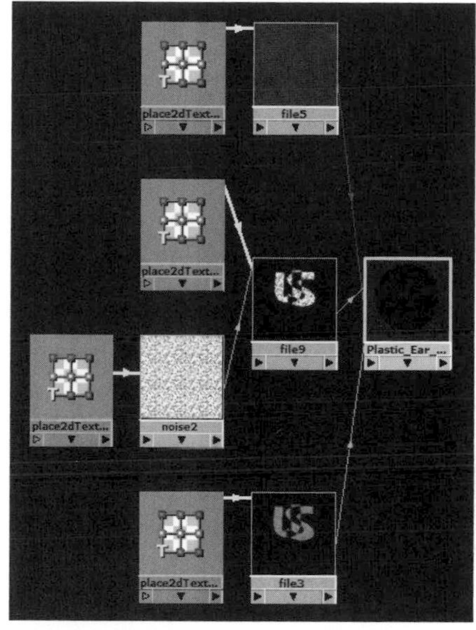

Figure 2.2
Final shading network for the material assigned to the ear cups

Figure 2.3
(Left) Incandescent pattern created by mapping a Noise texture to the Color Gain of the File texture carrying the logo mask. (Center) Pattern after Repeat UV is set to 8, 8. (Right) Pattern after Noise attributes are adjusted to provide more contrast

Animating a Sparkle

At this stage, the logo is given additional intensity through mapped Incandescence. However, the pattern provided by the Noise texture is fixed. That is, it will appear the same on every frame of the animation. You can add motion to the pattern by animating the Time attribute of the Noise node. Different Time values cause the program to select different "slices" of the noise pattern. If the Time value changes rapidly over the course of the animation, the dots within the noise pattern will appear to flicker, much like a sparkle. To animate the Time attribute, follow these steps:

1. Move the Timeline to frame 1. RMB+click the Time attribute's numeric cell. Choose Set Key from the menu. The cell turns pink, which indicates the addition of the key frame.
2. Move the Timeline to frame 36. Enter a value of **10** into the Time attribute's numeric cell. RMB+click the cell and choose Set Key. Scrub back and forth across the Timeline. The Noise pattern now shifts rapidly (see Figure 2.5).

To test the animation, it's best to render a short frame sequence. For example, render out frames 1 to 10. Testing a short sequence will allow you to judge whether this artificial sparkle occurs at a believable speed. For information on batch rendering, see the next section.

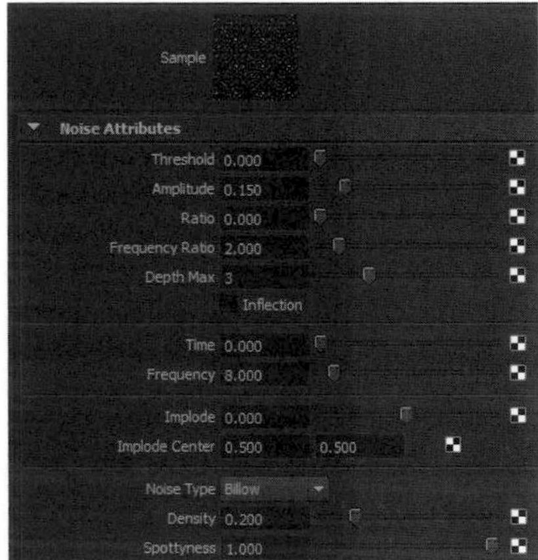

Figure 2.4

The Noise texture Attribute Editor tab after adjustment

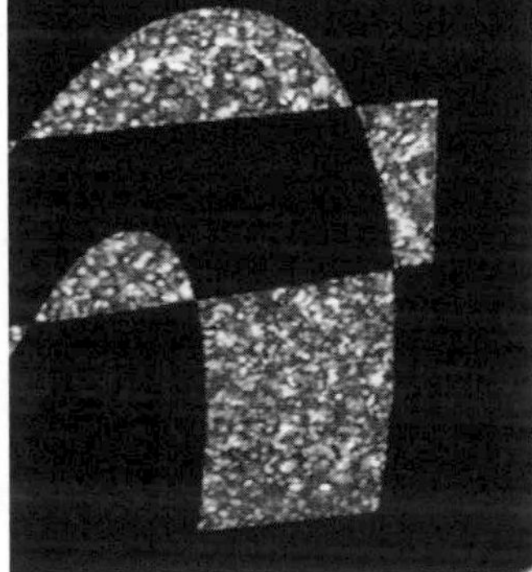

Figure 2.5

(Left) Detail of logo at frame 10 (Right) Detail of logo at frame 15. Note the slight variations in the Incandescent "sparkles." A sample Maya file is saved as `headphones-step14.ma` on the DVD. For a color version of this figure, see the color insert.

Adding a Sparkle to the Junction

To add an artificial sparkle to the logo appearing on the plastic junction, follow the steps in the previous two sections. Note that the smaller size of the junction will require different Repeat UV values on the place2dTexture node connected to the newest Noise texture. For example, a Repeat UV value of 7, 7 works well. An example file using these values is included as `headphones-step15.ma` on the DVD.

Batch Rendering

Thus far, you have created test renders through the Render View window. To create a rendered image sequence, it will be necessary to batch render. Before launching a batch render, you will need to set various attributes within the Render Settings window (see Figure 2.6).

Here are some tips:

- Choose a File Name Prefix that is easily understood, such as *headphones_test_1*.
- Through the Image Format menu, Maya gives you the option to render out a Windows AVI movie file. However, it's generally better to render image sequences. For example, Targa (`.tga`), TIFF (`.tif`), and OpenEXR (`.exr`) image sequences are commonly used in the animation industry. If you need to interrupt a batch render and are rendering an AVI, the AVI becomes truncated. In contrast, the rendered frames of an image sequence are unaffected by a canceled render. In addition, you can render out specific frame ranges to fill gaps in the image sequence; an AVI cannot be amended in the same way. AVI movies also suffer from compression, whereas a Targa or OpenEXR sequence does not suffer any loss of quality.

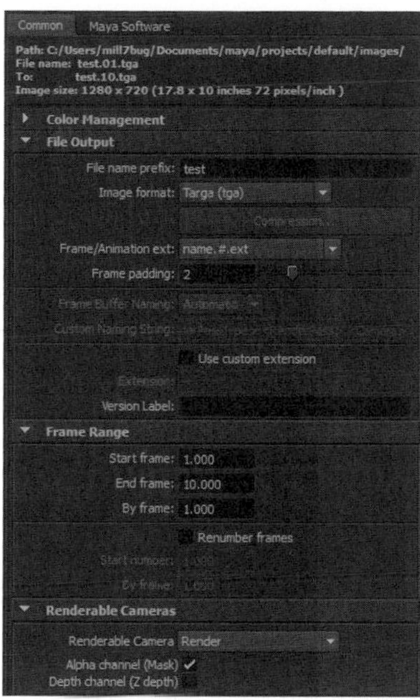

Figure 2.6

The Common tab of the Render Settings window

- In general, it's best to set Frame/Animation Ext to Name.#.ext. This will guarantee that external programs, such as compositors, will interpret the frame sequence correctly. For example, the Name.#.ext option creates frames with the names *`test.1.tga`*, *`test.2.tga`*, and so on.
- If an animation is longer than nine frames, you should adjust the Frame Padding attribute. Frame Padding sets the number of numeric placeholders that appear between the first and second periods in the filename. Proper padding will allow external programs, such as compositors, to load the frames in the proper order. For example, a Frame padding of 2 leaves two placeholders, as in *test.##.tga*. You can use Table 2.1 for choosing a Frame Padding value.

Table 2.1

Frame Padding settings

Animation Length	Frame Padding Value	Resulting Filenames
1 to 9 frames	1	`test.1.tga`, `test.9.tga`
1 to 99 frames	2	`test.01.tga`, `test.99.tga`
1 to 999 frames	3	`test.001.tga`, `test.999.tga`

- If there is more than one camera in the scene, set the Renderable Camera menu to the camera you want to render. The menu defaults to the persp camera.
- Set the anti-aliasing settings, in the appropriate renderer tab, to a level that's suitable for the particular render. For more information, see the section "Anti-Aliasing Theory" later in this chapter.

After you've adjusted the Render Settings attributes, you can launch a render by switching to the Render menu set and choosing Render → Batch Render. To monitor the progress of the render, choose Window → General Editors → Script Editor. The progress of each frame is printed. By default, the rendered frames are deposited in the default project directory. Before starting the render, you can select a new directory by choosing File → Project → Set. You can also edit the current directory structure by choosing File → Project → Edit Current. To cancel a render, choose Render → Cancel Batch Render. If you cancel the render, the current frame is broken; however, earlier frames will be left intact in the project directory.

To view a finished image sequence render, use Maya's FCheck viewer. Choose File → View Sequence and browse for the first frame. The FCheck viewer opens and carries standard playback controls. You can step through the sequence one frame at a time by using the keyboard's arrow keys.

Project: Adding Strategic Fill Light

At this point, the headphones are lit by a single area light. Although this provides attractive product lighting, you can add fill light to fine-tune the result. For example, the rear junction (Junction_L) and the head pad possess areas that are consistently dark with little detail showing. By strategically placing volume lights in these areas, you can provide a controlled fill and thereby add interest to otherwise uninteresting areas. To create and place the volume lights, follow these steps:

1. Choose Create → Lights → Volume Light. Select the new volume light and rename it **Fill_1**. Scale the light so it's approximately 6 units in diameter. Place it beside the Junction_L surface (see Figure 2.7).
2. Open the light's Attribute Editor tab. Change the Intensity to 5 and the Volume Light Dir to Inward. An Inward direction causes the light rays to move from the outer edge of the light volume shape to the light's center. Render a test. The junction receives a more distinct specular highlight, which helps to define the surface more clearly (see Figure 2.7). Experiment with different Intensity values. Try setting the Volume Light Dir to Outward and Downward to see variations in the light's effect. Even though the volume light shape intersects the floor, it will not light the floor as long as Volume Light Dir is set to Inward.

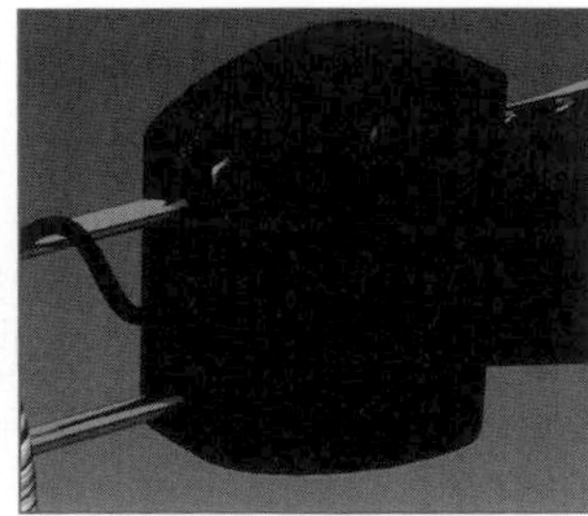
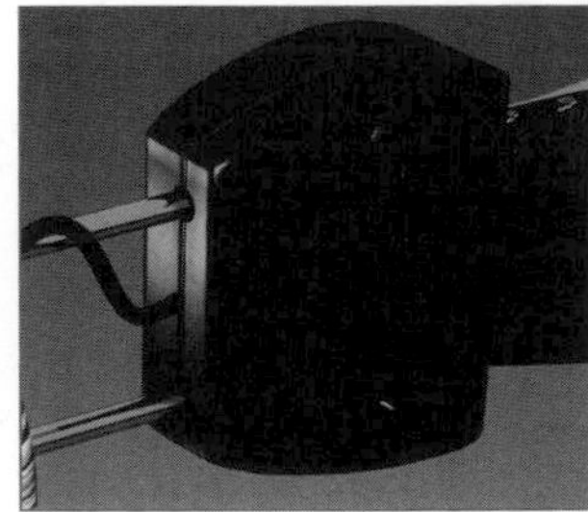

Figure 2.7
(Left) Placement of Fill_1 volume light. (Center) Junction_L surface without volume light. (Right) Surface with volume light

3. Choose Create → Lights → Volume Light. Select the new volume light and rename it **Fill_2**. Scale the light so it's approximately 7 units in diameter. Place it above the forward bend of the Head_Pad surface (see Figure 2.8).
4. Open the Attribute Editor for Fill_2. Change the Intensity to 20. By default, the light's Volume Light Dir is set to Outward. An Outward direction causes the light rays to move from the light's center to the outer edge of the light volume shape. Render a test. The top edge of the head pad receives a more distinct highlight, which helps define the curvature of the surface (see Figure 2.8). Because Volume Light Dir is set to Outward, the floor will receive extra illumination if the volume light shape is allowed to intersect the floor.

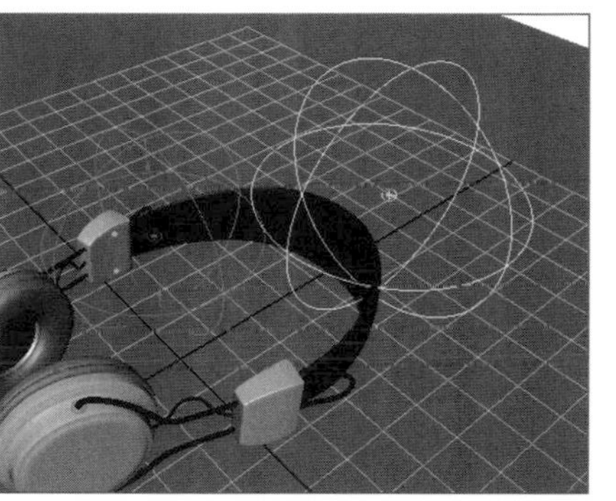

Figure 2.8
(Left) Placement of Fill_2 volume light. (Center) Head_Pad surface without volume light. (Right) Surface with volume light. A sample file is saved as `headphones-step16.ma` on the DVD.

Project: Splitting Material Assignments

The sample scene file provided in this chapter uses a minimum number of materials. Hence, similar surfaces share the same material. For example, the Leather_Ear_Pad material is assigned to the Pad_L and Pad_R surfaces. Although material sharing makes the adjustment of materials more efficient, it can lead to surfaces appearing poorly lit. By reexamining earlier example renders, it's clear that the pad surfaces suffer from this problem. While Pad_L looks appropriately bright, the back of Pad_R is overexposed and thus appears pure white (see Figure 2.9).

Figure 2.9
The back edge of the Pad_R surface is overexposed, making it appear as a pure white arc.

Figure 2.10
Pad_R is assigned to the duplicated material. The adjusted material attributes for both Pad_L and Pad_R improve the appearance and prevent overexposure. A sample file is saved as `headphones-step17.ma` **on the DVD.**

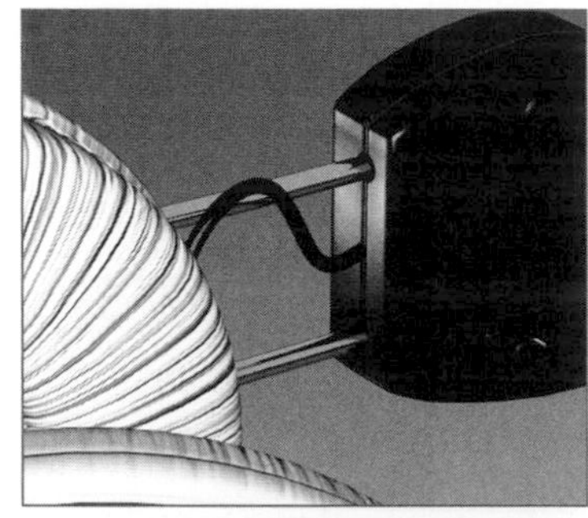

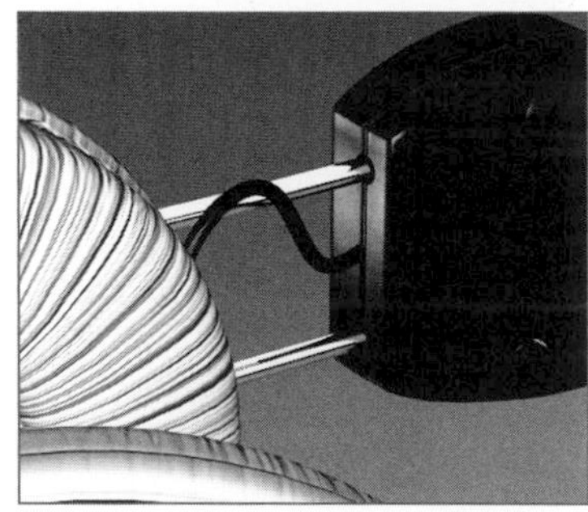

Figure 2.11
(Top) The reflection seen on the Slider_L surface is dim. (Bottom) Slider_L is assigned a duplicated material. The adjusted Reflectivity value increases the strength of the reflection. A sample file is saved as `headphones-step18.ma` **on the DVD.**

To solve this problem, it's best to assign a unique material to Pad_R. A quick way to do this is to duplicate Leather_Ear_Pad, thereby splitting it into a left and right version. To duplicate and adjust the resulting materials, follow these steps:

1. In the Hypershade, select the Leather_Ear_Pad material. From the Hypershade menu, choose Edit → Duplicate → Shading Network. The material, along with all its attribute settings and connections, is duplicated. Rename the original Leather_Ear_Pad material **Leather_Ear_Pad_L**. Rename the duplicated material **Leather_Ear_Pad_R**.
2. Assign the Leather_Ear_Pad_R material to the Pad_R surface. Adjust the material until the pad no longer appears overexposed. For example, in Figure 2.10, the Diffuse value is set to 0.2, Eccentricity is set to 0, and Ambient Color is set to 0.08, 0.08, 0.8 in RGB. By lowering the Diffuse values, the entire surface gets darker. However, this causes the far edge of the pad to become somewhat dirty and gray. To fight this, the Ambient Color is raised above 0. By doing this, the overall values for the material are raised; the darkened areas are thus brightened without overpowering the highlights. Changing the Eccentricity value to 0 shuts off the specular highlight. In this case, the highlight is not needed because it contributes to the overly bright edge.
3. Because the Pad_L surface now has its own material, it's a good time to fine-tune its look. For example, in Figure 2.10, the Leather_Ear_Pad_L material's Diffuse attribute is set to 0.35, Eccentricity is set to 0, and Ambient Color is set to 0.08, 0.08, 0.8 in RGB.

Another surface that suffers from a shared material is Slider_L. While Slider_R possesses a strong, bright reflection, Slider_L is dim and dingy. To fix this through a material split, follow these steps:

1. In the Hypershade, select the Chrome material. From the Hypershade menu, choose Edit → Duplicate → Shading Network. The material, along with all its attribute settings and connections, is duplicated. Rename the original Chrome material **Chrome_R**. Rename the duplicated material **Chrome_L**.
2. Assign the Chrome_L material to the Slider_L surface. Open the material's Attribute Editor tab and change Reflectivity to 2. Render a test. Slider_L gains a stronger, brighter reflection (see Figure 2.11).

Note that the material splitting demonstrated in this section is suitable for static objects. If the object undergoes deformation or other significant movement, as with character animation or a model spin test, the material splitting may not be appropriate as the surfaces may be exposed to different light and shadow intensities as the time line progresses. If material splitting proves ill-suited for a shot, more time must be spent placing lights and balancing the light and shadow intensities with the material attribute values.

Project: Fine-Tuning the Shadow

At this stage, the depth map shadow is equally smooth along its edge. The softening is provided by the Filter Size attribute of the area light. Unfortunately, the degree of softening is equal along all points of a depth map edge. In contrast, artificial light sources, such as lightbulbs, create shadows that naturally soften over distance. You can re-create such softness by switching to raytraced shadows. To do so, follow these steps:

1. Select the area light and open its Attribute Editor tab. Expand the Raytrace Shadow Attributes section and select the Use Ray Trace Shadows check box. The Use Depth Map Shadows check box is deselected automatically. Return the Shadow Color attribute to black.
2. Render a test. Because raytracing was activated in Chapter 1, the shadow appears. However, the shadow is very grainy (see Figure 2.12). To improve the quality, raise the Shadow Rays attribute from 1.0 to 40. Shadow Rays determines the number of samples taken along the shadow edge. Render a test. The shadow quality is improved. In addition, the shadow degrades over distance. That is, the farther the shadow-casting surface is from a shadow-receiving surface, the softer the shadow.

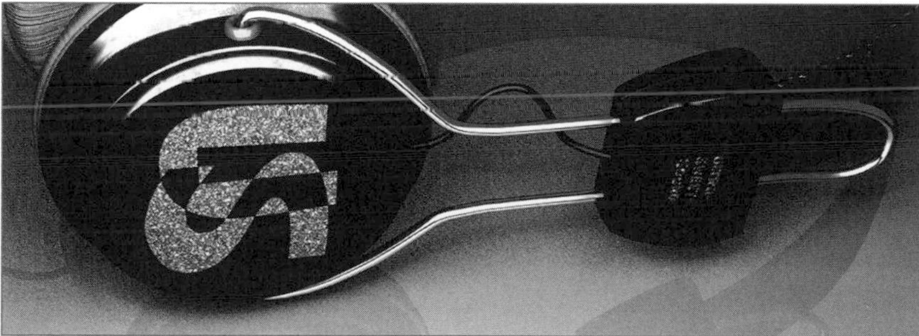

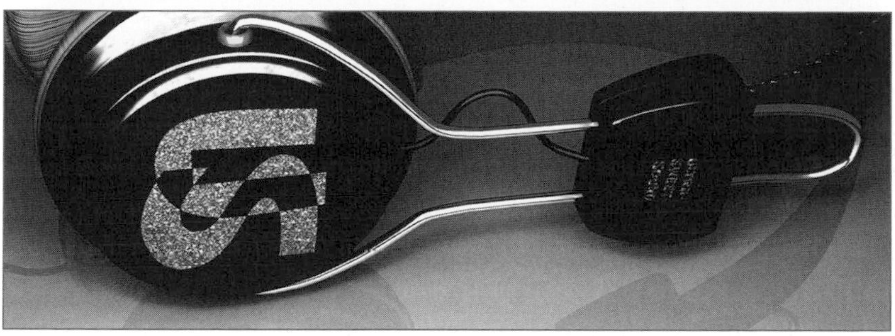

Figure 2.12
(Top) Raytraced shadow with Shadow Rays set to 1.0. (Bottom) Same shadow with Shadow Rays set to 40. A sample file is saved as `headphones-step19.ma` **on the DVD.**

Note that the render may slow significantly when raytracing shadows with an area light. To speed up the tests, consider reducing the render resolution and/or anti-aliasing quality through the Render Settings window. In addition, consider rendering small regions within the Render View to examine the shadow.

Light Width

Area lights are able to create shadow edge degradation because of the physically based lighting calculation they employ. (As discussed in Chapter 1, area lights function like an array of point lights whose rays overlap at the shadow edges.) Other light types do not produce the degradation, but instead produce hard-edged raytraced shadows by default. You can soften the shadow edges, however, by artificially increasing the light's width. The attribute that controls the width varies in name, as shown in Table 2.2.

Table 2.2
Light width attributes

LIGHT TYPE	ATTRIBUTE NAME	VALUE RANGE (HARD TO SOFT EDGED)
Ambient	Shadow Radius	0 to 1.0
Spot	Light Radius	0 to 1.0
Directional	Light Angle	0 to 180
Point	Light Radius	0 to 1.0
Volume	Light Radius	0 to 1.0

The light from a spot, point, or volume light emanates from a finite location in space. With a point or volume light, this location corresponds to the center of the light icon. With a spot light, the location is aligned to the origin of the cone. The directional component of an ambient light also emanates from the icon's center (hence, when Ambient Shade is set to 1.0, ambient lights are identical to point lights). Because the light rays extend from such a finite location, they do not overlap at the shadow edge (see Figure 2.13). By increasing the light width through the Shadow Radius or Light Radius attributes, the light rays are allowed to overlap. Overlapping rays create a soft-edged shadow. The distance the shadow-casting surface is from the shadow-receiving surface affects the degree of the softness. Hence, a shadow can degrade over distance.

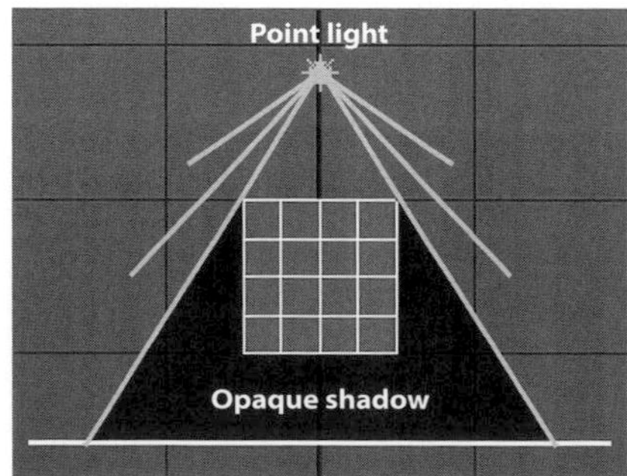

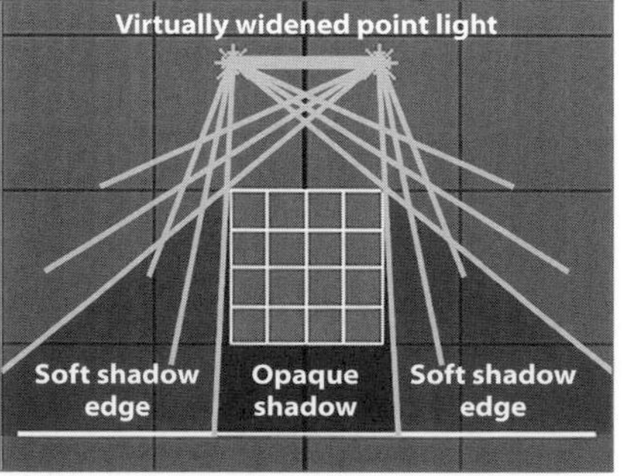

Figure 2.13
(Left) Rays from a point light fail to overlap at the shadow edge of a cube. (Right) Rays from a point light with a nonzero Light Radius value overlap at the shadow edge. (Although the light is illustrated with a greater width, the light icon does not change in Maya.)

For example, in Figure 2.14, the area light that serves as a key is changed temporarily to a point light. When Light Radius is set to the default 0, the shadow edge is perfectly hard. When Light Radius is set to 1.0, the shadow edge degrades over distance.

By default, directional lights create parallel rays of light while possessing direction without position. Hence, the Light Angle attribute allows you to make the rays divergent. Raising the Light Angle value is roughly analogous to increasing the cone diameter of an array of spot lights (see Figure 2.15).

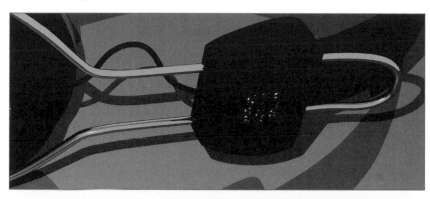

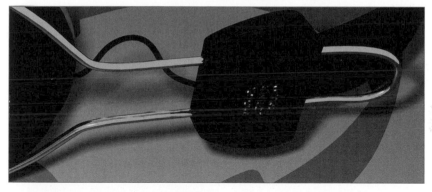

Figure 2.14

(Top) The area light that serves as a key is temporarily changed to a point light. Light Radius is left at the default 0, producing a hard-edged shadow. (Bottom) Light Radius is set to 1.0, creating a shadow that degrades (softens) over distance.

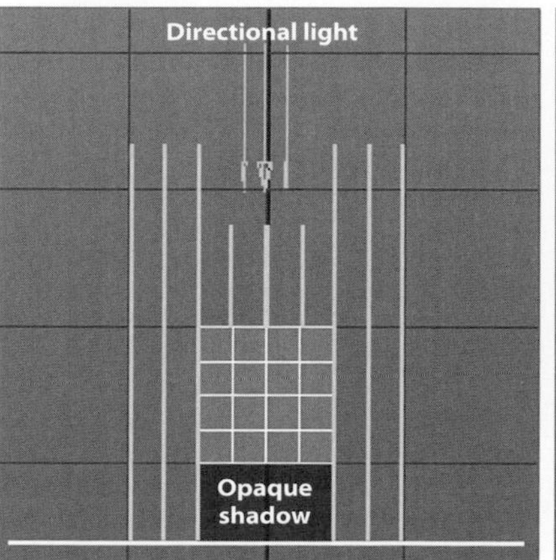

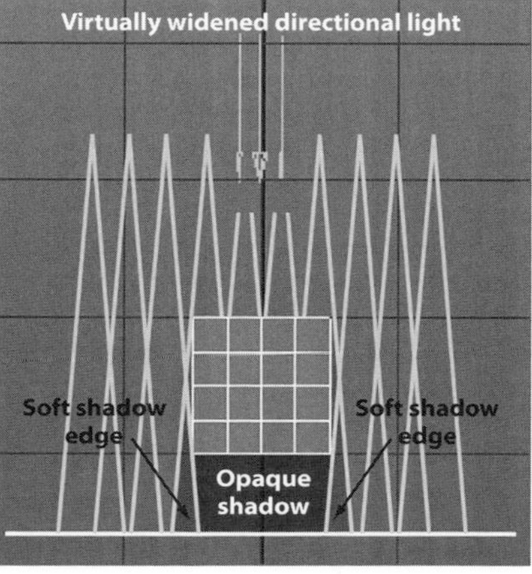

Figure 2.15

(Left) Rays from a directional light fail to overlap at the shadow edge of a cube. (Right) Rays from a directional light with a nonzero Light Angle overlap at the shadow edge.

Project: Switching to mental ray

The mental ray renderer offers a number of features that are not available to the Maya Software renderer. These include the blurring of reflections and the application of Final Gathering. (Other mental ray features are discussed in later chapters.)

To switch the renderer, change the Render Using menu, at the top of the Render Settings window, to mental ray. If mental ray does not appear as an option, its plug-in is disabled. To enable the mental ray plug-in, choose Window → Settings/Preferences → Plug-In Manager and select the Loaded check box beside *Mayatomr.mll* in the Plug-In Manager window.

By default, raytracing is activated for mental ray. You can find the Raytracing check box in the Raytracing section of the Quality tab of the Render Settings window. The Reflections, Refractions, and Shadows attributes, found in the same section, function in the same manner as they do for Maya Software (for more information, see the end of Chapter 1). The mental ray renderer, however, adds the Max Trace Depth attribute, which sets the maximum number of times any given ray is allowed to reflect *or* refract. For example, if Max Trace Depth is set to 5, a ray can reflect five times, refract five times, or reflect and refract up to five times. (Ultimately, Max Trace Depth trumps the Reflections and Refractions attributes.)

When switching the renderer, it's important to test the result. Although mental ray understands raytraced shadows and standard Maya Software materials, the results will be slightly different. For example, the raytraced shadow appears grainy with mental ray (see Figure 2.16). You can reduce the graininess by raising the Shadow Rays attribute of the area light to 128.

Additionally, the specular highlight along the top of the closest ear cup loses its detail (see Figure 2.17). In this situation, the Generic_Spec texture mapped to the Specular Roll Off of the Plastic_Ear_Cup material fails to have an effect. An alternative solution requires the mapping of the texture to the Specular Color instead.

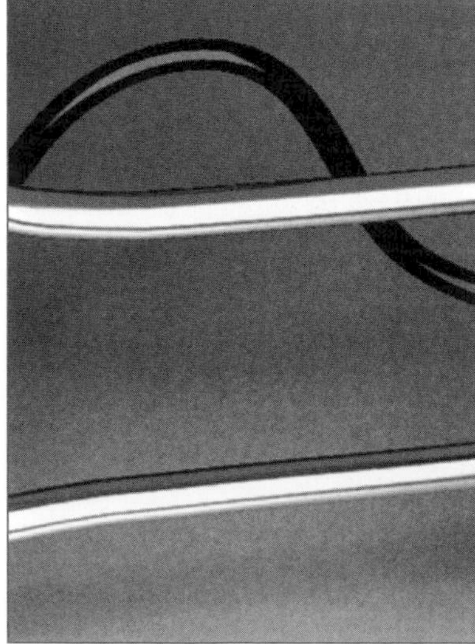

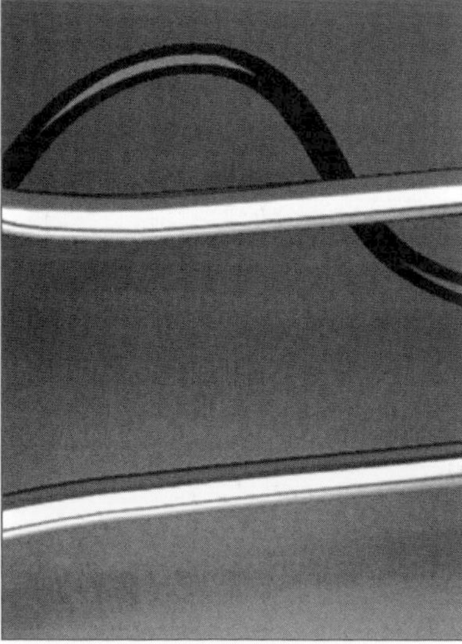

Figure 2.16

(Left) Close-up of the shadow after the switch to mental ray. (Right) The shadow after Shadow Rays is set to 128

Figure 2.17
(Left) Highlight after switch to mental ray. (Right) Highlight after the Generic_Spec texture is mapped to the Specular Color. A sample file is saved as `headphones-step20.ma` on the DVD.

To break the old texture connection and create a new one, follow these steps:

1. In the Hypershade, RMB+click the material assigned to the Cup_R geometry and choose Graph Network. The material's shading network appears in the work area. Click on the connection line between the File node carrying the Generic_Spec texture and the material. Use the Alt key and mouse buttons to change the view within the work area (Alt+RMB zooms in). After the connection is selected, it turns yellow. Press the Delete key. The connection is broken.
2. MMB+drag the newly freed File node and drop it on top of the material. The Connect Input Of menu appears. Choose specularColor from the menu. A new connection is drawn from the File node to the material node. The Generic_Spec texture is now affecting the specularColor of the material (see Figure 2.17).

Note that switching from Maya Software to mental ray forces a different set of anti-aliasing attributes upon the render; the attributes are set to low quality by default. For detailed information on these attributes, see the next section.

Anti-Aliasing Theory

By default, the Maya Software and mental ray renderers operate with draft anti-aliasing settings. When preparing high-quality renders, it's therefore important to understand how to adjust the anti-aliasing attributes.

Anti-aliasing is the process by which aliasing artifacts are reduced. Aliasing artifacts result when an image is constructed with a limited number of pixels. Even a large-resolution render suffers from aliasing problems. For example, a 2048×1556 render is limited to 3,186,688 pixels. Although 3 million pixels may seem like an excessive number, they may not be sufficient to reproduce all the fine detail found within a 3D scene (detail may stem from intricate geometry, textures, and/or lighting).

When a render is created, a view plane grid is laid over the scene from the point of view of the camera. The number of grid rows and columns is established by the render resolution. Hence, each grid square equates to 1 pixel. Whatever lies within a grid square must be sampled to create a single red, green, and blue color value for the corresponding pixel. If multiple pieces of geometry, complex textures, or detailed shadows lie within the view of a single grid square, they still must be sampled. If no anti-aliasing methods are applied, only a single sample can be taken at a single point within the grid square. Hence, the resulting render is never as accurate as the original scene. The limited sampling leads to aliasing artifacts, which include stair-stepping, Moiré patterns, and buzzing.

Stair-stepping forms step-like transitions along a surface or texture edge that is not perfectly parallel or perpendicular to a row of pixels (see Figure 2.18).

A *Moiré pattern* forms when a repeated design is not perfectly parallel or perpendicular to rows of pixels. This if often seen when texture is tiled and the surface carrying the texture is not perpendicular to the camera (see Figure 2.19).

Buzzing takes the form of abrupt variations in pixel values across sequential frames of an animation. Hence, the buzzing appears as additional random noise. The buzzing occurs when texture detail is significantly smaller than corresponding pixels and the color averaging for individual pixels becomes inaccurate. Buzzing is visible only if geometry and/or the camera moves through the scene.

Figure 2.18

(Left) Detail of surface edge. (Center) Portion of view plane grid laid over scene from the point of view of the camera. Each grid square corresponds to 1 pixel. (Right) Resulting rendered pixels. Each pixel can carry only one sampled color.

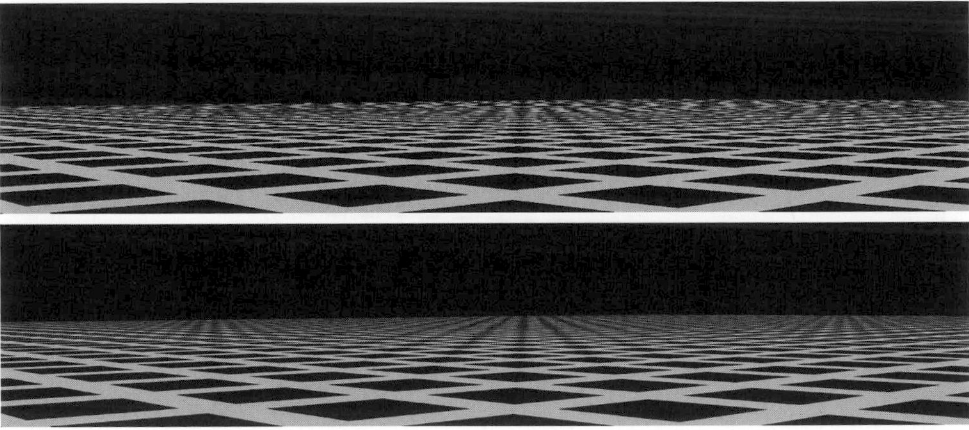

Figure 2.19

(Top) A noisy Moiré pattern forms along the far edge of a surface with a detailed texture. A sample file is included as `moire.ma` in the `ProjectFiles/Project1/Reference` folder. (Right) High-quality anti-aliasing settings significantly reduce the strength of the pattern and remove the visible noise.

The best way to combat aliasing artifacts is to take additional shading samples. That is, any given grid square in a view plane can be broken down into smaller squares. The smaller squares are commonly referred to as *subpixels*. Determining the color of each subpixel forces the renderer to take additional samples within the area originally covered by a single pixel. The additional sampling ensures that the final rendered pixel has a more representative color. The heightened accuracy minimizes the appearance of aliasing artifacts (see Figure 2.19).

Maya Software Anti-Aliasing Settings

The Maya Software renderer offers several presets for anti-aliasing. These are found within the Anti-Aliasing Quality section of the Maya Software tab in the Render Settings window (see Figure 2.20).

The Quality and Edge Anti-Aliasing menus present settings that run from draft quality to production quality. You can use either menu. Both menus remotely set the attributes within the Number Of Samples, Multi-Pixel Filtering, and Contrast Threshold sections. For more control, you can set the attributes to custom values. Each attribute's functionality is described here:

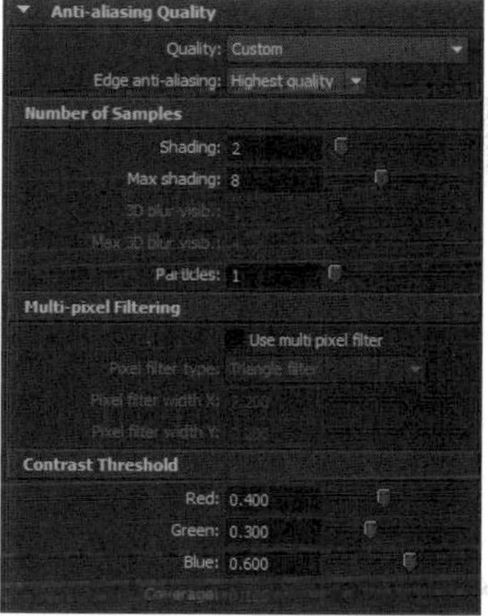

Figure 2.20
The Anti-Aliasing Quality section of the Maya Software renderer. These are the settings used to create high-quality renders at the beginning of this chapter.

Shading The Shading attribute sets the minimum number of subpixel samples taken for a given pixel. If set to 1, each pixel is sampled one time (in other words, there are no subpixels). If set to 4, each pixel is sampled four times with four subpixels.

Max Shading The Max Shading attribute sets the maximum number of subpixel samples taken for a given pixel. Max Shading is available only when Edge Anti-Aliasing is set to Highest Quality. When Max Shading is activated, the subpixel process becomes adaptive (that is, flexible for each pixel). The adaptivity is dependent on the Contrast Threshold section. Note that the higher the Max Shading value is, the more accurate the resulting render will be and the longer that render will take. For the example Maya Software renders in this chapter, Shading was set to 2, Max Shading was set to 8, multi-pixel filtering was left off, and the Contrast Threshold section was left with default values.

Contrast Threshold The Contrast Threshold section tests whether pixels sharing corners have a contrast value that is higher than the Red, Green, and Blue attribute values. For example, if a pixel has a red channel value of 0.7 and the neighboring pixel has a red channel value of 0.1, the contrast value for the red channel is 0.6. A contrast value of 0.6 is higher than the default Red attribute value of 0.4, which means the pixel becomes a candidate for subpixel subdivision. That said, the contrast must be tested for the blue and green channels before the subdivision criteria are fully met. The Contrast Threshold also tests the contrast between subpixels. Therefore, neighboring subpixels with high contrast are broken into smaller, recursive subpixels. Ultimately, the number of times a pixel is recursively broken down into smaller and smaller subpixels is capped by the Max Shading value.

Multi-Pixel Filtering Multi-pixel filtering is designed to blend neighboring pixels into a more coherent mass. Ultimately, the filtering softens the image and helps reduce aliasing artifacts. In particular, such softening can improve renders destined for video (the scanline nature of television tends to exaggerate stair-stepping). However, the filtering may not be desirable for renders destined for motion picture film stock or Web-based display. Although the Use Multi Pixel Filter check box is selected automatically when you change the Quality menu to Production Quality, you can deselect it at any time. If multi-pixel filtering is activated, Pixel Filter Width X and Pixel Filter Width Y set the size of the filter kernel; higher values increase the degree of softening. You can also choose different convolution filter types through the Pixel Filter Type menu. Each type creates a slightly different result. Of these, Box Filter creates the softest result, while Gaussian maintains the best detail.

Note that the 3D Blur Visib and Max 3D Blur Visib attributes determine the shading samples taken for the overlapping objects that use 3D motion blur. Coverage, in the Contrast Threshold section, also affects the overall quality of 3D motion blur.

mental ray Anti-Aliasing Settings

The mental ray renderer also takes advantage of subpixel sampling to minimize aliasing artifacts. However, mental ray stores the controlling attributes in the Anti-Aliasing Quality section of the Quality tab in the Render Settings window (see Figure 2.21).

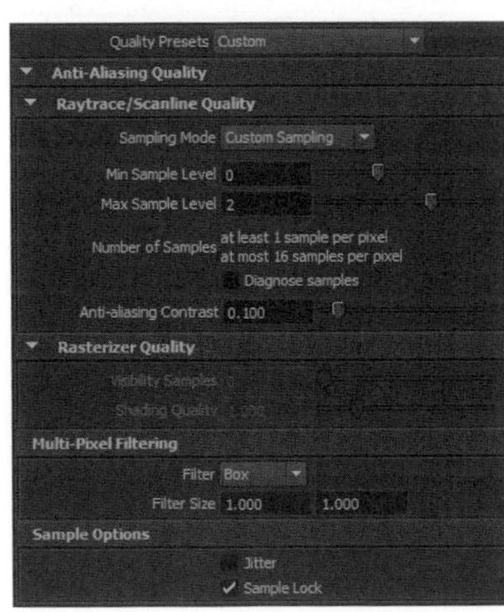

Figure 2.21 **The Anti-Aliasing Quality section for the mental ray renderer. These are the settings used to create high-quality renders throughout the remainder of this chapter.**

The mental ray renderer offers a long list of anti-aliasing presets through the Quality Presets menu at the top of the Quality tab. However, the menu affects sections outside the Anti-Aliasing Quality section, including Motion Blur, Final Gathering, and Global Illumination. Therefore, it's often better to manually set the anti-aliasing attributes. Descriptions of the attributes follow:

Sampling Mode The Sampling Mode menu sets the style of anti-aliasing sampling. The Fixed Sampling option uses a static number of subpixel samples per pixel. The Adaptive Sampling and Custom Sampling options use a different number of subpixel samples per pixel based on the contrast between neighboring pixels (or subpixels). Although Adaptive Sampling lets you adjust the Max Sample Level directly, Custom Sampling lets you adjust both the Min Sample Level and Max Sample Level.

Min Sample Level and Max Sample Level These two attributes set the minimum and maximum times a pixel is recursively subdivided into subpixel samples. A value of 0 equates to one sample per pixel (in other words, there are no subpixels). When Sampling Mode is set to Custom Sampling, you can set Min Sample Level to a negative number. This forces the renderer to skip some pixels in the pixel-sampling process. For example, a value of –2 forces the renderer to take only one sample per block of 16 pixels. In comparison, a Max Sample Level of 2 allows the renderer to sample a pixel 16 times (that is, take 16 subpixel samples). Hence, a Min Sample Level of –2 and a Max sample level of 0 is a low-quality render. A Min Sample Level of 0 and a Max Sample Level of 2 is a high-quality render. Whether or not the Max Sample Level is used is adaptively determined by the Anti-Aliasing Contrast value. If neighboring pixels or subpixels possess a contrast greater than the value, additional subpixel samples are taken. (With older versions of Maya, Anti-Aliasing Contrast is named Color Contrast or Contrast Threshold.) For a visual representation of the adaptive sampling process, you can select the Diagnose Samples check box. White lines represent the borders between regions with high contrast; additional subpixels are thereby required along those borders (see Figure 2.22).

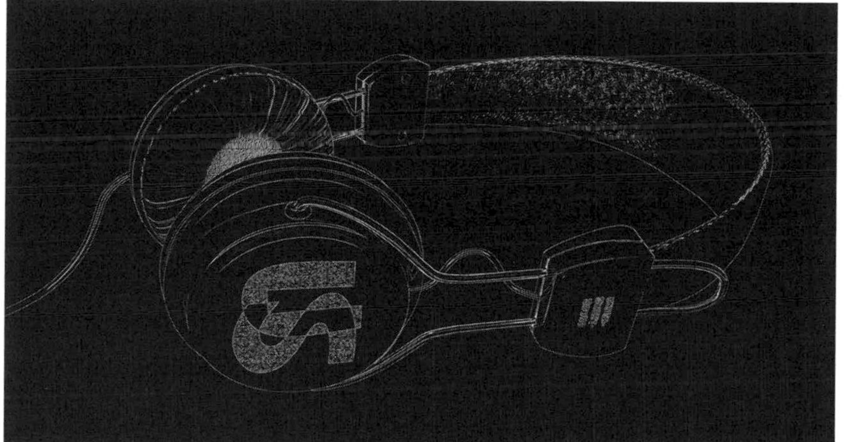

Figure 2.22
A test render with Diagnose Samples selected. White lines represent the borders between regions with high contrast.

Multi-Pixel Filtering The Multi-Pixel Filtering section controls the strength of the Multi-Pixel filter. Unlike the Maya Software variation, mental ray's Multi-Pixel filter cannot be turned off. However, you can lower the degree of softening by reducing the Filter Size X and Y cell values. Filter Size determines the size of the convolution filter applied to the render. The type of filter is set by the Filter menu. Box is the most efficient filter type, and Gauss (Gaussian) maintains important edge detail. Mitchell and Lanczos offer minor variations of the Gauss convolution curve.

Sample Options The Sample Options section includes Jitter and Sample Lock attributes. These attributes determine the exact point within a pixel or subpixel that is used for a sample. Jitter, when selected, introduces systematic variations to the sample points within pixels and subpixels (which would otherwise be at the pixel and subpixel corners). Sample Lock, when selected, ensures that sample points within a particular pixel or subpixel are identical across multiple frames of animation or multiple render layers for a single frame. Because changes to the Sample Options section create very minor changes to the render, it is generally fine to leave Jitter off and Sample on.

Project: Blurring Reflections

At this step of the project, the reflections are very sharp. To make the render more complex, you can blur the reflections through the assigned material. To do so, follow these steps:

1. Open the Attribute Editor tab for the material assigned to the bottom faces of the Light_Box surface. Expand the mental ray section. Change Mi Reflection Blur to 3. Render a test. The reflection is blurred but grainy (see Figure 2.23).
2. Raise the Reflection Rays attribute to 24. You can surpass the default limit of most Maya attributes by entering a value into the corresponding number cell. Render a test. The blur becomes smooth (see Figure 2.23).

Figure 2.23
(Left) Reflection Rays set to 1.0 creates a grainy reflection (the contrast has been exaggerated for print). (Right) The blurred reflection with Reflection Rays set to 24. A sample file is saved as `head-phones-step21.ma` **on the DVD.**

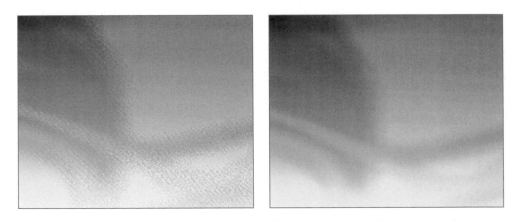

Note that the blur is heavier for surfaces farther away from the floor plane. Reflection Rays sets the number of samples used to calculate the blurred reflection. Reflection Blur Limit, which is the attribute directly between Mi Reflection Blur and Reflection Rays, determines the blur intensity of secondary or recursive reflections; that is, it determines the blurriness of reflections within reflections. Because the chrome sliders, which are the most reflective surfaces in the scene, do not reveal any coherent images, you can leave Reflection Blur Limit set to the default 1.0. In addition to the material Reflection Blur Limit, mental ray has a global Reflection Blur Limit attribute in the Raytracing section of the Quality tab of the Render Settings window; the smaller of the two values is used for any surface assigned to the material.

The Final Gathering System

Final Gathering, which is an optional rendering feature offered by mental ray, employs a variation of raytracing. Whereas standard raytracing allows a camera-eye ray to create secondary reflection and refraction rays at surface intersections, Final Gathering sends out Final Gather rays in a random direction within a hemisphere. When a Final Gather ray intersects a new surface, the light energy of the newly intersected point and its potential contribution to the initial surface intersected by the camera-eye ray are noted.

The net sum of Final Gather ray intersections stemming from a single camera-eye ray intersection is referred to as a *Final Gather point*. Final Gather points are stored in a Final Gather map and are ultimately added to the standard lighting calculation. The end result is a render that is able to emulate light bounce and color bleed. To better understand light bounce and color bleed, a closer look at the mechanics of light is necessary.

Light is a form of electromagnetic radiation that exists in a continuous range of wavelengths. Specific wavelengths are visible to the human eye and are perceived by the human brain as specific colors. When a light wave with a particular wavelength strikes an object, it is reflected, transmitted (refracted), or absorbed (converted to heat).

When light is reflected, its wavelength is affected by the object surface it reflects off. This is because color is not contained within the materials of objects. Instead, color is the result of particular wavelengths reaching the viewer through reflection or transmission. Different materials (wood, stone, metal, and so on) have different atomic structures and thereby reflect, transmit, and absorb light differently. Hence, the red of a red object represents a particular wavelength that the object reflects.

When light reflects off multiple objects with different material properties, *color bleed* occurs. For example, as seen in Figure 2.24, sunlight strikes a tomato. Some of the light rays, which inherit a red wavelength, are reflected back to the camera. Other light rays are re-reflected toward the table the tomato sits on. Some of those light rays are once again reflected toward the camera. However, the light rays that have reflected from the tomato to the table to the camera have altered wavelengths that are mixtures of the tomato's red and the table's white. Hence, color bleed occurs, and pink is visible on the table top. Note that real-world light reflection is often referred to as *light bounce*.

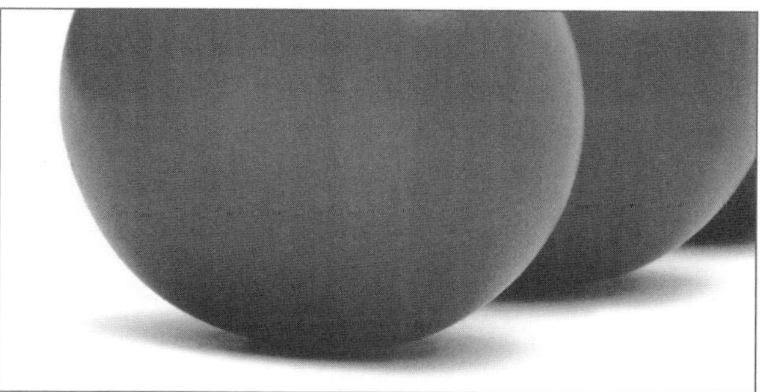

Figure 2.24
The red of a tomato "bleeds" onto a white table.

Final Gathering is able to re-create light bounce and color bleed by combining the Final Gather point information, which is indirect illumination, with the standard lighting model, which is direct illumination. The standard lighting model determines whether surface points are visible to various lights by comparing surface normals (lines drawn perpendicular to the surface) to light vectors (the direction the light is pointing in 3D space). If a light is visible, the light's vector, intensity, and color are combined with the surface's material attribute values to calculate the ultimate color value of the surface point. In contrast to Final Gathering, the Maya Software renderer uses direct illumination and does not employ any indirect illumination calculations.

In addition to re-creating light bounce and color bleed, Final Gathering is able to interpret specific material properties as virtual light sources. This is demonstrated in the next section.

Project: Activating Final Gathering

To activate Final Gathering, switch to the Indirect Lighting tab of the Render Settings window and select the Final Gathering check box in the Final Gathering section. Render a test. The render occurs in two stages. In the first stage, Final Gather points are calculated. After the points are calculated, a rough render pass is displayed in the Render View window. This occurs in tiles, causing the Render View to fill up incrementally. In the second stage, the Final Gather points are blended with the direct lighting calculation, and each tile is rendered with the final quality.

Final Gathering is able to interpret nonzero Incandescence or Ambient Color attributes of materials as light sources. In addition, Final Gathering is able to interpret the nonzero value of a Surface Shader material's Out Color attribute as a light source. Because the top and side faces of the Light_Box geometry are assigned to a Surface Shader material, you are thereby able to light the scene with the material alone. To test this ability, you will need to temporarily turn off the standard lights. Follow these steps:

1. Open the area light's Attribute Editor tab and deselect the Illuminates By Default check box, which is located below the Intensity slider. Repeat this process for the two volume lights that are contributing fill.
2. Return to the Render Settings window. Switch to the Common tab, expand the Render Options section, and deselect the Enable Default Light check box. If this check box is left selected, Maya will apply the generic default lighting when no other active lights are detected.
3. Render a test. The scene is lit solely by the Surface Shader's Out Color value. (In the sample scene files, this material is named Light_Box_Fabric.)

At this point, the render is dim. You can artificially increase the intensity of the Final Gathering lighting contribution by raising the Primary Diffuse Scale attribute above 1.0.

For example, the value is raised to 5 in Figure 2.25. Primary Diffuse Scale is found in the Final Gathering section of the Indirect Lighting tab of the Render Settings window. To raise the value above 1.0, click the attribute's color swatch, change the lower-right menu of the Color Chooser window to HSV, and enter a new value into the V (value) number cell.

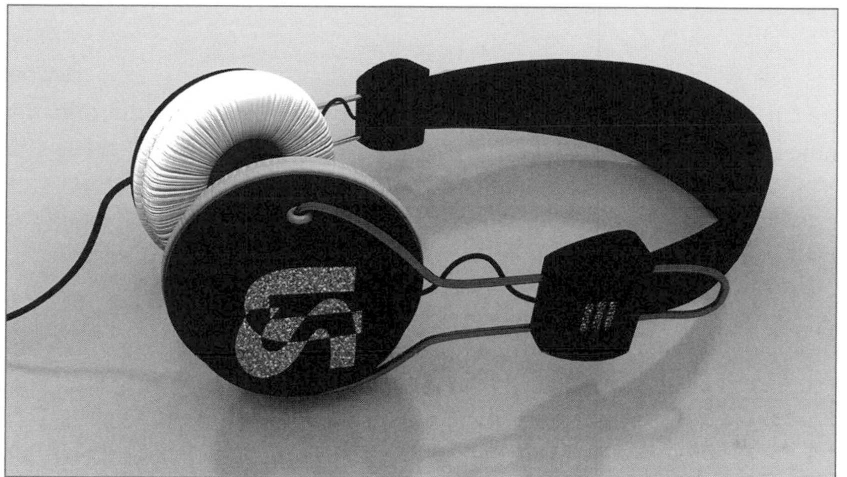

Figure 2.25

The scene rendered with Final Gathering and lit solely by the Out Color value of a Surface Shader material. A sample file is saved as `headphones-step22.ma` on the DVD.

Lighting with Final Gathering alone creates significant variations in the render:

- There are no cast shadows.
- Soft contact shadows exist where the headphone surfaces are close to the floor.
- The background becomes brighter as the light arrives from the top and sides of the Light_Box geometry.
- The specular highlight along the top of the forward ear cup is missing.
- There are no specular highlights to define the bump maps on the adjuster and the head pad surfaces.
- The Final Gathering process ensures that light is bouncing between surfaces. For example, the blue of the floor is subtly added to the black plastic of the ear cup.

To retrieve the cast shadow and bring back the specular highlights, you can reactivate the standard lights through the Illuminates By Default check boxes. However, the scene will become overlit. To use Final Gathering and standard lights, you will need to reduce the Primary Diffuse Scale and the area light's Intensity. For example, in Figure 2.26, primary Diffuse Scale is set to 2 and the area light's Intensity is set to 0.3.

Because of the new lighting setup, you will need to adjust various material attributes once again. For the render featured in Figure 2.26, the Specular Roll Off values are raised slightly for the materials assigned to the Cup_R, Wire_L, Wire_R, Cord, and Head_Pad surfaces. In addition, the Diffuse value for the Leather_Ear_Pad_L material is lowered to 0.3.

Figure 2.26
Final Gathering is combined with the area light and volume light illumination. The disc-shaped artifacts will be removed in the next section. A sample file is saved as `headphones-step23.ma` on the DVD. For a color version of the figure, see the color insert.

Fine-Tuning Final Gathering

Left to default settings, Final Gathering is liable to create rendering artifacts. The artifacts may take the form of small dark spots. More drastically, they can appear as bright discs, as shown in Figure 2.26. The bright discs are often a result of Final Gather points interacting with highly reflective surfaces (such as the chrome sliders on the headphones) and standard Maya lights.

To remove the Final Gathering artifacts, you can adjust the attributes found within the Final Gathering section of the Render Settings window. In particular, it's important to balance the Point Interpolation and Accuracy values. Point Interpolation determines the number of Final Gather points averaged to find the color value of a particular surface point. The higher the value, the more Final Gather points are averaged and the smoother the render will appear. In contrast, Accuracy sets the number of rays sent out into a hemisphere for each Final Gather point. The higher the value, the more accurate the indirect illumination and color bleed will be. However, high Accuracy values will significantly slow the render. Setting Point Interpolation and Accuracy to their maximum values does not necessarily guarantee the best quality. For example, if Point Interpolation is set to 50, the attribute may continue to create rendering artifacts because Final Gather points located at a significant distance from each other may be averaged together. A more controlled approach requires the testing of different value combinations. Hence, you might test each of the following combinations:

Accuracy: 512 Point Interpolation: 20

Accuracy: 512 Point Interpolation: 30

Accuracy: 512 Point Interpolation: 40

Accuracy: 512 Point Interpolation: 50

You can test small regions that contain the rendering artifacts to save render time. If artifacts stubbornly persist, you can adjust the Filter attribute (in the Final Gathering Quality subsection). The Filter attribute applies additional averaging to the Final Gather map. More specifically, Filter is able to target the bright discs. For this project, an Accuracy of 512, a Point Interpolation of 40, and a Filter of 1.0 works well (see Figure 2.27).

You will use Final Gathering in other tutorials in this book. Hence, the remaining Final Gathering attributes are presented in greater detail in the following chapters.

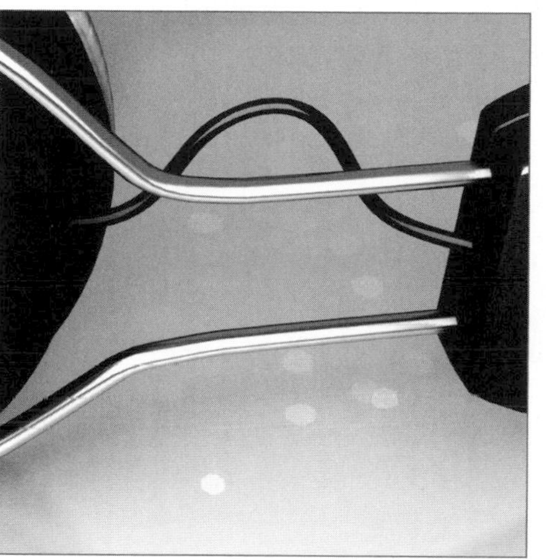

Figure 2.27

(Left) Close-up of Final Gathering artifacts. (Right) The artifacts are removed by setting Accuracy to 512, Point Interpolation to 40, and Filter to 1.0. A sample file is saved as `headphones-step24.ma` **on the DVD.**

Lighting with a Texture

Final Gathering is not limited to solid colors when converting material attributes into a source of light. That is, you can map a procedural or bitmap texture to the Incandescence, Ambient Color, or Out Color of a material. Such mapping will make the light pattern more complex (although it will not create a sharp-edged pattern that you might find with a real-world projector). To map the Out Color of the Surface Shader assigned to the Light_Box geometry, follow these steps:

1. Open the Surface Shader's Attribute Editor tab. (The material is named Light_Box_Fabric in the sample scene files.) Click the checkered Map button beside Out Color. In the Create Render Node window, click the Grid texture icon.
2. Render a test. The black-and-white pattern of the Grid texture changes the light quality. Some areas will appear darker, while others will retain their original intensity (see Figure 2.28).
3. To adjust the resulting light, you can tweak the Grid texture's attributes. Before doing so, however, it will pay to examine the UV texture space of the Light_Box geometry. Select the geometry and choose Window → UV Texture Editor. Note that the floor,

walls, and ceiling overlap. To test this, return to a view panel and RMB+click the Light_Box surface. Choose Face from the marking menu. Proceed to select the faces of one wall. (Switch the view panel to the persp camera view to make the selection of the faces easier.) Return to the UV Texture Editor. Note the position of the wall's UV points. The four corners of the wall correspond to the four corners of the valid 0-to-1 UV texture space (indicated by the dark gray box). To determine how the wall is oriented, RMB+click in the UV Texture Editor and choose UV from the menu. Select the UV points along the right side of the UV space. The corresponding vertices are highlighted in the view panel. The location of the corresponding vertices along the top edge of the wall indicates that the wall is rotated 90 degrees in the UV space. You can test other sections of the Light_Box geometry. Before selecting new faces in the view panel, however, clear the section by clicking on an empty area of the scene.

Figure 2.28

A Grid texture mapped to the Out Color of the Surface Shader material affects the light quality and creates a reflected pattern in the background. A sample file is saved as `headphones-step25.ma` on the DVD.

4. Return to the Hypershade, select the new Grid texture node, and open its Attribute Editor tab. Change U Width to 0 and V Width to 0.35. Select the place2dTexture node connected to the Grid node and open its Attribute Editor tab. Change Repeat UV to 8, 8. These steps create a series of horizontal lines. Because the wall faces are offset by 90 degrees in the UV texture space, the lines will run vertically from the walls' bottom to top. Return to the Grid node and change the Filler Color to dark blue. Any change to the Line Color or Filler Color will change the color of the light generated by Final Gathering. In addition, the new colors will appear in the floor's reflection of the walls and ceiling. Render a test. The vertical lines appear in the background as a reflection (see Figure 2.29). In addition, the light provided through Final Gathering takes on a deeper blue hue.

Note that the specific pattern contained within the Grid does not appear as sharp shapes across the headphones and floor. Instead, the colors within the Grid pattern are softly merged as part of the lighting calculation.

Figure 2.29
Changes to the Grid texture attributes create a different background reflection and subtle shift to the overall lighting. A sample file is saved as `headphones-step26.ma` on the DVD.

Optimizing the Scene

When preparing for a final render, it's important to optimize the scene. Optimization will guarantee that the render progresses efficiently. Aside from setting various attributes in the Common tab of the Render Settings window (see the "Batch Rendering" section earlier in this chapter), critical optimization steps follow:

- Delete construction history. Choose Edit → Delete All By Type → History.
- Delete unneeded geometry, such as curves used for NURBS modeling.
- Delete unused nodes, such as empty group nodes and unassigned materials. An empty group node is created when the children nodes are deleted or are removed from the hierarchy. In the Hypershade, you can delete unassigned materials by choosing Edit → Delete Unused Nodes.
- You can automate such deletion by choosing File → Optimize Scene Size → r. The Optimize Scene Size tool offers a long list of optimization options (see Figure 2.30). You can choose a single optimization by clicking one of the Optimize Now buttons. You can also activate all the selected optimization check boxes by

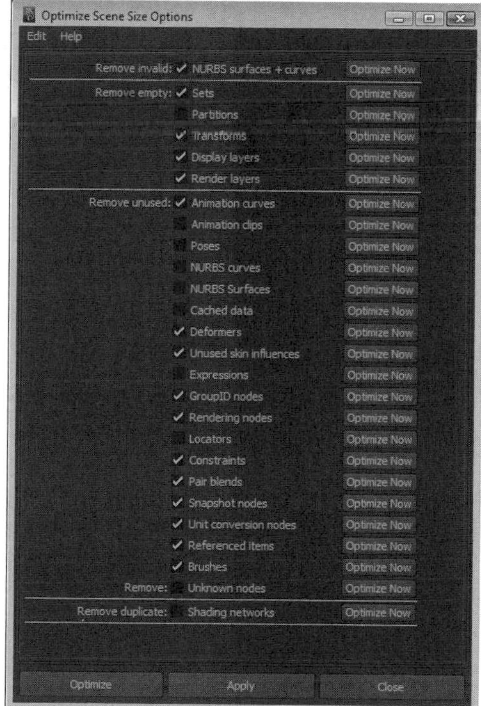

Figure 2.30
The Optimize Scene Size Options window

clicking the window's Optimize button. Note that empty group nodes are removed by the Transforms check box. Unassigned materials are removed by the Rendering Nodes check box.

Aside from deleting unneeded components, it's also important to check various quality settings. For example:

- Check the Resolution and Filter Size attributes of any light that creates depth map shadows. Set the Resolution value only as high as necessary to create a high-quality shadow.
- Check the Shadow Rays attribute of any light creating raytraced shadows. Set the Shadow Rays value only as high as needed to create high-quality shadows.
- Check the anti-aliasing settings in the appropriate render tab of the Render Settings window. Raise the shading attributes only as high as is needed to create high-quality anti-aliasing.
- If raytracing, check the raytracing quality settings in the appropriate render tab of the Render Settings window. Let the rays reflect or refract only as many times as necessary to make surfaces appear realistic.

Adjusting shadow, anti-aliasing, or raytracing attribute values may require additional render tests. Generally, you can render small regions in the Render View to determine whether the chosen values will work.

If Final Gathering is activated for a scene in which no animation exists for the objects or lights, you can reuse a previously created Final Gather map and thereby reduce the overall rendering time. To do so, follow these steps:

1. Render a test frame (for example, frame 1). Make adjustments to the various Final Gathering attributes found in the Indirect Lighting tab of the Render Settings window, such as Accuracy and Point Interpolation, until you are satisfied with the render.
2. Expand the Final Gathering Map subsection and change the Rebuild option to Off. This change forces mental ray to use the Final Gather map of the previous render *unless* the Final Gathering attributes are adjusted. If the attributes are adjusted, the Final Gather file is appended. You can also set Rebuild to Freeze, which prevents any update to the Final Gather file. You can choose a Final Gather filename through the Primary Final Gather File name cell. Final Gather files are saved to the `renderData/mentalray/finalgMap/` folder within the project directory.

Project: Creating the Final Render

Now that you've fine-tuned the lights, shadows, and reflections in the second part of the headphones project, you are ready to create a final batch render for the full length of the 36-frame animation. Keep in mind that many of the steps in this chapter are optional. For example, blurred reflections and Final Gathering add their own unique look to the scene, but they are by no means mandatory. Hence, you should consider what combination of texturing and lighting steps create an aesthetic look without taking an unduly long time to render.

After you're satisfied with the texturing and lighting setup and have optimized the scene for efficiency (see the previous section), batch render an image sequence (see Figure 2.31). For example, choose TIFF or Targa as the image format. To play back the frames, use FCheck; otherwise, import the frames into a program, such as Apple's QuickTime Pro or Adobe After Effects, that is able to convert an image sequence into a movie. For more information on render settings, see the sections "Batch Rendering" and "Anti-Aliasing Theory" earlier in this chapter.

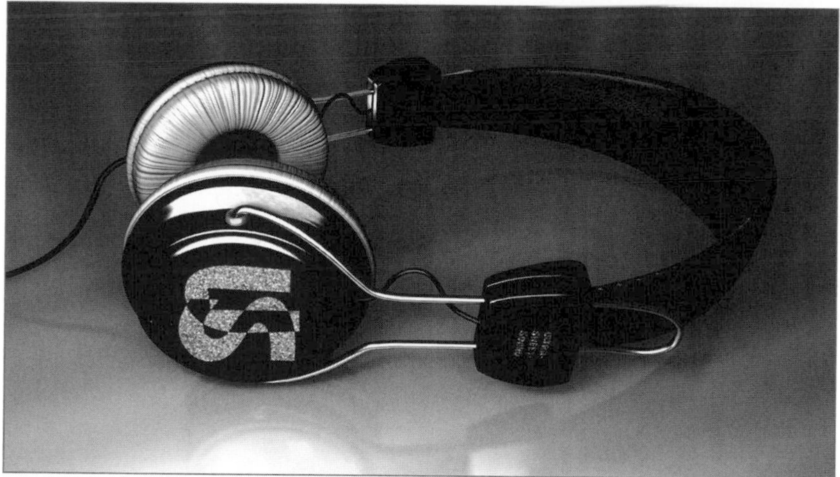

Figure 2.31

Final headphones render, as seen in frames 15 and 30. A sample file is saved as `headphones-final.ma` on the DVD. For a color version of this figure, see the color insert.

Texturing and Lighting a Character, Part 1

In this chapter and Chapter 4, "Texturing and Lighting a Character, Part 2," you will texture and light the bust of a woman. This chapter, which contains part 1 of the project, will guide you through the following steps:

- **Preparing the scene**
- **Assigning materials**
- **Roughing in the lighting**
- **Roughing in the textures**
- **Creating a custom skin bitmap**
- **Switching to mental ray**

In addition, important lighting and texturing theory is included as follows:

- **1-, 2-, and 3-point lighting**
- **The UVs of NURBS surfaces**
- **Translucence**

Project: Preparing the Scene

Before starting the texturing process, review the scene file and its contents. Open the `woman-start.ma` scene file from the `ProjectFiles/Project2` folder on the DVD.

Because the scene is designed for a still render, the character is only partially modeled. For example, the head ends behind the ears. The shoulders end below the camera view. The visible portion of the hair is represented by several isolated tufts. A primitive plane serves as a backdrop. The character model itself is constructed from multiple NURBS and polygon surfaces.

Once again, two cameras are included in the scene file. You can use the default persp camera for examining the model and setting lights. The Render camera, on the other hand, is positioned for the final render. Note that the Render camera has its Resolution Gate activated, which indicates the area to be rendered.

Note that the sample scene files included for this chapter and Chapter 4 assume that the bitmap textures are located within the `Textures` folder of the `ProjectFiles/Project2` project directory. Before opening a sample scene file, choose File → Project → Set and browse for the `Project2` folder, whether the folder remains at its original location on the DVD or is located on a drive after the DVD contents have been copied.

Adjusting Surface Smoothness

At this stage, the woman's face remains faceted (see Figure 3.1). This is not an unusual condition for models imported into Maya from another 3D program, such as 3ds Max or Softimage. You can smooth the polygons' surfaces by adjusting the vertex normals of each surface. To do so, select the Face surface. Switch to the Polygons menu set, and choose Normals → Soften Edge. Render a test. The face surface renders smoothly. The Soften Edge tool sets the vertex normal angle to 180 degrees. This causes the vertex normals at the shared corners to be averaged. The averaging forces the render to treat the transition from polygon face to polygon face smoothly. When a surface is faceted, the vertex normal angle is 0 and no smoothing occurs; instead, there is an abrupt change in shading intensity at each shared polygon edge. By default, vertex normals are vectors that run perpendicular to the surface face. The Soften Edge tool essentially "bends" the vertex normals so they are no longer perpendicular.

NURBS surfaces, in contrast, never appear faceted along their interiors. However, they can appear faceted along their edges. During a render, the NURBS surfaces are converted discretely to polygons. Hence, if the NURBS surfaces do not carry enough subdivisions in the U or V directions, they may pick up angular edges. To defeat this trait, Maya temporarily tessellates the NURBS surfaces in anticipation of the polygon conversion. The tessellation is controlled through the Tessellation section of each NURBS surface's shape node Attribute Editor tab.

When examining the `woman-start.ma` scene file, faceting is visible along the edge of the sweatshirt shoulder seams (see Figure 3.2). To appropriately judge the faceting, open the Render Settings window, switch to the Maya Software tab, change the Edge

Anti-Aliasing Quality menu to High Quality, and render a test through the Render View window.

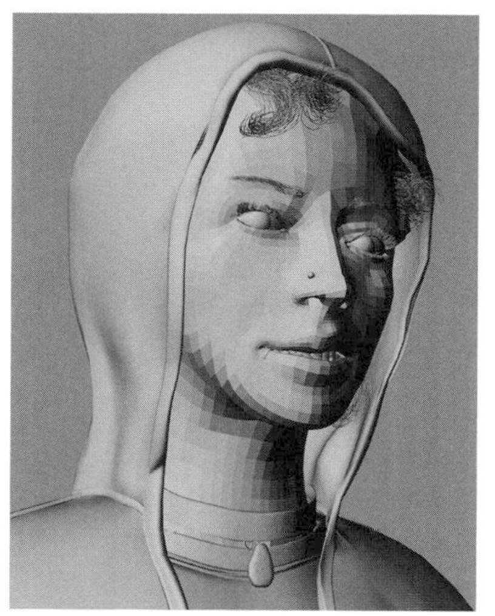
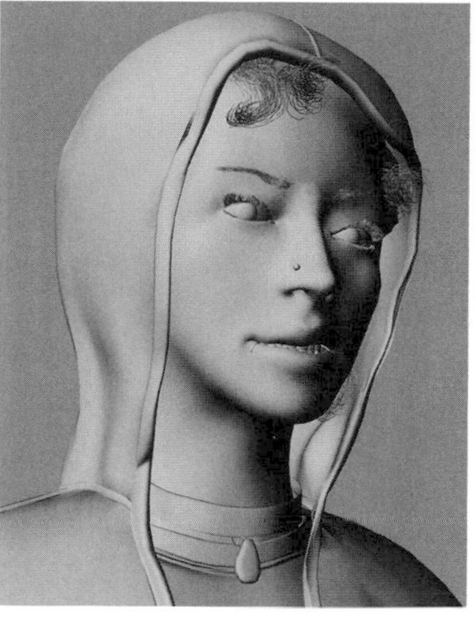

Figure 3.1
(Left) Faceting on the Face surface. (Right) Smoothed result of the Soften Edge tool

To smooth out the seams, and the sweatshirt in general, follow these steps:

1. Select all the surfaces composing the sweatshirt model. You can Shift+click the surface nodes in the Hypergraph: Hierarchy or Outliner windows.
2. With the surfaces selected, choose Window → General Editors → Attribute Spread Sheet. In the Attribute Spread Sheet window, switch to the Tessellation tab. Enter **3** into each cell of the U Divisions Factor and V Divisions Factor columns (see Figure 3.3).

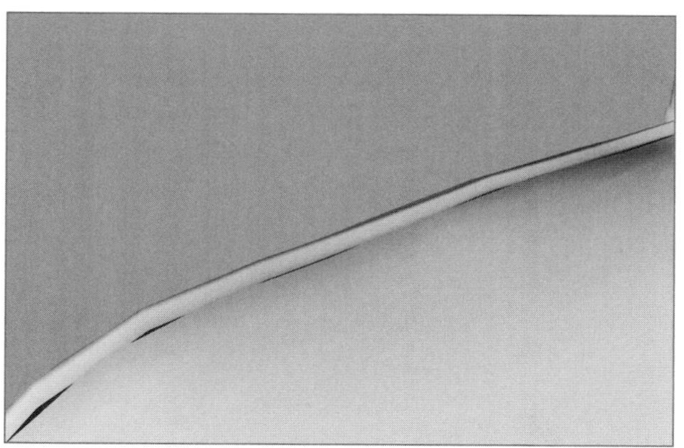

Figure 3.2
Close-up of faceting along NURBS surface edges

Attribute Spread Sheet
Names Layouts Key Layer Help
Keyable Shape Keyable Transform Translate Rotate Scale Render

	Explicit Tessellation Attributes	U Divisions Factor	V Divisions Factor	Curvature Tolerance	Sm
Front_Rshape	off	1.5	1.5	Medium Quality	off
Hood_RShape	off	1.5	1.5	Medium Quality	off
Hood_LShape	off	1.5	1.5	Medium Quality	off
Seam_NeckShape	off	1.5	1.5	Medium Quality	off
Seam_RShape	off	1.5	1.5	Medium Quality	off
BackShape	off	1.5	1.5	Medium Quality	off
Seam_LShape	off	1.5	1.5	Medium Quality	off
Front_LShape	off	1.5	1.5	Medium Quality	off
Seam_TopShape	off	1.5	1.5	Medium Quality	off
Seam_FrontShape	off	1.5	1.5	Medium Quality	off

Figure 3.3
U Division Factor and V Division Factor columns highlighted in the Attribute Spread Sheet window

A U Divisions Factor and V Divisions Factor of 3 subdivides each NURBS surface three times for each NURBS face in the U and V direction. This is a sufficient number of subdivisions to avoid significant faceting along the surface edges (see Figure 3.4). Render out a test to examine the result. Note that the subdivisions are added only during the render and are not visible in any of the view panels.

Examining and Exporting the UVs

To produce convincing textures for the woman's face, it will be necessary to examine and export the UVs of the Face surface. To do so, select the surface and choose Window → UV Texture Editor. The UV points are visible in the 0-to-1.0 UV range (see Figure 3.5).

Like many character models, the UVs of the face are pelted. UV pelting "unwraps" the UVs in such a way that the entire face is flattened into a single "pelt." (Although there are no UV pelting tools in the standard release of Maya, various pelting plug-ins are available, such as Hydralab's Pelting Tools.) Although pelting offers the advantage of minimizing the number of separate UV shells and potential seams, it does require the construction of very specific texture maps to match the UV layout. As such, it is necessary to export the UVs so they may be brought into a digital paint program as a reference. To export the UVs for the face and prepare them for use in Photoshop, follow these steps:

1. While the Face surface is selected as an object, choose Polygons → UV Snapshot through the UV Texture Editor menu. In the UV Snapshot window, change the Size X and Size Y to 2048, change the Image Format menu to JPEG, and choose a filename and location through the File Name cell. Click the OK button and exit the window. (If you choose an Image Format type that supports alpha, such as Targa or TIFF, the UV lines will be written simultaneously to the RGB and alpha channels.)
2. Launch Photoshop. (Any recent edition of Photoshop will work.) Open the UV snapshot file you created through Maya. By default, the image is converted to a Background layer, which cannot be moved in the layer stack. In the Layers panel,

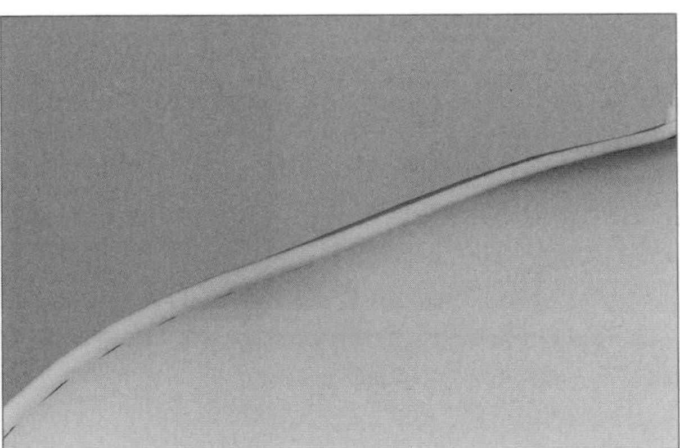

Figure 3.4

Close-up of NURBS surface edges after U Divisions Factor and V Divisions Factor values are changed to 3. A sample file is included as `woman-step1.ma` on the DVD.

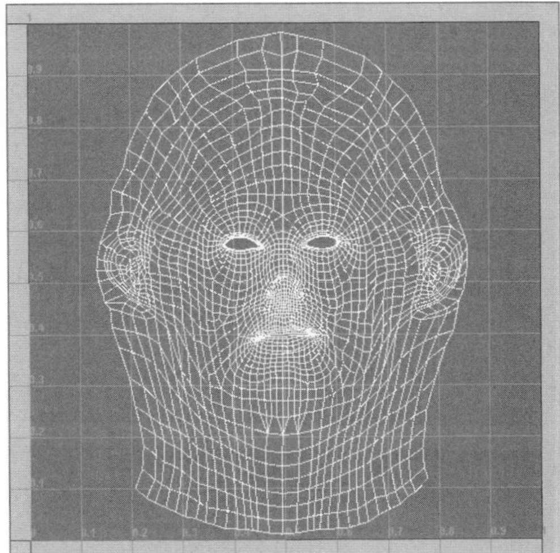

Figure 3.5

The UV layout of the Face surface as seen in the UV Texture Editor

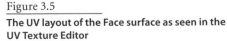

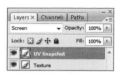

double-click the Background layer. The New Layer window opens. Enter a new layer name, such as **UV Reference**, and click OK. This converts the Background layer into a new, editable layer.

3. In Photoshop, choose Layer → New → Layer. In the New Layer window, enter a new name, such as **Texture**. You will paint the texture on this layer. LMB+drag the UV Reference layer to the top of the layer stack. Switch its Blending Mode menu from Normal to Screen. This causes the white lines of the UV snapshot to appear over the lower texture layer. To see this work, temporarily paint or fill the texture layer with a solid color (see Figure 3.6).
4. Save the file in the Photoshop PSD format. We will return to this file at a later step.

With the UV layout visible in Photoshop, you are ready to paint the texture. However, before doing so, it is best to assign basic materials and rough in the lighting.

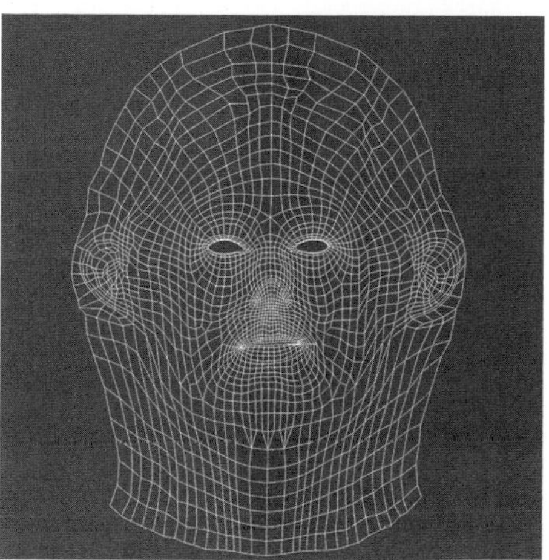

Figure 3.6

(Top) Photoshop CS3 Layers panel. The UV snapshot is imported and placed on a higher layer with the Screen blending mode. The lower layer is created to hold the new face texture and is temporarily filled with red. (Bottom) The resulting image. A sample Photoshop file is included as `Face-start.psd` **in the** `ProjectFiles/Project2/Reference` **folder on the DVD.**

Project: Assigning Materials

The first stage of texturing requires the basic assignment of materials. As discussed in Chapter 1, "Texturing and Lighting a Product, Part 1," you can either assign a unique material to each surface or allow surfaces to share material assignments. For this scene, it's best to combine both techniques. For example, in Figure 3.7, a set of assigned materials is shown. A number of materials are assigned to single surfaces. The Back_ material is assigned to the Back surface, the Collar_ material is assigned to the Collar surface, and so on. Note that these materials have an underscore (_) added as a suffix. (Maya does not allow duplicate names.)

Figure 3.7

Assigned materials. A sample file is included as `woman-step2.ma` **on the DVD.**

Table 3.1

Surfaces that share a material

SURFACE NAMES	ASSIGNED MATERIAL NAME
Choker_Ring	Gold
Pendant _Ring	
Lip_Ring	
Stud	
Eyebrow_L	Eyebrows_
Eyebrow_R	
Lash_Lo_L	Eyelashes_
Lash_Hi_L	
Lash_Lo_R	
Lash_Hi_R	
Cornea_L	Corneas
Cornea_R	
Eye_Black_L_	Eye_Black_
Eye_Black_R_	
Eye_Wet_In_L	Eye_Wet_
Eye_Wet_Out_L	
Eye_Wet_In_R	
Eye_Wet_Out_R	
Seam_L	Seam
Seam_R	
Seam_Top	
Hood_L	Hood
Hood_R	
Front_L	Front
Front_R	
Tooth_1	Teeth_
Tooth_2	
Tooth_3...	
Curl_1	Hair_
Curl_2	
Curl_3...	

At the same time, there are a number of surfaces that share a material; a list is included in Table 3.1.

The majority of the materials are Blinn shaders. A few of the materials are Phong shaders. The Phong materials include Corneas, Eye_Gloss_L_, Eye_Gloss_R_, Eye_Wet_, and Pendant_. In addition, the Eyelashes_, Eyebrows_, and Hair_ materials are Anisotropic shaders, and the Eye_Black_ material is a Surface Shader.

To ensure that you are assigning materials to all the surfaces in the scene, use the Hypergraph: Hierarchy or Outliner windows to make surface sections. Some of the surfaces, such as the four Eye_Wet surfaces in the corners of the eyes, are relatively small. For additional tips and tricks for material assignment, see Chapter 1.

1-, 2-, and 3-Point Lighting

As discussed in Chapter 1, lights used for stage, motion picture, and 3D lighting are often classified by their roles. Thus, a key light is the most intense light in the scene, such as the sun. A fill light is a weaker, secondary light or is light from the key that has bounced off a surface. A rim, back, or hair light is a stylistic light used to outline the edge of a person or object. Whether a lighting setup uses 1-, 2-, or 3-point lighting depends on the number of lights used; that is, the setup is dependent on whether it uses a key, fill, and/or rim light.

The 1-point lighting scheme is dramatic, sometimes stark, and often foreboding. The lighting involves a single, easily identifiable key light source with no significant supplemental sources. You can find 1-point lighting in the following situations:

- A man lights a cigarette in an otherwise dark room.
- A theater audience is illuminated by the light of a movie screen.
- A woman drives on a moonless night, but is lit by the car's instrument panel.

The motion-picture genre that most closely emulates 1-point lighting is film noir. Film noir is a style historically associated with crime dramas of the 1940s and 1950s. The style is typified by black-and-white film stock, sparely lit characters, and deep black shadows. In addition, 1-point lighting can be found in various horror films made over the last 80 years. Often, a single light source is placed at an odd angle to create unnatural or disturbing shadows (see Figure 3.8).

1-point lighting need not remain disturbing. If a light is placed near or around the camera, the 1-point lighting becomes a form of product or glamour lighting. As demonstrated in Chapter 1, this type of lighting minimizes unattractive shadows (see Figure 3.8).

Figure 3.8

(Left) 1-point lighting used to create a horror look. The light is placed above the model's head, preventing the eyes from being lit. (Right) 1-point lighting used for glamour photography. The light is placed close to the top-right side of the camera.

The 2-point lighting scheme matches many of the lighting scenarios we encounter in our everyday lives. The scheme uses a strong key light and an extremely diffuse (soft) fill. The following are examples of 2-point lighting:

- Sunlight streams through a window. The light bouncing from the interior walls and floor serves as fill light.
- Office workers sit in a windowless room lit by overhead fluorescent lights. The light bounce from the walls, desks, and floors serves as the fill light.
- A couple walks down a sidewalk on a sunny day. The light bounces off the concrete, providing fill.

2-point lighting is very common in painted and photographed portraits. In such portraits, the figure is lit from the left or right by a strong key, while the opposite side is lit by a weaker light or light bounced off a nearby wall or similar surface. 2-point lighting can also be found in any painting or photograph of an outdoor, daytime scene. In this situation, the sun is the key light, and the net sum of all the bounced sunlight serves as the fill light (see Figure 3.9).

Perhaps the most commonly discussed and applied lighting technique is 3-point lighting. Descriptions can be found in numerous 3D, film, and video instructional materials. Although 3-point lighting is a reliable way to light many scenes, it has inherent drawbacks.

In a standard 3-point lighting scheme, a strong key is placed to one side of a subject (approximately 15 to 45 degrees off the axis between the camera and the subject). A fill light is placed on the opposite side and is at least half the intensity of the key. A rim light is placed behind the subject so that it grazes the subject's edge (see Figure 3.10). The 3-point lighting scheme is popular in the realm of 3D because it lends depth to a potentially flat subject.

Figure 3.9

(Left) 2-point lighting used in a photography studio. The key light is placed left, and a weaker fill light is placed right. (Right) 2-point lighting found in the outdoors. The sun serves as a key light and arrives from the upper right. The net sum of bounced sunlight serves as fill and arrives from the lower center and left. The bounced light prevents the shadows from becoming pure black.

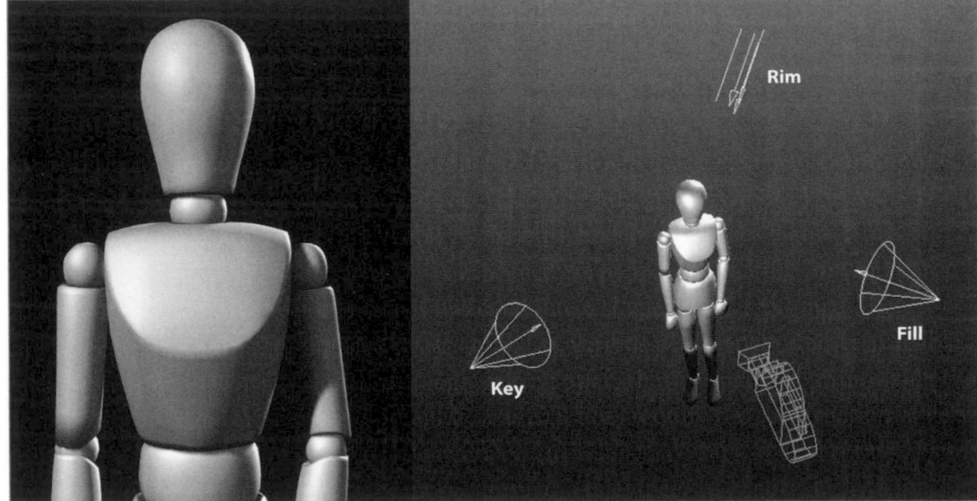

Figure 3.10

(Left) 3-point lighting applied to a mannequin in Maya (Right) Light position as seen from a perspective view

When applied to photography or cinematography, both 2-point lighting and 3-point lighting create an aesthetic result on the human face (see Figure 3.9 and Figure 3.11). The position of the key and fill light form an attractive transition from the key side of the face to the fill side of the face. In addition, the shadows formed by the key light are not overly long and do not interfere with the eyes or mouth. With 3-point lighting, the rim light helps separate the subject from the background. This is particularly useful when the background is dark or cluttered with detail.

One disadvantage of 3-point lighting is the stylistic nature of the rim light. You rarely see 3-point lighting in nature that has a distinct key, fill, and rim. If there is a rim light, the lighting tends to be 2-point lighting; in that situation, the rim is actually the key, and the fill is bounced light (see Figure 3.12).

For this reason, classically trained painters tend to choose 2-point lighting when creating portraits and outdoor scenes. This is especially true for any painting created before the advent of artificial light. Lacking strong artificial light, painters were forced to use the sun, a torch, an oil lamp, or a set of candles as a key light (see Figure 3.13). Bounced light from a nearby wall often served as the fill.

Figure 3.11

(Left) 3-point lighting. The key is placed right, the fill is placed left, and the rim light arrives from the back left. (Right) 3-point lighting. The key is placed right but is slightly lower than the camera. The fill is placed left. The rim light arrives from directly behind the subject.

Figure 3.12

(Left) Natural rim light formed by the sun arriving from behind the girl. Bounced sunlight forms a fill and arrives from the direction of the camera. (Right) Natural rim light formed by the sun arriving from behind the antelope. Bounced sunlight forms a fill and arrives from the direction of the camera.

A second disadvantage of 3-point lighting is the rigidity of the key and fill placement. Hence, many contemporary cinematographers and photographers eschew the 3-point scheme in favor of more flexible setups. When lighting pushes past a fixed number of lights and light positions, it is often referred to as *naturalistic*. We will explore naturalistic lighting in more detail in the last four chapters of this book.

Figure 3.13

(Left) Rembrandt. *Man in a Golden Helmet*. c. 1650. Oil on canvas. Staatliche Museen, Berlin. (Right) Hals. *The Laughing Cavalier*. 1624. Oil on canvas. The Wallace Collection, London. In both examples, a natural key light arrives from the left while weaker bounced fill light arrives from the right. Photos © 2011 Jupiterimages Corporation.

Project: Roughing in the Lighting

Before proceeding with the texturing process, you can rough in the lighting. A rough pass on the lighting will help you make sound decisions when adjusting materials and mapping textures. For this project, we will apply 3-point lighting, as discussed in the prior section. You can follow these steps:

1. Create a spot light. Rename the light **Key**. Position the light to the left of the model so that it's approximately 20 degrees off the axis that runs between the camera and the model (see Figure 3.14). You can look through the light by selecting the light icon and choosing Panels → Look Through Selected Camera from a view panel menu. After the view is activated, you can use the standard Alt+LMB, Alt+MMB, and Alt+RMB camera shortcuts to move the light. To deactivate the view, choose Panels → Perspective → *camera name* or Panels → Orthographic → *camera name*. In addition, you can roughly gauge the influence of a light by choosing Shading → Smooth Shade All and Lighting → Use All Lights.
2. Open the light's Attribute Editor tab. Set the Cone Angle to 90 and the Penumbra to 10. In the Depth Map Shadow Attributes section, select the Use Depth Map Shadows check box. Set the Resolution to 512 and the Filter Size to 4. Render a test. The result should look similar to Figure 3.15. The goal is to create aesthetically shaped shadows

that don't occlude the character's eyes or lips. Minor changes to the position of the Key light will cause the shadows to take on different shapes.

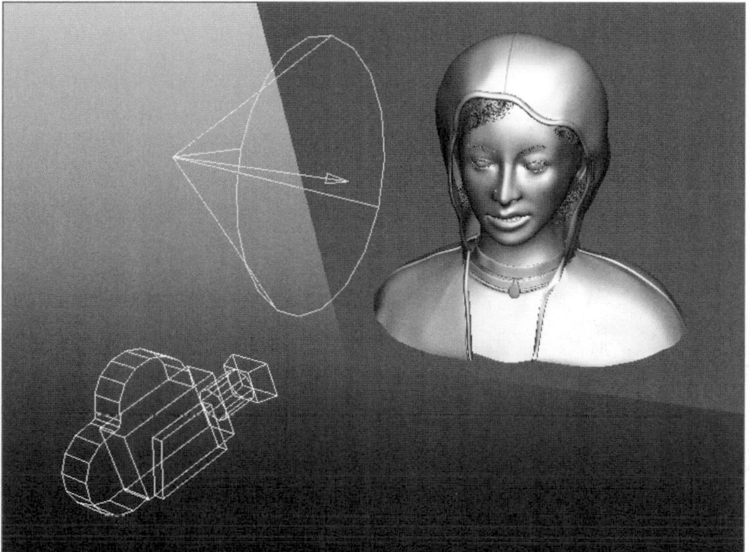

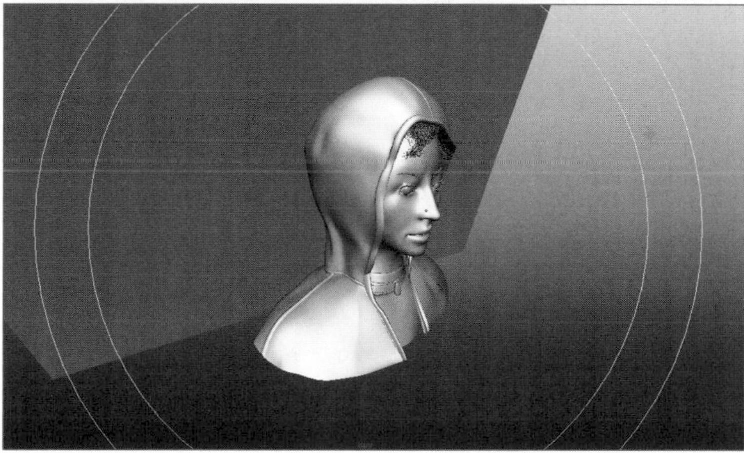

Figure 3.14
(Top) Positioned spot light. (Bottom) View of light after Look Through Selected Camera is activated

3. Although the presence of the spot light automatically prevents the Maya Software renderer from using the default light, it's a good idea to manually disable the default light. To do so, open the Render Settings window, expand the Render Options section in the Common tab, and deselect the Enable Default Light check box. If the Enable Default Light check box is left selected, it will interfere with eventual application of the mental ray renderer.
4. Create a directional light. Rename the light **Fill**. Position the light to the right of the model so that it's approximately 60 degrees off the axis that runs between the camera

and the model (see Figure 3.16). Point the light upward slightly. Open the light's Attribute Editor tab and reduce the Intensity to 0.2. Deselect the Emit Specular check box. This will prevent the light from producing a second set of specular highlights. Render a test.

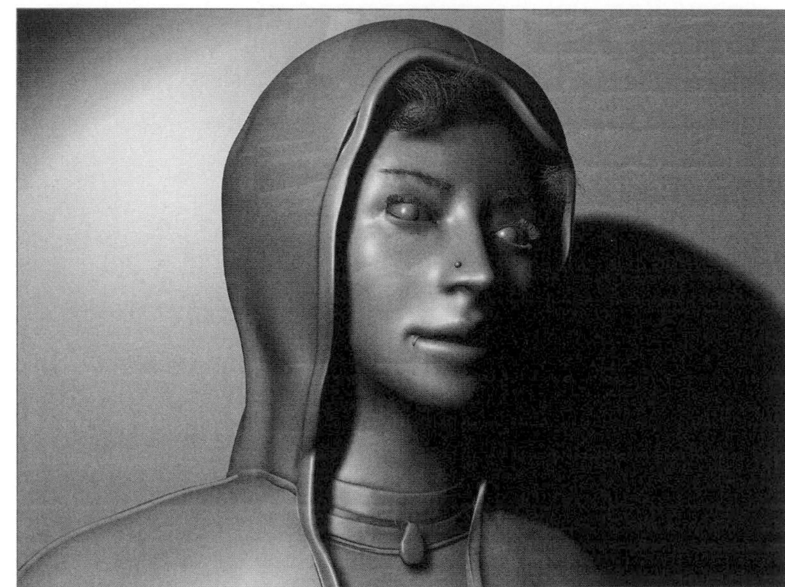

Figure 3.15
Render after the addition of the Key light and depth map shadows. A sample scene file is included as `woman-step3.ma` **on the DVD.**

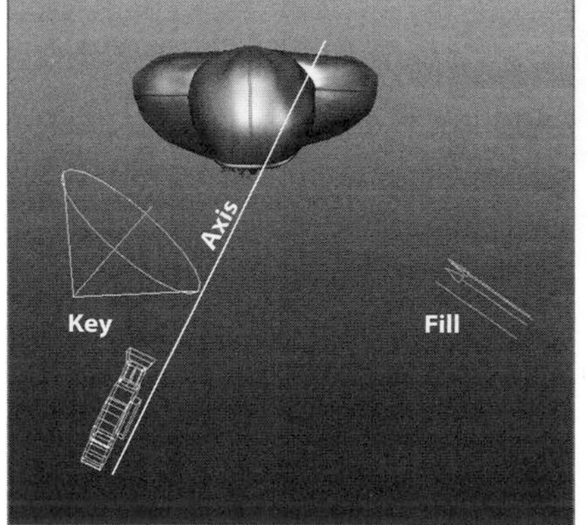

Figure 3.16
(Left) Top view showing position of the Key and Fill lights. (Right) Resulting render. A sample file is included as `woman-step4.ma` **on the DVD.**

5. Create a new directional light. Rename the light **Rim**. Position this light behind the character model so that it points back toward the spot light (see Figure 3.17). Rotate the light until it creates a thin sliver along the woman's left cheek, the edge of the sweatshirt hood, and the left shoulder. Open the light's Attribute Editor. Change the Intensity to 0.5 and the Color to cyan. The nonwhite light color will help tie the model to the background plane, which will be textured at a later step. The nonwhite color also makes it easier to see the influence of the Rim light. Select the Use Depth Map Shadows check box and set

Resolution to 512 and Filter Size to 6. Casting a shadow prevents the light from illuminating areas that would be blocked in real life. Render a test. The Rim light should create a rim similar to Figure 3.17.

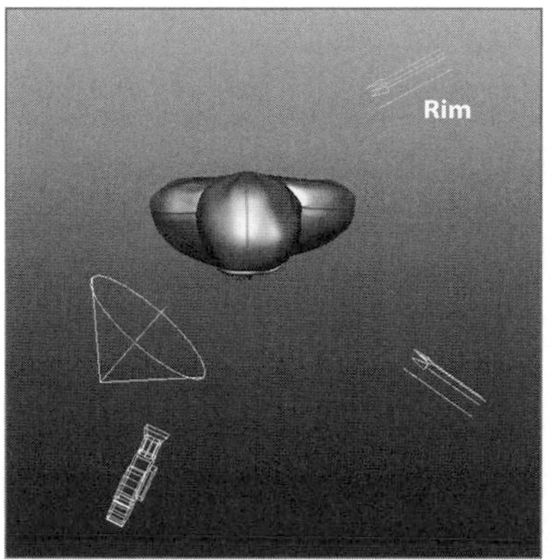

Figure 3.17

(Left) Top view showing position of Rim light. (Right) Resulting render. A sample file is included as `woman-step5.ma` **on the DVD.**

Examining the UVs of NURBS Surfaces

NURBS surfaces automatically receive UV coordinates when they are created. 0, 0 in UV texture space occurs at the origin box of the surface. The two vertices appearing closest to the origin box are represented by a tiny U and V, indicating the U and V direction (see Figure 3.18). Hence, you can check the UV orientation of a NURBS surface in the wireframe view of a view panel. If the vertices prove too difficult to see, you can choose Display → NURBS → Surface Origins. U and V symbols are displayed, as well as red (U axis) and green (V axis) edge lines. The surface normal direction is indicated by a blue line drawn from the UV origin. Either approach will help you choose appropriate values for the U and V tiling of a texture. The U and V tiling is controlled by the Repeat UV attribute of the texture's connected place2dTexture node.

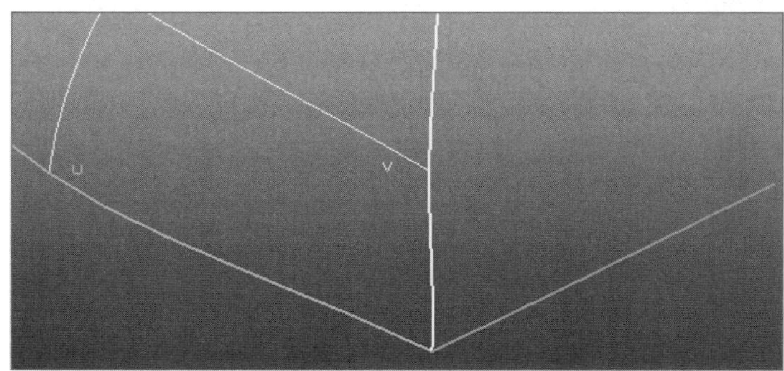

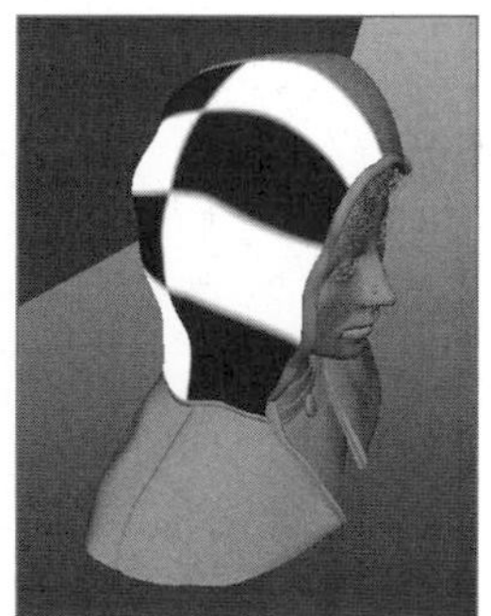

Figure 3.18

(Left) The U and V directions of a NURBS surface are indicated by UV symbols drawn by the Surface Origins display option. (Right) Surfaces temporarily assigned to a Surface Shader material with a Ramp mapped to its Out Color. A sample file is included as `Uv_texture.ma` **in the** `ProjectFiles/Project2/Reference` **folder on the DVD.**

If you are unable to determine appropriate tiling values by examining the wireframe alone, you can assign a temporary material to a surface or surfaces. For example, in Figure 3.18, the Hood_R surface is assigned to a Surface Shader that has a Checker texture mapped to its Out Color. To get the material to appear roughly square, the Repeat UV values of the connected place2dTexture node are adjusted. The adjusted UV values are then applied to the final texture. To make the texture appear in a view panel, choose Shading → Smooth Shade All and Shading → Hardware Texturing from the view panel menu.

If a NURBS surface is unduly stretched during the modeling process, its UV distribution may not be even. The stretching may occur if vertices are manually moved apart from each other. The stretching may also be the result of uneven isoparm distribution stemming back to the initial construction. Minor variations are not overly harmful to the texturing process. Significant stretching, however, can affect the quality of the render. Although it's best to construct the surfaces to avoid such a problem, it's possible to repair the stretching during the texturing process with the Texture Warp tool. This tool is demonstrated in Chapter 4.

Translucence

The Translucence attribute carried by Lambert, Blinn, Phong, Phong E, and Anisotropic materials simulates the diffuse penetration of light into a solid surface. In the real world, you can see the effect when holding a flashlight to the back of your hand. Translucence naturally occurs in hair, fur, wax, paper, leaves, and human flesh.

The higher the Translucence value, the more the scene's light penetrates the surface (see Figure 3.19). A Translucence value of 1.0 allows 100 percent of the light to pass through the surface. A value of 0 turns the translucent effect off. The Translucence Depth attribute sets the virtual distance into the object to which the light is able to penetrate. The attribute is measured in world units and may be raised above 5. Translucence Focus controls the scattering of light through the surface. A value of 0 makes the scatter of light random and diffuse; high values focus the penetrated light into a point.

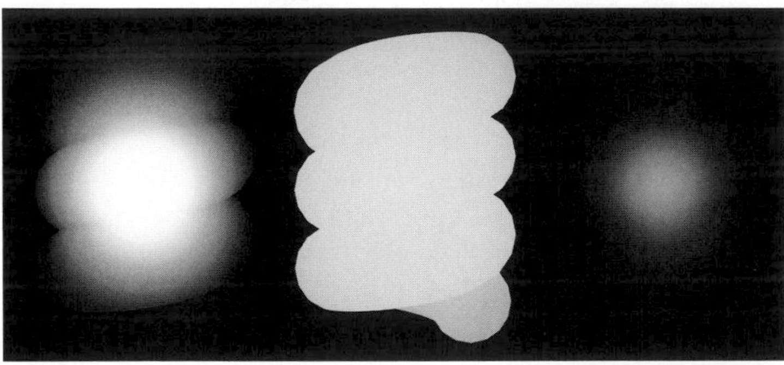

Translucence = 1.0
Translucence Depth = 0.5
Translucence Focus = 0.95

Translucence = 0.7
Translucence Depth = 1.0
Translucence Focus = 0.5

Translucence = 0.5
Translucence Depth = 0.2
Translucence Focus = 0.98

Figure 3.19

Different combinations of Translucence, Translucence Depth, and Translucence Focus values. A point light is placed behind the surface and is given a yellow Color value. The surface itself is assigned to a Blinn with its Color set to gray. A sample file is included as `translucence.ma` in the `ProjectFiles/Project2/Reference` folder on the DVD.

Project: Roughing in the Textures

With the basic lighting established, you can now adjust the materials and add various color, specular, and bump maps.

Texturing the Choker

The woman's choker is composed of four surfaces: Choker_Band, Choker_Ring, Pendant_Ring, and Pendant. To make the choker look like black vinyl with gold rings and a semi-transparent red pendant stone, follow these steps:

1. Select the Blinn material assigned to Choker_Band and open its Attribute Editor tab (in the sample scene files, the material is named Choker_Band_). Change the Color to black, the Eccentricity to 0.2, and the Specular Roll Off to 2.0. Render a test. The band's specular highlight makes very even vertical stripes (see Figure 3.20).

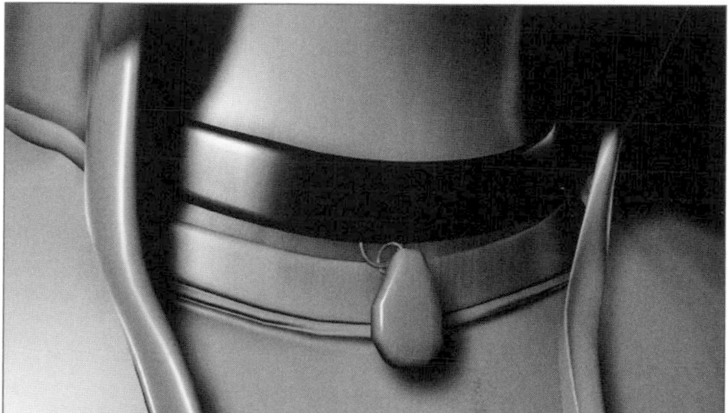

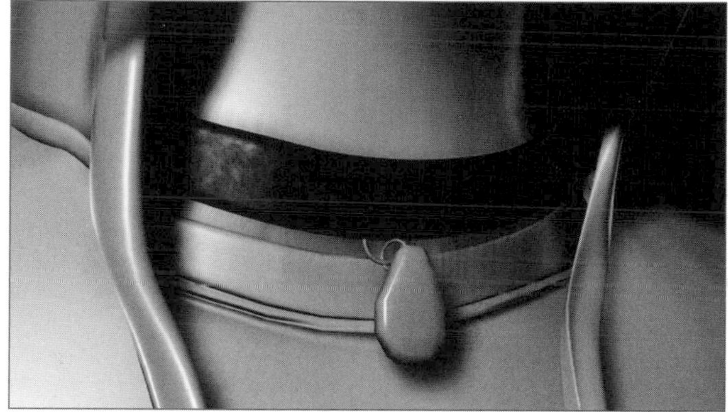

Figure 3.20
(Top) Initial specular highlight on the choker band. (Bottom) Result of Fractal texture mapped to the Specular Color attribute. A sample file is included as `woman-step6.ma` **on the DVD.**

2. To break up the highlight and thus make the band more worn and weathered, click the checkered Map button beside Specular Color. Click the Fractal texture icon in the Create Render Node window. In the new Fractal node's Attribute Editor tab, change Amplitude to 0.5 and Threshold to 0.25. This reduces the contrast within the fractal pattern. In the Color Balance section, reduce the Color Gain to dark gray (0.25, 0.25, 0.25 in RGB). This darkens the texture. Open the Attribute Editor tab for the place2dTexture node attached to the new Fractal node. Change Repeat UV to 3, 0.5. This is required to prevent horizontal stretching. The Choker_Band NURBS surface is longer than it is tall. Because U runs along the length and V runs along the height, the texture must be tiled more times in the U direction than in the V direction. (For tips on how to identify U and V directions on NURBS surfaces, see the section "Examining the UVs of NURBS Surfaces" earlier in this chapter.) Render a test. The specular highlight is now more random. Additional detail will be added to the surface when raytracing is activated in a later step.
3. Select the Blinn material assigned to Choker_Ring and Pendant_Ring (in the sample scene files, the material is named Gold). Open the material's Attribute Editor tab. Change the Color to goldish yellow, the Eccentricity to 0.2, the Specular Roll Off to 0.7, and the Specular Color to a brighter yellowish white. Render a test. The rings

appear gold. Additional realism will be added when raytracing is activated in a later step. You can also assign this material to the Stud and Lip_Ring surfaces.

4. Select the Phong material assigned to the Pendant surface (in the sample scene files, the material is named Pendant_). Open the material's Attribute Editor tab. Change the Color to a ruby red, the Transparency to gray (0.5, 0.5, 0.5 in RGB), and Specular Color to pinkish red. Render a test. The pendant appears glass-like (see Figure 3.21). Additional realism will be added when raytracing is activated in a later step.

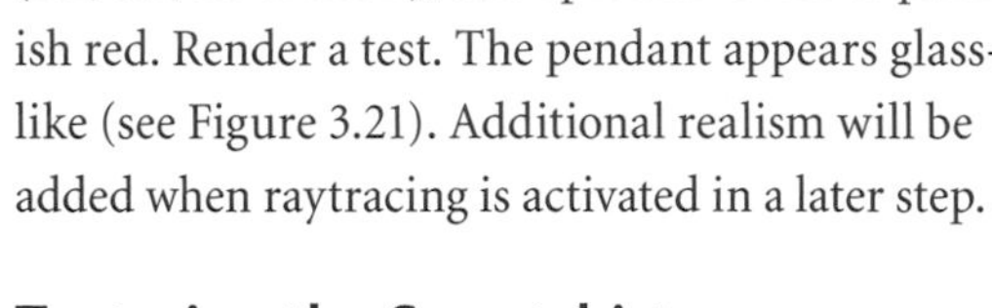

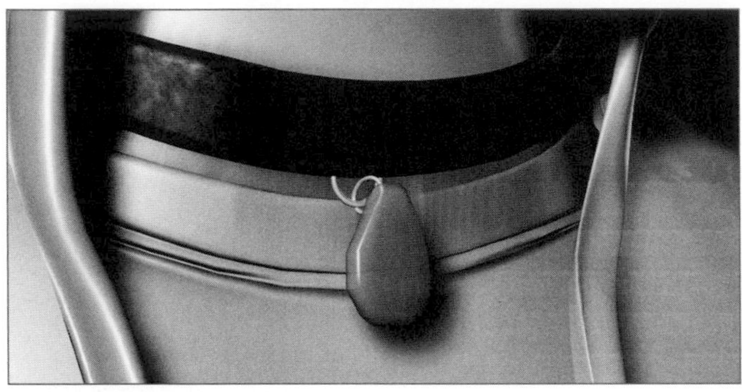

Figure 3.21

Textured rings and pendant. Raytraced reflections will be added in a later step. A sample file is included as `woman-step7.ma` on the DVD.

Texturing the Sweatshirt

The woman's sweatshirt is composed of 10 NURBS surfaces. These are all grouped under the Sweatshirt group node. To make the sweatshirt components look like slightly rough, heavy, blue cloth, follow these steps:

1. Select the Blinn material assigned to the Hood_L and Hood_R surfaces and open its Attribute Editor tab (in the sample scene files, the material is named Hood). Change Diffuse to 0.5, Eccentricity to 0.75, Specular Roll Off to 0.1, and Specular Color to purple. A large Eccentricity and a small Specular Roll Off value make the surface appear more matte-like. If the Specular Color is different from the Color, the surface takes on a subtle iridescent look. Click the checkered Map button beside Color. Click the File texture icon in the Create Render Node window. In the new File texture's Attribute Editor tab, click the Image Name browse button and load a bitmap that features a piece of cloth.
2. You can create your own cloth bitmap through one of the following techniques:
   - Photograph a piece of cloth laid out flat or taped to a wall.
   - Scan a piece of cloth on a flatbed scanner.
   - Use a preexisting cloth bitmap from a website that specializes in 3D textures.

   If the cloth bitmap you've created or secured is not blue, tint it in Photoshop or a similar digital paint program. In Photoshop, you can tint an image by choosing Image → Adjustments → Hue/Saturation and either shifting the Hue slider toward blue or by selecting the Colorize check box and adjusting the Hue, Saturation, and Lightness sliders. For example, in Figure 3.22, a cloth bitmap was created from a scan. Note that color variation was maintained so that the blue is not consistent at all points. The bitmap resolution is 1600×1600.

Figure 3.22

A cloth bitmap is created from a digital scan of real cloth. The bitmap file is included as `Cloth_Color.tga` in the `ProjectFiles/Project2/Textures` folder on the DVD. For a color version of this figure, see the color insert.

3. After you've loaded a cloth bitmap into the new File node, render a test. At this juncture, you must determine whether the tiling of the bitmap is appropriate for the assigned surfaces. For example, the `Cloth_Color.tga` file requires a UV Repeat of 1.0, 2 for the

Hood_L and Hood_R surfaces. After you've set the Repeat UV values in the connected place2dTexture nodes, return to the material's Attribute Editor tab and click the checkered Map button beside Bump Mapping. Click the File texture icon in the Create Render Node window. A new Bump 2d node and File node are added to the material's shading network. In the Bump 2d node's Attribute Editor tab, change the Bump Depth to 0.2. In the new File texture's Attribute Editor tab, click the Image Name browse button and load a bitmap that can be used as a cloth bump. The easiest way to create such a bitmap is to make a high-contrast, grayscale version of the cloth bitmap used as a Color map. You can create a grayscale version of an image in Photoshop by choosing Image → Adjustments → Desaturate. You can adjust the contrast by choosing Image → Adjustments → Brightness/Contrast. For example, in Figure 3.23, a grayscale version of `Cloth_Color.tga` is included as `Cloth_Bump.tga`. After you've created a bitmap for the bump map, adjust the UV tiling through the connected place2dTexture nodes. You can use the same Repeat UV values you used for the Color map. The end result should be a cloth-like render (see Figure 3.23).

4. Repeat steps 1 to 3 for the remaining sweatshirt components. To save time, you can copy the Hood material shading network and assign the copy to a different surface. To make a copy, select the material in the Hypershade and choose Edit → Duplicate → Shading Network. The material, along with all the connections and loaded bitmaps, is copied. The new copy is simply named Hood1. The copied material must be renamed and assigned to a different surface. In addition, the Repeat UV values for the connected File nodes must be adjusted to match the newly assigned surface. For example, a list of materials utilizing `Cloth_Color.tga` and `Cloth_Bump.tga` are listed in Table 3.2 with associated Repeat UV values.

Figure 3.23

(Top) A bump bitmap is created by desaturating and adjusting the contrast of the bitmap used as a Color map. The bitmap file is included as `Cloth_Bump.tga` in the `ProjectFiles/Project2/Textures` folder on the DVD. (Bottom) The resulting render of the Hood_R surface. A sample scene is included as `woman-step8.ma` on the DVD.

The shading group node connected to a duplicated shading network will receive a name similar to the material when copied. For example, the shading group node for the Hood material is named HoodSG; therefore, the copied shading group node is automatically named HoodSG1. Although renaming the shading group nodes will make for better organization, it's not necessary for the steps laid out in this chapter and Chapter 4.

You may need to render a series of tests to determine the most appropriate Repeat UV values for the various sweatshirt surfaces. Ideally, the size of the "threads" or bumps on each surface should be fairly consistent. Additionally, you want to avoid any obvious seams created by tiling. To some degree, you can disguise seams by selecting the Stagger, Mirror U, and/or Mirror V check boxes carried by the place2dTexture nodes. Stagger, Mirror U, and Mirror V offset each tile iteration to make the final pattern appear more random. It's also possible to paint small fixes along tiling seams with the 3D Paint tool, which is demonstrated in Chapter 4. As you apply the various Repeat UV values, you may notice some texture stretching due to an uneven distribution of UVs. This problem will be addressed in Chapter 4. For additional suggestions concerning NURBS surfaces and UV distribution, see the "Examining the UVs of NURBS Surfaces" section earlier in this chapter.

At this stage, a large portion of the model is textured. Hence, it's a good idea to readjust the Intensity values of the lights in the scene. For example, in Figure 3.24, the Intensity of the Key light is raised to 1.2.

Table 3.2
Sweatshirt materials and associated Repeat UV values

MATERIAL	ASSIGNED SURFACES	REPEAT UV VALUES
Back_	Back	3, 1.0
Hood	Hood_L	1.0, 2
	Hood_R	
Seam	Seam_L	0.2, 2
	Seam_R	
	Seam_Top	
Seam_Front_	Seam_Front	0.2, 10
Seam_Neck_	Seam_Neck	6, 0.2
Front	Front_L	1.0, 1.0
	Front_R	

Figure 3.24
The remaining surfaces of the sweatshirt are textured. The Intensity of the Key light is raised to 1.2. A sample file is included as `woman-step9.ma` on the DVD. For a color version of the figure, see the color insert.

Texturing the Shirt

The woman's shirt is composed of two surfaces: Shirt and Collar. To make the shirt look like finely woven green cloth, follow these steps:

1. Select the Blinn material assigned to the Shirt surface and open its Attribute Editor tab (in the sample scene files, the material is named Shirt_). Change Eccentricity to 0.5, Specular Roll Off to 0.1, and Specular Color to purple. Click the checkered Map button beside Color. Click the File texture icon in the Create Render Node window. In the new File texture's Attribute Editor tab, click the Image Name browse button and

load the cloth bitmap created for the sweatshirt in the previous section. Even though the bitmap is blue, you can tint it through the Color Balance section. To do so, change the Color Gain to orange-yellow (1.0, 0.78, 0.27 in RGB). The Color Gain values are multiplied by the bitmap values to produce a final color result for the texture. Open the Attribute Editor tab for the new place2dTexture node connected to the new File node. Set Repeat UV to 1, 0.5. Render a test. The shirt appears green, but there is no appearance of fine threads (see Figure 3.25).

2. Return to the shirt material's Attribute Editor tab. Click the checkered Map button beside Bump Mapping. Click the Cloth texture icon in the Create Render Node window. A Bump 2d node, along with a new Cloth node, is added to the material's shading network. In the Bump 2d node's Attribute Editor tab, change the Bump Depth to 0.03. Open the Attribute Editor tab for the new place2dTexture node connected to the Cloth node. Change Repeat UV to 180, 4. The high U repeat creates the illusion that the shirt is woven fabric (see Figure 3.25). To make the selection of nodes easier, you can RMB+click a material in the Hypershade and choose Graph Network from the marking menu. The shading network for the material is revealed in the work area. You can click any node in the work area to bring up its Attribute Editor tab (if the Attribute Editor is closed, double-click).

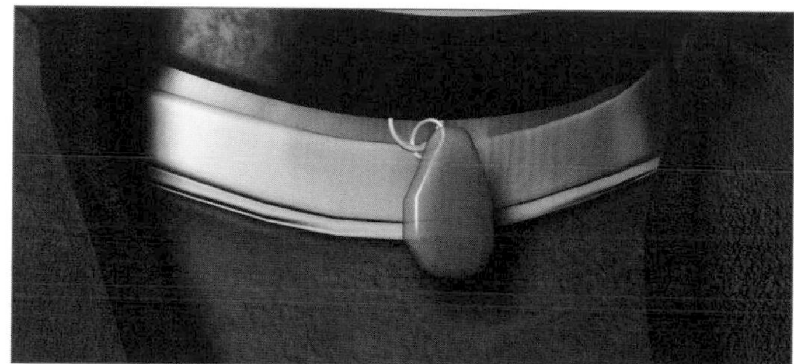

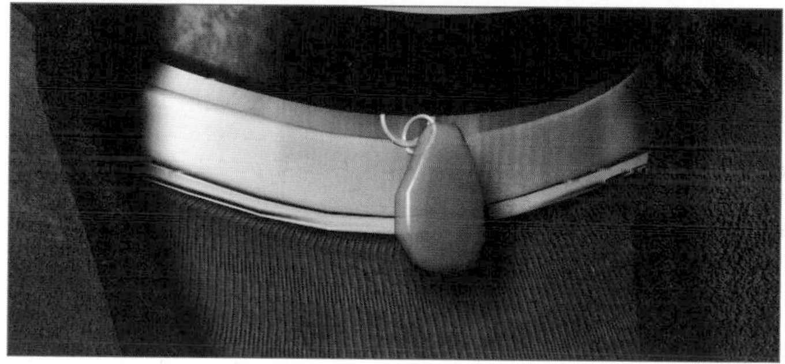

Figure 3.25

(Top) Close-up of shirt without bump map. (Bottom) Shirt with bump map

3. Select the Blinn material assigned to the Collar_ surface and open its Attribute Editor tab (in the sample scene file, the material is named Collar_). Change the Eccentricity to 0.5, the Specular Roll Off to 0.1, and the Specular Color to purple. Click the checkered Map button beside Color. Click the File texture icon in the Create Render Node window. In the new File texture's Attribute Editor tab, click the Image Name browse button and load the cloth bitmap created for the sweatshirt in the previous section. Change the File node's Color Gain to orange-yellow (1.0, 0.78, 0.27 in RGB). Open the Attribute Editor tab for the new place2dTexture node connected to the new File node. Set Repeat UV to 1.0, 0.2.
4. Return to the material's Attribute Editor tab and click the checkered Map button beside Bump Mapping. Click the Water texture icon in the Create Render Node window. A new Bump 2d node and Water node are added to the material's shading network. In the Bump 2d node's Attribute Editor tab, change the Bump Depth to –0.25.

In the Water node's Attribute Editor tab, change Wave Amplitude to 4. This increases the contrast within the water pattern. Open the Attribute Editor tab for the new place2dTexture node connected to the Water node. Change Repeat UV to 36, 0.4. Render a test. A series of fine vertical lines are added to the collar (see Figure 3.26). This emulates the elastic found in cotton T-shirt collars.

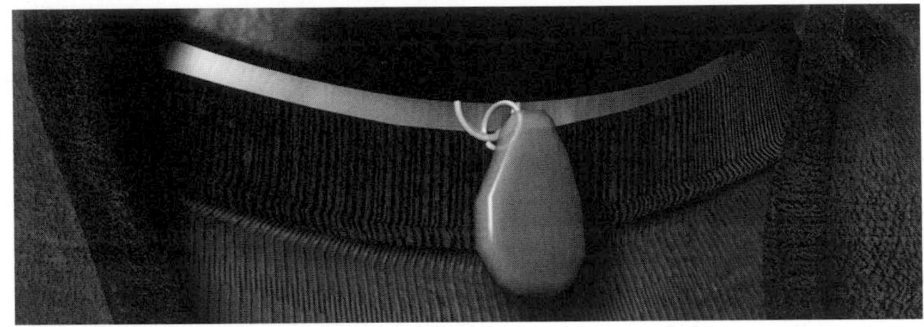

Figure 3.26
Close-up of shirt collar. A sample file is included as `woman-step10.ma` on the DVD.

Texturing the Eyes

Each of the woman's eyes is constructed from seven NURBS and polygon surfaces (see Figure 3.27).

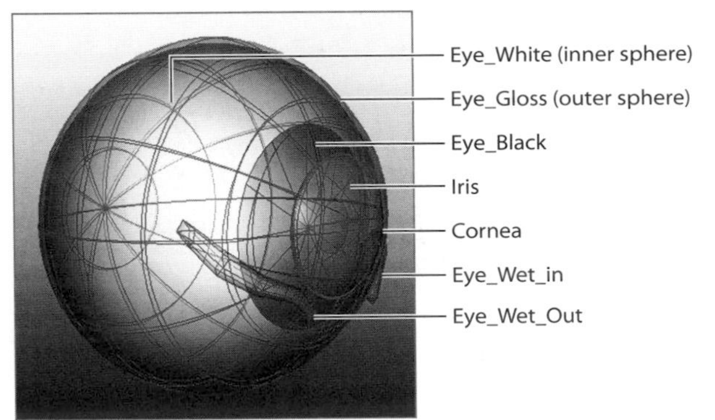

Figure 3.27
The various surfaces making up the eye geometry

Of the eye surfaces, the Eye_Black_L and Eye_Black_R are the easiest to texture. Because they are designed to fill the open part of each iris with black, you can leave them assigned to a Surface Shader with a black Out Color. The Surface Shader material is unaffected by lights and shadows, so the assigned surfaces will remain pure black regardless of the lighting setup.

The Iris_L and Iris_R surfaces can benefit from a bitmap texture of a real iris. Because the geometry is composed of a NURBS surface that has two edge borders meeting across its width, it's necessary to project the texture map to avoid stretching. To apply a projection to one iris, follow these steps:

1. Select the Cornea_L surface. Press Ctrl+H to hide the surface. If the Cornea_L surface is left visible, it will block the view of the Iris_L surface in the view panels. Select the Blinn material assigned to the Iris_L surface and open its Attribute Editor tab. Set Eccentricity to 0.2, Specular Roll Off to 0.4, and Specular Color to medium gray (0.4, 0.4, 0.4 in RGB). Click the checkered Map button beside Color. In the Create Render Node window, click the Projection utility icon, which you can find in the Utilities section. With the new Projection node's Attribute Editor tab open, click the checkered Map button beside Image. In the Create Render Node window, click the File texture

icon. In the new File texture's Attribute Editor tab, click the Image Name browse button and load a bitmap that features an iris. You can create your own bitmap by adapting a photograph. For example, in Figure 3.28, an iris bitmap is created by editing a close-up photo of a model. Note that the iris bitmap is unobstructed by any eyelid, eyelashes, or reflections, and the transition from the iris to the white of the eyeball is soft.

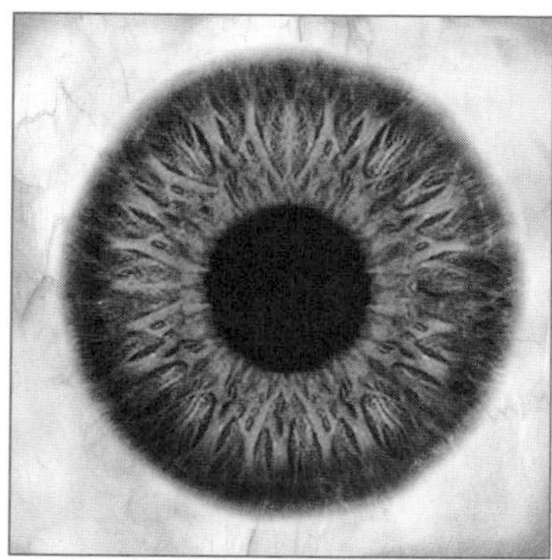

Figure 3.28

A bitmap of an iris. The bitmap file is included as `Iris_Color.tga` in the `ProjectFiles/Project2/Textures` folder on the DVD.

2. Return to the Projection node's Attribute Editor tab. Click the Fit To BBox button. An error message pops up, warning that the projection cannot be manipulated without a placement utility. Click the Create A Placement Node button. A place3dTexture node is automatically connected to the Projection node (see Figure 3.29). The place3dTexture utility allows you to interactively transform the projection. Return to the Projection node's Attribute Editor tab. Click the Fit To BBox button. This time, the projection handle appears in the view panels and is snapped to the bounding box of the surface it's assigned to. To aid the placement of the projection, choose Shading → Smooth Shade All and Shading → Hardware Texturing from the menu of the view panel you are working in. This displays a rough version of the assigned textures in the 3D view. Scale the projection handle by LMB+dragging a corner box. To transform the handle, click the small "T" at the bottom-left corner and LMB+drag one of the axis handles. To return to the handle's initial state, click the "T" handle again. Position the projection handle so that it is centered on the Iris_L surface. Scale the handle until the dark area of the iris touches the edge of the Iris_L surface (see Figure 3.29).
3. When you're satisfied with the projection position, open the Hypergraph: Hierarchy window. Select the place3dTexture node first and the Eye_L group node second and choose Edit → Parent from the main menu. Parenting the place3dTexture node to the eye group node will allow the texture to stay in place even when the eye group is rotated.
4. To apply a projection to the Iris_R surface, repeat steps 1 through 3.

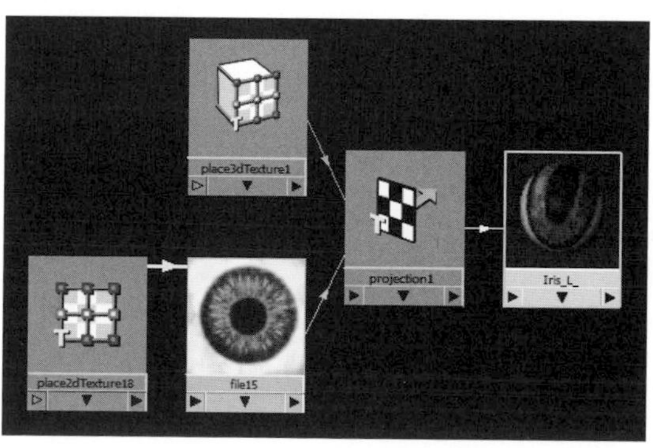

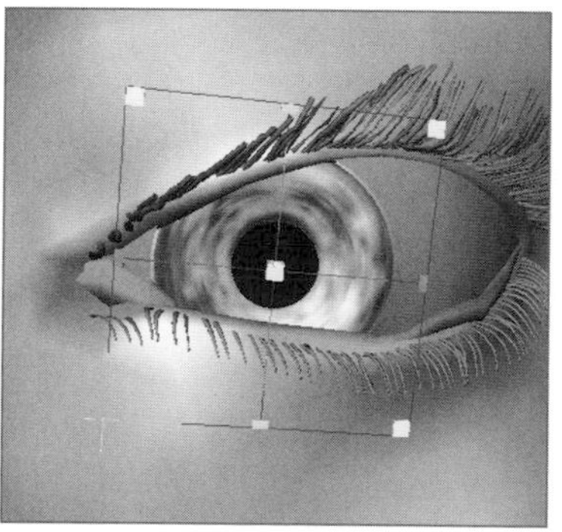

Figure 3.29

(Left) The final shading network for the Iris_L_ material. (Right) A hardware shaded view with the place3dTexture projection handle visible. A sample file is included as `woman-step11.ma` on the DVD.

The Eye_White surfaces can also benefit from projections. Much like the Iris surfaces, the Eye_White surfaces are constructed from NURBS surfaces and have a visible seam where two edges meet. To map the surfaces with Projection nodes, follow these steps:

1. In the Hypergraph: Hierarchy or Outliner window, select the Eye_Gloss_L surface and press Ctrl+H to hide the surface. If Eye_Gloss_L surface is left visible, it will block the view of the Eye_White_L surface in the view panels. Select the Blinn material assigned to the Eye_White_L surface and open its Attribute Editor tab (with the sample scene files, the material is named Eye_White_L_). Set Diffuse to 0.6, Ambient Color to dark gray (0.05, 0.05, 0.05 in RGB), Eccentricity to 0.2, Specular Roll Off to 0.4, and Specular Color to tan (0.8, 0.8, 0.6 in RGB). A nonzero Ambient Color will brighten the eye even if it's in shadow. A nonwhite Specular Color will prevent the eye from appearing pure white. Click the checkered Map button beside Color. In the Create Render Node window, click the Projection utility icon, which you can find in the Utilities section. With the new Projection node's Attribute Editor tab open, click the checkered Map button beside Image. In the Create Render Node window, click the File texture icon. In the new File texture's Attribute Editor tab, click the Image Name browse button and load a bitmap that features the white of an eye. You can create your own bitmap by combining multiple photographs of eyes. For example, in Figure 3.30, an eye bitmap is created by editing close-up photos of a model.

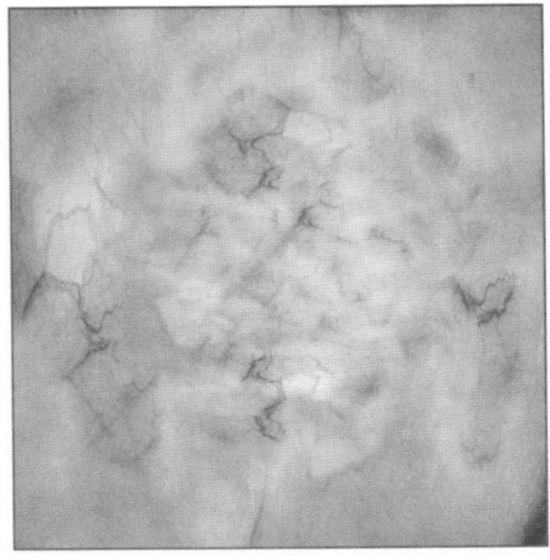

Figure 3.30

A bitmap of an eye surface. The bitmap file is included as `Eye_White.tga` in the `ProjectFiles/Project2/Textures` folder on the DVD.

2. Return to the Projection node's Attribute Editor tab. Click the Fit To BBox button. An error message pops up, warning that the projection cannot be manipulated without a placement utility. Click the Create A Placement Node button. A place3dTexture node is automatically connected to the Projection node. Return to the Projection node's Attribute Editor tab. Click the Fit To BBox button. This time, the projection handle appears in the view panels and is snapped to the bounding box of the surface it's assigned to. In the Projection node's Attribute Editor tab, change Proj Type to Spherical. Change the U Angle to 360 and the V Angle to 180. This extends the projection so that it completely surrounds the Eye_White_L surface. In a view panel, interactively rotate the projection handle so that its axis lines up with the axis of the surface. Open the Hypergraph: Hierarchy window. Select the newest place3dTexture node first and the Eye_L group node second and choose Edit → Parent from the main menu.

3. To apply a projection to the Eye_White_R surface, repeat steps 1 and 2. To prevent the same exact vein pattern from appearing on both eyes, open the place2dTexture node connected to the material's shading network and change Repeat UV to –1, 1; this mirrors the bitmap in the U direction. You can also mirror the V direction or use the Rotate UV attributes to further offset the bitmap. Render a test. If the Eye_White_R surface appears too dark (despite the fact that it's lit directly by the Key light), you

can give the material a unique set of attribute values. For example, set Diffuse to 1.0, Ambient Color to dark gray (0.1, 0.1, 0.1 in RGB), Eccentricity to 0.4, Specular Roll Off to 0.7, and Specular Color to tan (0.8, 0.8, 0.6 in RGB). Note that the application of different attribute values to the left and right eye surfaces is permissible because the woman is static and the render is a still frame. If the woman was animated, moving about the scene, dissimilar material assignments to the eyes would create inconsistent results; in such a case, it would be necessary to assign identical materials to the left and right eye surfaces and to spend additional time balancing the material attributes with the light positions and intensities.

The Eye_Gloss, Eye_Wet, and Cornea surfaces are designed to add additional specularity to the render without providing any diffuse quality. Thus, their assigned materials should be given a Transparency value of pure white, or 1.0. Follow these steps to adjust the materials:

1. Unhide the Cornea_L, Cornea_R, Eye_Gloss_L, and Eye_Gloss_R surfaces by choosing Display → Show → All.
2. Select the Phong material assigned to the Eye_Gloss_L surface and open its Attribute Editor tab (with the sample scene files, the material is named Eye_Gloss_L_). Set the Transparency to white, the Cosine Power to 40, and the Specular Color to dark gray (0.15, 0.15, 0.15 in RGB). Repeat step 2 for the Phong material assigned to the Eye_Gloss_R surface.
3. Select the Phong material assigned to the Eye_Wet surfaces and open its Attribute Editor tab (with the sample scene files, the material is named Eye_Wet_). Set the Transparency to white, the Cosine Power to 10, and the Specular Color to light gray (0.75, 0.75, 0.75 in RGB). Render a test. Additional specular highlights appear over the Eye_White and Iris surfaces (see Figure 3.31). Reflections will be added at the end of this chapter.

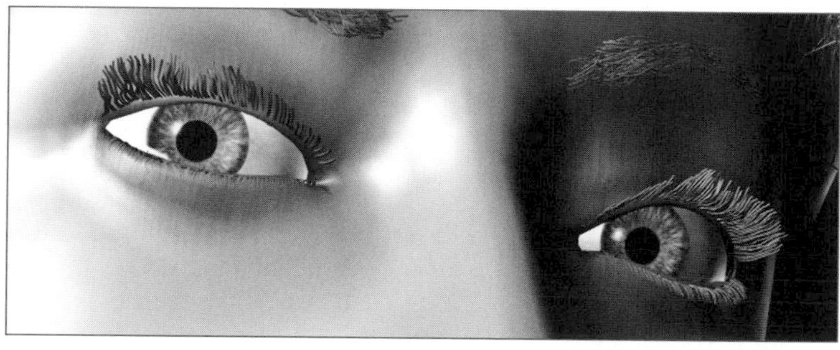

Figure 3.31

Close-up of textured eyes. A sample scene is included as `woman-step12.ma` **on the DVD. For a color version of the figure, see the color insert.**

Texturing the Hair, Eyelashes, and Eyebrows

The visible portion of the woman's hair is composed of several tufts of polygons tubes. The tubes were originally Paint Effects hair brushes, but were converted with the Paint Effects

To Polygons conversion tool. A similar process was used to create the polygon eyebrows and eyelashes. To texture these parts, follow these steps:

1. Select the Anisotropic material assigned to the hair surfaces (named Curl_1, Curl_2, and so on) and open its Attribute Editor tab (in the sample scene files, the material is named Hair_). Change Color to a dark brown (0.18, 0.12, 0.04 in RGB), Diffuse to 0.5, Translucence to 0.8, Translucence Depth to 1.0, Translucence Focus to 0.3, Angle to 180, Spread X to 7.4, Spread Y to 3.3, Roughness to 0.56, and Specular Color to light brown (0.65, 0.54, 0.47 in RGB). Nondefault Translucence values cause the light to penetrate and pass through the hair surfaces. An Angle of 180 rotates the specular highlight so that it appears perpendicular to the direction of individual hairs (see Figure 3.32). For more information on the Anisotropic material, see Chapter 1. For more information on translucence, see the section "Translucence" earlier in this chapter.
2. Using the attribute setting established by step 1 as a starting point, adjust the materials assigned to the Eyebrow_L, Eyebrow_R, Lash_Hi_L, Lash_Lo_L, Lash_Hi_R, and Lash_Lo_R surfaces. The sample scene files use the Eyebrows_ and Eyelashes_ materials. Render a test. The render should appear similar to Figure 3.32.

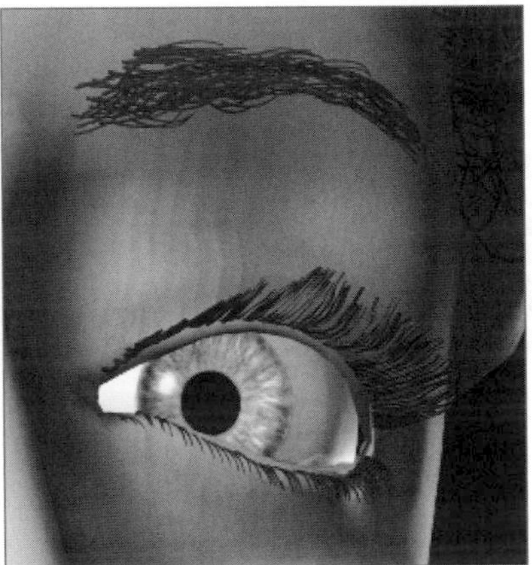

Figure 3.32

(Left) Close-up of hair tuft after material adjustment. (Right) Close-up of right eye after similar material adjustments are applied to eyebrow and eyelash materials. A sample scene is included as `woman-step13.ma` **on the DVD.**

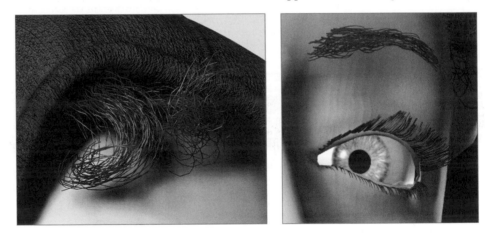

Texturing the Teeth

The woman's teeth are composed of 16 primitive polygon surfaces. Although the teeth are barely seen through the lips, they should be textured nevertheless. Select the Blinn material assigned to the Teeth surfaces and open its Attribute Editor tab (in the sample scene files, the material is named Teeth). Change Color to an off-white (0.8, 0.8, 0.6 in RGB), Diffuse to 0.5, Translucence to 0.6, Translucence Depth to 0.4, Translucence Focus to 0.6, Eccentricity to 0.5, Specular Roll Off to 0.5, and Specular Color to white. Render a test. The teeth will appear less gray (see Figure 3.33). At this point, the upper lip fails to cast a clean shadow on the teeth; the shadow will be fine-tuned during the last step of this chapter.

Project: Creating a Custom Skin Bitmap

Although you can use Photoshop's various brush tools to paint a skin bitmap from scratch, it's easier to sample photos of a real person. Whereas an animation studio might convert laser scans or high-resolution digital photographs into texture maps and polygon geometry, an individual animator can create texture maps from more mundane photos. For example, a front photo and profile photo can be utilized (see Figure 3.34). Ideally, the lighting should be very even and diffuse to avoid any distinct or heavy shadows from appearing. In addition, the digital resolution should be as large as possible. If you are unable to take your own photos, `www.3d.sk` offers a wide range of photos designed for use by animation professionals.

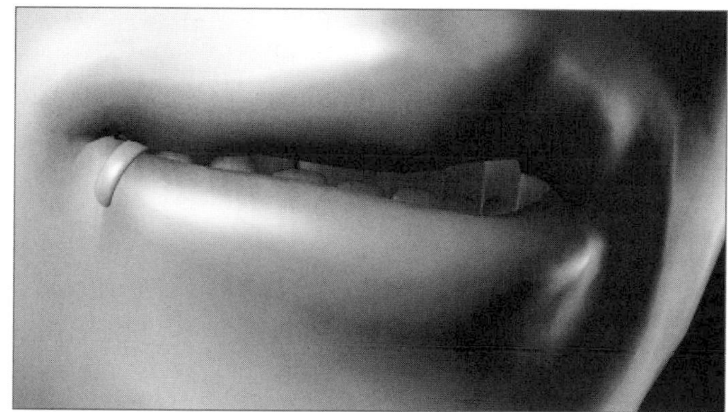

Figure 3.33

Teeth after material adjustment. A sample scene is included as `woman-step14.ma` **on the DVD.**

Painting the Face in Photoshop

Using the UV snapshot you exported as part of the "Examining and Exporting the UVs" section earlier in this chapter, follow these steps to construct a skin bitmap from digital photographs:

1. Open the UV snapshot PSD file in Photoshop. The UV snapshot sits on the top layer and is blended with the lower layer through the Screen blending mode. The lower layer, which contains only a solid color, will hold the newly created skin texture.
2. Open the source photographs. You need only two high-resolution stills—one taken in front of the person and one taken of the person's profile. Select the front photo. Using the Lasso tool, draw a selection around the face so that the background is left out. Press Ctrl+C to copy the selection. Switch to the UV snapshot PSD. With the lower layer selected in the Layers panel, press Ctrl+V to paste the copied face. Because of the Screen blending mode of the upper layer, the pasted face is visible under the white lines of the UV snapshot (see Figure 3.35).

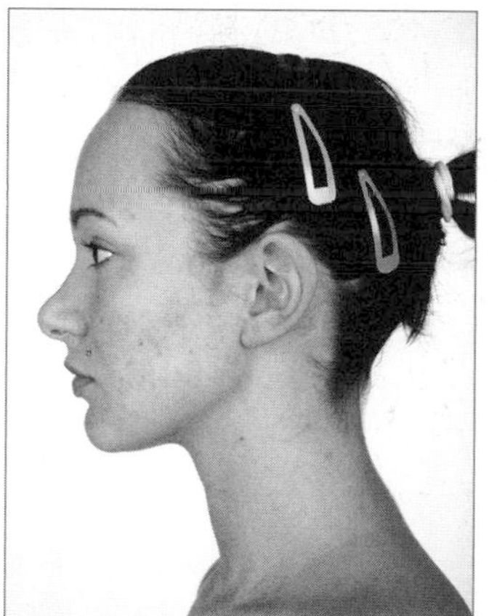

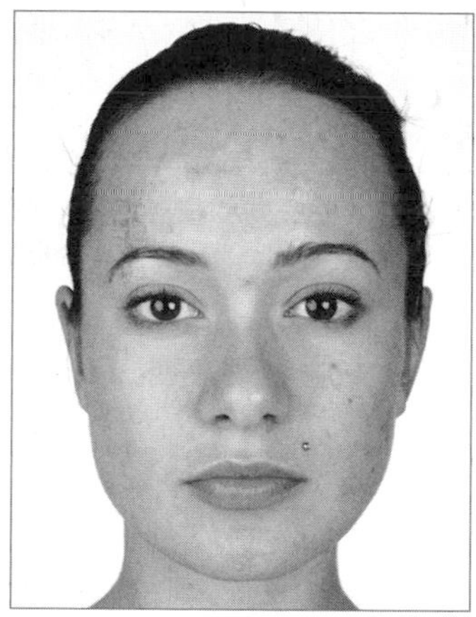

Figure 3.34

High-resolution profile and front photo of a model provide good sources for texture painting. Note that the even, diffuse lighting prevents distinct shadows from forming and thereby interfering with the lighting in Maya.

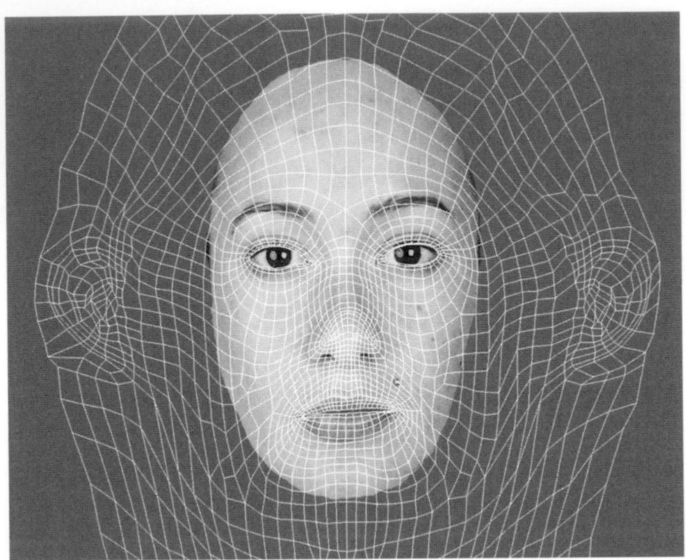

Figure 3.35
A section of a front photo pasted under the UV snapshot layer

3. Use Photoshop's various transform tools to position and scale the pasted face so that it lines up with the features of the UV snapshot. For example, the eyes of the photo should line up with the eyes of the snapshot. Because the UVs were pelt mapped and were relaxed in the UV mapping process, it will be impossible to get a perfect fit. However, you can use Photoshop's Liquify tool to push pixels around for a better match. Choose Filter → Liquify to activate the tool. In the Liquify window, choose a Brush Size and LMB+drag in the view area. The pixels are pushed as you drag the mouse. When you are satisfied with the result, click the OK button at the top right of the window.
4. If Liquify proves difficult to use (you can't see the UV snapshot layer while using it) or the tool is unavailable, you can cut, paste, and transform smaller areas. For example, use the Lasso tool to select one eye. Press Ctrl+C to copy the selection. Click outside the selection to undo the selection. Press Ctrl+V to paste the eye back onto a new layer. Press Ctrl+T to enter the transform mode and reposition the eye to a new location. You can rearrange the layers at any time by LMB+dragging a layer name up or down in the layer stack of the Layers panel.
5. After you've fit the face to the UV snapshot, switch to the profile photo. Select the ear, cheek, and jaw and press Ctrl+C. Switch to the UV snapshot PSD and press Ctrl+V to paste the selection. Using the Liquify and transform tools, move and scale the side of the face until it lines up with the UV lines and the pasted front of the face (see Figure 3.36).
6. Continue the process of copying sections from the source's photos until all the areas of the face are filled in. Use the Brush, Eraser, and Clone Stamp tools to blend the borders between the pasted sections. If you need to mirror one section, select it, copy it, paste it onto a new layer, and choose Edit → Transform → Flip Horizontal. When you're satisfied with the result, delete the UV snapshot layer by selecting it in the Layers panel and choosing Layer → Delete → Layer. Flatten the PSD file by choosing Layer → Flatten image. Save the file in a format supported by Maya. For example, save the file as `Face_Color.tga`.

Any part of the bitmap that lies outside the edge of the UV shell will not appear on any surface in Maya. Therefore, those areas need not be painted. The same holds true for the eyes. Although the example bitmap leaves the eyes intact, the eye geometry receives textures from different materials and bitmap textures. That said, you can leave the eyebrows in the bitmap. Although the Maya scene file includes eyebrow geometry, using an underlying texture that includes the brow hairs will make the end result more realistic. On the other hand, you should remove the eyelashes. If left, the eyelashes will appear inappropriately flat against the face. Figure 3.37 features a completed example. In this case, the overall brightness and contrast were adjusted to exaggerate the pores, blemishes, and other detail.

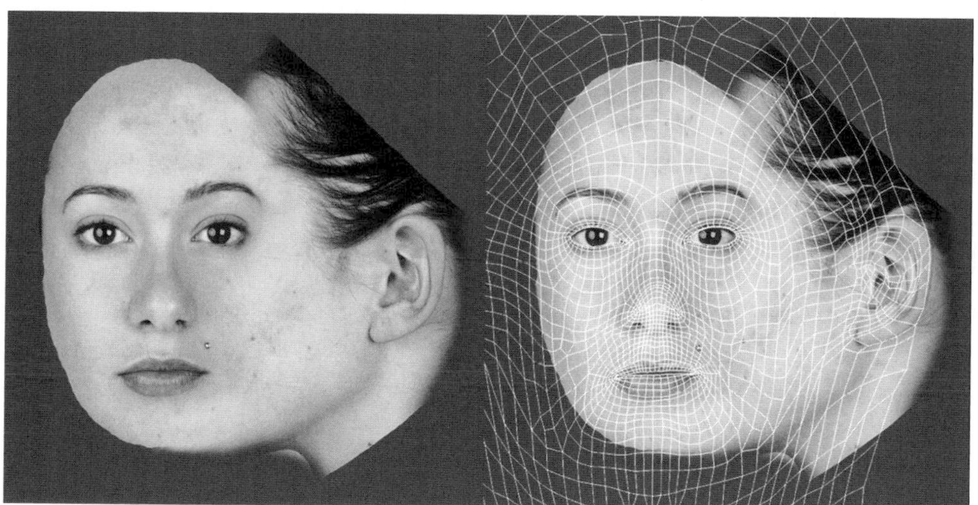

Figure 3.36
A section of a profile photo blended with the front photo by using the Clone Stamp tool, as seen with and without the UV snapshot layer

After you've completed the skin bitmap, you can alter it to create a bump map. To do so, create a high-contrast, grayscale version and save it under a different filename. Choose Image → Adjustments → Desaturate to remove the color and Image → Adjustments → Brightness/Contrast or Image → Adjustments → Curves to adjust the contrast. The color bitmap and bump bitmap need not be perfectly identical. For example, you can add additional detail to the bump bitmap, such as wrinkles. At the same time, you can blur or simplify areas of the bump bitmap to reduce the severity of the bump in particular areas. For example, Figure 3.38 features a complete bump bitmap.

Setting Up the Face Material

After you've created the color and bump texture bitmaps for the woman's face, you can map them to the assigned material. You can follow these steps:

1. Select the Blinn material assigned to the Face surface and open its Attribute Editor tab (with the sample scene files, the material is named Face_). Set Eccentricity to 0.25 and Specular Roll Off to 0.55. Click the checkered Map button beside Color. In the Create Render Node window, click the File texture icon. In the new File texture's Attribute Editor tab, click the Image Name browse button and load the skin color bitmap you created as part of the previous section. Render a test. The face takes on a greater degree of realism, but remains perfectly smooth (see Figure 3.39).

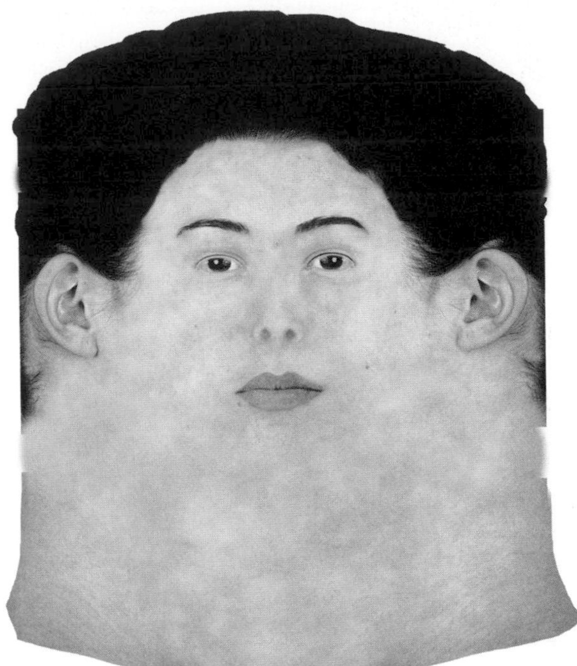

Figure 3.37

A final skin bitmap. The bitmap file is included as `Face_Color.tga` in the `ProjectFiles/Project2/Textures` folder on the DVD. For a color version of the figure, see the color insert.

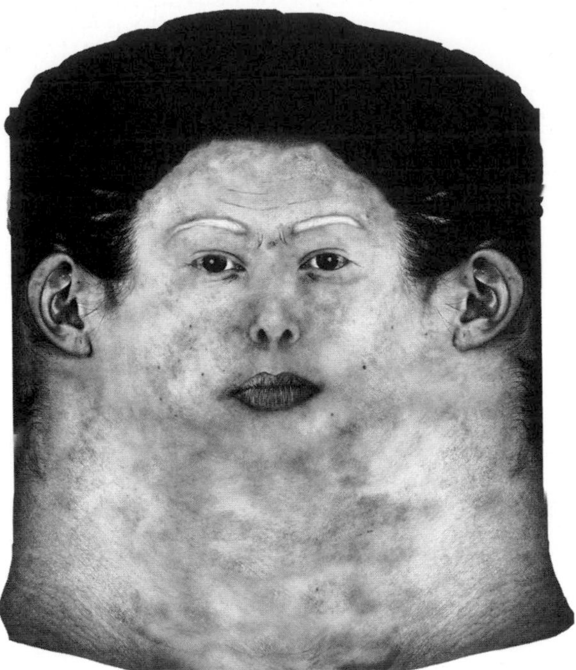

Figure 3.38

A final bump bitmap. The bitmap file is included as `Face_Bump.tga` in the `ProjectFiles/Project2/Textures` folder on the DVD.

2. Return to the material's Attribute Editor tab. Click the checkered Map button beside Bump Mapping. In the Create Render Node window, click the File texture icon. In the new Bump 2d node's Attribute Editor tab, set Bump Depth to 0.008. Open the Attribute Editor tab for the File node connected to the Bump 2d node. Click the Image Name browse button and load the skin bump bitmap you created as part of the previous section. Render a test. The bump map breaks up the specularity and prevents the skin from becoming too smooth (see Figure 3.39). Note that the bump is fairly subtle. To properly view the bump, use a 1:1 zoom ratio. You can jump to a 1:1 zoom ratio by clicking the 1:1 button at the top of the Render View window. The specularity will be further broken up by mapping the Specular Color and building custom connections in Chapter 4.

Project: Switching to mental ray

At this stage, all the surfaces of the scene have been textured (minus the background plane). However, the shadow quality remains fairly poor. The depth map shadow of the Key light creates artifacts across the face. These appear as dark vertical bands above and below the eyes (see Figure 3.31 earlier in this chapter) and the right side of the pendant (see Figure 3.21 earlier in this chapter). Small surfaces, such as the Stud or Lip_Ring, fail to produce distinct shadows. Although you can adjust each shadow-casting light's Bias attribute to reduce the artifacts, high Bias values will further erode the edges to the shadows.

Figure 3.39

(Left) Textured face without bump map. (Right) Face with bump map. A sample scene is included as `woman-step15.ma` **on the DVD. For a color version of this figure, see the color insert.**

To avoid the depth map artifacts, you can switch to raytraced shadows. Raytraced shadows are not immune to artifacts, however. For example, at the point where a surface turns from the shadow-casting light, a raytraced shadow may cause a shadowed polygon triangle to appear directly beside an unshadowed polygon triangle without any kind of smooth transition. Fortunately, the mental ray renderer is able to reduce such raytracing artifacts. Thus, this step will call for you to switch renderers. You can follow these steps:

1. Open the Render Settings window. Change the Render Using menu to mental ray. Switch to the Quality tab. Change the Anti-Aliasing menu to Custom Sampling. Change the Samples to 0 and the Max Sample to 2. This is equivalent to Maya's High Quality Anti-Aliasing setting. Note that Raytracing is automatically selected for mental ray.
2. Select the Key light and open its Attribute Editor tab. In the Raytrace Shadow Attributes section, select the Use Ray Trace Shadows check box. Raise the Light Radius to 5 and the Shadow Rays to 40. Render a test. The depth map artifacts disappear. The spotlight shadow takes on a soft edge that changes over the surface based on the distance from the shadow-casting surface (see Figure 3.40). The mental ray renderer and raytraced shadows add a significant amount of time to the render; if necessary, test the settings by rendering regions or by reducing the render resolution through the Render Settings window.
3. By default, all Maya materials that possess specularity are given a Reflectivity value of 0.5. Hence, when Raytracing is selected in the Render Settings window, all the Blinn, Phong, and Anisotropic materials begin to reflect. Although some surfaces should reflect their surroundings, such as the gold pieces and portions of the eyes, other surfaces should be nonreflective. Therefore, you must adjust the current set of materials.

For each material assigned to a nonreflective surface, set the Reflectivity value to 0. For each material assigned to a reflective surface, leave the Reflectivity value set to 0.5. You will readjust the reflective surfaces in Chapter 4 when an image-based lighting system is added to the scene. Aside from contributing light, the system will provide a surrounding environment appropriate for reflections.

4. The mental ray renderer tends to render bump maps more softly than Maya Software. To restore the previous degree of "bumpiness" to the face surface, update the assigned material's Bump 2d node with a Bump Depth value of 0.015.

The addition of raytraced shadows concludes Part 1 of this project. As such, your render should look similar to Figure 3.40. In Chapter 4, you'll add an image-based lighting node, adjust reflections, texture the background plane, build more complex shading networks to add warmth to the skin, and render the scene with simple render layers.

Figure 3.40

Scene with raytraced shadows. This project continues in Chapter 4. A sample scene is included as `woman-step16.ma` **on the DVD. For a color version of this figure, see the color insert.**

CHAPTER 4

Texturing and Lighting a Character, Part 2

In Chapter 3, "Texturing and Lighting a Character, Part 1," you textured and lit the bust of a woman. In this chapter, you'll continue to fine-tune the texturing and lighting to add detail and realism. This part of the project will guide you through the following steps:

- **Adjusting the skin-shading network**
- **Activating image-based lighting**
- **Deactivating shadows**
- **Addressing texture warp**
- **Fine-tuning**

In addition, important lighting and texturing theory is included as follows:

- **Creation of custom connections in the Hypershade**
- **Color space and monitor calibration**
- **Maya color profiles**

Custom Connections in the Hypershade

Although mapping various attributes of materials is fairly straightforward, a more powerful method of building shading networks requires the creation of custom connections. Before a custom connection can be made, however, it's necessary to understand node outputs and inputs.

Any node connected to any other node is considered upstream or downstream. An upstream node is a node that outputs information. A downstream node inputs information. The node icons themselves will show whether an upstream or downstream connection exists. If the bottom-left arrow is solid, the node is downstream of another node and therefore receives an input from that node. If the bottom-right arrow is solid, the node is upstream of another node and therefore provides an output to that node. If an arrow is hollow, a connection does not exist in a corresponding upstream or downstream direction (see Figure 4.1).

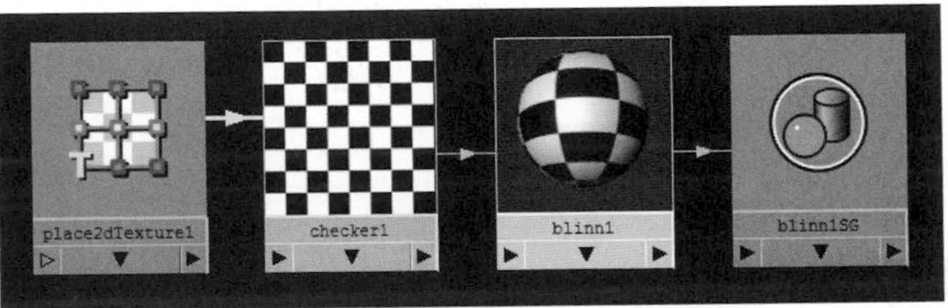

Figure 4.1

Four nodes connected in a row. In this example, place2dTexture1 is furthest upstream, and blinn1SG is furthest downstream. The connection line arrows also indicate the flow of information. There is a node downstream from blinn1SG, but it is not visible in this view (you can use the Input And Output Connections button to show hidden nodes).

Dragging and dropping one node on top of another by using the MMB automatically opens the Connect Input Of menu (see Figure 4.2). The default attribute of the output (upstream) node is used for a connection. The default output attribute is generally Out Color. Out Color is a vector attribute. That is, Out Color carries three channels: Out Color Red, Out Color Green, and Out Color Blue. Another common output attribute is Out Alpha. Out Alpha is a single-channel attribute whereby alpha information is carried as grayscale. UV-related attributes carry dual channels—for example, Repeat UV carries Repeat U and Repeat V. The Connect Input Of menu does not differentiate between vector attributes, dual-channel attributes, and single-channel attributes. However, if you select a menu item that does not correspond to the output, the menu automatically opens the Connection Editor and waits for the connection to be made manually. Hence, you cannot connect a vector output to a single-channel input or connect a single-channel output to a vector input.

You can connect vector attributes directly to other vector attributes through the Connect Input Of menu. For example, if you MMB+drag a File texture node and drop it on a Blinn node, you can choose Color from the menu. Hence, a connection is made between the File node's Out Color and the Blinn node's Color, both of which are vector attributes. In addition, you can connect single-channel attributes directly to single-channel attributes through the Connect Input Of menu. For example, if you MMB+drag a Bump 2d texture node and drop it on a Blinn node, you can choose Bump Map from the menu. Hence, a connection is made between the Bump 2d node's Out Normal and the Blinn node's Bump Map, both of which are single-channel attributes.

The default output attribute selected by the Connect Input Of menu may not be the one you want to use. To avoid this problem, you can select a specific output by RMB+clicking the bottom-right arrow of the output node. This displays the Connect Output Of menu (see Figure 4.3). If you choose an output from the menu, a connection string is drawn from the node to the mouse pointer. If you click another node, the Connect Input Of menu opens. After you select an input from the menu, a connection line is drawn between the two nodes. Note that the menu displays the attribute's "long name" as opposed to the attribute's "nice name." A long name has no spaces, such as outColor, whereas a nice name usually contains spaces, such as Out Color. Out Color and outColor refer to the same attribute.

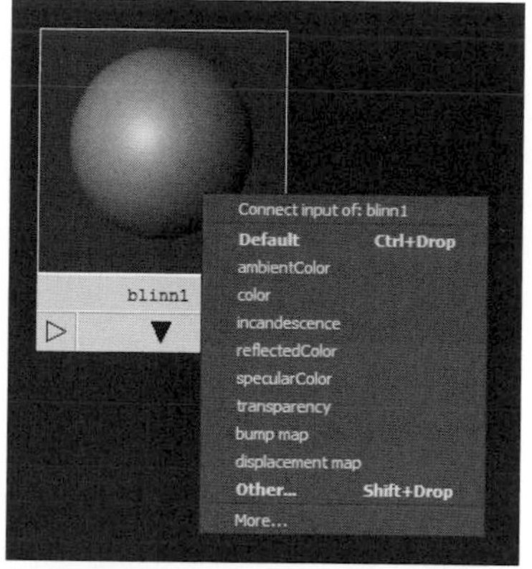

Figure 4.2
Connect Input Of menu of a Blinn node

You can read the outputs and inputs of a preexisting connection by placing your mouse over the connection line. A small box appears with the output channel listed on the left and the input channel listed on the right. The channels are written in the following format: *node.channel*. You can delete a connection by clicking the connection line so that it turns yellow and then pressing the Delete key.

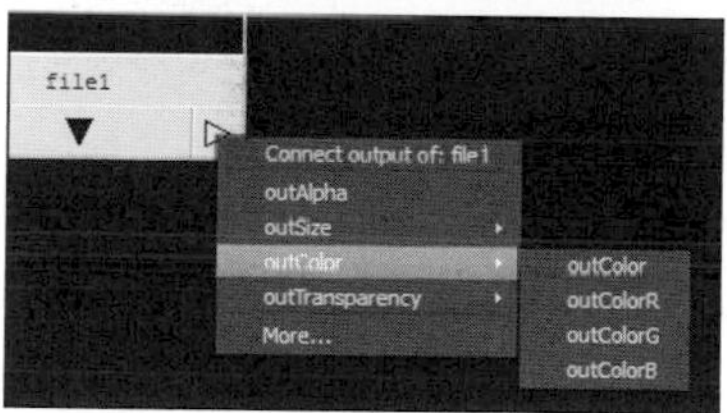

Figure 4.3
Connect Output Of menu of a File node. The vector attribute outColor is listed along with the single-channel outputs outColorR, outColorG, and outColorB.

One disadvantage of using the Connect Output Of or Connect Input Of menus is the limited number of attributes you can choose. Any given node carries many attributes that are not listed by the menus. To access these attributes for connections, you can use the Connection Editor. There are several ways to launch the editor:

- MMB+Shift+drag one node on top of another. The Connect Input Of menu opens.
- MMB+drag one node on top of another. The Connect Input Of menu opens. Choose Other from the menu. The Connection Editor opens.
- RMB+click the bottom-right arrow of a node and choose an output from the Connect Output Of menu. A connection string is attached to the mouse pointer. Click a second node. The Connect Input Of menu opens. Choose Other from the menu. The Connection Editor opens.
- Select a node you wish to use as an output. Shift+select a node you wish to use as an input. Choose Window → General Editors → Connection Editor from the main Maya menu.

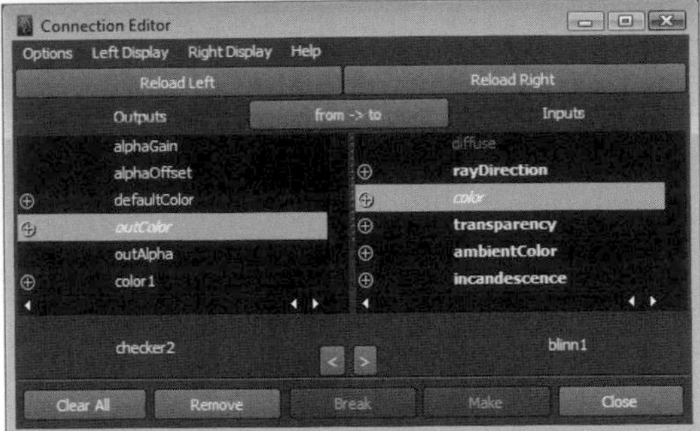

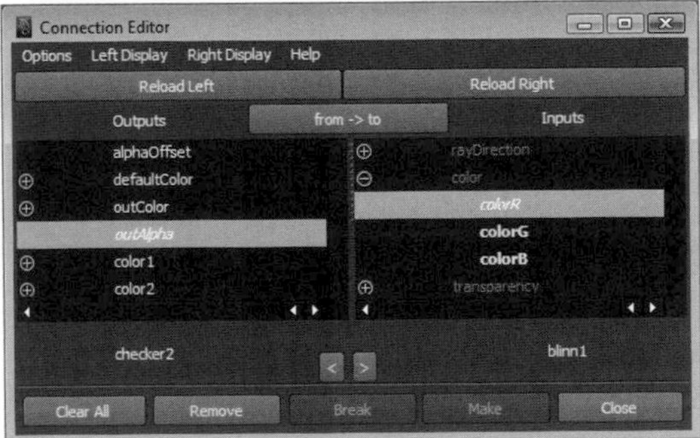

Figure 4.4

(Top) The vector attribute outColor is connected to the vector attribute Color. (Bottom) A single-channel attribute, outAlpha, is connected to one channel of the vector attribute Color.

The Connection Editor is divided into two sections. By default, the left side contains output attributes of the upstream node, and the right contains input attributes of the downstream node. To make a connection, select an attribute name on the left and an attribute name on the right. If the connection is successful, both attribute names become italicized (see Figure 4.4). If an input name is grayed out, it cannot be used. All vector and dual attributes carry a small plus sign. If you click the plus, the individual channels are revealed and are available for connections. For example, clicking the plus beside outColor reveals outColorR, outColorG, and outColorB.

In the editor, you can make the following connections:

- Vector attribute to vector attribute
- Single-channel attribute to single-channel attribute
- Dual-channel attribute to dual-channel attribute
- One channel of a vector attribute or one channel of a dual-channel attribute to a single-channel attribute

A number of attributes are hidden by default. To reveal all the attributes for a given node, choose Left Display → Show Hidden (or Right Display → Show Hidden) from the Connection Editor menu. You can remove a connection by clicking an attribute or channel name so that it is no longer italicized.

Project: Adjusting the Skin-Shading Network

To begin this phase of the tutorial, open the scene file you created for the last step of Chapter 3. A completed sample file is saved as `woman-step16.ma` in the `ProjectFiles/Project2` folder on the DVD.

Note that the sample scene files included for this chapter and Chapter 5 assume that the bitmap textures are located within the `Textures` folder of the `ProjectFiles/Project2` project directory. Before opening a sample scene file, choose File → Project → Set and browse for the `Project2` folder, whether the folder remains at its original location on the DVD or is located on a drive after the DVD contents have been copied.

Mapping the Ambient Color

At this stage, the woman's skin appears gray and somewhat lifeless. In real life, skin develops a subtle translucence as light bounces through the various subcutaneous layers. Common Maya materials carry Translucence attributes. However, with complex geometry, such as a face, the Translucence attribute is difficult to control and often leads to artifacts along convolutions in the surface. Alternatively, you can emulate translucence by mapping the Ambient Color attribute. Ambient Color determines the color of a surface when no light hits it. If the Ambient Color is given a low value, the surface appears to take on a subtle glow. Although you can simply raise the Ambient Color slider above 0, you can add more complexity by connecting the bitmap used as a bump map. Follow these steps:

1. Open the Hypershade window. RMB+click the material assigned to the Face surface and choose Graph Network. The shading network is revealed in the work area.
2. In the work area, identify the File node that carries the texture bitmap used as a bump map. MMB+drag the node and drop it on top of the material node. The Connect Input Of menu opens. Choose ambientColor from the menu. A connection line is created between the two nodes, and the Ambient Color attribute is thus mapped. With the example scene file, you would MMB+drag the file20 node to the Face_ node (see Figure 4.5).

Render a test. The skin becomes excessively bright. This is because of the high values contained within the texture bitmap. To avoid this, you could reduce the corresponding File node's Color Gain value. However, this would affect the bump mapping. Instead, you can insert a Multiply Divide utility into the network. To revise the shading network, follow these steps:

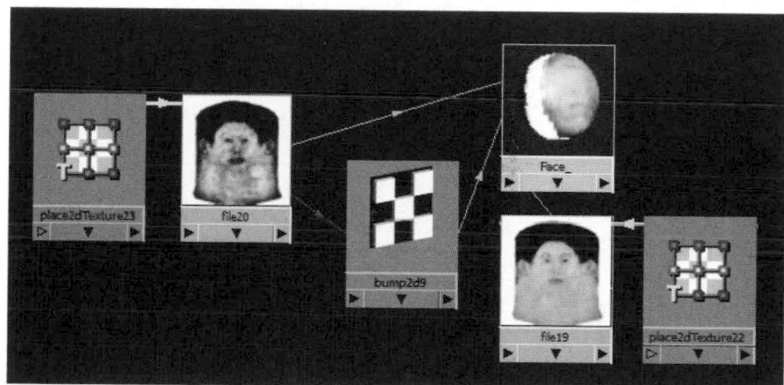

Figure 4.5

The new connection line between file20 and Face_ nodes is shown in yellow; the file texture is thus mapped to the Bump Value attribute of the bump2d9 node and the Ambient Color of the Face_ material node.

1. Click the new connection line so it turns yellow. Press the Delete key. The connection line is removed, and the Ambient Color attribute is no longer mapped.
2. Click the word *Utilities* in the Create tab. This reveals a list of utility nodes. Click the Multiply Divide utility icon. A new Multiply Divide node, named multiplyDivide1, is placed in the work area; however, the node is not connected to any other node. Reposition the multiplyDivide1 node so it sits between the File node and the material node. MMB+drag the File node and drop it on the multiplyDivide1 node. Choose Input1 from the Connect Input Of menu. Using the example scene file, you would MMB+drag file20 onto multiplyDivide1. MMB+drag multiplyDivide1 and drop it on top of the material node. Choose ambientColor from the Connect Input Of menu. Using the example scene, you would MMB+drag multiplyDivide1 onto Face_. Thus, the output of the File node is passed through the multiplyDivide1 node before it reaches the Ambient Color attribute (see Figure 4.6).

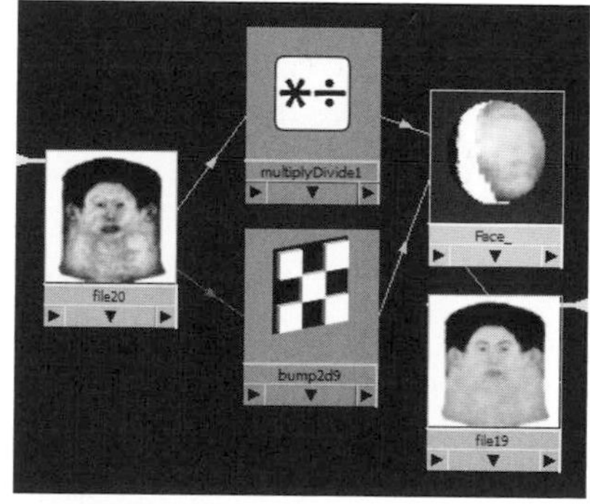

Figure 4.6

The updated network with the output of file20 passed through the multiplyDivide1 node before reaching the Ambient Color of the Face_ material.

The Multiply Divide utility applies a mathematical operation to an input before passing the output to another node. Ultimately, you can think of any input or output as a value that can be adjusted. For example, Out Color carries three channels; each channel carries a single value, such as 0.5 or 1.0. Thus, pure red is 1.0, 0, 0; middle gray is 0.5, 0.5, 0.5; dark green is 0, 0.2, 0; and so on.

3. Open the multiplyDivide1 node's Attribute Editor tab. Change Input2 to 0.2, 0.1, 0.1. The default Operation setting for the node is Multiply. Hence, the values output by the File node are multiplied by 0.2, 0.1, 0.1. This causes a darker, slightly red version of the File texture to be mapped to the Ambient Color. Render a test. The skin takes on a subtle red glow (see Figure 4.7).

   If the contribution of the Ambient Color map is difficult to see, bring the render into a program such as Photoshop and read the values within the shadow areas. (You can export an image from the Render View by choosing File → Save Image from the Render View menu.) In Photoshop, you can see the RGB values of any given point by placing the mouse over the image and watching the Info tab readout. When the Ambient Color attribute was left at its default value of 0, the shadow along the woman's right cheek had RGB values of 0, 0, 0. With the mapping of Ambient Color, the shadow area takes on values around 25, 10, 8 (on a 0 to 255 scale).

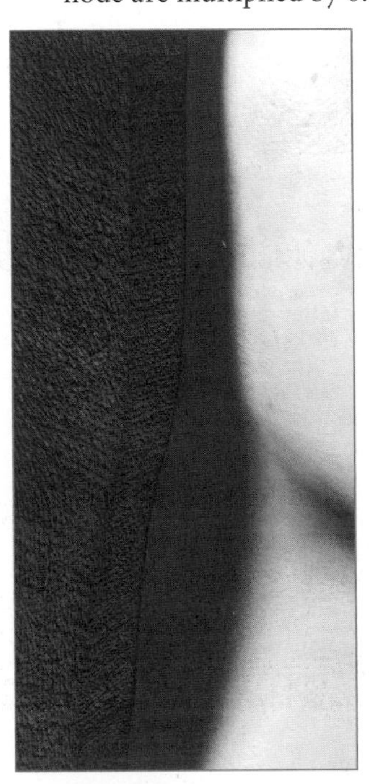

Figure 4.7

Result of revised shading network. The shadow areas pick up a red glow. (Note that the brightness has been exaggerated for print; the actual result is more subtle.) A sample file is saved as `woman-step17.ma` **on the DVD. For a color version of this figure, see the color insert.**

Adding a Neck Tattoo

You can add a tattoo to the skin by mapping the Color Gain of the File node that carries the skin texture bitmap. You can follow these steps:

1. Using the skin bitmap as a guide, create a new texture that represents a tattoo design. The tattoo should be aligned so that it covers the lower neck. The empty space around the tattoo should be left white. To make the tattoo appear faded, pick a tattoo color that is not too dark. For example, in Figure 4.8, the tattoo is a washed-out blue-purple. Save the new texture.

2. Open the Attribute Editor tab for the File node that carries the skin bitmap. In the example scenes, the node is named file19. Expand the Color Balance section and click the checkered Map button beside Color Gain. In the Create Render Node window, click the File texture icon. In the new File node's Attribute Editor tab, browse for the newly created tattoo bitmap. Render a test. The tattoo appears on the neck (see Figure 4.9). If the tattoo colors are fairly bright, the tattoo will appear faded or as if the tattoo pigments are buried within the skin. Because the tattoo bitmap values are multiplied by the skin bitmap via the Color Gain attribute, white areas of the tattoo bitmap have no effect on the skin (the skin bitmap is multiplied by 1.0 in those

areas). Areas of the tattoo bitmap that are darker than the skin bitmap ultimately darken the skin bitmap.

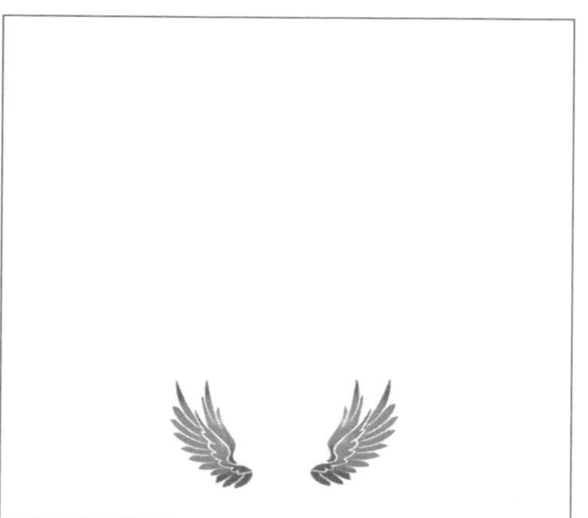

Figure 4.8
A tattoo design is aligned to the neck and is surrounded by white. A sample texture is saved as `Tattoo.tga` **in the** `ProjectFiles/Project2/Textures` **folder on the DVD.**

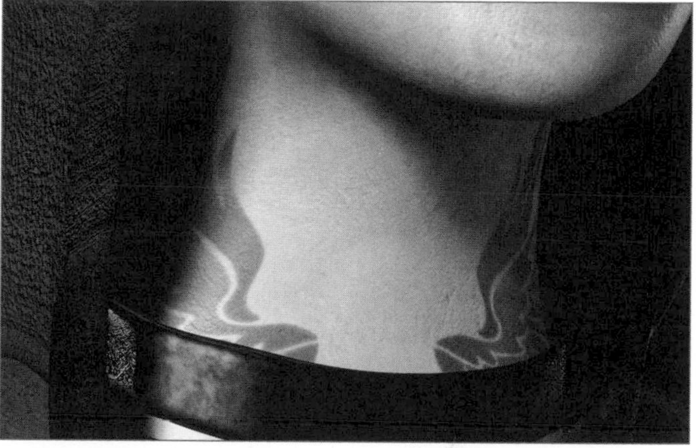

Figure 4.9
The tattoo is added to the neck. A sample file is saved as `woman-step18.ma` **on the DVD.**

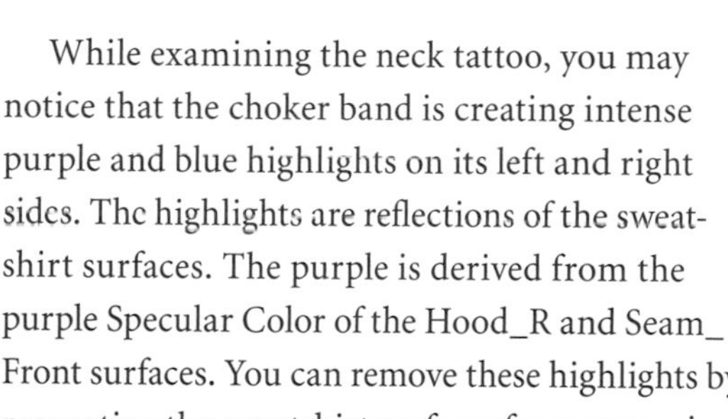

While examining the neck tattoo, you may notice that the choker band is creating intense purple and blue highlights on its left and right sides. The highlights are reflections of the sweatshirt surfaces. The purple is derived from the purple Specular Color of the Hood_R and Seam_Front surfaces. You can remove these highlights by preventing the sweatshirt surfaces from appearing in reflections. To do so, select a sweatshirt surface, open the Attribute Editor tab for its shape node, expand the Render Stats section, and deselect the Visible In Reflections check box. For example, in Figure 4.10, Visible In Reflections is deselected for the Hood_R, Hood_L, and Seam_Front surfaces.

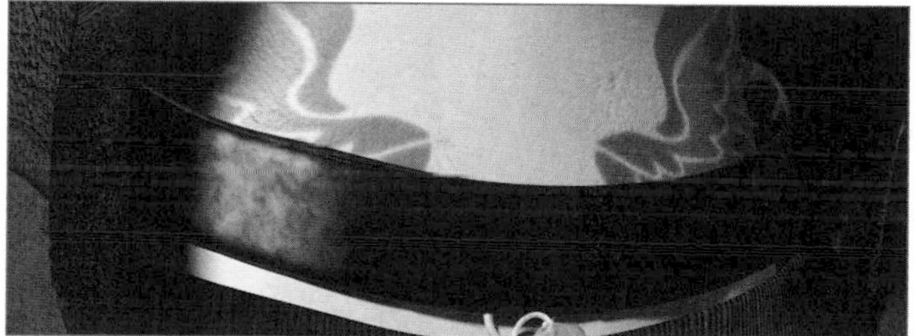

Figure 4.10
The intense purple and blue highlights on the choker band are removed by deselecting the Visible In Reflections check box for the Hood_R, Hood_L, and Seam_Front surfaces.

Mapping the Specularity

At this stage of the tutorial, the specularity of the skin is controlled by the values of the Eccentricity, Specular Roll Off, and Specular Color attributes. You can exert greater control, however, by mapping the Specular Color. To do so, follow these steps:

1. In Photoshop or a similar program, create a new texture to control the Specular Color. To save time, you can adapt the bitmap used for bump mapping. For example, in Figure 4.11, the bump bitmap is adapted so that regions of the face take in different specular intensities. Because this tutorial is designed to create a still image, there is no

penalty for creating inconsistent specular regions. However, if the model was intended for animation, such a trick might not be appropriate. Nevertheless, you can use such a texture to exaggerate small regions of specularity (for example, the glossiness of the lips) or reduce the specularity in certain areas (for example, the shadow side of the woman).

2. Open the Attribute Editor tab for the material assigned to the Face surface. Click the checkered Map button beside Specular Color. In the Create Render Node window, click the File texture icon. In the new File node's Attribute Editor tab, browse for the newly created bitmap. Render a test. Because the Specular Color is mapped, the overall specular intensity of the skin is reduced. To combat this, open the Attribute Editor tab for the material assigned to the Face surface and adjust the Eccentricity and Specular Roll Off. For example, if you use the sample texture illustrated in Figure 4.12, set the Eccentricity to 0.5 and Specular Roll Off to 0.6.

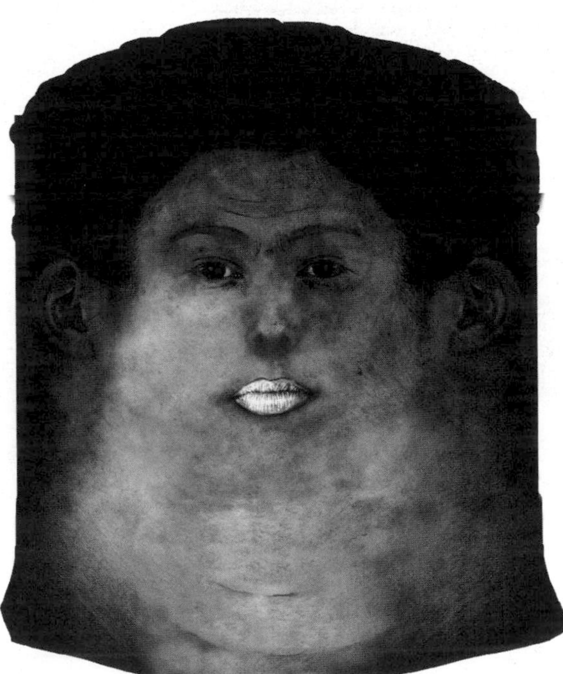

Figure 4.11

The bitmap used for bump mapping is adapted to control the Specular Color of the skin material. A sample texture is saved as `Face_Spec.tga` in the `ProjectFiles/Project2/Textures` folder on the DVD.

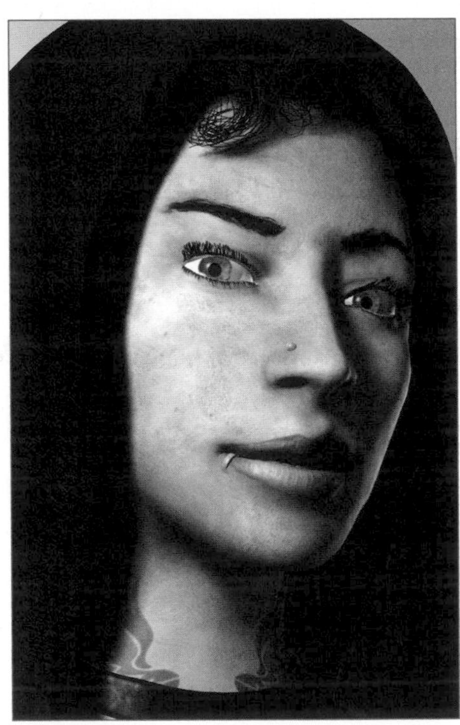

Figure 4.12

The Specular Color is mapped, thus affecting the specular intensity across the skin. A sample file is saved as `woman-step19.ma` on the DVD. For a color version of this figure, see the color insert.

Project: Activating Image-Based Lighting

Thus far, you have lit the scene with standard spot lights and directional lights. You can add more complexity to lighting by activating an image-based lighting system through mental ray and Final Gathering. As was demonstrated in Chapter 2, "Texturing and Lighting a Product, Part 2," Final Gathering incorporates bounced light and color bleed. In addition, Final Gathering is able to light with a bitmap if the bitmap is loaded into an image-based lighting (IBL) node.

Creating an IBL Node

To create an IBL node, follow these steps:

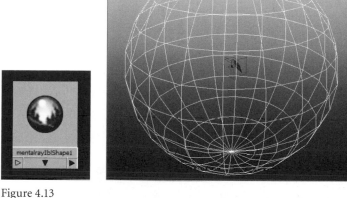

1. Open the Render Settings window. Switch to the Indirect Lighting tab. In the Environment section, click the Create button beside the Image Based Lighting attribute. An IBL shape node is automatically created and is listed in the Lights tab of the Hypershade (see Figure 4.13). The node provides the orange (yellow if selected) projection sphere.

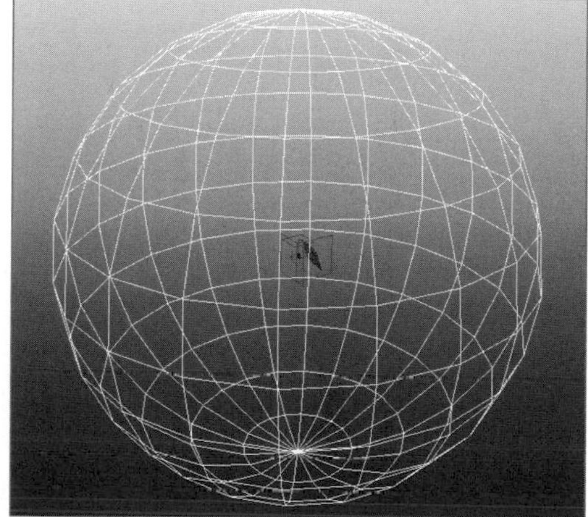

Figure 4.13

(Left) IBL shape node. (Right) Projection sphere created by node

2. Open the Attribute Editor tab for the new IBL shape node, which is named mentalrayIblShape1. Click the File browse button beside Image Name and search for a bitmap you would like to use as a lighting source. A sample bitmap is included as `Background.tga`; this features a blurry photo of a brightly colored room (see Figure 4.14). Expand the Render Stats section and deselect Primary Visibility; this prevents the sphere from appearing in the background of renders.

3. Return to the Render Settings window. Select the Final Gathering check box in the Indirect Lighting tab. Render a test. The Final Gathering system uses the loaded bitmap as a light source. When Final Gather rays encounter the projection sphere, the pixels within the bitmap are interpreted as light intensities. Because the projection sphere surrounds the woman, additional light is generated from all directions. Initially, the lighting contribution of the IBL node is fairly subtle. You can increase the contribution by returning to the IBL node's Attribute Editor tab and raising the Color Gain value above 1.0.

Figure 4.14

A blurry photo of a room is used as a lighting source through an IBL shape node. A sample bitmap is saved as `Background.tga` in the `ProjectFiles/Project2/Textures` folder on the DVD.

In addition, you can temporarily deactivate the standard spot lights and directional lights by deselecting their Illuminates By Default check boxes (found in the top section of their Attribute Editor tabs). For example, in Figure 4.15, Color Gain is set to 3.0 and Illuminates By Default has been deselected for the lights.

4. Reactivate the standard lights by selecting their Illuminates By Default check boxes. Balance the Intensity of the Key spot light with the Color Gain of the IBL node. For example, in Figure 4.15, the Color Gain is returned to 1.0 and the Key spot light Intensity is lowered to 1.0.

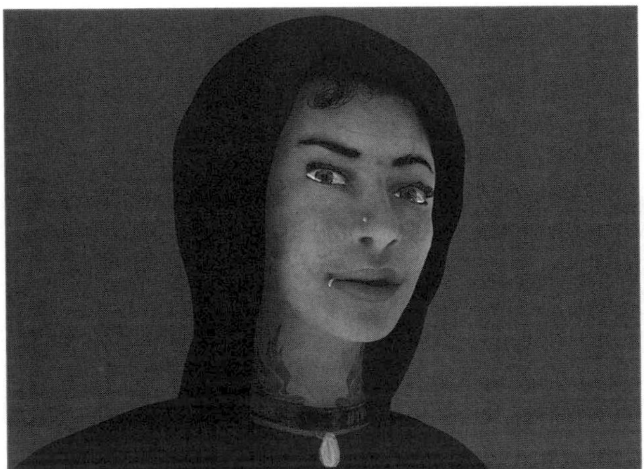

Figure 4.15

(Left) To test the IBL lighting contribution, the IBL node's Color Gain is raised to 3.0, and the scene's standard lights have been deactivated. (Right) The IBL node's Color Gain is returned to 1.0, and the Intensity of the Key spot light is lowered to 1.0. For a color version of this figure, see the color insert. A sample file is saved as `woman-step20.ma` on the DVD.

By default, the IBL projection sphere is infinite. That is, the scale of the projection sphere has no effect on the resulting light. However, rotation will cause the lighting to shift as the bitmap is rotated along with the sphere. Note that the IBL node is designed for images that have specific mappings that vary from standard bitmap textures. Hence, the loaded bitmap will become pinched at the poles of the projection sphere. The pinching, however, will have a minor impact on this scene.

Adding a Background

At this point, the background plane remains a default gray. In the absence of more complex background geometry, you can map a photographic texture to the plane's material. Follow these steps:

1. Using Photoshop or a similar program, prepare a photograph that will serve as a texture for the background plane. The photo may be as simple as a section of a painted or stuccoed wall. Alternatively, you can select a more complex wall that displays paintings, posters, and so on. For example, in Figure 4.16, a photo of a densely decorated wall is chosen. As shown in this example, you can blur the photo in Photoshop to emulate a narrow depth of field. Although Maya can render depth of field, blurring the photo in advance will save render time.

2. Open the Attribute Editor tab for the material assigned to the background plane. In the example scenes, the material is named Wall_. Click the checkered Map button beside Color. Click the File texture icon in the Create Render Node window. In the new File node's Attribute Editor tab, browse for the newly created wall bitmap. Render a test. The scene is now full-textured (see Figure 4.17). Depending on the bitmap you choose, however, you may need to adjust the specular qualities of the material assigned to the plane. For example, in Figure 4.17, the Eccentricity is set to 0.1, the Specular Roll Off is set to 0.1, and the Specular Color is set to 0.1, 0.1, 0.1 in RGB. The goal, in this case, is to match the blacks (darkest areas) of the wall to the blacks of the woman.

Figure 4.16

A blurry photo of a decorated wall is used to texture the background plane. A sample bitmap is saved as `Wall.tga` in the `ProjectFiles/Project2/Textures` folder on the DVD.

Figure 4.17

The textured background plane becomes a more complex wall. A sample file is saved as `woman-step21.ma` on the DVD.

Adjusting the Reflectivity

In addition to providing lighting information for Final Gathering, the IBL shape node creates a virtual environment that is reflected by any reflective surface. For example, the various surfaces of the eyes reflect (see Figure 4.18).

Thus, the Reflectivity values of various surfaces in the scene should be adjusted. Table 4.1 includes recommended Reflectivity values; if a surface is not listed, it should be given a Reflectivity of 0.

Note that Anisotropic materials use the Anisotropic Reflectivity attribute by default. Anisotropic Reflectivity sets the material's reflectivity as a percentage of the Roughness value; Roughness determines its namesake, whereby higher values cause the specular highlight to spread out. You can deselect the Anisotropic Reflectivity check box in the material's Attribute Editor tab. You are then free to adjust the standard Reflectivity slider.

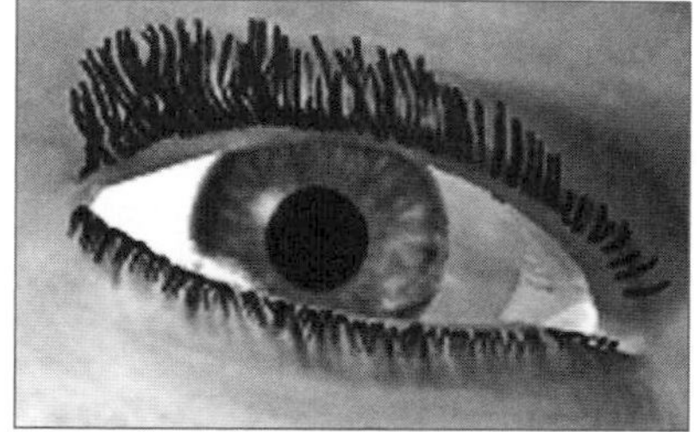

Figure 4.18

The bitmap loaded into the IBL node is reflected by the reflective surfaces of the right eye.

Table 4.1

Materials and associated Reflectivity values

MATERIAL	ASSIGNED SURFACE(S)	REFLECTIVITY VALUE
Pendant_	Pendant	1
Gold	Choker_Ring	1.5
	Pendant_Ring	
	Lip_Ring	
	Stud	
Choker_Band_	Choker_Band	0.25
Corneas	Cornea_L	0.75
	Cornea_R	
Eye_Wet	Eye_Wet_In_L	0.5
	Eye_Wet_Out_L	
	Eye_Wet_In _R	
	Eye_Wet_In_L	
Eye_Gloss_L_	Eye_Gloss_L	0.3
Eye_Gloss_R_	Eye_Gloss_R	0.1
Eye_White_L_	Eye_White_L	0.1
Eye_White_R_	Eye_White_R	0.1

The most reflective surfaces in the scene should be those made of gold. Although the white of the eye is as reflective as the eye cornea, the cornea reflections are generally more visible because the iris is darker and provides better contrast for the reflection. After the Reflectivity values are adjusted for the eye surfaces, the Diffuse and various specular values should be reevaluated. For example, in Figure 4.19, the Diffuse value of the Eye_White_R_ material is lowered to 0.8 while Specular Roll Off is lowered to 0.6. In addition, the Cosine Power of the Eye_ Wet_ material is raised to 30, which shrinks the specular highlight size.

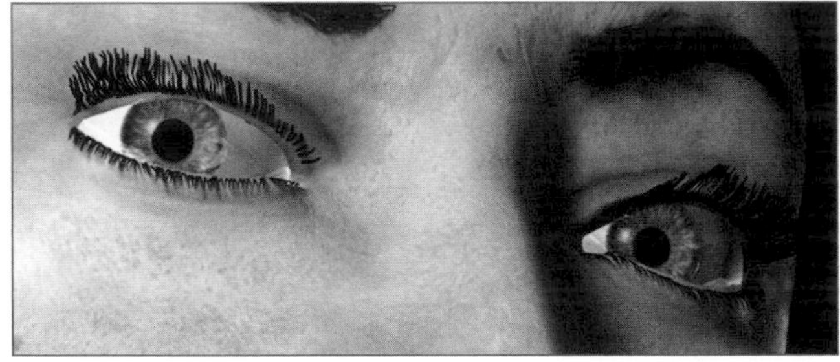

Figure 4.19

Eyes after the adjustment of Reflectivity, Diffuse, and various specular values. A sample file is saved as `woman-step22.ma` on the DVD.

Project: Deactivating Shadows

By default, all surfaces within Maya cast and receive shadows. However, you can change this behavior per surface to help improve the results of a render. Each surface carries a Casts Shadows and a Receive Shadows attribute, which you can find in the Render Stats section of the surface shape node Attribute Editor tab.

By default, the surface shape node receives an Attribute Editor tab directly to the right of the surface transform node. By default, shape nodes carry the *Shape* suffix. For example, Face is the transform node, and FaceShape is the shape node. By default, transform nodes appear in the Hypergraph: Hierarchy window, while both shape and transform nodes appear in the Hypergraph: Connections window. Transform nodes carry all the transform information for a surface, while shape nodes carry all the nontransform attributes. When you create a surface, the two nodes are created automatically.

Surfaces that can benefit from the lack of received and cast shadows include Cornea_L, Cornea_R, Iris_L, Iris_R, Eye_White_L, Eye_White_R, Eye_Gloss_L, Eye_Gloss_R, and Lash_Hi_R. The sample scene files included with this chapter feature deselected Casts Shadows and Receive Shadows check boxes for these surfaces. If Casts Shadows and Receive Shadows check boxes are selected for these surfaces, the eye will develop unaesthetic shadows (see Figure 4.20).

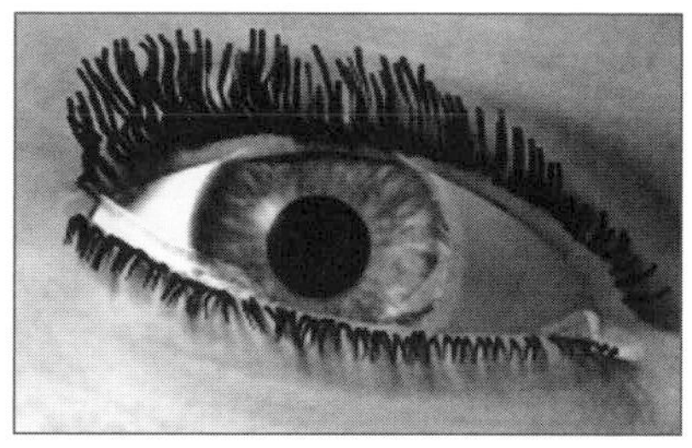

Figure 4.20

Render with Casts Shadows and Receive Shadows selected for all the eye surfaces. Note the uneven shadows cast by the upper eyelash, the thin shadow at the top of the iris, and the more distinct division between the iris and the eye white.

Project: Addressing Texture Warp

One disadvantage of NURBS surfaces is the potential for texture warping. This warping can lead to unwanted texture softness, stretching of texture detail, or uneven scale in repeating texture patterns. In these cases, the model is constructed or adjusted in such a way that the UV texture space is not distributed evenly over the surface.

Identifying Warped Areas

As demonstrated in Chapter 3, you can use a Checker texture to examine UV alignment on a surface. A Checker texture is equally useful for identifying texture warp. You can follow these steps to identify warping on the NURBS surfaces of the sweatshirt:

1. Through the Hypergraph: Hierarchy or Outliner window, select all the surfaces that make up the sweatshirt. (Do not select the Sweatshirt group node.) Switch to the Render Layer Editor at the bottom-right of the Maya main window (click the Render tab). With the surfaces selected, choose Layers › Create Layer From Selected from the Render Layer Editor menu. A new layer, layer1, is created. Click the *layer1* name in the layer stack (see Figure 4.21). The surfaces are revealed in the view panels as the only members of layer1.
2. RMB+click the *layer1* name in the layer stack and choose Overrides → Create New Material Override → Lambert. A new Lambert material is created and is assigned to the surfaces. The assignment is nondestructive, however, and affects only layer1.
3. Open the Hypershade. Identify the new Lambert material. Open the material's Attribute Editor tab. Click the checkered Map button beside Color. In the Create Render Node window, click the Checker texture icon. Close the Hypershade. If the view of the persp camera is not visible in a view panel, choose Panels → Perspective → Persp from one of the view panel menus. Choose Shading → Smooth Shade All and Shading → Hardware Texturing. The Checker pattern is revealed across the surfaces in the 3D view.
4. Move the persp camera around the model and identify the surfaces that have the most uneven distribution of Checker squares. Of the surfaces that face the Render camera, Front_L, Front_R, and Seam_Front have poor distribution (see Figure 4.22).

Figure 4.21

The Render Layer Editor with the newly created layer1 layer. The masterLayer layer, which contains all the scene's surfaces and lights, is provided automatically.

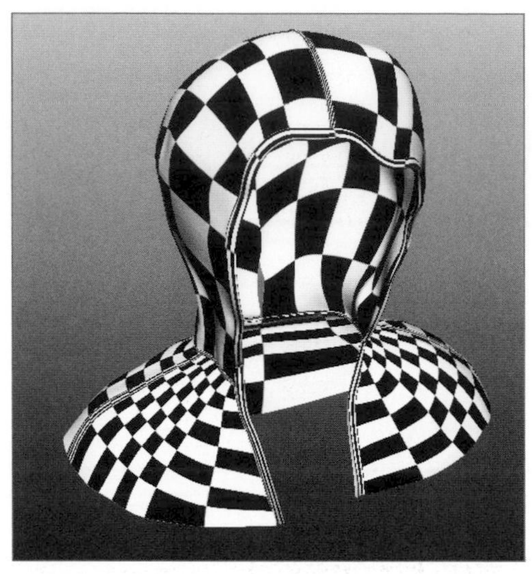

Figure 4.22
The sweatshirt surfaces assigned a material override with a Checker texture. Of the forward-facing surfaces, Front_L, Front_R, and Seam_Front have the worst UV distribution. A sample file is saved as `woman-step23.ma` on the DVD.

By default, Hardware texturing uses a scaled-down version of the Checker texture, which results in a slightly blurry render in the 3D view. You can increase the resolution of the texture and thereby sharpen the result by opening the Attribute Editor tab for the Lambert material, expanding the Hardware Texturing section, and changing Texture Resolution to a larger size such as Highest (256×256).

Using Fix Texture Warp

Ideally, surfaces should be remodeled to avoid texture warping. If remodeling is not practical, however, you can fix the warping by using the Fix Texture Warp attribute. Unfortunately, the attribute is supported by only the Maya Software renderer. Nevertheless, you can apply the Fix Texture Warp attribute and render the problem surfaces with Maya Software if they are assigned to a separate layer with the Render Layer Editor. Follow these steps to fix the Front_L, Front_R, and Seam_Front surfaces:

1. Select the Front_L surface. Open the Attribute Editor. By default, the surface's shape node is displayed. (The shape node occupies the tab to the immediate right of the surface's transform node.) Expand the Texture Map section and select the Fix Texture Warp check box (see Figure 4.23). Although the Hardware Texturing view does not change, the UVs will be remapped during the Maya Software render. Repeat this process for the Front_R and Seam_Front surfaces. To improve the quality and accuracy of the UV remapping applied by the Fix Texture Warp attribute, you can raise the values of Grid Div Per Span U and Grid Div Per Span V. These attributes control a virtual grid that's laid over the surface when calculating the new UV point values.
2. Return to the Render Layer Editor. Click the *layer1* name in the layer stack. Select all the surfaces of the sweatshirt *except* Front_L, Front_R, and Seam_Front. RMB+click the *layer1* name in the layer stack and choose Remove Selected Objects. Only the Front_L, Front_R, and Seam_Front surfaces are left on the layer.
3. Open the Render Settings window. The window indicates that the settings affect layer1 by displaying the layer name in the Render Layer menu (see Figure 4.24). RMB+click the Render Using attribute name, choose Create Layer Override, and change the Render Using menu to Maya Software. The *Render Using* attribute name turns orange to indicate a render override. Whereas the default masterLayer layer will continue to render with mental ray, layer1 will render with Maya Software.

4. Click the *masterLayer* name in the layer stack. Because all the surfaces and lights belong to masterLayer by default, they become visible once again in the view panels. Shift+select all the lights in the scene. Over the *layer1* name in the layer stack, RMB+click and choose Add Selected Objects. This adds the lights to layer1. In order to render the sweatshirt surface appropriately on layer1, it's necessary to have all the lights present. Note that the IBL projection sphere is not assigned to layer1 because the Maya Software renderer cannot use it for lighting information.

Figure 4.23

The Texture Map section carried by a surface's shape node

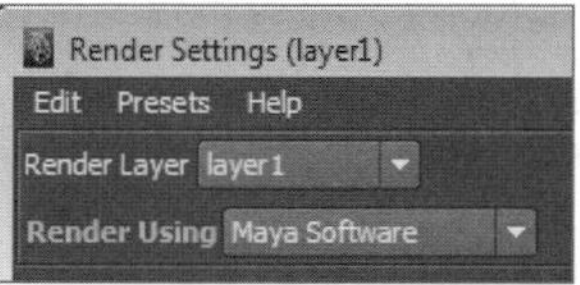

Figure 4.24

The top-left corner of the Render Settings window. The orange *Render Using* text indicates that a render override is applied to the Render Using attribute.

5. Click the Renderable button beside the *layer1* name so that its icon carries a green "on" check mark. (The Renderable button features a small image of a motion picture clapboard; see Figure 4.21 earlier in this chapter.) Click the Renderable button beside the *masterLayer* name so that its icon carries a red "off" x mark. Render a test with the Render View. The layer1 layer is rendered. The Front_L, Front_R, and Seam_Front surfaces show improved UV distribution thanks to the Fix Texture Warp attribute (see Figure 4.25).

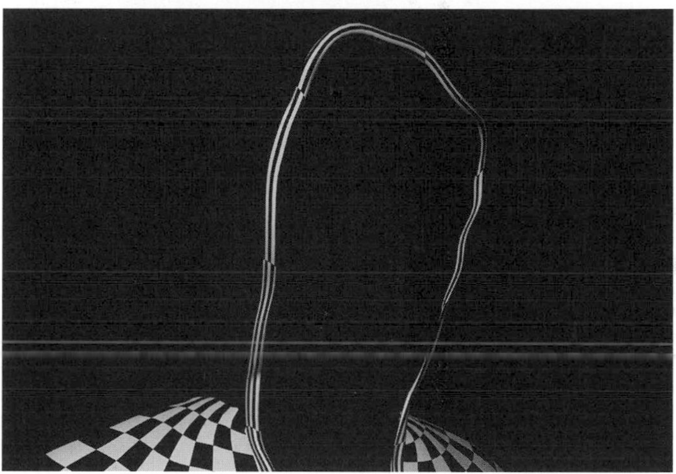

Figure 4.25

Front_L, Front_R, and Front_Seam surfaces with Fix Texture Warp applied

6. The Render Layer Editor can serve as a simple compositing tool. If masterLayer and layer1 are permitted to render, the Render View can combine both renders into a single image. To use the compositing feature, choose Options → Render All Layers → ❐ from the Render Layer Editor menu. In the Render All Layers Options window, select the Composite Layers radio button and click the Apply And Close button. Choose Options → Render All Layers from the Render Layer Editor menu (the compositing will not take place unless Render All Layers has a check mark beside it in the menu).
7. Over the *layer1* name in the layer stack, RMB+click and choose Overrides → Remove Material Override. This removes the Checker from the surfaces and returns the original cloth material.
8. Click the Renderable button beside *layer1* and *masterLayer* names so that both icons carry a green "on" check mark. Render a test frame. Because Render All Layers was selected and both layers have Renderable buttons set to the on position, each layer is rendered before both layers are combined into a single image. The sweatshirt sur-

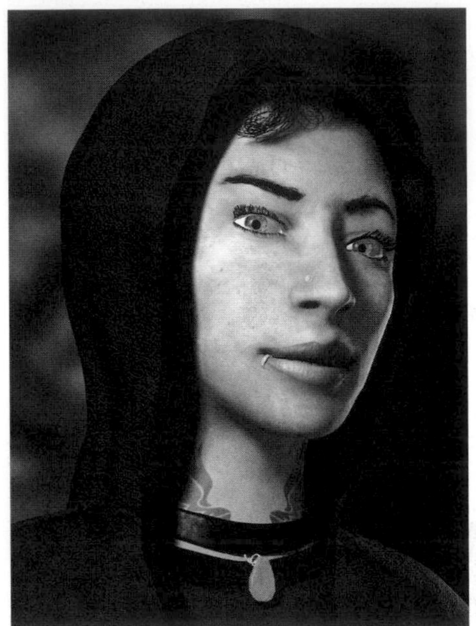

Figure 4.26
The resulting composite created by the Render View after layer1 and masterLayer are rendered. A sample file is saved as `woman-step24.ma` on the DVD.

faces belonging to layer1 are placed on top of the masterLayer, which contains all the geometry for the scene (see Figure 4.26).

In this case, the compositing process works because the isolated sweatshirt surfaces sit in front of all the other geometry. If some of the surfaces on layer1 were behind surfaces on the masterLayer, the composite would not be able to fit them together properly. Hence, a more complex setup is often required when using the Render Layer Editor with multiple layers. Such a process is detailed in Chapter 6, "Texturing and Lighting a Vehicle, Part 2," along with more information on the Render Layer Editor's basic functionality.

As a final step, adjust the Repeat UV values for the place2dTexture nodes connected to the shading networks assigned to the Front_L, Front_R, and Seam_Front surfaces. For example, a Repeat UV value of 0.4, 5 creates a suitably sized color and bump-mapping detail for the Seam_Front surface.

Project: Fine-Tuning

At this juncture, all the basic lighting and texturing is complete. Nevertheless, if you double-check the material attribute settings and examine the custom bitmap quality, you are more likely to achieve an acceptable level of technical and aesthetic quality.

Duplicating Materials

For some surfaces, you may need to create duplicate materials so you can fine-tune the attributes independent of other surfaces. For example, the tuft of hair that appears at the woman's left eye is too bright and translucent. To avoid this problem, you can assign the tuft to a duplicate of the hair material and reduce the duplicate's Translucence value. To create a duplicate, select a material and choose Edit → Duplicate → Shading Network from the Hypershade menu.

Choosing Attribute Values

Examine all the parts of the render and ask yourself whether any of the attributes can be adjusted to further improve the result. For example, here are a few suggested attribute changes and the problems they are addressing:

- Darken the Color of the material assigned to the Pendant surfaces. The pendant appears too bright.
- Reduce the Bump Value of the material assigned to the Hood_L and Hood_R surfaces. The cloth appears too rough, especially when compared to other sweatshirt surfaces.

- Lower the Diffuse value of the material assigned to the Eye_White_R surface. The left side of the right eye is rendering pure white.
- Brighten the Color and raise the Diffuse value of the material assigned to the Eyebrow_L and Eyebrow_R surfaces. The eyebrow hairs are too dark compared to the eyebrows that are integrated into the color bitmap used by the Face surface.
- Raise the Reflectivity of the material assigned to the Choker_Band surface. The choker has no detail beyond the far left and far right sides.
- Darken the Color of the material assigned to the gold surfaces, such as the Stud surface. The gold appears too bright.

Figure 4.27 illustrates the result of these adjustments.

Figure 4.27

Render after the adjustment of various material attribute values

Fixing the Eyelashes

The eyelashes, despite any adjustment to their assigned materials, remain somewhat thick and faceted. In particular, the upper eyelashes suffer from this quality issue. You can take several steps to alleviate this problem:

1. Select the Lash_Hi_R and Lash_Hi_L surfaces. Switch to the Polygons main menu and choose Mesh → Smooth. The Smooth tool subdivides the surfaces and therefore induces smoother transitions between polygon faces along the lash lengths. Although this changes the way in which the character was modeled, the Smooth tool is useful for last-second fixes during the rendering process.
2. Duplicate the material assigned to the eyelashes and assign the duplicate to the Lash_Hi_R and Lash_Hi_L surfaces. Open the duplicated material's Attribute Editor tab. Click the checkered Map button beside Transparency. In the Create Render Node window, click the Ramp texture icon. In the Ramp node's Attribute Editor tab, change Interpolation to Smooth. Delete the center color handle by clicking the handle's right-side x box. Change the color of the top handle to white. Change the color of the bottom handle to black. Change the Selected Position of the bottom handle to 0.45. This creates a half-black and half-white Ramp pattern with a semisoft transition between the two colors (see Figure 4.28).
3. Render a test. The eyelashes appear tapered and softer. The mapped Transparency causes the upper lashes to become transparent near the lash tips (see Figure 4.29).

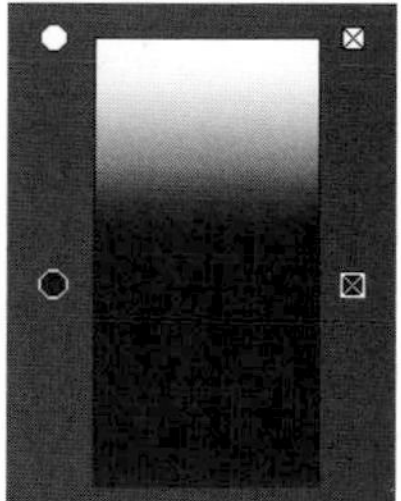

Figure 4.28

Adjusted Ramp mapped to the Transparency of the upper eyelash material

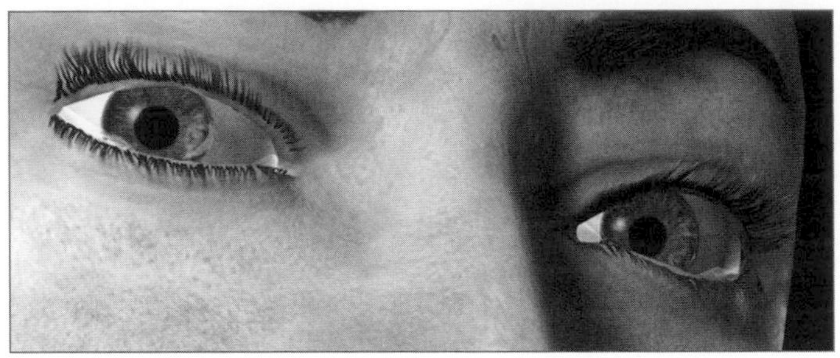

Figure 4.29

Softer upper eyelashes are created with the polygon Smooth tool and the mapping of the assigned material's Transparency. A sample file is saved as `woman-step25.ma` on the DVD.

Revising Bitmaps with the 3D Paint Tool

You can return to the various custom bitmaps and make final adjustments in Photoshop. As an alternative to painting in Photoshop, you can use Maya's 3D Paint tool to interactively update the texture bitmaps. For example, if you choose to update the bitmap used for the color of the Face surface, you can follow these steps:

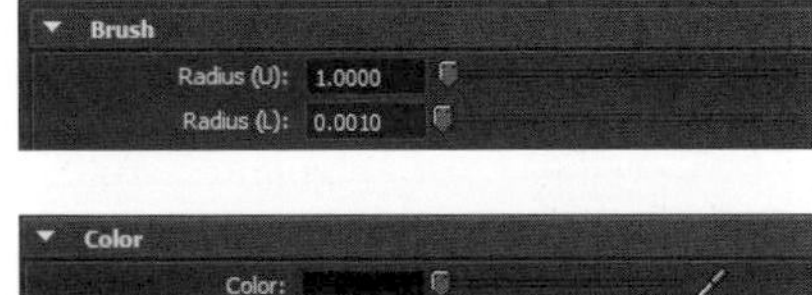

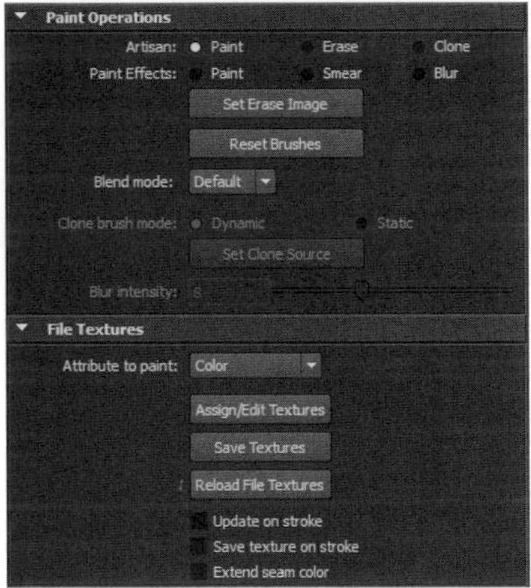

Figure 4.30

Sections of the 3D Paint Tool panel used in this chapter

1. Hide all the surfaces in the scene *except* for Face. Choose Display → Hide → Hide Selection to hide any selected surface. From one of the view panel menus, choose Panels → Perspective → Persp, as well as Shading → Smooth Shade All and Shading → Hardware Texturing. Select the Face surface. Switch to the Rendering main menu. Choose Texturing → 3D Paint Tool → ❐. The 3D Paint Tool panel opens in the Attribute Editor (see Figure 4.30).

2. Drag your mouse over the Face surface. A brush is attached to the mouse pointer and automatically follows the undulations of the surface. You can change the brush size by changing the Radius (U) value in the 3D Paint Tool panel. LMB+drag over the face to paint a test stroke. A black line is immediately drawn. Press Ctrl+Z to undo the stroke. To change the brush color, click the Color swatch in the Color section of the 3D Paint Tool panel.

3. To save the strokes, click the Save Textures button in the File Textures section. The original bitmap is duplicated, updated with the strokes, and saved to the following directory: *`project folder`*`/3dPaintTextures/`*`scene file name`*. At the same time, the new bitmap is loaded into the File texture that carried the original. The original bitmap remains unmolested and in its original location. If you would like the bitmap to be saved automatically with each stroke that's painted, select the Update On Stroke check box in the File Textures section.

4. Continue to paint strokes. You can erase strokes by switching the Artisan attribute, in the Paint Operations section, to Erase. You can clone a preexisting section of the texture by switching the Artisan attribute to Clone. To choose a clone source, click the Set Clone Source button and then click on the surface.
5. When you've finished painting, deselect the surface to exit the tool. Keep in mind that the updated bitmap is in a default directory that might not be optimal for your project. If necessary, move the bitmap to a new directory and reload it into the File texture by using the File's browse button. To display all the surfaces once again, choose Display → Show → All.

The 3D Paint tool paints on the Color bitmap by default. You can change this, however, by changing the Attribute To Paint menu. If you choose an attribute that is already mapped, such as Bump Mapping, the bitmap is displayed in the 3D view (see Figure 4.31). If you choose an attribute that is not mapped, the surface is shaded default gray and you can paint a new bitmap from scratch.

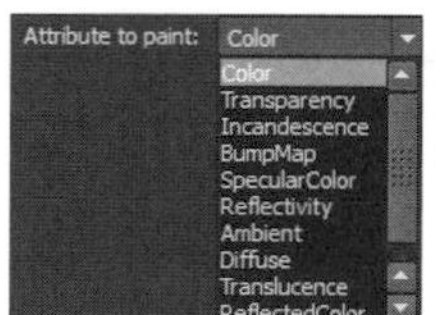

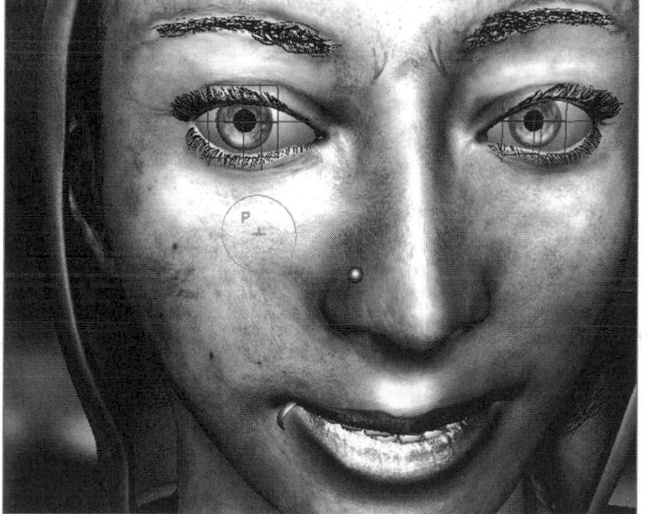

Figure 4.31
(Left) Attribute To Paint menu with list of attributes. (Right) Bump Mapping bitmap displayed in the 3D view with 3D Paint tool brush positioned over cheek.

Figure 4.32 shows the result of final fine-tuning, including the adjustment of various bitmaps. Sample bitmaps are include in the `ProjectFiles/Project2/Texture` folder on the DVD and carry the `_Final` suffix.

Many of the steps presented in Chapter 3 and in this chapter produce fairly subtle results. As such, it's important to be aware of your monitor's color space and to know whether your monitor has been calibrated. A monitor that is uncalibrated has the potential to show color values in a false manner and thus interfere with suitable adjustments to the texturing and lighting. Hence, the following two sections discuss color space, monitor calibration, and Maya's own built-in color profiles.

Figure 4.32
The final render. For a color version of this figure, see the color insert. A sample file is saved as `woman-final.ma` on the DVD.

Color Space and Monitor Calibration

Gamut represents all the colors that a device can produce. *Color space* refers to a gamut that utilizes a particular color model. A *color model* establishes primary colors, combinations of which form all other visible colors. For example, the red-yellow-blue (RYB) color model is used extensively throughout the nondigital arts. The red-green-blue (RGB) color model is the standard for digital arts and computer animation. The color space available to various output devices varies greatly. Hence, the color space of a high-definition television is significantly different from the color space available to a computer monitor or an inkjet printer. The variations in color space necessitate the calibration of equipment to guarantee correct results when it comes to color reproduction. In addition, calibration can help ensure that colors look identical across multiple iterations of the same device; for example, calibration can make the color output of a dozen identical computer monitors consistent.

More specifically, monitor calibration ensures that a monitor is using brightness, contrast, gamma correction, and color temperature settings that are suitable for the type of work being done on the computer and the environment in which the computer is located. *Gamma correction* applies a special curve to neutralize a monitor's nonlinear voltage-to-brightness relationship. If gamma correction is not applied, displayed images receive additional contrast through their midtones and lose details in the shadows and dark areas; the result is inaccurate and usually unaesthetic. *Color temperature*, which is the color of light as measured on the Kelvin scale, determines the white point of the hardware. A *white point* is a coordinate in color space that defines what is "white."

Maya Color Gallery

On the following pages, you will find images from the book in color to better showcase their nuances and details. Note that copies of the majority of the book's color figures are also included in the ColorFigures folder on the DVD.

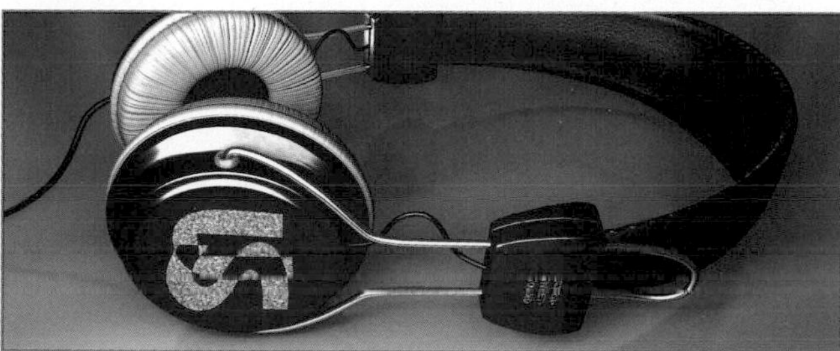

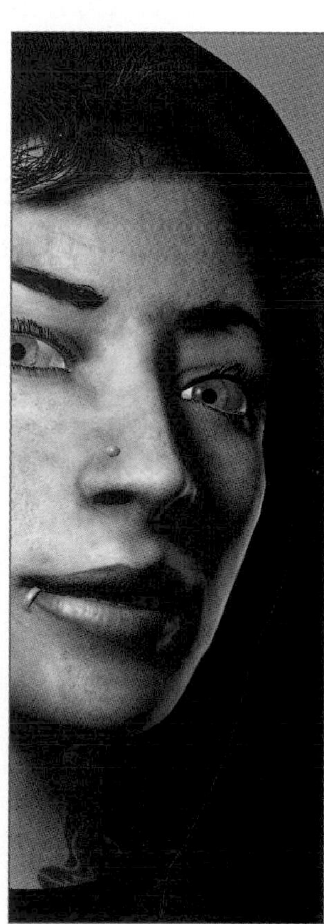

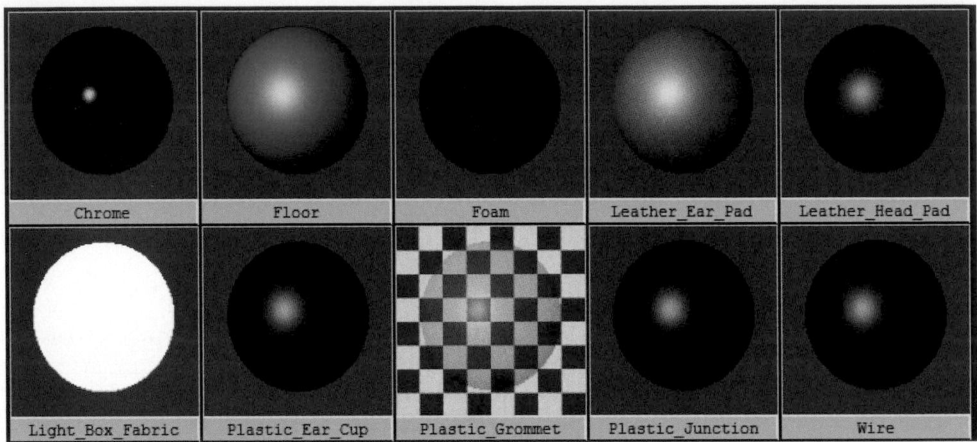

From Chapter 1, Figure 1.12: (Top) Materials created for the headphones scene. Each material is assigned to surfaces that share the same look. For example, the Wire material is assigned to the Wire_L, Wire_R, and Cord surfaces. Note that the material names are easy to interpret. ■ Figure 1.18: (Bottom) Eccentricity, Specular Roll Off, and Specular Color attributes of materials are adjusted.

Figure 1.31: (Top) Custom bitmap texture applied to Junction material (as seen on frame 36) ■ Figure 1.40: (Bottom) The final render of the headphones

From Chapter 2, Figure 2.5: (Top Left) Detail of logo at frame 10. (Top Right) Detail of logo at frame 15. Note the slight variations in the Incandescent "sparkles." ■ Figure 2.6: (Bottom) Final Gathering is combined with the area light and volume light illumination. (The disc-shaped artifacts are not yet removed here.)

Figure 2.31: The final headphones render, as seen in frames 15 (Top) and 30 (Bottom)

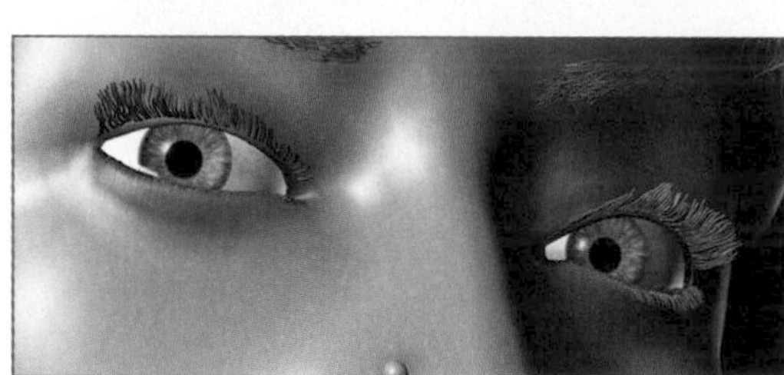

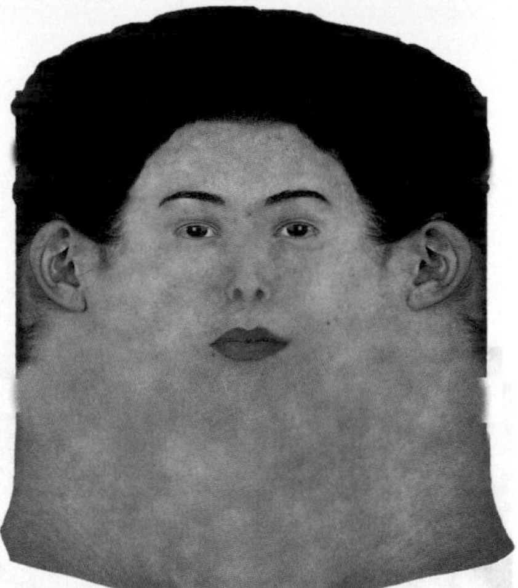

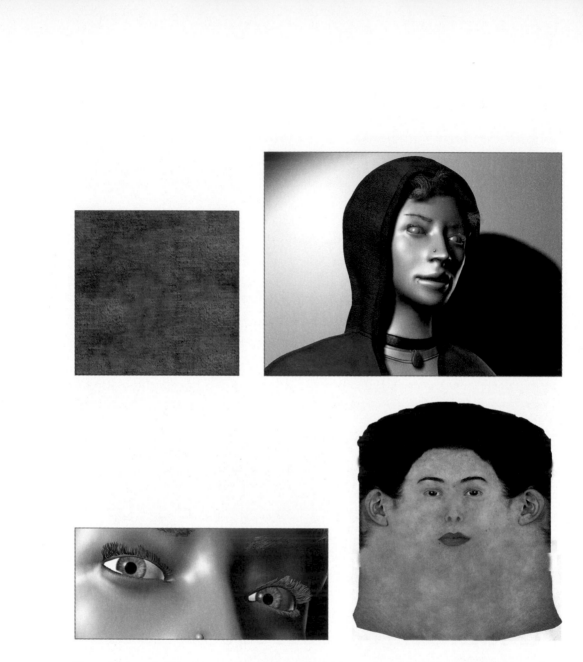

From Chapter 3, Figure 3.22: (Top Left) A cloth bitmap is created from a digital scan of real cloth. ■ Figure 3.24: (Top Right) The remaining surfaces of the sweatshirt are textured. The Intensity of the Key light is raised to 1.2. ■ Figure 3.31: (Bottom Left) Close-up of textured eyes. ■ Figure 3.37: (Bottom Right) A final skin bitmap

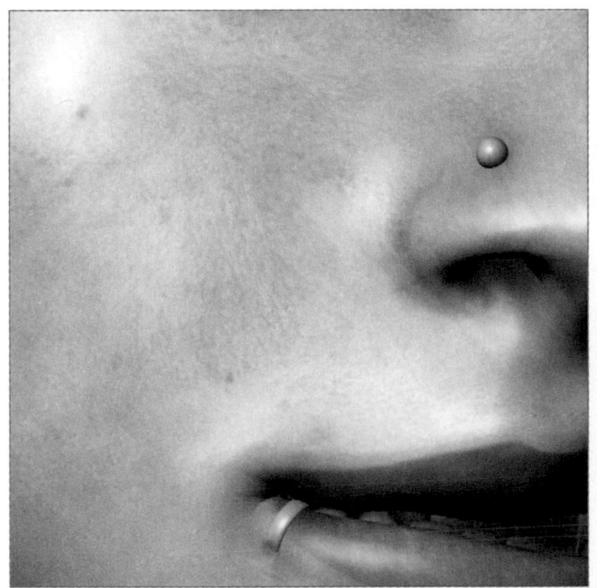

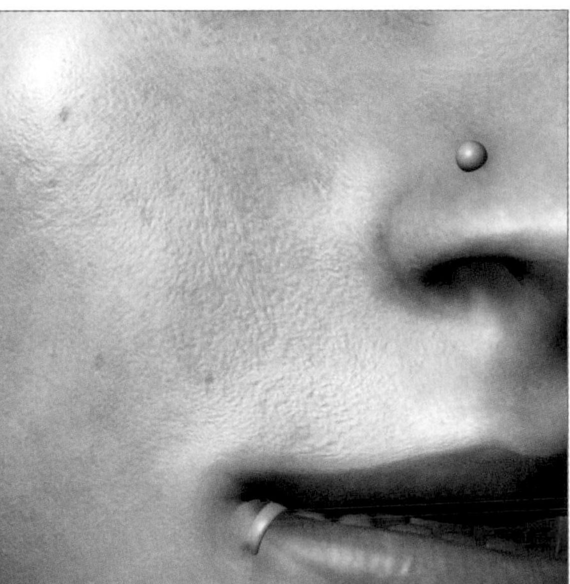

Figure 3.39: (Top Left) Textured face without bump map. (Top Right) Face with bump map. ■ Figure 3.40: (Bottom) Scene with raytraced shadows

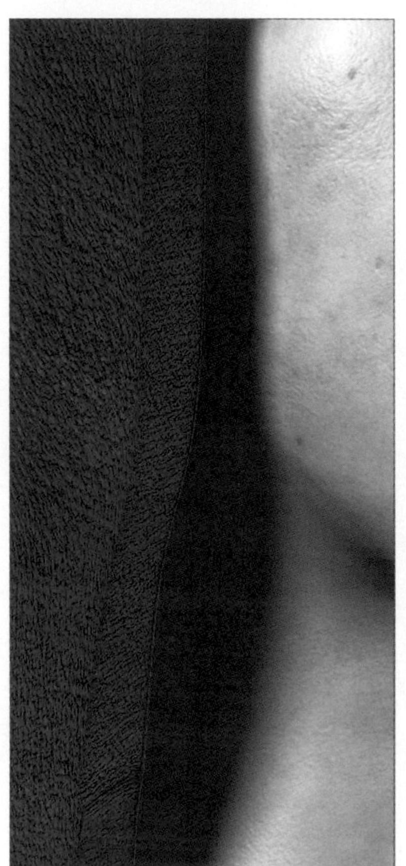

From Chapter 4, Figure 4.7: (Left) Result of revised shading network. The shadow areas pick up a red glow. (Note that the brightness has been exaggerated for print; the actual result is more subtle.) ■ Figure 4.12: (Right) The Specular Color is mapped, thus affecting the specular intensity across the skin.

Figure 4.15: (Top) To test the IBL lighting contribution, the IBL node's Color Gain is raised to 3.0, and the scene's standard lights have been deactivated. (Bottom) The IBL node's Color Gain is returned to 1.0, and the Intensity of the Key spot light is lowered to 1.0.

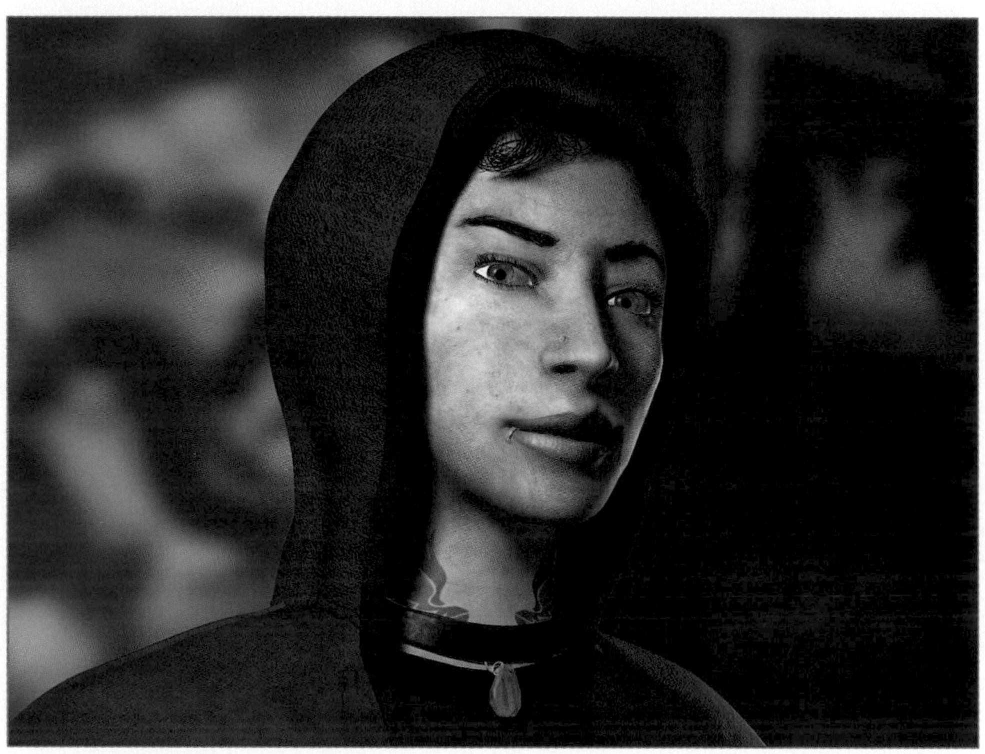

From Chapter 4, Figure 4.32: The final render of the woman

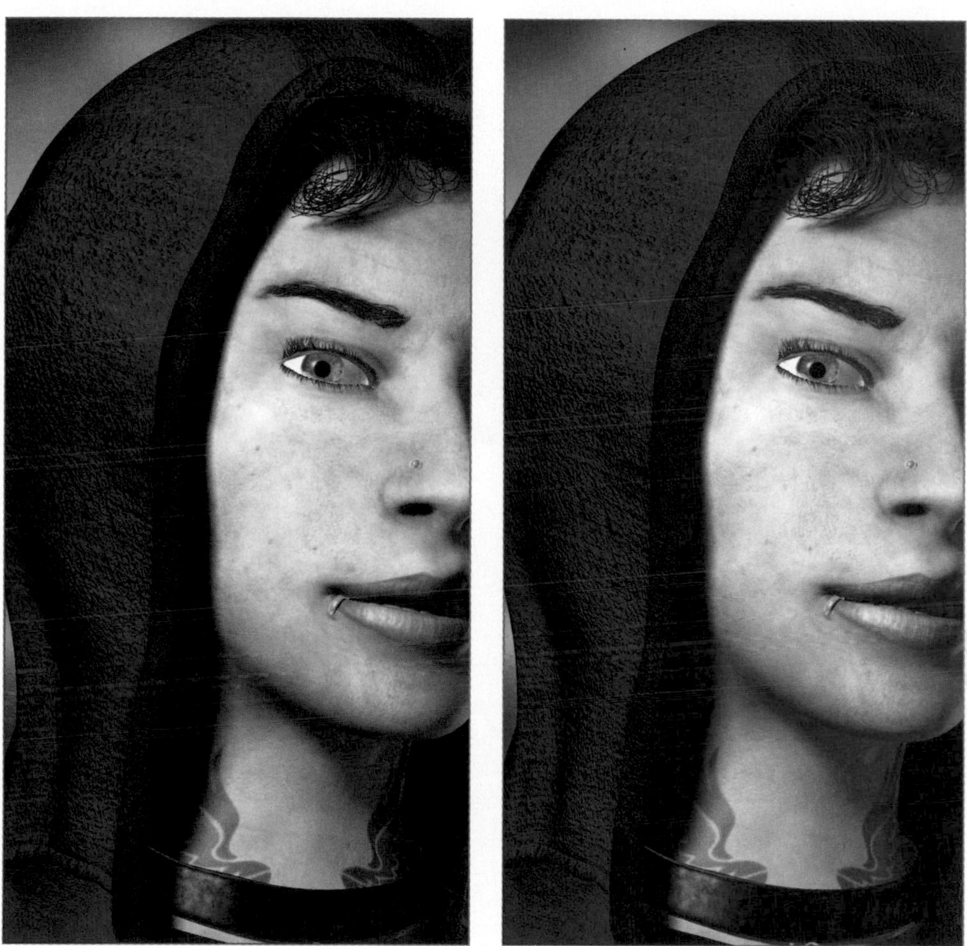

Figure 4.37: (Left) Render with Default Output Profile set to Linear. (Right) Render with Default Output Profile set to CIE RGB. In both examples, the Default Input Profile is set to Linear.

From Chapter 6, Figure 6.1: (Top) Bitmap created as a Color map for the ambulance body. (Bottom) Resulting render. The displacement of the hill is temporarily turned off to save render time.

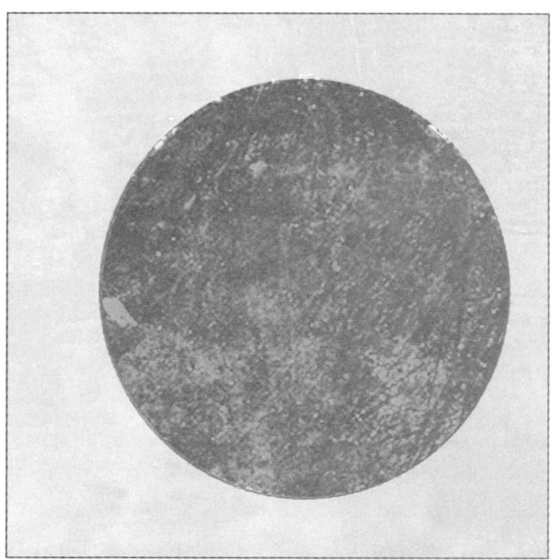

Figure 6.8: (Top) Bitmap created to establish the reflectivity of the lens and outer ring for the headlights and fog lights. (Bottom) Resulting render. To add reflections of dark objects, such as the bumper or ground, it will be necessary to activate raytracing.

From Chapter 6, Figure 6.35: Frame 1 (Top) and frame 48 (Bottom) from the final render of the vehicle

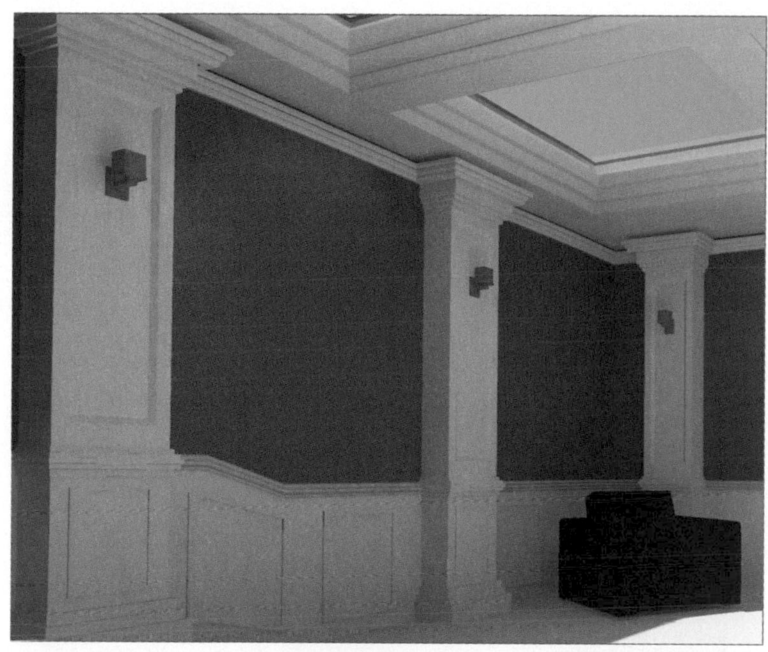

From Chapter 7, Figure 7.12: (Top) Anisotropic reflections give the walls a specular sheen without a distinct reflection. ■ Figure 7.20: (Bottom) The final render for part 1 of the room project. Room model © Nolan Miller, Graphite Digital, `www.graphite3d.com`.

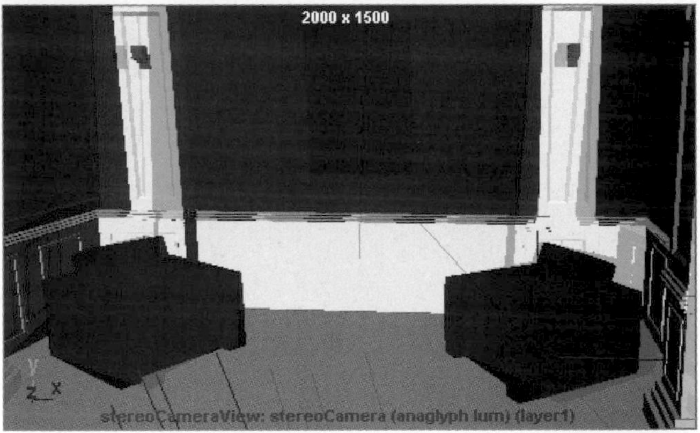

From Chapter 8, Figure 8.10: (Top) The final beauty render of the room. ■ Figure 8.12: (Bottom) The Anaglyph mode, as seen in a panel view

Accurate monitor calibration requires two items: color calibration software and a colorimeter. Colorimeters take the form of a physical sensor that is suction-cupped or otherwise positioned over the monitor screen. Monitor calibration generally follows these steps:

1. The calibration software outputs color patches of known values to the monitor. The colorimeter reads the monitor's output values. To reduce the disparity between the values, the user is instructed to adjust the monitor's contrast and brightness controls as well as the system's gamma and color temperature.
2. The calibration software compares the measured values to the known values and creates a monitor profile. A *monitor profile* describes the color response of the tested monitor within a standard file format determined by the International Color Consortium (ICC). The profile includes data for a lookup table (LUT) for each color channel. A LUT is an array used to remap a range of input values. The system graphics card is able to extract gamma correction curves from the LUTs. As part of the monitor calibration process, the user may decide to choose a white point different from the system default.
3. When an image is displayed, it is first loaded to a framebuffer (a portion of RAM storage). Each pixel is remapped through the LUTs before its value is sent to the monitor. When LUTs are used, the original pixel values are temporarily changed and the original image file remains unchanged.

By default, operating systems supply a default monitor profile so that the computer system can be used before calibration. Although the profile is functional, it is not necessarily accurate or appropriate for specific work (such as computer animation destined for video). In addition, the system supplies a default gamma correction value and color temperature.

Colorimeters are generally bundled with matching calibration software. Manufacturers that include Datacolor, Pantone, and X-Rite offer models ranging from those suitable for home use to those designed for professional artists (see Figure 4.33).

If you do not have access to calibration software and a colorimeter, you can use a chip chart to determine appropriate brightness and contrast settings. Chip charts often take the form of grayscale rectangles lined up in a row and/or a continuous grayscale gradient (see Figure 4.34).

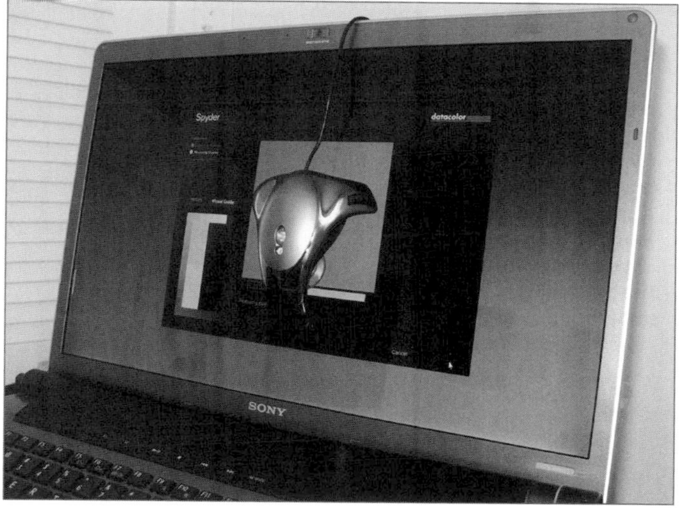

Figure 4.33

A Datacolor Spyder colorimeter used to calibrate a laptop monitor

The Default Output Profile attribute determines the profile that is applied to an image rendered through the Render View or batch-rendered to disk. Default Output Profile affects the entire render and not just the textures. For example, if the `woman_final.ma` file is rendered with Default Output Profile set to CIE RGB, the resulting image is destaurated (see Figure 4.37).

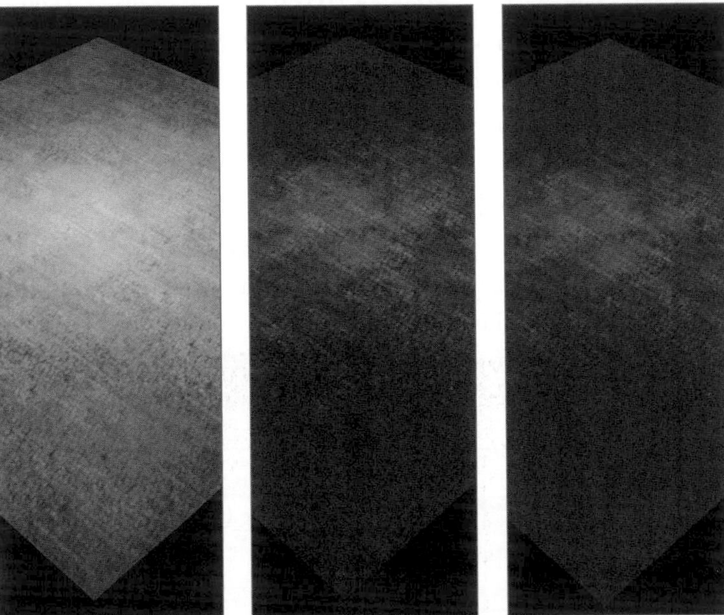

Figure 4.36

(Left) Cloth texture rendered with mental ray with Default Input Profile set to Linear. (Center) Same texture with Default Input Profile set to sRGB. (Right) Same texture with Default Input Profile set to Rec. 709. A sample file is saved as `test_profile.ma` in the `ProjectFiles/Project2/Reference` folder on the DVD.

Figure 4.37

(Left) Render with Default Output Profile set to Linear. (Right) Render with Default Output Profile set to CIE RGB. In both examples, the Default Input Profile is set to Linear. For a color version of this figure, see the color insert.

If you choose to use set Default Output Profile to a profile other than Linear, you should be aware of the color profile and color space options within Photoshop and compositing programs such as Adobe After Effects and The Foundry's Nuke. Here is a summation of those programs:

- Photoshop allows you to work within a specific color space. This is set by selecting a color profile from the RGB menu in the Working Spaces section of the Color Settings window (choose Edit → Color Settings). For example, if you set Default Output Profile to Rec. 709 in Maya, you can set the RGB menu in Photoshop to HDTV (Rec. 709). Matching the profile will guarantee that the render appears the same in Maya and Photoshop.
- After Effects allows you to choose a working color space through the Working Space menu in the Color Settings section of the Project Settings window (choose File → Project Settings).
- Nuke interprets the color space of each imported image through the Colorspace menu of the File node. You can apply a specific color space interpretation to any file written to disk through the Colorspace menu of the Write node. The working color space is determined by the Display_Lut menu, which is provided by the viewer.

Last, here are descriptions of various color profiles offered by Maya. Each profile uses a specific color space:

sRGB sRGB is shorthand for the sRGB IE6 1966-2.1. The sRGB color space was developed by Hewlett-Packard and Microsoft in the 1990s. Since its creation, it has become an international standard for computer monitors, scanners, digital cameras, and the Internet. The Maya profile includes gamma correction.

Rec. 709 The standard color space of HDTV. The Maya profile includes gamma correction.

HDTV The HDTV profile without gamma correction.

CIE XYZ The CIE XYZ color space was developed in 1931 and served as the forerunner of all modern RGB-based color space. The X, Y, and Z components correspond to red, green, and blue primary colors. Although somewhat esoteric, the CIE RGB color space is made available by Photoshop and Nuke.

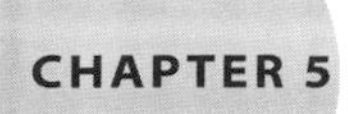

Texturing and Lighting a Vehicle, Part 1

In this chapter and Chapter 6, "Texturing and Lighting a Vehicle, Part 2," you will texture and light an all-terrain ambulance. This chapter, which contains Part 1 of the project, will guide you through the following steps:

- **Preparing the scene**
- **Assigning materials**
- **Roughing in the lighting**
- **Creating a sky in Maya**
- **Roughing in the textures**
- **Displacing the hill**
- **Painting grass**

In addition, important lighting and texturing theory is included as follows:

- **UV maps**
- **Displacement maps**
- **Paint Effects**

Project: Preparing the Scene

Before starting the texturing process, review the scene file and its contents. Open the `ambulance-start.ma` scene file from the `Project3` folder on the DVD.

The scene features a four-wheel-drive ambulance driving over a rocky hill top. The ambulance is composed of 38 polygon surfaces. The hill is a single-polygon surface that has numerous undulations. The ambulance is animated driving forward for a two-second animation. In addition, the Render camera is animated panning and craning up.

Note that the sample scene files included for this chapter and Chapter 6 assume that the bitmap textures are located within the `Textures` folder of the `ProjectFiles/Project3` project directory. Before opening a sample scene file, choose File → Project → Set and browse for the `Project3` folder, whether the folder remains at its original location on the DVD or is located on a drive after the DVD contents have been copied.

Examining the UVs

Many of the ambulance surfaces carry carefully prepared UVs. Various Maya UV projection tools were used to unwrap and arrange the UV points in the UV texture space. For example, the Body surface is split into front, back, left, right, and top views of the fenders, hood, cab, and enclosed gurney area (see Figure 5.1). Other surfaces have been flattened into single UV shells. For example, the cylindrical Axle_Rear surface is unfolded as if it were once a rolled-up piece of paper.

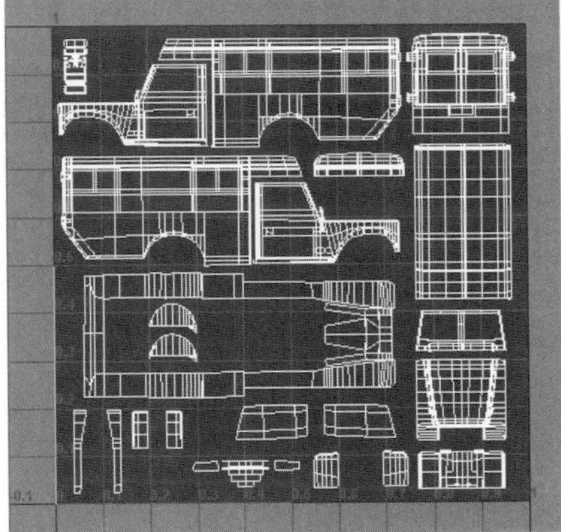

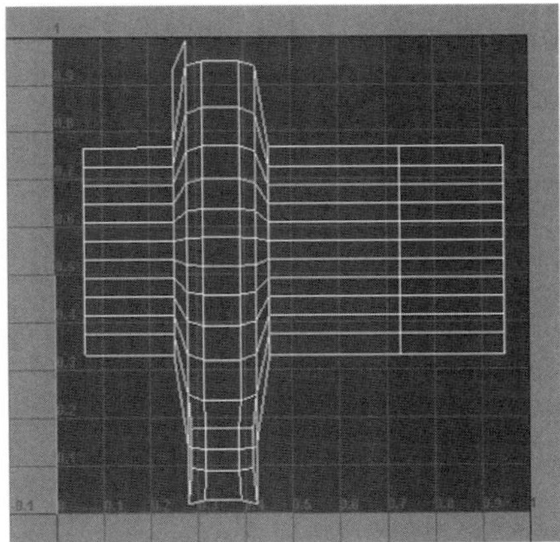

Figure 5.1

(Left) Body surface, as seen in the UV Texture Editor. (Right) The Axle_Rear surface

One surface that varies from the others, however, is the Frame. Because of an intricate design consisting of frame rails, floor pans, spring shackles, and bumper surfaces, the Automatic Mapping tool was applied. By default, Automatic Mapping re-projects the UV points from six different vantage points (as if surrounded by a cube). With a complicated surface, this leads to numerous, small UV shells (see Figure 5.2). Such a UV layout makes the creation of a custom bitmap texture difficult because many edges are split apart. In addition, it's difficult to tell which part of the model is covered by a particular shell. However, these issues are not a detriment when the surface is assigned to a generic texture with consistent color or a texture that uses the same degree of detail at all points. For example, as a step in this chapter, you will create a texture for the Frame surface that emulates dirty, rusty, black-painted metal. The dirt and rust will not be specific to any single part of the Frame, but will be equally heavy across the entire surface.

For more information on Automatic Mapping and other UV mapping tools provided by Maya, see the section "UV Maps" later in this chapter.

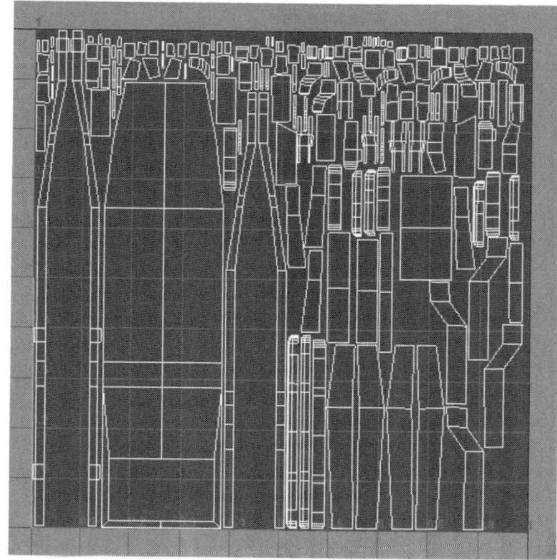

Figure 5.2

The Frame surface, as seen in the UV Texture Editor. The numerous UV shells are a product of the Automatic Mapping tool.

Exporting the UVs

To produce convincing bitmap textures on a complex man-made object, such as a truck, it will be necessary to create UV snapshots of the various surfaces. This is particularly critical for any part that needs specifically located features, such as seams, bolts, decals, signs, and so on. The snapshots will serve as an invaluable guide after texture painting has begun in a digital paint program such as Photoshop. Because of the complexity of the Ambulance model hierarchy, however, you will need to take the additional steps to create UV snapshots. Follow these steps:

1. Open the Hypergraph: Hierarchy or Outliner window. Select all the nodes that make up the hierarchy of the Ambulance model. Choose Display → Hide → Hide Selection from the main Maya menu. The ambulance is hidden from view. The node names are grayed out in the Hypergraph: Hierarchy and Outliner. Choose Window → UV Texture Editor. The UV Texture Editor appears empty.
2. Return to the Hypergraph: Hierarchy or Outliner and select one surface node, such as Body. Choose Display → Show → Show Selection. The Body node is no longer grayed out; however, the parent nodes (Frame and Ambulance) remain hidden. Because the Body node is selected, only the Body surface is revealed in the UV Texture Editor. No other surface is shown. If all the transform nodes were left visible, the selection of the Body node would cause the Body node and the node's children (glass, rim, tire, mirror, and light nodes) to be simultaneously shown in the UV Texture Editor (see Figure 5.3). Alternatively, you can isolate a single surface in the UV Texture Editor by selecting its shape node; you can access shape nodes through the Hypergraph: Connections window.

Figure 5.3

When working with a complex hierarchy, the selection of a transform node causes its children nodes to be seen simultaneously in the UV Texture Editor. To avoid this, you can either hide every node but the one you want to examine, or simply select a surface's shape node.

Choose Polygons → UV Snapshot from the UV Texture Editor menu. In the UV Snapshot window, change Size X and Size Y to 2048, change the Image Format menu to an image format of choice, and choose a filename and location through the File Name cell. Click the OK button and exit the window. (If you choose an image format that supports alpha, such as Targa or TIFF, the UV layout will appear in the alpha channel. You can delete this unneeded channel in Photoshop by RMB+clicking the alpha channel in the Channels panel and choosing Delete Channel from the menu.)

3. Launch Photoshop. (Any recent edition of Photoshop will work.) Open the UV snapshot file you created through Maya. By default, the image is converted to a Background layer, which cannot be moved in the layer stack. In the Layers panel, double-click the Background layer. The New Layer window opens. Enter a new layer name, such as **UV Reference**, and click OK. This converts the Background layer into a new, editable layer.

4. In Photoshop, choose Layer → New → Layer. In the New Layer window, enter a new name, such as Texture. You will paint the texture on this layer. Click+drag the UV Reference layer to the top of the layer stack. Switch its Blending Mode menu from Normal to Screen (see Figure 5.4). This causes the white lines of the UV snapshot to appear over the lower texture layer. Save the image as a Photoshop PSD file.

5. Return to Maya. While the surface transform node remains selected, choose Display → Hide → Hide Selection from the main Maya menu. Select the next surface node for which you wish to snapshot UVs. Choose Display → Show → Show Selection. Return to step 2 and repeat the UV snapshot process for the newly displayed surface. Continue the process until you've exported a UV snapshot for every surface that has unique UVs. When you have finished exporting the UVs, you can redisplay all the surfaces by choosing Display → Show → All from the main Maya menu.

Many of the surfaces that make up the ambulance share identical UV distributions. For example, the UVs of each tire surface are identical (during the modeling phase, a single tire was duplicated three times). Therefore, it's not necessary to export UVs for every single surface. A list of suggested UV snapshots is included in Table 5.1. In addition, it's not necessary to make each UV snapshot the same resolution. You can map smaller, less complex

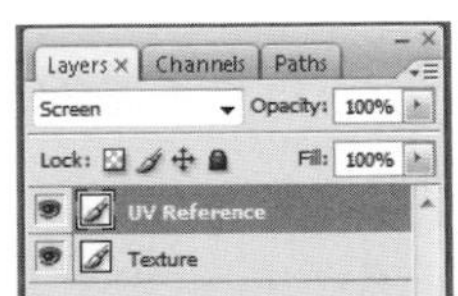

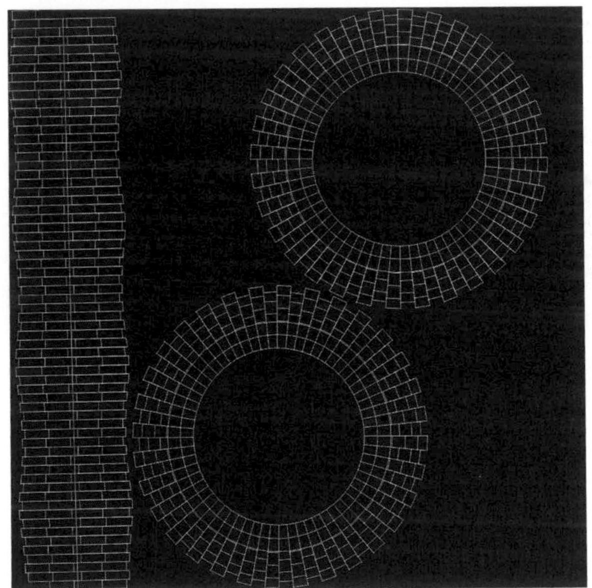

Figure 5.4

(Top) Photoshop CS3 Layers panel with arranged layers. The UV snapshot layer is renamed UV Reference, is moved to the top, and has its blending mode set to Screen. The lower layer, named Texture, is empty and serves as a place to paint a new texture. (Bottom) Resulting appearance of UV snapshot of a tire surface. A sample Photoshop file is included as `Tire_UVs.psd` in the `ProjectFiles/Project3/Reference` folder on the DVD.

surfaces with smaller texture bitmaps; larger, more intricate surfaces require larger resolutions to hold an appropriate level of detail. Sample UV snapshot bitmaps are included in the `ProjectFiles/Project3/Reference` folder and are named after their associated surfaces.

Table 5.1
UV snapshot breakdown

SURFACE REQUIRING UV SNAPSHOT	SURFACES THAT SHARE IDENTICAL UV DISTRIBUTION	RECOMMENDED SNAPSHOT RESOLUTION
Body	None	2048×2048
Interior	None	1024×1024
Headlight_L	Headlight_R Foglight_L Foglight_R Signal_Bottom_L Signal_Bottom_R Signal_Top_L Signal_Top_R	512×512
Mirror_L	Mirror_R	512×512
Rim_Front_L	Rim_Front_R Rim_Rear_L Rim_Rear_R	1024×1024
Spring_Front_L	Spring_Front_R Spring_Rear_L Spring_Rear_R	512×512
Tire_Front_L	Tire_Front_R Tire_Rear_L Tire_Rear_R	1024×1024
Warning_Light	None	512×512

Throughout this book, UV snapshot and bitmap texture resolutions have followed predictable sizes: 512, 1024, and 2048. These resolutions are used commonly in the animation industry and stem from the historical use of binary-based computing. 1024 is 2^10 and is the number of bytes in a kilobyte. 512 is simply half of 1024. 2048 is twice as large as 1024. 1024 and 2048 are also referred to as 1K and 2K, respectively. With this usage, IK and 2K refer to the number of horizontal pixels carried by a render resolution, film scanner resolution, or digital projection resolution. For example, the render resolution of this chapter's project is 1024×768, which is 1K with a 1.33 aspect ratio (the resolution width is 1.33 times greater than the height).

UV Maps

When a polygon model is created from scratch in Maya, it carries no UV information. That is, there are no UV points when examining the surface in the UV Texture Editor. In addition, the surface is unable to carry a texture and will render out as a solid color. Some polygon models start out as polygon primitives. As such, they automatically receive an initial UV mapping. However, numerous applications of various polygon editing tools leave the UVs chaotic and unusable (see Figure 5.5). This results in stretched and illegible texture maps appearing in the render.

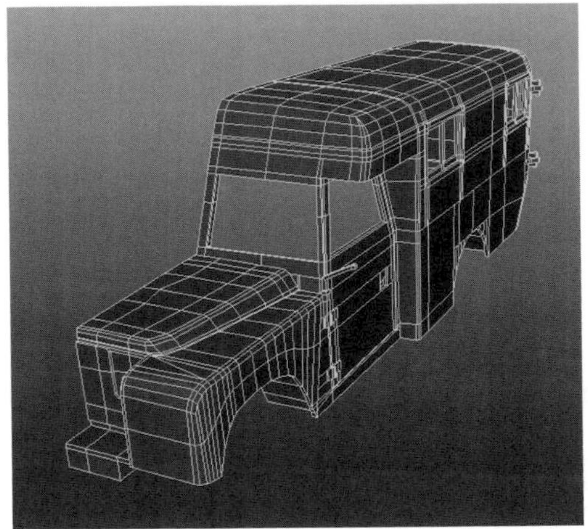
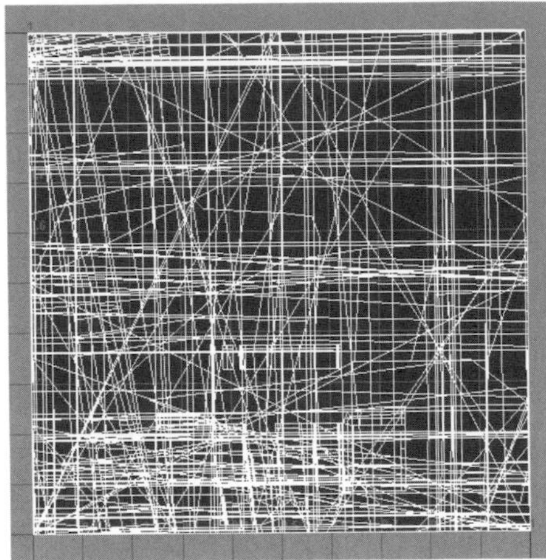

Figure 5.5
(Left) An early iteration of the ambulance body. (Right) The corresponding UV layout before the application of UV mapping tools

Mapping Tool Overview

To impart UV information to a surface or repair an existing UV layout, you can use Maya's UV mapping tools, which are located in the Create UVs menu. The tools map surface vertex positions onto two-dimensional UV texture space. Hence, the vertex positions are transformed into UV point positions. To undertake the mapping, each tool creates a unique projection node, each of which is described here:

Planar Mapping Planar Mapping projects from a flat plane. Hence, the tool is suitable for surfaces or sets of faces that are essentially flat. If you apply Planar Mapping to a convoluted or spherical surface, UV points will overlap and faces will share the same section of a texture.

Cylindrical Mapping Cylindrical Mapping projects from an open cylinder (you can think of the cylinder as a rolled-up plane that has two opposite edges meeting along a seam). Cylindrical Mapping is appropriate for any tube-like surface or set of faces. Note that the success of the mapping is dependent on the projection's scale, which is determined by the projection manipulator. If the UV layout looks twisted or overlaps, the projection manipulator should be re-scaled (see the next section for manipulator information).

Spherical Mapping Spherical Mapping projects from a sphere, although the projection shape takes the form of a sphere fragment by default. To ensure that the projection manipulator covers 360 degrees in U and 180 degrees in V, you must raise the manipulator's Horizontal Sweep and Vertical Sweep attribute values. (The Cylindrical Mapping manipulator also possesses a Horizontal Sweep attribute.) The Spherical Mapping projection is similar to a Cylindrical Mapping projection with the top and bottom edges pinched into poles. Spherical Mapping is appropriate for any ball-like surface or set of faces.

Automatic Mapping As mentioned in the "Examining the UVs" section earlier in this chapter, the Automatic Mapping tool projects from six different planes arranged like a cube. This leads to the creation of numerous UV shells. You can reduce or increase the number of planes by adjusting the tool's Planes attribute.

Create UVs Based On Camera By using the Create UVs Based On Camera tool, you can create a projection from the current camera view. (The selected view panel determines which camera is used.)

Best Plane Texturing Tool The Best Plane Texturing tool enables you to define a projection plane based on the locations of vertices on the surface. When the tool is applied, it prompts you to select faces to remap and vertices that define the projection.

Applying a Mapping Tool

You can apply a UV mapping tool with the following basic steps:

1. Select an entire surface or a limited number of polygon faces. Switch to the Polygons main menu and choose Create UVs → *UV mapping tool*.
2. A projection manipulator appears in the view panel (see Figure 5.6). The manipulator's attributes appear in an Attribute Editor tab. For example, the Planar Mapping tool provides a manipulator named polyPlanarProj. Translate, scale, and rotate the manipulator to face and/or surround the surface so that a nonoverlapping UV layout is achieved. You can interactively see the result of the projection by opening the UV Texture Editor. To interactively scale the manipulator in a view panel, click+drag the red, cyan, and green cubes. To rotate or translate the manipulator, click the red T-shaped icon at the corner to reveal the rotation circle and translation axis; you can also update the Projection Center and Rotate values in the manipulator's Attribute Editor tab. If you are using Spherical Mapping or Cylindrical Mapping, adjust the sweep of the projection in the manipulator's Attribute Editor tab.

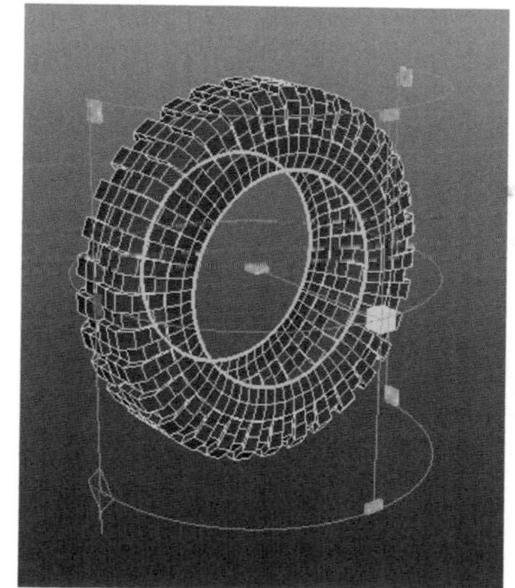

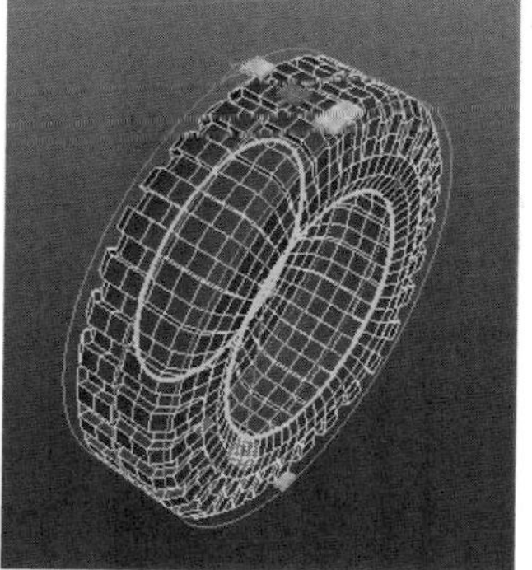

Figure 5.6

(Top Left) A Cylindrical Mapping manipulator in its default state after the tool's application to a tire surface. (Top Right) The same manipulator after its Rotate attribute is set to 90, 0, 0 and its Projection Horizontal Sweep is set to 360. (Bottom) The manipulator's Projection Attributes section, as seen in the Attribute Editor

3. When you are finished adjusting the projection manipulator, deselect the surface. The manipulator disappears. The projection is included as history until you choose Edit → Delete By Type → History.
4. If you applied a mapping tool to polygon faces but not the entire surface, the corresponding UV points are "broken off" the main UV layout and become a new UV shell. You can move this shell away from other shells in the UV Texture Editor by RMB+clicking, choosing UV from the menu, selecting the UV points of the shell, and using Maya's standard Move tool to move the shell aside. You can apply different UV mapping tools to different sets of faces. For example, you can apply the Cylindrical Mapping tool to the tread of a truck tire and then apply a Planar Mapping tool to the face of the same tire.

Using Mapping Alternatives

Aside from the polygon mapping tools provided by Maya, various plug-ins are available to help simplify or expedite the process. While some of these build upon the basic UV mapping work flow presented by Maya, other use pelt mapping techniques. Pelt mapping unfolds the surface so that it becomes a single large shell with a minimal number of seams (for more information, see Chapter 3, "Texturing and Lighting a Character, Part 1"). On the other hand, large animation studios that are able to support proprietary software have recently turned to Ptex technology. *Ptex*, which stands for *per-face texture mapping*, does not require UV mapping but is able to store separate texture maps for each polygon face in a specialized file format. Nevertheless, because Ptex and pelt mapping are not a part of Maya's standard UV tool set, it pays to understand the basic UV mapping process discussed in this book.

In addition to using UV mapping tools, you can manipulate UV points and UV edges inside the UV Texture Editor. This includes the ability to move, scale, and rotate selected UV points or sets of points with the standard Maya transform tools. The UV Texture Editor's Polygons menu also includes a long list of automated tools that scale, rotate, and redistribute UV points; in addition, you can separate or "sew" (recombine) edges. Although it is beyond the scope of this book to discuss these tools in more detail, they are worth investigating (Maya's built-in Help files can provide important information for their basic use).

Project: Assigning Materials

The first stage of texturing requires the basic assignment of materials. As discussed in Chapter 1, "Texturing and Lighting a Product, Part 1," you can either assign a unique material to each surface or allow surfaces to share material assignments. For this scene, it's best to combine both techniques.

Because the ambulance model is composed of multiple surfaces grouped together in a hierarchy, the assignment process will present additional difficulties. For example, if you assign a material to a node that is the parent of second node, the assignment is applied to both nodes. In other words, the assignment is carried downstream in the hierarchy. There are several ways to avoid such an assignment:

- Assign materials to surface nodes before grouping them together in a hierarchy. Unfortunately, this will not be practical for the ambulance scene because animation already exists.
- Assign materials to the topmost surface nodes in the hierarchy and then work your way downstream. By working in such a direction, the lower nodes are reassigned to new materials without affecting the assignments of the nodes that serve as parents.
- Assign materials directly to surface shape nodes. You can access shape nodes in the Hypergraph: Connections window. For example, select a surface through a view panel, the Hypergraph: Hierarchy or Outliner window, switch to the Hypergraph: Connections window, select the corresponding shape node (which appears to the right of the transform node), and assign it to a material in the Hypershade.

For example, in Figure 5.7, a set of assigned materials is shown. A number of materials are assigned to single surfaces. The Hill_ material is assigned to the Hill surface, the Frame_ material is assigned to the Frame surface, and so on. Note that some of the materials have an underscore (_) symbol added as a suffix; this distinguishes the material names from the surface transform or group node names.

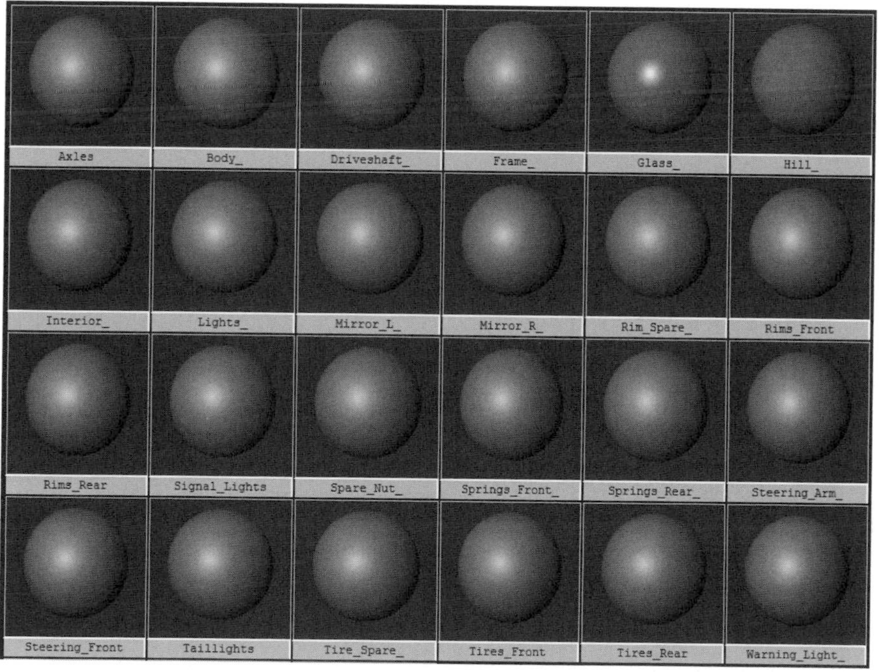

Figure 5.7

Assigned materials. A sample scene is included as `ambulance-step1.ma` **on the DVD.**

The majority of the materials featured in Figure 5.7 are Blinns. The Glass surface is assigned to a Phong material. The Hill surface is assigned to a Lambert material. At the same time, there are several surfaces that share a material; a list is included in Table 5.2.

Table 5.2
List of surfaces that share a material

SURFACE NAMES	ASSIGNED MATERIAL NAME
Axle_Front	Axles
Axle_Rear	
Headlight_L	Lights
Headlight_R	
Foglight_L	
Foglight_R	
Rims_Front_L	Rims_Front_
Rims_Front_R	
Rims_Rear_L	Rims_Rear_
Rims_Rear_R	
Signal_Bottom_L	Signal_Lights
Signal_Bottom_R	
Signal_Top_L	
Signal_Top_R	
Spring_Front_L	Springs_Front_
Spring_Front_R	
Spring_Rear_L	Springs_Rear_
Spring_Rear_R	
Steering_Front_L	Steering_Front
Steering_Front_R	
Tire_Front_L	Tires_Front
Tire_Front_R	
Tire_Rear_L	Tires_Rear
Tire_Rear_R	

When assigning materials, it pays to determine which surfaces are visible from the viewpoint of the camera. If the subject, such as the ambulance, is seen from only one angle, you can save time by assigning unseen or poorly seen surfaces to materials shared by their more visible counterparts. For example, Tire_Rear_L is assigned to the same material as Tire_Rear_R because Tire_Rear_L is barely seen past the bumpy surface on the hill. The same is true of Spring_Rear_L, which is assigned to the material shared by Spring_Rear_R.

In other cases, surfaces are allowed to share a material until the materials are adjusted and mapped. For example, the Headlight and Foglight surfaces are assigned to the Lights material. After the Lights material is adjusted and mapped, duplicates of the shading network can be made and adjusted individually. By duplicating the shading network of the Lights material, less time will be spent setting up materials that are assigned to surfaces that share identical surface topology and real-world surface appearance.

Project: Roughing in the Lighting

In Chapter 3, 1-, 2-, and 3-point lighting schemes were discussed. When lighting a scene set in a sunlit exterior, 2-point lighting is appropriate. In such a scenario, the sun serves as a strong key, and the net bounced light from the ground serves as a fill. You can follow these steps to place a key and fill light:

1. Create a directional light. Rename the light **Key**. Rotate the light so it points down and roughly forms a 45-degree angle between the light icon and the XZ grid plane. The position of the directional light icon does not affect the lighting. You can also scale up the light icon to make it easier to manipulate. To help determine the best rotation of the light, choose Shading → Smooth Shade All and Lighting → Use All Lights..
2. Afternoon sunlight arriving from a cloudless sky produces hard-edged shadows. Hence, you should activate key light shadows before adding any fill. To do so, open the light's Attribute Editor tab, expand the Depth Map Shadow Attributes section, and select the Use Depth Map Shadows check box. Set the Resolution to 2048 and the Filter Size to 3. A large Resolution and a small Filter size will keep the shadow edge fairly hard while removing the depth map's potential roughness. Render a test. At

this stage, the render appears pixelated. Open the Render Settings window, switch to the Maya Software tab, and change the Edge Anti-Aliasing menu to Highest Quality. To save render time, you can temporarily reduce the Width and Height values in the Common tab (Maintain Width/Height Ratio should remain selected to avoid distorting the aspect ratio of the render resolution). Re-render a test. The result should look similar to Figure 5.9. The goal is to create aesthetically shaped shadows that fall across the ambulance and hill and that allow the viewer to determine the source of light and the general time of day. Minor changes to the rotation of the Key light will cause the shadows to take on different shapes. In fact, you should create test renders at different frames of the timeline (such as 1, 24, and 48) to make sure the light's rotation is optimal.

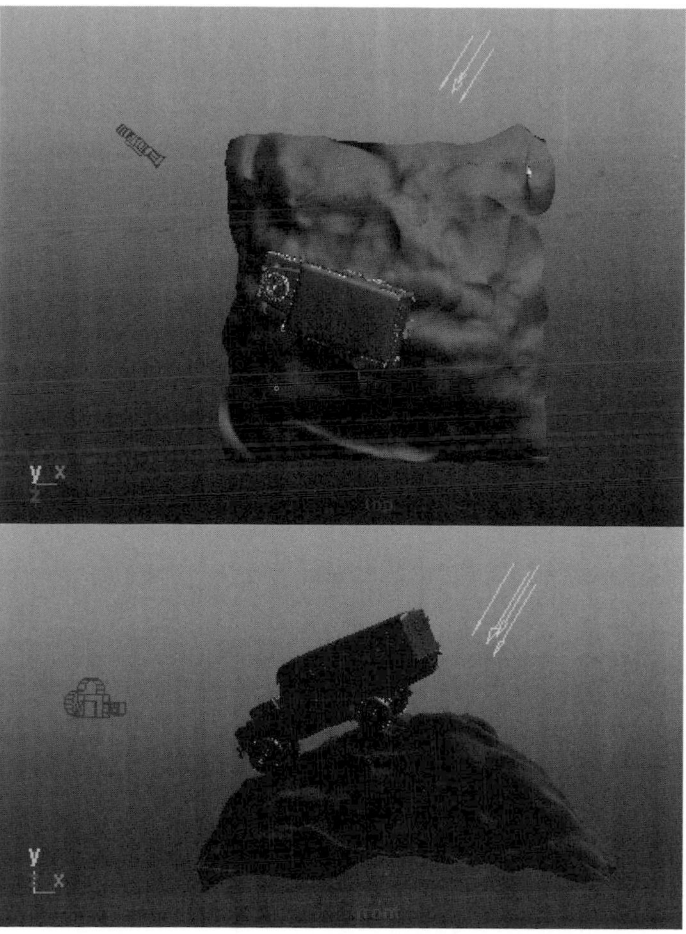

Figure 5.8

Top and Front view showing position of Key light. The Render camera icon appears on the left.

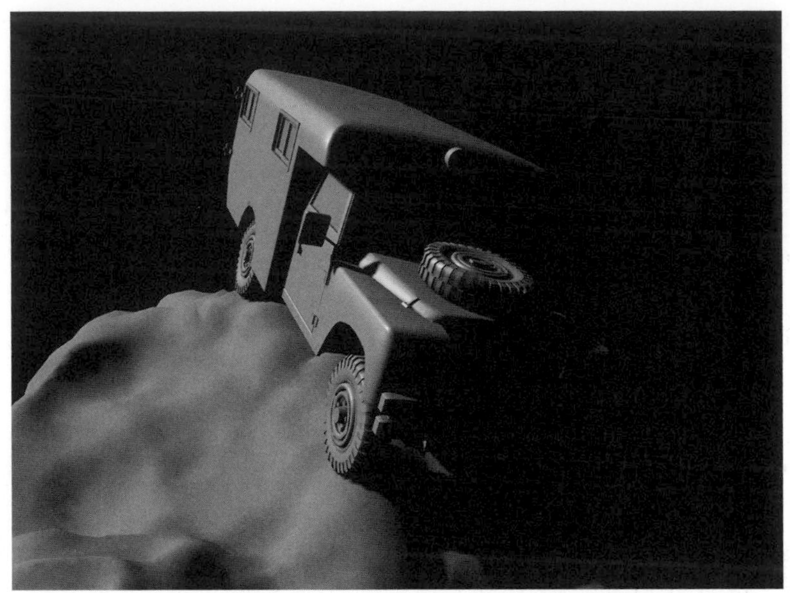

Figure 5.9
Scene lit with Key light, as seen on frame 48. A sample scene is included as `ambulance-step2.ma` **on the DVD.**

3. Create a new directional light. Rename the light **Fill**. Rotate the light so its light arrives from a direction opposite that of the Key light (see Figure 5.10). While the Key re-creates light arriving from the sun in the sky, the Fill should re-create sunlight that has bounced off the hill. Open the new light's Attribute Editor tab and set the Intensity to 0.2. Render a test. Because directional lights create parallel light rays, the fill arrives from one direction. Although this allows the front of the truck to be dimly illuminated, several areas of the geometry receive no light at all and remain black. For example, the inner camera-left fender and the hood suffer from the lack of light (see Figure 5.10). To solve this, two additional fill lights must be added. Technically, the lighting will remain 2-point lighting in that the scene emulates two sources of light: the sun and the bounced sunlight. However, because such a lighting setup will require four different Maya lights, it's better to refer to the lighting style as *naturalistic*. Naturalistic lighting attempts to re-create a real-life lighting situation but places no limit on the number of lights used, the light types, or their various settings. As such, successful naturalistic lighting does not betray the exact lighting setup used in the 3D program (or on the motion picture set or the theater stage).
4. Create an Ambient light. Rename the light **Fill_2**. Position the light to the camera-left side of the hill (roughly –4, –4, –20 in X, Y, Z). Open the light's Attribute Editor tab and set the Intensity to 0.05. Create a new Ambient light. Rename the light **Fill_3**. Position the new light to the front of the hill (roughly –18, –8, 7 in X, Y, Z). Open the new light's Attribute Editor tab and set the Intensity to 0.05. Render a test. Areas that previously received no light are now dimly lit (see Figure 5.11). By default,

ambient lights create a mixture of directional and omnidirectional light, so the light provided by Fill_2 and Fill_3 reach all parts of the model. (For information on the Ambient Shade attribute, which controls the directional and omnidirectional mixture, see Chapter 1.)

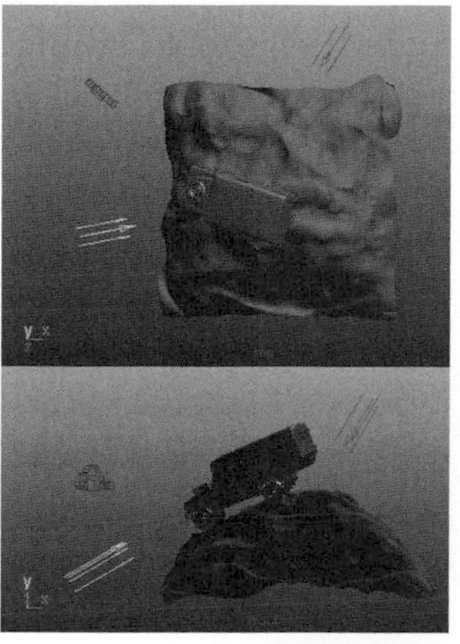

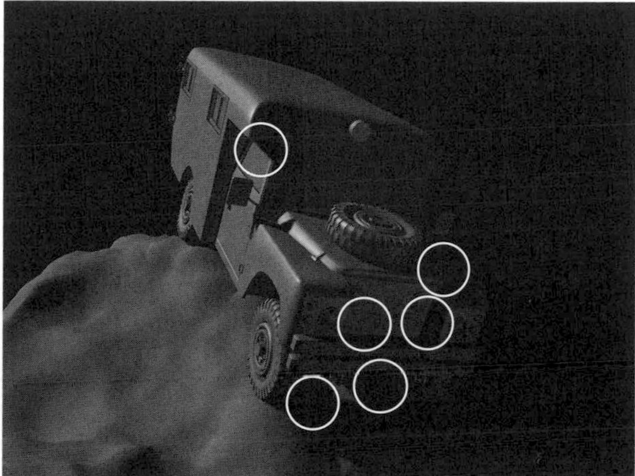

Figure 5.10

(Left) Top and Front view showing position of selected Fill light. (Right) Render after the addition of the Fill light. Areas circled in yellow remain unlit. A sample scene is included as `ambulance-step3.ma` **on the DVD.**

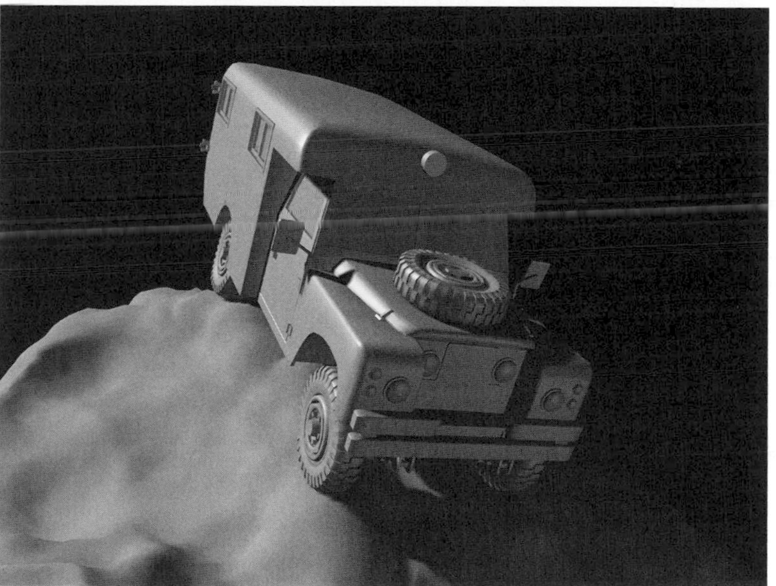

Figure 5.11

Render after the addition of two additional fill lights. A sample scene is included as `ambulance-step4.ma` **on the DVD.**

Project: Creating a Sky in Maya

When lighting a daylight scene, it's difficult to judge the overall success of the render when the background remains black. To avoid this, you can add a sky while working in Maya. There are several approaches you can take.

Changing the Environment Color

By default, empty space in Maya is colored 0, 0, 0 black. To change the color that is used, open the rendering camera's Attribute Editor tab, expand the Environment section, and change the Background Color. Although the resulting render will show no color variation in the empty areas of the scene, a blue Background Color does provide a sense of sky. Note that a nonblack Background Color can interfere when compositing an alpha channel (the fourth channel that encodes transparency for a rendered frame). For example, if you wish to render an object surrounded by empty space for the purpose of compositing it over the top of another render, it's best to leave the Background Color set to black. Black is assumed to be the color of empty space by such compositing programs as Adobe After Effects.

Importing an Image Plane

If a solid color doesn't provide a realistic sky, you can import a bitmap photo as an image plane. Image planes are connected to a camera and serve as a permanent backdrop. You can add an image plane to a camera by choosing View → Image Plane → Import Image through a view panel menu. After a bitmap is chosen, an imagePlane node appears in the Cameras tab of the Hypershade window, and the image plane becomes visible in all the view panels (see Figure 5.12).

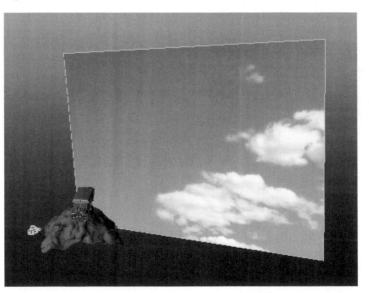

Figure 5.12

An image plane is added to the scene to provide a background sky. In this example, the image plane's Width and Height are set to 35 after the Fixed option is selected. A sample scene is included as `image_plane.ma` in the `ProjectFiles/Project3/Reference` folder on the DVD.

By default, the image plane is attached to the camera and is scaled to fit the camera's Resolution Gate. If the camera moves, the image plane moves along with it. If this behavior is not suitable for the scene, you can fix the image plane to a specific location in space by selecting the Fixed radio button in the image plane's Attribute Editor tab. You can choose the image plane's location by changing the Center X, Y, Z attribute, which is found in the Placement Extras section. In addition, you can scale the image plane by adjusting Width and Height, which are found in the same section. Note that, despite the use of the Fixed option, the image plane continues to orient itself toward the camera as the camera moves. If you wish to delete an image plane, delete its node in the Hypershade.

Adding Background Geometry

An alternate solution for adding a bitmap to a scene background requires the texturing of primitive geometry. Follow these steps:

1. Choose Create → Polygon Primitives → Interactive Creation and deselect the Interactive Creation option. Choose Create → Polygon Primitives → Sphere. A sphere is placed at 0, 0, 0.
2. Select the sphere. Open the UV Texture Editor. Because the sphere is a primitive, it has a predefined UV layout. By default, the poles of the sphere, which lie at the top and the bottom of the UV texture space, are separated in a "sawtooth" fashion. In the UV Texture Editor, RMB+click and choose Face from the menu. Select all the faces that lie along the bottom half of the UV texture space. Press the Delete key. The faces are deleted in the UV Texture Editor and in the view panels. The top half of the sphere remains. In the UV Texture Editor, select the faces that occupy the top-right half of the UV texture space. Press the Delete key. A quarter sphere remains (see Figure 5.13). Select the remaining faces and choose Polygons → Normalize from the UV Texture Editor menu. Normalize expands the remaining faces so they fill the entire 0-to-1 texture space. Close the UV Texture Editor.

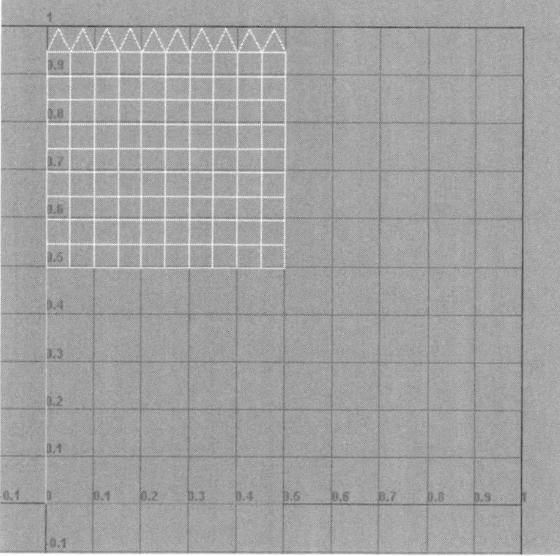

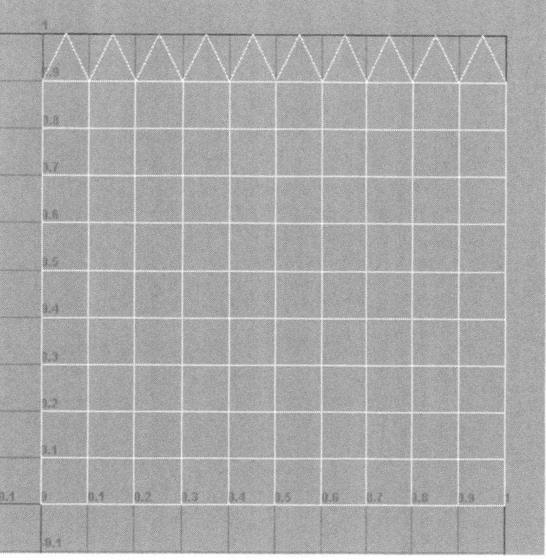

Figure 5.13

(Left) UV texture space of a sphere after the bottom half and top-right half of faces are deleted. (Right) The surviving faces are expanded to the full 0-to-1 UV texture space with the application of Normalize.

3. Using the Channel Box, scale the remaining quarter-sphere to 60, 60, 60. Translate the sphere to 0, –30, 0 and rotate it to 0, 200, 0. This places and orients the quarter-sphere so it covers the background from the point of view of the Render camera (see Figure 5.14). The quarter-sphere's remaining pinched pole, which sits at the top, is kept out of view. Rename the quarter-sphere **Sky_Dome**.

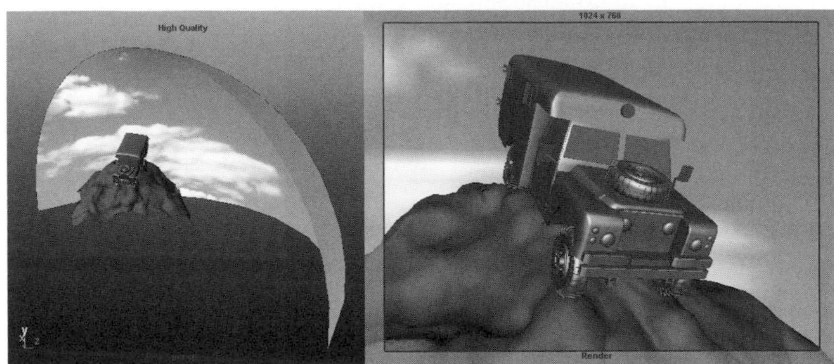

Figure 5.14
The quarter-sphere is translated, rotated, and scaled to fill the view of the Render camera. Smooth Shading and Hardware Texturing are activated for the view panels, allowing the sky bitmap to be seen.

4. Assign Sky_Dome to a new Surface Shader material. Rename the material **Sky**. The Surface Shader material is unaffected by lights and shadows and therefore does not have to be lit (for more information on this quality, see Chapter 1). Open the material's Attribute Editor tab. Click the checkered Map button beside Out Color. Click the File texture icon in the Create Render Node window. In the new File node's Attribute Editor tab, browse for a photo bitmap of a sky. An example bitmap is included as `sky.tga` in the `Project3/Textures` folder on the DVD. Render a test. A sky appears in the background (see Figure 5.15). Even though the Surface Shader material is unaffected by lights and shadows, the Sky_Dome geometry continues to cast shadows. Therefore, select Sky_Dome, open the Attribute Editor, switch to the Sky_DomeShape tab, expand the Render Stats section, and deselect the Casts Shadows check box.

Figure 5.15
(Left) Render of frame 1 with Sky_Dome. (Right) Render of frame 48. A sample scene is included as `ambulance-step5.ma` on the DVD.

Project: Roughing in the Textures

Before adjusting the assigned materials and mapping textures, determine what real-world surface qualities each part of the ambulance should strive to replicate. A suggested list of qualities is included in Table 5.3.

Table 5.3
Ambulance parts and suggested real-world surface qualities

AMBULANCE PART(S)	SURFACE QUALITY
Body	White-painted metal with red-painted cross logo on each side; dirt near wheel wells
Frame (with springs, axles, drive-shaft, and steering components)	Semigloss black paint covered with scratches, rust spots, and caked-on dirt
Rims	White-painted steel with scratches and caked-on dirt
Tires	Semiworn rubber with raised markings and caked-on dirt
Lights	Glass lenses (either clear or colored) with stainless steel edge loops
Glass	Clear glass with minor dirt and smudges
Interior	Brown leather seat, white-painted metal steering wheel, white-painted dash, and white-painted back wall with vents and access panel

After you determine the desired surface qualities, adjust the Color, Transparency, Eccentricity, Specular Roll Off, and Specular Color attributes of all the assigned materials. For example, Figure 5.16 shows a render after each material has been adjusted. Note that the windows are assigned 100 percent Transparency; reflections will be added in the next section.

Figure 5.16
Render after the adjustment of common material attributes. A sample scene is included as `ambulance-step6.ma` on the DVD.

Establishing Window Reflections

Although the Sky_Dome surface created in the previous section provides a background for the render, it cannot provide a suitable reflection for the glass of the ambulance. Even if raytracing is activated in the Render Settings window, much of the empty space surrounding the ambulance and hill will render as a black reflection. To create reflection that surrounds the model completely, you can map an environment texture to the glass material's Reflected Color attribute. The Reflected Color attribute simulates a reflection without requiring the use of raytracing. You can follow these steps:

1. Open the Attribute Editor tab for the material assigned to the Glass surface. In the example scene files, the material is named Glass_. Scroll down to the Specular shading section. Click the checkered Map button beside Reflected Color. In the Create Render Node window, click the phrase *Env Texture* in the Create tab. Click the Env Sphere texture icon.

2. In the new envSphere node's Attribute Editor tab, click the checkered Map button beside the Image Name attribute. In the Create Render Node window, click the File texture icon. In the new File node's Attribute Editor tab, browse for a bitmap that features a sky. You can use the same bitmap mapped to the Sky_Dome's material or use a new one that possesses similar colors.

3. When you create an envSphere node, a place3dTexture utility is automatically connected to the shading network (see Figure 5.17). The place3dTexture utility controls the scale, rotation, and position of a projection sphere. The sphere is represented as two interlocking circles in the view panels and is placed at 0, 0, 0. The bitmap loaded into the File texture is thereby projected from the projection sphere toward the center of the sphere. Because the sphere is only 1 unit high by default, you must scale it so it surrounds the model. You can select the place3dTexture node in the Hypergraph, Outliner, or the Utilities tab of the Hypershade. After the place3dTexture node is selected, change its scale to 40, 40, 40 in the Channel Box; accordingly, the projection sphere becomes large enough to surround the ambulance.

4. Render a test. A reflection appears across the glass surfaces. To increase the intensity of the reflection, return to the

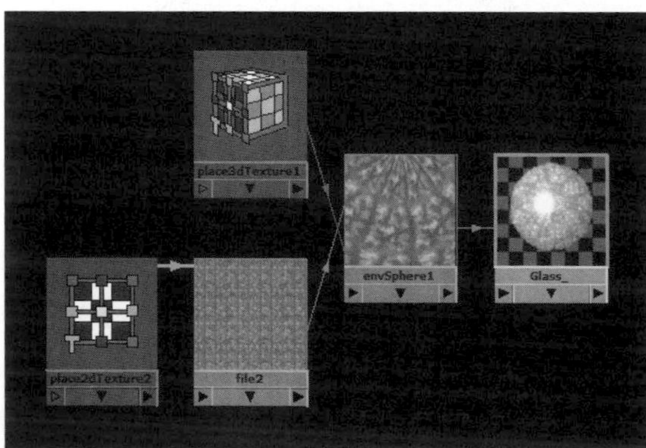

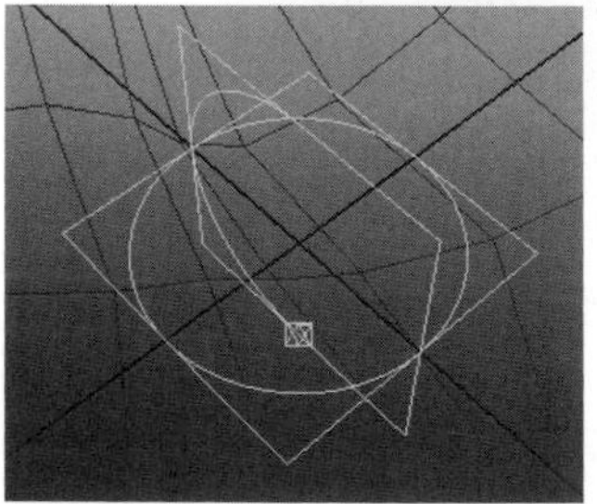

Figure 5.17

(Top) envSphere, place3dTexture, File, and place2dTexture nodes connected to the Glass_ material node. (Bottom Left) Projection sphere in its default state at 0, 0, 0. The diamond shape at the bottom represents the point at which all four edges of the mapped texture are pinched at one pole. (Bottom Right) Projection sphere scaled and rotated to surround the ambulance

glass material's Attribute Editor tab and lower the Transparency value and raise the Reflectivity value. To further increase the strength of the reflectivity, adjust the Specular Color value. Specular Color serves as a multiplier for the Reflected Color value. In turn, the Reflected Color value is added to the material's Color value. For example, in Figure 5.18, Transparency is set to 0.4, 0.4, 0.4 in RGB; Specular color is set to 1.0, 1.0, 1.0; and Reflectivity is set to 0.8.

Figure 5.18

An Env Sphere texture mapped to the Reflected Color attribute creates reflections in the windows, as seen on frame 43. A sample scene is included as `ambulance-step6.ma` on the DVD.

5. Because of the size of the projection sphere, the detail within the bitmap may be difficult to see within the reflections. To shrink the size of the detail, you can adjust the UV tiling of the File texture connected to the shading network. To do so, return to the Hypershade. RMB+click the material assigned to the Glass surface, and choose Graph Network. In the work area, click the place2dTexture node connected to the File node. In the Attribute Editor, increase the place2dTexture node's Repeat UV values. Render tests at different frames to determine the best Repeat UV values. For example, in Figure 5.18, the Repeat UV value is set to 10, 10. Note that high Repeat UV values may cause the edges of the repeated tiles to become visible in the reflections. To avoid this, use a bitmap that has similar color values along its top, bottom, left, and right edges. In Figure 5.19, such a bitmap is painted in Photoshop and features a number of soft clouds.

Figure 5.19

Bitmap mapped to the Env Sphere via a File texture. The top, bottom, left, and right edges carry similar color values that help disguise UV tiling. This file is included as `Sky_Reflection.tga` in the `Project3/Textures` folder on the DVD.

6. As a final touch, rotate the projection sphere by selecting the place3dTexture node and entering

different Rotate values in the Channel Box. Different Rotate values will create different reflection patterns. Test the reflections at different frames along the timeline. In Figure 5.18, Rotate is set to 2, 9, 20.

Texturing the Interior

The visible interior of the ambulance is represented by a single surface (named Interior). The surface includes the top of the driver's bench seat, the inner front door panels, the steering wheel, a portion of the dash, and the wall dividing the driver's area from the rear of the ambulance. Because these parts require several types of textures (painted metal, leather, mechanical details, and so on), you will need to paint a custom bitmap. Using the UV snapshot of the surface created in the section "Exporting the UVs" earlier in this chapter, create the bitmap in Photoshop or a similar program. When the bitmap is complete, load it into a File texture mapped to the Color of the material assigned to the Interior surface. For example, in Figure 5.20, a bitmap is created with leather seats and door panel inserts, seams along the door edges, and an access panel and pair of vents installed in the dividing wall. Photos of distressed metal, worn fabric, and various architectural details were cut, copied, pasted, and adjusted in Photoshop.

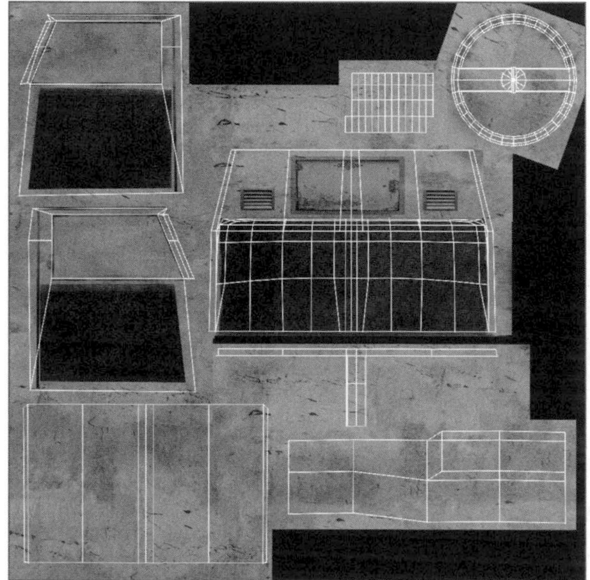

Figure 5.20

(Top) Bitmap painted for Interior surface. The UV snapshot is overlaid for reference, but was deleted before the bitmap was saved to disk. Dark brown areas represent the leather seat and door panels. (Bottom) Resulting render. A sample scene is included as `ambulance-step7.ma` on the DVD.

Texturing the Frame

As discussed earlier in this chapter, the Automatic Mapping tool was applied to the Frame surface, creating myriad small UV shells. As such, it's not necessary to paint a detailed bitmap for the surface. Instead, you can create a generic bitmap that contains the same degree of detail throughout. One trick is to layer various photos of rusty metal in Photoshop to produce a complex result (see Figure 5.21).

After you create a similar bitmap, load it into a File texture mapped to the Color of the material assigned to the Frame surface. When you map a Color attribute, you may need to adjust the material's Diffuse, Eccentricity, Specular Roll Off, and Specular Color attributes. For example, in Figure 5.22, the Frame_ material has its Diffuse value set to 1.0, Eccentricity set to 0.5, Specular Roll Off set to 0.2, and Specular Color set to 0.5, 0.5, 0.5.

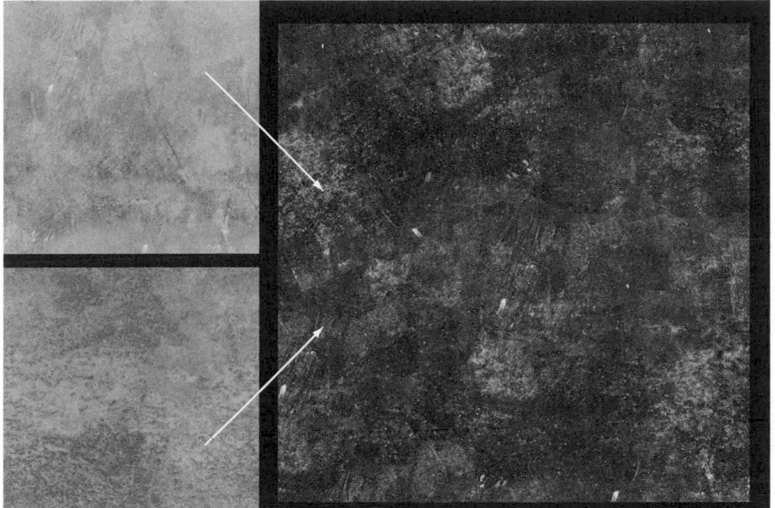

Figure 5.21
Two photo bitmaps of rusty metal are combined and adjusted in Photoshop, producing a new bitmap that will become the color of the Frame surface. The bitmap is included as `Frame_Color.tif` in the `Project3/Textures` folder on the DVD.

Figure 5.22
Detail of bumper, which is part of the Frame surface, after the mapping of a custom bitmap to the material's Color. A sample scene is included as `ambulance-step8.ma` on the DVD.

Texturing the Tires

Each of the ambulance's tires is represented by a single surface (named with the Tire prefix). In order to place dirt on the tire tread and add the tire model name in weathered text on the sidewall, you will need to paint a custom bitmap. Using the UV snapshot of the surface created in the section "Exporting the UVs" earlier in this chapter, construct the bitmap in Photoshop or a similar program. When the bitmap is complete, load it into a File texture mapped to the Color of the materials assigned to the tire surfaces.

To maximize realism, you can create several variations of the bitmap. For example, the first variation is assigned to the front left tire, the second variation is assigned to the front right tire, and so on. In addition, you can make the variations fairly different. The spare tire

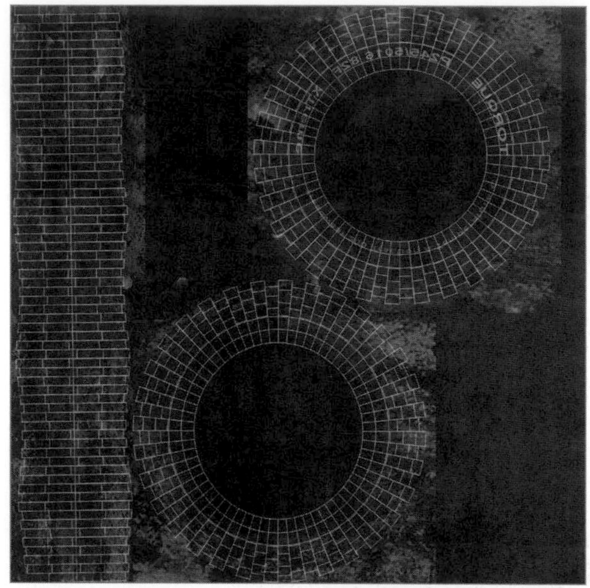

Figure 5.23

(Top) `Tire_1_Color.tga` **bitmap, which is assigned to the front tires through the Tires_Front material. The UV snapshot is overlaid for reference, but was deleted before the bitmap was saved to disk. (Bottom) Resulting render. A sample scene is included as** `ambulance-step9.ma` **on the DVD.**

on the hood might receive a clean texture, while the tires on the ground receive dirtier textures. In Figure 5.23, three variations of the tire bitmap are created: `Tire_1_Color.tga`, `Tire_2_Color.tga`, and `Tire_3_Color.tga`. `Tire_1_Color.tga` is assigned to the front two tires through the Tires_Front material. `Tire_2_Color.tga` is assigned to the rear two tires through the Tires_Rear material. `Tire_3_Color.tga` is assigned to the spare tire through the Tire_Spare material. The initial mapping of the bitmaps caused the text to be mirrored on the tire sidewalls. To correct this, the text layer was flipped horizontally in Photoshop. During the UV mapping process, the UV points of the sidewalls were inadvertently flipped. Hence, before you spend a great deal of time painting bitmap detail, it's best to test the bitmap in Maya to make sure the UV layout holds no surprises.

Displacement Maps

Displacement maps distort geometry at the point of render. That is, the assigned surface is tessellated, and the resulting vertices are translated. The distance the vertices are translated is based on values within the source texture. Although displacement maps are processor intensive, they are more realistic than bump maps. As such, displacement maps provide two main advantages:

- The surface's silhouette is displaced.
- Displaced details cast and receive shadows.

Displacement maps cannot be created through the standard material connections. Instead, you must connect a Displacement Shader to a shading group node. Follow these steps:

1. Select a material node in the Hypershade and open its Attribute Editor tab. Click the Go To Output connection button at the top of the tab (the button is to the left of the Presets button). The tab for the material's shading group node is loaded into the Attribute Editor. Switch to the Shading Group (SG) tab if it's not already selected.
2. Click the Displacement Mat. checkered Map button in the Shading Group Attributes section. Choose a texture from the Create Render Node window. (If you decide to use a File texture, load a bitmap through the File node's Attribute Editor tab.) A displacementShader node is created. The displacement output of the displacementShader is connected to the displacementShader input of the Shading Group node (see Figure 5.24). The outAlpha of the texture node is connected to the displacement input of the displacementShader node. (The displacementShader's input and output channels carry the same name.)

3. Render a test frame. The surface is displaced. (See the next section for example renders.) To reduce the intensity of the displacement, reduce the Alpha Gain attribute, which is found in the Color Balance section of the texture node's Attribute Editor tab (see Figure 5.25). To increase the intensity, raise the Alpha Gain value. If necessary, you can enter values above 2.0 or below 0 in the attribute's number cell. Note that Alpha Gain offers the only ready-made attribute within Maya with which you can adjust the intensity of the displacement. The texture used by the displacementShader node is converted to scalar (grayscale) values through the Out Alpha channel.

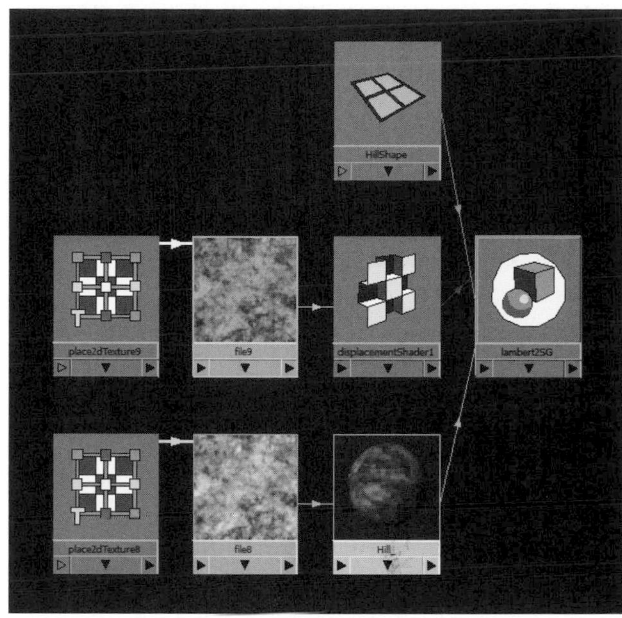

Figure 5.24

A displacementShader node in a shading network

Alpha Gain is a multiplier that's applied to the texture's Out Alpha channel. If Alpha Gain is set to 1.0, the Out Alpha values are unaffected. An Alpha Gain of 0.5 cuts the Out Alpha values in half. An Alpha Gain value of –1 reverses the Out Alpha value; as such, the displacement thereby becomes inverted. An Alpha Gain value of 0 converts the Out Alpha to 0 black, which effectively turns the displacement off. Because the displacement adds a significant amount of time to the render, consider temporarily turning off the displacement as you test other surfaces in the scene.

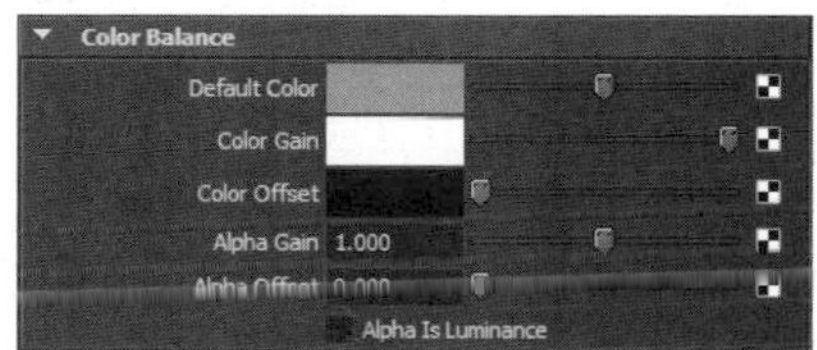

Figure 5.25

The Color Settings section of a texture's Attribute Editor tab

You can also fine-tune the displacement through the Alpha Offset, which is found below Alpha Gain in the Color Balance section. Alpha Offset is an offset for the texture's Out Alpha channel. The Alpha Offset value is added to the Out Alpha value, thus offsetting the displacement; essentially, this raises or lowers the rendered surface in the direction of the polygon faces' surface normals. Note that both Alpha Gain and Alpha Offset also affect the intensity of bump mapping.

In addition to the texture's Attribute Editor tab, you can adjust the attributes found within the Displacement Map section of the displaced surface's shape node Attribute Editor tab (see Figure 5.26).

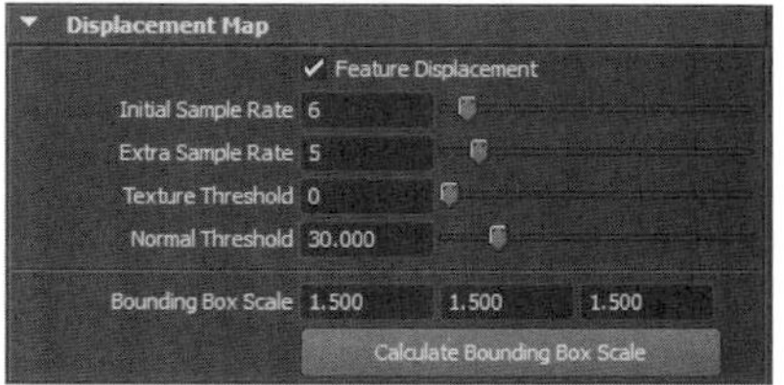

Figure 5.26

The Displacement Map section of a surface shape node's Attribute Editor tab

The attributes found in this section control the way in which the surface is tessellated and shaded during the displacement process. Descriptions of the most critical attributes follow:

Feature Displacement Feature Displacement toggles on or off feature-based displacement. If selected, the Displacement Shader tessellates the assigned surface in only those areas where displaced features occur. If deselected, the Displacement Shader adds no additional tessellation; in this case, the detail in the displacement map may be lost if the surface does not have a sufficient number of subdivisions. Maya attempts to make up for the loss of detail inherent with non-feature-based displacement by simultaneously treating the displacement map as a bump map.

Initial Sample Rate and Extra Sample Rate Initial Sample Rate determines the size of the sampling grid laid over each polygon triangle (a quadrangular face is made up of two triangles). The grid is used to determine whether the triangle should be subdivided into additional triangular faces (that is, tessellated). Subdivision is deemed necessary if the contrast between neighboring pixels in the displacement texture is sufficient. Extra Sample Rate adds additional sampling. In effect, Extra Sample Rate further subdivides the sampling grid applied by the Initial Sample Rate.

Texture Threshold Texture Threshold eliminates unneeded vertices and aims to reduce noise within the displacement. The Texture Threshold value is a percentage of the maximum height variation within a displacement. A vertex is removed if its difference in height with neighboring vertices is below the Texture Threshold value. The default value of 0 leaves this feature off. When raising the value, do so incrementally. If possible, eliminate any fine noise with the texture before mapping it to the Displacement Shader.

Normal Threshold Normal Threshold controls the "softness" of the resulting displacement. The attribute's functionality is identical to Set Normal Angle (Set → Set Normal Angle in the Polygons menu set). If the angle between two adjacent triangles is less than the Normal Threshold value, the triangles are rendered smoothly. If not, the triangles are rendered with a sharp edge between them.

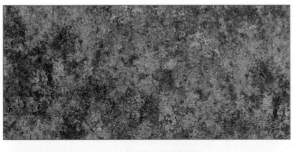

Figure 5.27

(Top) Bitmap created as a color map for the hill. The file is included as `Hill_Color.tif` in the `Project3/Textures` folder on the DVD. (Bottom) Resulting render

Project: Displacing the Hill

Although the Hill surface is modeled with a number of undulations, it does not carry fine detail. To create the illusion that the hill is covered by rocks, stones, and dirt, as well as cracks and crevices, you can create the custom color bitmap. Because there are no specific features of the hill that require isolation or exaggeration, you can create a generic bitmap that features an organic pattern. Once again, combining photos of varied surfaces in Photoshop can give you a complex result. For example, in Figure 5.27, a bitmap is created by combining photos of small rocks, dirt, and rusty metal. When the bitmap is loaded into the File texture mapped to the Color of the material assigned to the Hill surface, the render becomes more realistic. Because the hill is the largest surface in the scene and occupies a large portion of the rendered frame, the size of the bitmap is set to 3072×3072. A smaller size would reveal blockiness (pixelization) within the texture.

Unfortunately, a texture mapped to the Color of a material cannot affect the bumpiness of a surface. As an additional step, you can map the bitmap to the Bump Mapping attribute. However, a bump map is unable to perturb the silhouette edges of a surface. Hence, a displacement map may be the most suitable solution. Following the steps outlined in the previous section, add a displacement map to the material assigned to the Hill surface. You can reuse the bitmap created for the Color attribute or you can create a brand new bitmap. One trick is to desaturate the color bitmap, increase its contrast, and save it under a new name. For example, in Figure 5.28, such an approach creates a suitable displacement.

Figure 5.28

(Top) Bitmap created as a displacement map for the hill. The file is included as `Hill_Displace.tif` in the `Project3/Textures` folder on the DVD. (Bottom) Resulting render. A sample scene is included as `ambulance-step10.ma` on the DVD.

If the intensity of the displacement is too severe or too subtle, adjust the Alpha Gain attribute in the File node's Attribute Editor tab. The render illustrated by Figure 5.28 has the Alpha Gain set to 0.35. (At this stage, the surface's Displacement Map attributes have not been adjusted; they will be fine-tuned in Chapter 6.)

Adding a displacement will slow the render significantly. When you proceed to texture other parts of the scene, consider temporarily turning off the displacement by setting the Alpha Gain to 0.

Paint Effects

Paint Effects is a powerful tool that allows you to interactively paint specialized strokes that create complex geometry as a post-process. Numerous Paint Effects brushes are included with Maya and are grouped in such categories as trees, flowers, weather, and fire (see Figure 5.29).

To create a Paint Effects stroke, follow these steps:

1. Select a surface with valid UVs. Switch to the Rendering menu set. Choose Paint Effects → Make Paintable.
2. Choose Paint Effects → Get Brush. The Visor window opens. Select a brush folder, such as Grasses. Select a brush style by clicking a Paint Effects icon. Close the Visor.

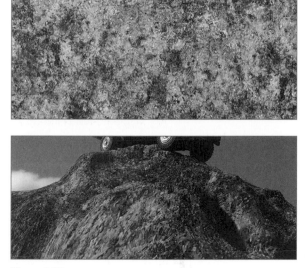

Figure 5.29

Various Paint Effects grass brushes, as shown in the Visor

3. Click+drag the mouse over the chosen surface. The Paint Effects stroke is laid over the surface, and the Paint Effects tube will grow from it. When you release the mouse button, the stroke is ended. You can add additional strokes by click+dragging again. You can retrieve a new brush style at any time by choosing Paint Effects → Get Brush. You can delete a stroke by selecting the associated stroke node in the Hypergraph or Outliner.
4. Render a test (Paint Effects is supported by Maya Software, but not mental ray). The Paint Effects brush is laid over the geometry after the initial render is complete.

Although Paint Effects brushes can create convincing results, they are unable to cover large areas effectively. For example, you can use the tool to paint patches of grass, weeds, or trees, but filling the entire park, meadow, or forest would be impractical in terms of render times and render stability.

Project: Painting Grass

To add plant life to the ambulance scene, you can paint several Paint Effects strokes. Following the steps in the previous section, choose the Cactus Grass Paint Effects brush (in the `Grasses` folder) and paint on the hill surface. Make your strokes fairly short, as multiple individual plants are spaced along the stroke. Initially, the plants will appear too small. You can adjust the size, and other render properties, through the brush tab in the Attribute Editor. You can access the tab by selecting a stroke node in the Hypergraph. The tab is to the right of the strokeShape tab and is named after the brush type (for example: cactusGrass1). Note that each stroke receives its own brush node, and thereby its own set of attributes.

The second topmost attribute in the brush tab is Global Size, which controls the size of the plants or other painted objects. Set Global Size to a value between 5 and 10 (see Figure 5.30).

By default, the plants are grown along the surface normal. Thus, the plants may appear to grow sideways out of the hill. To override this property, adjust the values in the Width Scale subsection. To access the subsection, expand the Tubes section first. In particular, adjusting the Elevation Min and Elevation Max will affect the orientation of the plants along their stroke. Appropriate values depend on the location of the stroke. Interactively adjusting the sliders will have an immediate effect on the plants shown in the view panels. An additional problem befalling Paint Effects plants is the similarity between plant iterations. You can add a greater degree of randomness by raising the Random attribute value in the Forces subsection. You can access the subsection by expanding the Growth section first.

Figure 5.30

Three Cactus Grass strokes painted on the hill surface. Their Global Size attributes have been adjusted to values between 5 and 10. In addition, their Elevation Min, Elevation Max, and Random values have been adjusted so the plants grow upright and in a nonpredictable fashion. A sample scene is included as `ambulance-step11.ma` on the DVD.

By default, Paint Effects brushes do not cast shadows. However, you can activate several shadow types through the Shadow Effects section (see Figure 5.31). The Cast Shadows check box, if selected, forces the Paint Effects geometry (which is composed of primitive tubes) to be included in depth map shadow calculations. However, unless the depth map shadow Resolution is very large, the shadow will become blocky and pixelated. Alternatively, if the Fake Shadow attribute is set to 3D Cast, a simulated cast shadow is added without affecting the original depth map. 3D Cast shadows lack the fine detail of a high-resolution depth map shadow but render quickly. For this stage of the tutorial, 3D Cast shadows is sufficient. You can fine-tune the appearance of the 3D Cast shadow by adjusting the Shadow Diffusion and Shadow Transp. settings. Shadow Diffusion controls the softness of the shadow edge, and Shadow Transp. controls the shadow opacity.

The addition of Paint Effects strokes concludes step 1 of "Lighting and Texturing a Vehicle." As such, your render should look similar to Figure 5.30. In Chapter 6, we'll continue to build and refine texture maps for the ambulance, improve the shadows, and adjust the hill displacement.

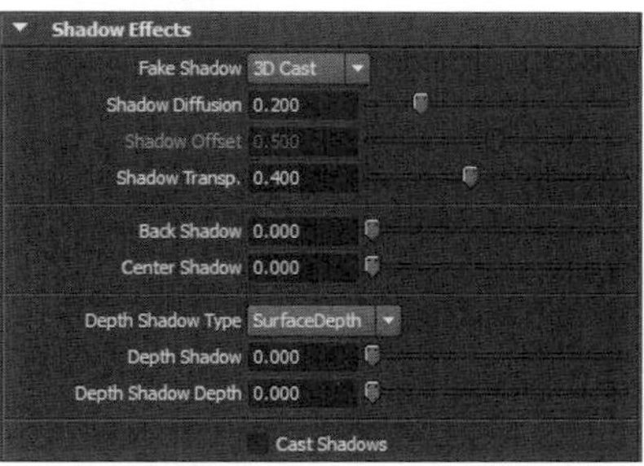

Figure 5.31

The Shadow Effects section of a brush node's Attribute Editor tab

Texturing and Lighting a Vehicle, Part 2

In Chapter 5, "Texturing and Lighting a Vehicle, Part 1," you textured and lit an ambulance on a hill. In this chapter, you'll continue the texturing process and fine-tune the render settings. Part 2 of the project will guide you through the following steps:

- **Completing the texture maps**
- **Refining the materials**
- **Adding motion blur**
- **Breaking the scene into render layers**
- **Adding reflectivity**
- **Creating the final render**

In addition, important lighting and texturing theory is included as follows:

- **Motion blur**
- **The Render Layer Editor**

Project: Completing the Texture Maps

To begin this phase of the tutorial, open the scene file you created for the last step of Chapter 5. A completed sample file is saved as `ambulance-step11.ma` in the `ProjectFiles/Project3` folder on the DVD.

When opening sample scene files for this chapter and Chapter 5, you can avoid missing bitmap textures by first choosing File → Project → Set and browsing for the `Project3` folder, whether the folder remains at its original location on the DVD or is located on a drive after the DVD contents have been copied.

Texturing the Body

The Body surface of the ambulance model possesses the most complex UV layout. Fortunately, the UV shells are laid out in such a manner that most parts of the vehicle are easily recognizable. As with other complex parts of the ambulance, the best solution for texturing requires a custom bitmap. Using the UV snapshot of the surface created in the section "Exporting the UVs" in Chapter 5, construct the bitmap in Photoshop or a similar program. When the bitmap is complete, load it into a File texture mapped to the Color of the material assigned to the Body surface. An example is illustrated in Figure 6.1.

Texturing the Side Mirrors

The side mirrors are separate surfaces. To make the surfaces appear as if they are covered with distressed chrome, you can map a dark bitmap texture to the material Color attribute and connect the Reflected Color attribute to the environment texture used by the Glass surface material. Follow these steps:

1. In the Hypershade, select the material assigned to the Mirror_R surface and open its Attribute Editor tab. Click the checkered Map button beside Color. In the Create Render Node window, click the File texture icon. In the new File node's Attribute Editor tab, browse for a bitmap. The bitmap should feature a dark, noisy pattern. For example, in Figure 6.2, a photo of dark metal is used.
2. Return to the material's Attribute Editor tab. Set the Eccentricity to 0. Because the Reflected Color attribute will be mapped, it's not necessary to see a specular highlight. (In reality, specular highlights are reflections of bright light sources.) Set Specular Roll Off to 1.0. Set Specular Color to 2.0, 2.0, 2.0 in RGB. This increases the intensity of the reflections.
3. Return to the Hypershade window. MMB+drag the material assigned to the Mirror_R surface into the work area. MMB+drag the material assigned to the Glass surface into the work area. In the example scene files, the materials are named Mirror_R_ and Glass_. In the work area, Shift+click the two material nodes. Click the Input And Output

Connections button. This reveals the shading networks for both materials (see Figure 6.3). MMB+drag the envSphere node connected to the glass material and drop it on top of the mirror material node. The Connect Input Of menu opens. Choose reflectedColor from the menu. A connection is made between the envSphere node's Out Color attribute and the mirror material's Reflected Color attribute (see Figure 6.3). With this step, the environment texture of the glass material provides a reflection to the mirror material.

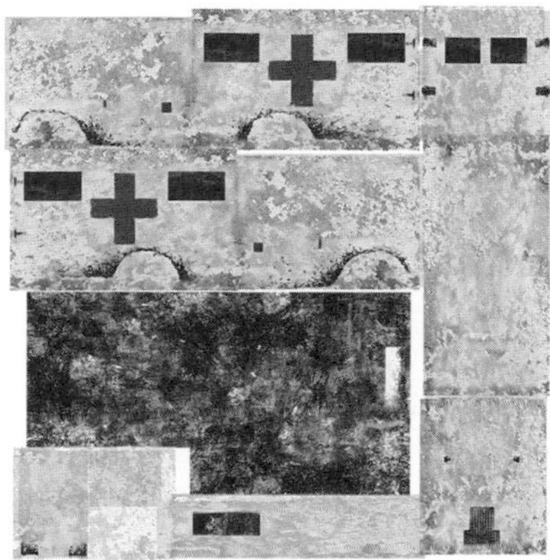

Figure 6.1

(Left) Bitmap created as a Color map for the ambulance body. The file is included as `Body_Color.tif` **in the** `ProjectFiles/Project3/Textures` **folder on the DVD. (Right) Resulting render. The displacement of the hill is temporarily turned off to save render time. A sample file is included as** `ambulance-step12.ma` **on the DVD. For a color version of this figure, see the color insert.**

4. In the Hypershade work area, MMB+drag the File texture node created in step 1 and drop it on top of the mirror material node. The Connect Input Of menu opens. Choose Other from the menu. The Connection Editor opens. In the left column, click the word *Out Alpha.* In the right column, all the attributes that require three channels are grayed out. In the right column, scroll down and click the word *Reflectivity.* A connection is made; a grayscale version of the File texture controls the reflective strength of the Mirror_R surface. Mapping the Reflectivity creates the illusion that the chrome surface is aged or dirty (see Figure 6.4).
5. Repeat steps 1 to 4 for the Mirror_L surface.

Figure 6.2

Bitmap used as a Color map for the Mirror surfaces. The file is included as `Mirror_Color.tif` **in the** `ProjectFiles/Project3/Textures` **folder on the DVD.**

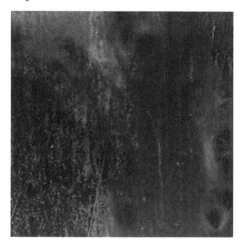

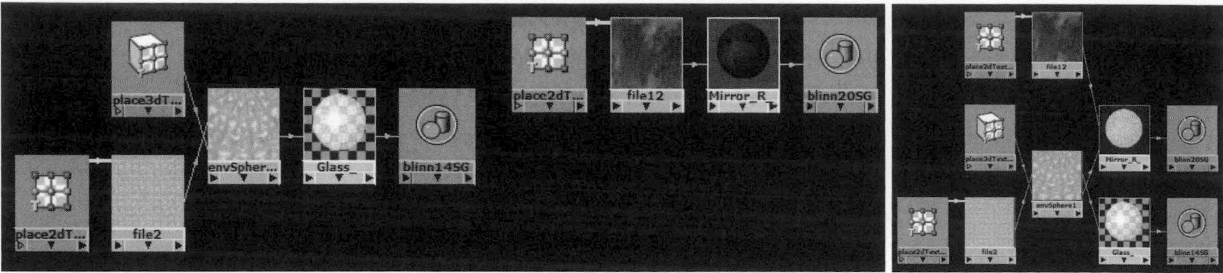

Figure 6.3

(Left) The shading networks for the Glass_ and Mirror_R_ materials, as seen in the Hypershade work area. (Right) Shading networks after the Out Color attribute of the envSphere node is connected to the Reflected Color attribute of the Mirror_R_ material.

Figure 6.4

The side mirrors reflect unevenly through a custom shading network. A sample file is included as `ambulance-step13.ma` **on the DVD.**

Texturing the Headlights, Fog Lights, and Signal Lights

The headlight, fog light, and signal light surfaces require complex texturing. For example, to make the headlight and fog light rings appear chrome-like and the center lenses appear glass-like, you will need to create custom bitmaps for the assigned materials' Color, Transparency, Bump Mapping, and Reflectivity attributes. Follow these steps:

1. Using Photoshop or a similar program, open the UV snapshot of a light surface created in the section "Exporting the UVs" in Chapter 5 (see Figure 6.5). The headlights, fog lights, and signal lights possess identical geometry, so a UV snapshot of any single light can be used for all the lights. Paint the bitmap to represent the transparency of the light lens. To make the lens appear dirty, vary the gray tone used for the bitmap. For example, in Figure 6.5, a bitmap features dark specks in the lens area. When the bitmap is complete, map it to the Transparency attribute of the material assigned to the headlight and fog light surfaces. In the example scene files, a material named Lights is assigned to all the headlight and fog light surfaces.
2. Return to Photoshop. Create a new bitmap that represents the color of the lights. Paint a noisy brown pattern in the lens area and a dark gray pattern in the edge ring areas (see Figure 6.6). Because the lens portion of the geometry receives transparency information from the transparency bitmap, the brown color will show only in the areas

where the transparency bitmap is gray. When the color bitmap is complete, map it to the Color attribute of the material assigned to the headlight and fog light surfaces. Render a test. The lights possess transparency in the lens area (see Figure 6.6).

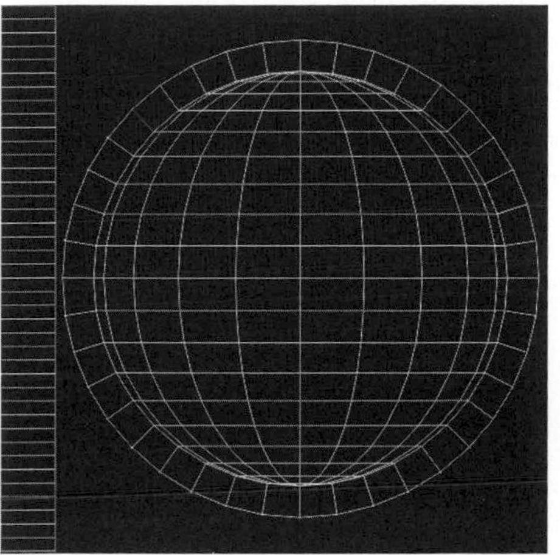

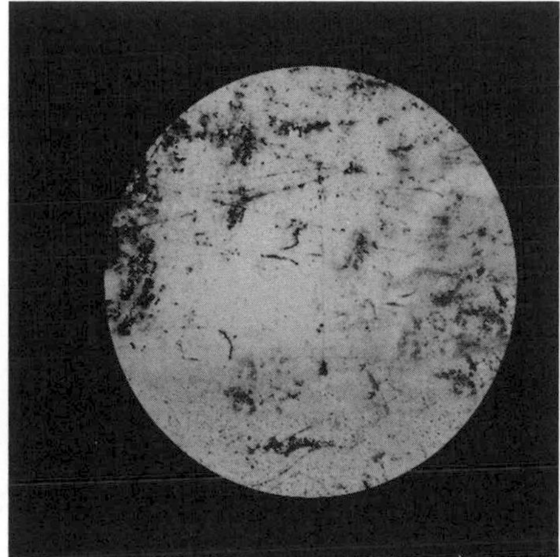

Figure 6.5

(Left) A UV snapshot that's usable for all headlight, fog light, taillight, and signal light surfaces. (Right) Bitmap created to establish the light lens transparency. The file is included as `Headlight_Trans.tif` in the `ProjectFiles/Project3/Textures` folder on the DVD.

3. Return to the Hypershade window. MMB+drag the material assigned to the headlight and fog light surfaces into the work area. MMB+drag the material assigned to the Glass surface into the work area. In the example scene files, the materials are named Lights and Glass_. In the work area, Shift+click the two material nodes. Click the Input And Output Connections button. This reveals the shading networks for both materials. MMB+drag the envSphere node connected to the glass material and drop it on top of the headlight material node. The Connect Input Of menu opens. Choose reflectedColor from the menu. A connection is made between the envSphere node's Out Color attribute and the material's Reflected Color attribute (see Figure 6.7). With this step, the environment texture of the glass material provides a reflection to the material assigned to the headlight and fog light surfaces. Render a test. The blue of the sky appears on the headlights and fog lights.
4. If you wish to vary the amount of reflectivity between the headlight and fog light rings and

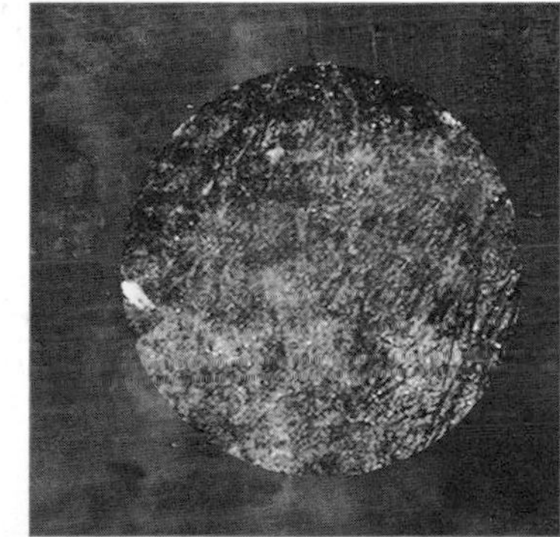

Figure 6.6

(Top) Bitmap created to establish the color of the lens and outer ring for the headlights. The file is included as `Headlight_Color.tif` in the `ProjectFiles/Project3/Textures` folder on the DVD. (Bottom) Resulting render

lenses, you will need to create a Reflectivity bitmap. For example, in Figure 6.8, such a bitmap gives the ring areas the maximum default reflectivity by carrying values that are close to 1.0 white. In contrast, the lens area carries values close to 0.5 gray. The resulting render improves the illusion that the rings are chrome. However, the Reflected Color attribute provides only blue and white for the reflection. This is due to the Reflected Color deriving its values from the envSphere of the glass material. A more convincing chrome must include darker reflection of surrounding ambulance surfaces and the ground. To do this, you must activate raytracing; this will be carried out in a later section of this chapter.

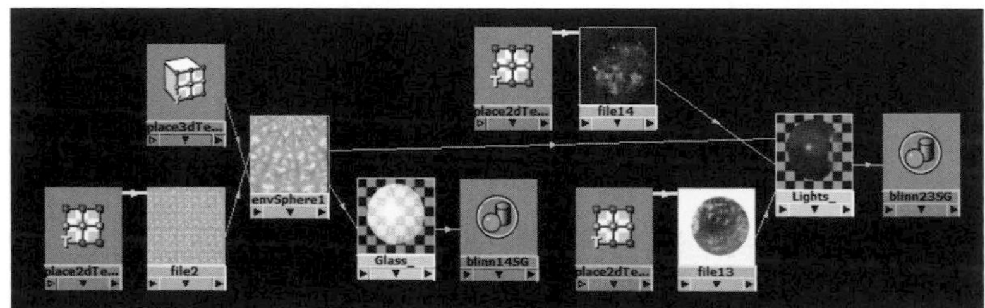

Figure 6.7
(Top) Shading networks after the Out Color attribute of the envSphere node is connected to the Reflected Color attribute of the Lights material, which is assigned to the headlight and fog light surfaces. (Bottom) Resulting render

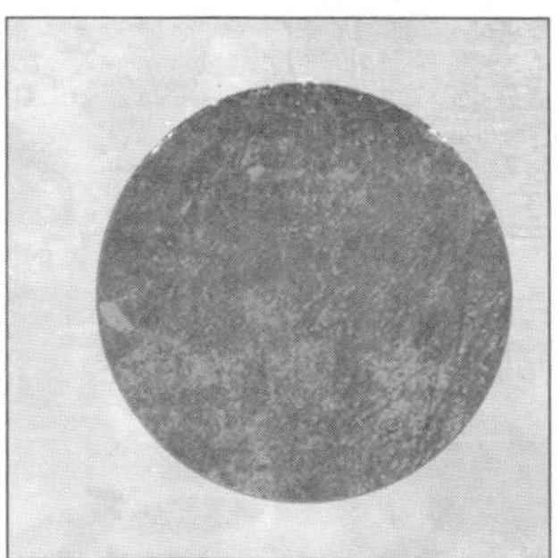

Figure 6.8
(Left) Bitmap created to establish the reflectivity of the lens and outer ring for the headlights and fog lights. The file is included as `Headlight_Ref.tif` in the `ProjectFiless/Project3/Textures` folder on the DVD. (Right) Resulting render. To add reflections of dark objects, such as the bumper or ground, it will be necessary to activate raytracing; this will be carried out in a later section of this chapter. For a color version of this figure, see the color insert.

Adding Light Buckets

Unfortunately, the transparency of the light lenses reveals that there is no geometry to represent the light bucket or lightbulb. You can create the illusion that there is an internal structure to the lights by revising the color bitmap employed by the ambulance body. For example, in Figure 6.9, steel light buckets are added to the section of the body color bitmap that includes the front of the ambulance. Because the UV layout vertically stretches the front of the ambulance, the light buckets require an oval shape. In this case, the overall reflectivity of the headlights and fog lights is lowered to allow the bucket detail to show through. A quick way to reduce the overall reflectivity is to lower the assigned material's Specular Color value. For the render in Figure 6.9, the Specular Color of the Lights_ material is set to 0.4, 0.4, 0.4 in RGB.

Figure 6.9

(Top) Detail of the revised ambulance body color bitmap. The light buckets appear elongated because the UV layout stretches the ambulance front in a vertical manner. The file is included as `Body_Color_Headlights.tif` in the `ProjectFiles/Project3/Textures` folder on the DVD. (Bottom) Resulting render. A sample file is included as `ambulance-step14.ma` on the DVD.

Because there is no direct correlation between the ambulance geometry and the positions of the light buckets, it may be difficult to line up such detail on the revised bitmap. Here are two tips for making the process easier:

- Activate Smooth Shading and Hardware Texturing through a view panel menu. The color bitmap detail will appear in the 3D view. After the revised color bitmap is loaded, you will be able to see whether the newly painted detail is misaligned with the headlight and fog light geometry (see Figure 6.10).

- Temporarily re-add the UV snapshot to the color bitmap. You can use the UV layout as a rough reference. For example, each fog light sits over the edge between two faces; the edge runs horizontally across the lower quarter of the Foglight geometry. To re-add the UV snapshot, open the UV snapshot bitmap in Photoshop, draw a selection marquee around the entire bitmap, choose Edit → Copy, open the body color bitmap, choose Edit → Paste, and change the new layer's Blending Mode menu to Screen.

Figure 6.10

Smooth Shading and Hardware Texturing are activated for a view panel. The detail within the ambulance body's color bitmap becomes visible. With this view, the misalignment of the detail of the headlight bucket at the right of the screen becomes obvious.

Texturing the Signal Lights

To texture the signal lights, you can follow the steps outlined in the previous two sections. To color the lights orange, reduce the strength of the material's specularity, reflectivity, and transparency while tinting the bitmap mapped to the Color attribute.

A quick way to create an appropriate material for the signal lights is to duplicate the material assigned to the headlights and adapt it. You can follow these steps to create a material for the signal light surfaces:

1. In the Hypershade, select the material assigned to the headlight geometry. From the Hypershade menu, choose Edit → Duplicate → Shading Network. The material is duplicated along with all its connections.
2. In the Hypershade, select the material assigned to the signal light surfaces. In the example scene files, the material is named Signal_Lights. From the Hypershade menu, choose Edit → Select Objects With Materials. All the signal light surfaces are selected automatically. RMB+click the newly duplicated material and choose Assign Material To Selection. You can delete the material the signal lights were once assigned to, which is now unneeded, by selecting the node icon and pressing the Delete key. Rename the newly duplicated material a logical name. You can use the same name that the deleted material once had.
3. RMB+click the newly duplicated material and choose Graph Network from the marking menu. The material's shading network is revealed in the work area. Open the

Attribute Editor tab for the File node that is connected to the material's Color attribute. Change the Color Offset to orange. This tints the entire bitmap. Locate the File node connected to the material's Transparency attribute. Select the node and delete it. Open the Attribute Editor tab for the material. Change the Transparency to 0.15, 0.15, 0.15 in RGB. Deleting the transparency map and reducing the Transparency value allows the orange tint to show. Change Specular Roll Off to 0.2 and Specular Color to 0.25, 0.25, 0.25 in RGB. This reduces the strength of the Reflected Color, which would otherwise interfere with the orange tint. (The Reflected Color values are added to the Color values of a material.) Open the Attribute Editor tab for the File node connected to the material's Reflectivity attribute. Change the Color Gain to 0.25, 0.25, 0.25 in RGB. By reducing the overall reflectivity of the surface, the orange tint is strengthened once again. Render a test. The result should appear similar to Figure 6.11.

Texturing the Suspension

At this stage of the project, several of the suspension components lack detail. The components include the Steering Arm, Steering Front_L, Steering_Front_R, Axle_Front, Axle_Rear, Driveshaft, Spring_Front_L, Spring_Front_R, Spring_Rear_L, and Spring_Rear_R surfaces. Because these surfaces are barely seen by the camera and fall within the ambulance's shadow, you can apply a generic texture to the assigned materials. For example, in Figure 6.12, a section of the `Body_Color.tif` bitmap is copied to a new bitmap named `Suspension_Generic.tif`. The new bitmap is mapped to the Color attribute of the Axles, Driveshaft, Spring_Front, Springs_Rear, Steering_Arm_, and Steering_Front materials. To create variation between these materials, the `Suspension_Generic.tif` bitmap is offset by changing the Repeat UV and Rotate UV values of the associated `place2dTexture` nodes.

Figure 6.11

Detail of signal lights. A duplicate of the material assigned to the headlight surfaces is tinted orange via the Color Offset attribute. A sample file is included as `ambulance-step15.ma` **on the DVD.**

Figure 6.12

Generic color bitmap created for various suspension components. The file is included as `Suspension_Generic.tif` **in the** `ProjectFiles/Project3/Textures` **folder on the DVD.**

Texturing the Warning Light

The Warning_Light surface, which sits above the ambulance window, features a UV texture space that carries four UV shells. To place a cross logo on the forward lens, you must create a custom bitmap (see Figure 6.13).

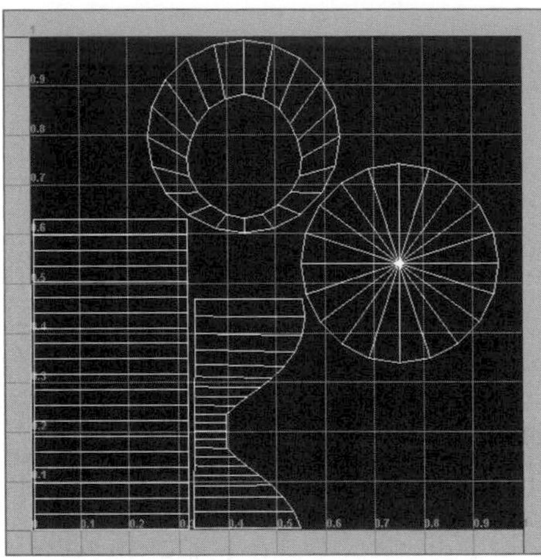

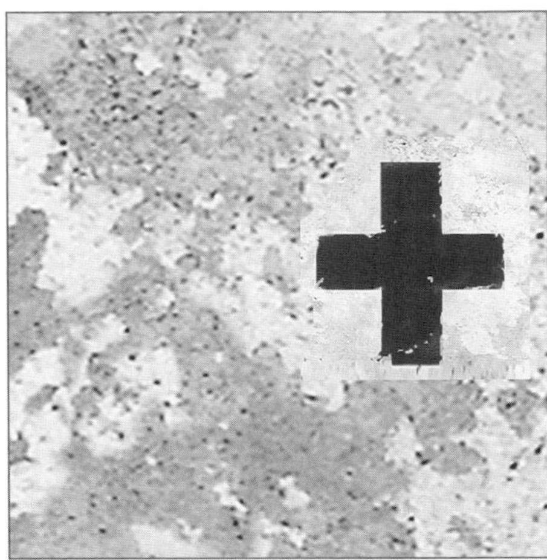

Figure 6.13

(Left) The UV layout of the Warning_Light surface. (Right) Custom bitmap used as a Color map for the Warning_Light surface. The file is included as `Warning_Color.tif` in the `Project Files/Project3/Textures` folder on the DVD.

To create the illusion that the Warning_Light surface surrounds a light source, such as a lightbulb, you can map the assigned material's Incandescence attribute. In such a situation, the black part of the map represents no incandescent strength, while gray represents moderate incandescent strength (see Figure 6.14). High Incandescence map values will wash out the surface and make it appear white.

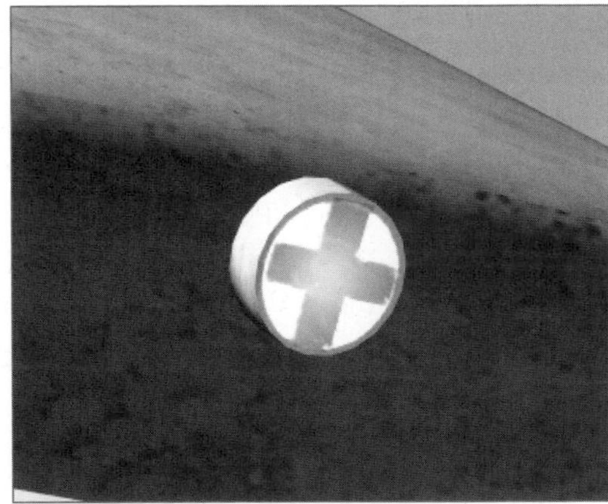

Figure 6.14

(Left) Custom bitmap used as an Incandescence map for the Warning_Light surface. The file is included as `Warning_Incan.tif` in the `Project Files/Project3/Textures` folder on the DVD. (Right) Resulting render. A sample file is included as `ambulance-step16.ma` on the DVD.

Note that the ambulance taillight surfaces carry their own unique UV layout. As such, you can create custom Color and Incandescence bitmaps for the taillights. However, because the taillights are not visible from the Render camera view, they are not textured as part of this project.

Texturing the Rims

The wheel rims are the last surface to require custom bitmaps. As with the bitmap created for the ambulance body, the inclusion of dirt and general wear-and-tear will add additional realism. Note that the UV layout for the front rims and rear rims is slightly different. This requires the creation of two different color bitmaps (see Figure 6.15). The Rim_Spare surface shares the same UV layout as the rear rim surfaces (minus the central faces); however, because the spare tire is mounted on the hood, the color texture need not be as dirty (see Figure 6.15).

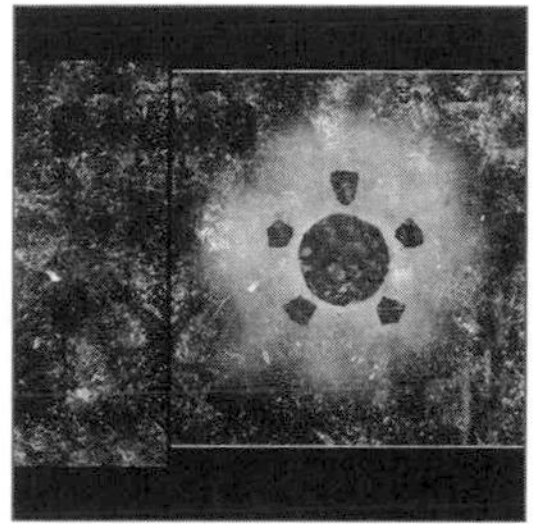

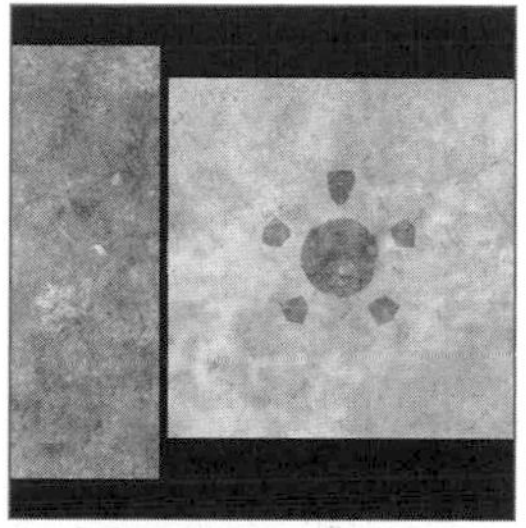

Figure 6.15

(Top Left) A custom color bitmap created for the Rim_Rear_L and Rim_Rear_R surfaces. The file is included as `Rim_Rear_Color.tif` in the `ProjectFiles/Project3/Textures` folder on the DVD. (Top Center) Color bitmap created for the Rim_Front_L and Rim_Front_R surfaces. The file is included as `Rim_Front_Color.tif`. (Top Right) Color bitmap created for the Rim_Spare surface. The file is included as `Rim_Spare_Color.tif`. (Bottom) Resulting render. A sample file is included as `ambulance-step17.ma` on the DVD.

Project: Refining the Materials

Thus far, you've created custom color, transparency, reflectivity, and incandescence bitmaps for the majority of surfaces in the ambulance scene. Although this has provided a suitable render, you can continue to refine the various materials. In particular, the addition of bump maps and specular maps will increase the realism. In addition, you can add greater variation to the surfaces by duplicating materials and adjusting the attributes of the duplicates.

Adding Bump Maps

Bump maps can add missing roughness to a surface. Whereas displacement maps displace the positions of surface vertices, bump maps simply perturb surface normals at the point of render. This makes bump maps very efficient. Hence, you can add bump maps to many of the ambulance surfaces without unduly impacting render times. Although you can create custom bump map bitmaps from scratch, you can also reuse bitmaps previously mapped to Color attributes. For example, use the following steps to reuse the color bitmap created for the ambulance body:

1. In the Hypershade, locate the material assigned to the Body surface. RMB+click the material and choose Graph Network. The material's shading network is revealed in the work area.
2. In the work area, MMB+drag the File node that carries the color bitmap and drop it on top of the material icon. The Connect Input Of menu opens. Choose Bump Map from the menu. A Bump 2d node is inserted automatically into the network (see Figure 6.16). Hence, the File node's output is sent to the Bump 2d node and the material node simultaneously. Whereas the Out Color attribute of the File node is connected to the Color attribute of the material node, the Out Alpha attribute of the File node is connected to the Bump Value attribute of the Bump 2d node. Because Out Alpha is a scalar channel, the color RGB values of the bitmap are converted to alpha values. For example, 0.2, 0.5, 0.4 in RGB (dark green) is converted 0.399 by Out Alpha.

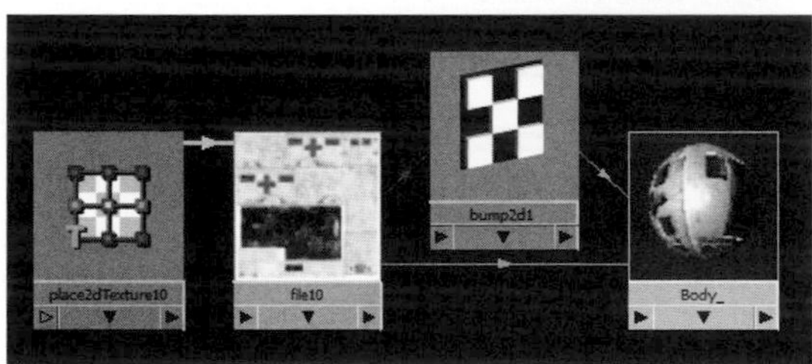

Figure 6.16
A Bump 2d node is inserted into the shading network of the Body_ material.

3. Render a test. The bump appears too strong (see Figure 6.17). To reduce the strength, lower the Bump Value attribute, which is found in the Bump 2d node's Attribute Editor tab. You can also reverse the effect of the bump by giving the Bump Value a negative number. For example, a Bump Value of –0.02 adds a subtle roughness to the ambulance body. This is most noticeable around the wheel wells, where the dirt splatters present the most contrast and thus "bump up" the most.

Other ambulance surfaces can benefit from the reutilization of color bitmaps as bump bitmaps. These include the rims, tires, the frame, and various visible suspension components. Table 6.1 includes a list of materials used in the sample scene files, their assigned surfaces, and the Bump Value amounts used for the Bump 2d node inserted into their shading networks.

Figure 6.17

(Left) The initial application of a bump map makes the ambulance appear extremely rough. (Right) A Bump Value of –0.02 makes the bump more subtle and believable. A sample file is included as `ambulance-step18.ma` on the DVD.

Table 6.1

Materials, assigned surfaces, and Bump Value amounts

MATERIAL NAME	ASSIGNED SURFACES	BUMP VALUE AMOUNTS
Body_	Body	–0.2
Frame_	Frame	0.3
Rims_Front	Rim_Front_L	0.3
	Rim_Front_R	
Rims_Rear	Rim_Rear_L	0.3
	Rim_Rear_R	
Springs_Front	Springs_Front_L	0.4
	Springs_Front_R	
Springs_Rear	Springs_Rear_L	0.4
	Springs_Rear_R	
Steering_Front	Steering_Front_L	0.4
	Steering_Front_R	
Tires_Front	Tire_Front_L	1
	Tire_Front_R	
Tires_Rear	Tire_Rear_L	1
	Tire_Rear_R	

Layering Bump Maps

One disadvantage of reutilizing color bitmaps as bump bitmaps is the lack of variation. That is, only detail contained in the color bitmap is applied as a bump, and no new information is provided. You can overcome this trait, however, by layering together textures in the Hypershade to create a more complex bump result. For example, to add rivets to the side of the ambulance body, follow these steps:

1. In Photoshop or a similar program, paint a bitmap that represents rows of rivets. To emulate rivets, you can create rows and columns of gray dots or circles against an otherwise white background (see Figure 6.18). Use the UV snapshot of the ambulance as a reference when choosing the rivet positions.
2. Return to Maya and open the Hypershade window. RMB+click the material assigned to the Body surface and choose Graph Network from the marking menu. The material's shading network is revealed in the work area.
3. In the work area, click the connection line between the Bump 2d node and the File node that carries the color bitmap. In the sample scene files, the connection line runs between file10 and bump2d1. When the connection line is selected, it turns yellow. Press the Delete key. The connection is broken. Click the phrase *2D Textures* in the Create tab of the Hypershade. Click the File texture icon. A new File node (and matching place2dTexture node) appears in the work area but remains unconnected to any shading network. MMB+drag the new File node and drop it on top of the Bump 2d node. The Connect Input Of menu opens. Choose Default from the menu. The Out Alpha attribute of the File node is connected to the Bump Value attribute of the Bump 2d node.

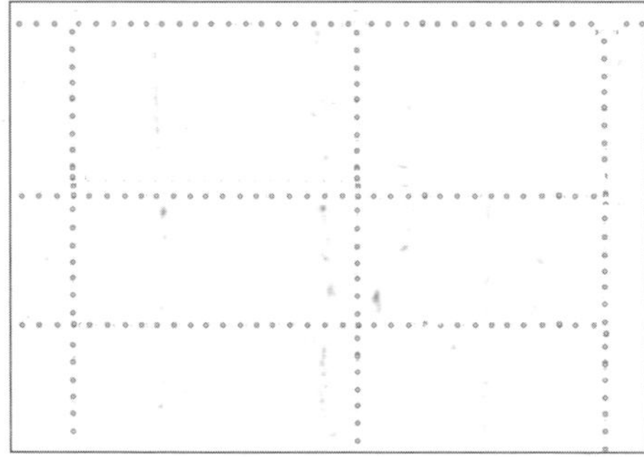

Figure 6.18
Detail of custom bump bitmap created to create rows and columns of rivets. The file is included as `Body_Rivets_Bump.tif` in the `ProjectFiles/Project3/Textures` folder on the DVD.

4. Open the new File node's Attribute Editor tab. Browse for the bitmap you created in step 1. Return to the Hypershade work area. MMB+drag the original File node that carries the color bitmap and drop it on top of the new File node that now carries the rivet bitmap. The Connect Input Of menu opens. Choose Other from the menu. The Connection window opens. In the left column, click the word *outAlpha*. In the right column, click the word *alphaGain*. Close the Connection Editor window. (See Figure 6.19 for the final shading network configuration.) By connecting the Out Alpha attribute of the color bitmap to the Alpha Gain attribute of the rivet bitmap, the rivet bitmap Out Alpha values are multiplied by the color bitmap Out Alpha values. This darkens the rivet bitmap and essentially combines both bitmaps so they can be used by a single Bump 2d node. Render a test. The rivet pattern appears on the ambulance side as a bump map (see Figure 6.20). In addition, the bump information provided by the color bitmap continues to appear. For example, the dirt splotches by the wheel wells remain "bumped out."

Applying Procedural Bump Maps

Although Maya's procedural textures cannot take the place of custom bitmap textures in many situations, they can be useful for small details. For example, to give the headlight, fog light, and signal light lenses the appearance that they are formed of molded, ridged glass, you can apply Bulge and Ramp textures as bump maps. To do so, follow these steps:

1. In the Hypershade window, identify the material assigned to the headlight surfaces and open its Attribute Editor tab. In the sample scene files, the material is named Lights_. Click the checkered Map button beside Bump Mapping. In the Create Render Node window, click the Bulge texture icon. A new Bulge node, along with a new Bump 2d node, is added to the material's shading network. Open the Bulge node's place2dTexture node in the Attribute Editor tab. Change the Repeat UV value to 20, 10. This creates a larger number of bulge squares, which will be suitable for the ridges found on many headlights' lenses.
2. Open the new Bulge node's Attribute Editor tab. Click the checkered Map button beside Alpha Gain (in the Color Balance section). In the Create Render Node window, click the Ramp texture icon. Open the new Ramp node's Attribute Editor tab. Change Type to Circular Ramp and Interpolation to None. Delete the center ramp handle by clicking the small x box on the handle's right side. Change the bottom ramp handle to white. You can change a handle color by clicking the circular control on the handle's left side and choosing a new color through the Selected Color attribute. Change the top ramp handle to black. With the top handle selected (select a handle by clicking its circular control), change the Selected Position attribute to 0.55. This lowers the handle and causes the ramp to appear as a white circle over a black background (see Figure 6.20).

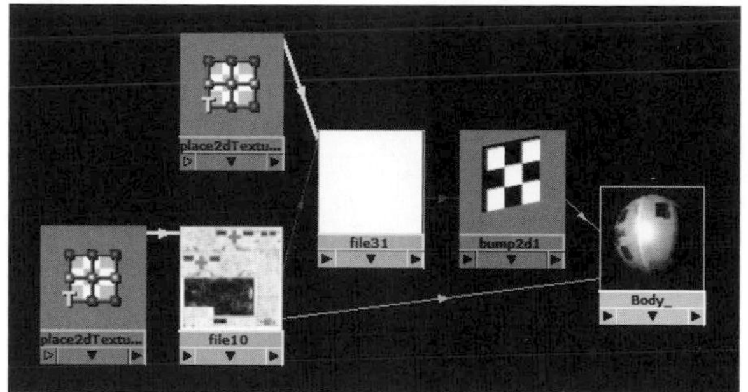

Figure 6.19

(Top) Shading network after update (Bottom) Resulting render. A sample file is included as `ambulance-step19.ma` **on the DVD.**

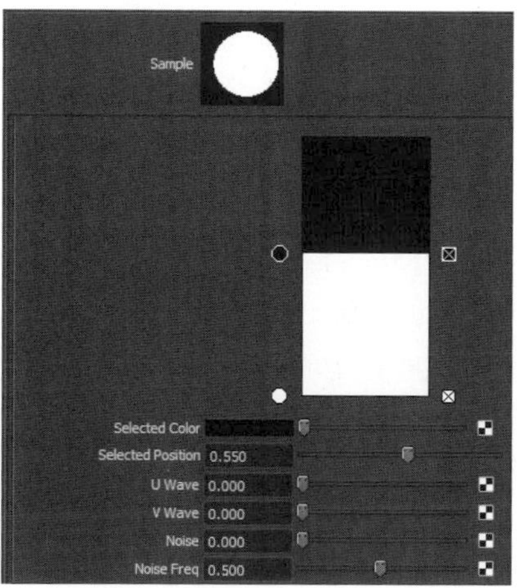

Figure 6.20

The adjusted attributes and handles of a Ramp texture create a white circle over a black background. The circle is slid to the right by changing the connected place2dTexture node's Offset UV value to –0.5, 0.

3. Open the Attribute Editor tab of the place2dTexture node connected to the Ramp node. Change Offset UV to –0.5, 0 (the attribute is listed as Offset with two number cells, U and V). This scoots the ramp pattern slightly to the right (see Figure 6.20). This aligns the white circle to the UV shell of the headlight lens. Ultimately, the adjusted Ramp serves as a cutout matte for the Bulge. Through the Alpha Gain attribute, the Ramp's Out Alpha values are multiplied by the Bulge's Out Alpha values. Hence, values in the black, zero-value areas of the Ramp force the Bulge to take on the same black, zero-value areas. Render a test. The headlights appear bumpy in the lens area (see Figure 6.21). In this case, the RGB values of the Bulge are not important because the Bump 2d node's Bump Value attribute uses only Out Alpha or similar single-channel values.
4. Repeat steps 1 to 3 for any separate materials assigned to the fog lights and signal lights.

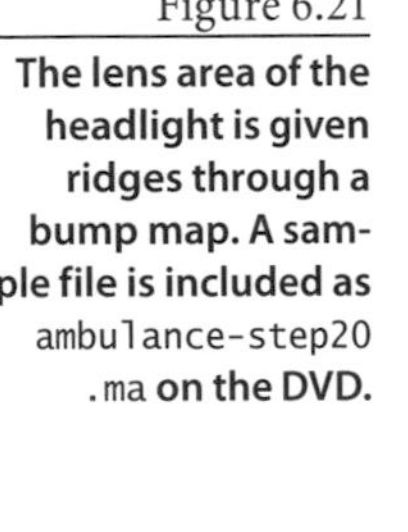

Figure 6.21

The lens area of the headlight is given ridges through a bump map. A sample file is included as `ambulance-step20.ma` **on the DVD.**

Alternatively, you can connect the output of the Bump 2d node used by the headlight material node to other materials. For example, to connect the Bump 2d node output to both the headlight material and signal light material simultaneously, follow these steps:

1. In the Hypershade, MMB+drag the material assigned to the headlights into the work area. MMB+drag the icon of the material assigned to the signal lights into the work area. In the example scene files, these materials are named Light_ and Signal_Lights. In the work area, Shift+click both material icons. Click the Input And Output Connections button. Both shading networks are revealed.
2. MMB+drag the headlight material's Bump 2d node and drop it on top of the signal light material node. The Connect Input Of menu opens. Choose Other from the menu. The Connection Editor opens. In the left column, click the word *outNormal*. In the right column, click the word *normalCamera*. A connection is made, and the bump map is applied to both materials. The Out Normal attribute passes surface normal information while the Normal Camera attribute relates the information to the camera position.

Adding Specular Maps

One material shading component that is often overlooked when texturing is the specularity. By default, Blinn, Phong, and Phong E specular highlights are predictably shaped. That is, the resulting highlights take on a smooth shape as if created by a perfectly smooth surface. This creates the familiar circular highlight on a spherical object. Although the highlight may taper from the edge to the core, there is no other variation in intensity. Ultimately, Maya's specular highlights are a simplified representation of specular reflections. Real-world specular reflections are as varied as the bright light sources that create them and the surfaces on which they appear. Hence, when mimicking a real-world surface, the perfection of Maya's specular highlight is unsatisfactory. Although you can make the specular highlight elongated with an Anisotropic material, the result is still artificial. Mapping the material's Eccentricity, Specular Roll Off, and/or Specular Color with either procedural or bitmap textures can disguise this limitation by adding variation to the specular highlight intensity.

The one ambulance surface that can benefit the most from specular mapping is the Body. Without mapping, the specular highlights are broad and tend to obscure the texture detail. In this case, you can map procedural textures to the Specular Roll Off attributes. Follow these steps:

1. Open the Attribute Editor tab for the material assigned to the Body surface. Click the checkered Map button beside Specular Roll Off. In the Create Render Node window, click the Noise texture icon. In the Attribute Editor tab for the new Noise texture, set Threshold to 0.1 and Amplitude to 0.6. This darkens the noise pattern and reduces the overall contrast.
2. Render a test. The intensity of the specular highlight is diminished (see Figure 6.22). Open the Attribute tab for the place2dTexture node connected to the Noise node. Change Repeat UV to 2, 2. This causes the individual noise "grains" to become smaller and the intensity of the specular highlight to become more subtly varied across the surface.

Motion Blur

Motion blur is the streaking of objects in motion as captured by motion picture, film, or video mediums. The effect is an artifact of the time required to chemically expose film stock or electronically process light through a video CCD chip. If an object moves 1 foot during the 1/60 of a second required by a camera to create one frame, the motion blur appears 1 foot in length on that frame. Motion blur is also perceived by the human eye when motion is rapid. Although the human brain processes information continuously and does not perceive "frames" per se, rapid motion is seen as blurry through various physiological and psychological mechanisms.

Figure 6.22
(Top) Ambulance side, as seen on frame 1, without a Specular Roll Off map. (Bottom) Same render with a Noise texture mapped to the Specular Roll Off. The change is most noticeable across the front fender and roof line above the door. A sample file is included as `ambulance-step21.ma` **on the DVD.**

By default, motion blur is disabled in Maya. To activate it, select the Motion Blur check box in the Motion Blur section of the Maya Software tab in the Render Settings window (see Figure 6.23). You can choose the style of motion blur by selecting either the 2D or 3D radio button for the Motion Blur Type attribute.

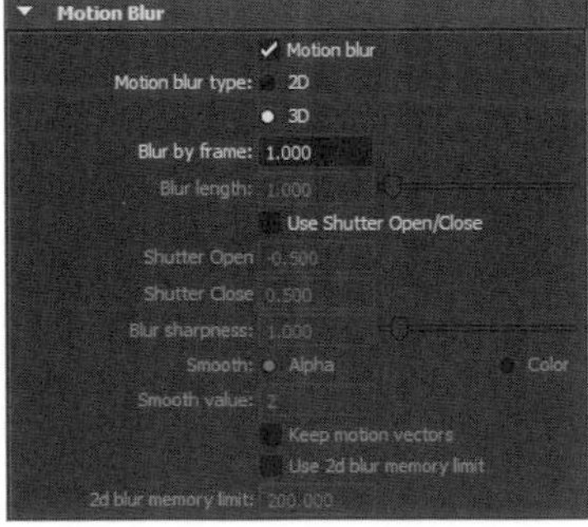

Figure 6.23
The Motion Blur section of the Maya Software tab in the Render Settings window

2D motion blur applies a post-process blur to the render. The blur is laid between the object's start point and end point in a linear fashion. Thus, 2D motion blur is not accurate if an object rapidly changes direction or deforms during the course of one frame. Nevertheless, 2D motion blur is efficient and convincing for many animations (and the default settings work quite well). 3D motion blur, on the other hand, samples the moving object along multiple points along its path and is sensitive to rapid direction changes and surface deformation.

A list of the most critical motion blur attributes follows:

Blur By Frame and Shutter Angle Blur By Frame controls the time range within which the motion blur for one frame is calculated. Raising the value will artificially lengthen the blur trail. Lowering the value will have the opposite effect. Note that Blur By Frame is influenced by the Shutter Angle attribute, which is carried by the rendering camera in the Special Effects section of its Attribute Editor tab. The following formula is used to determine an object's start and end point when calculating the motion blur trail for one frame: ((Shutter Angle / 360) × Blur By Frame) / 2. Thus, if Shutter Angle is set to the default 144, and Blur By Frame is set to the default 1.0, the start point is 0.2 frames back in time, and the end point is 0.2 frames forward in time. Shutter Angle emulates the spinning aperture disc used by motion picture cameras to control the duration that one frame of film is exposed.

Use Shutter Open/Close, Shutter Open, and Shutter Close Use Shutter Open/Close, when selected, makes Shutter Open and Shutter Close available. Shutter Open determines the start point for an object when calculating the motion blur trail. When set to 0.5, Maya goes back in time half a frame to establish the start point. Shutter Close determines the end point for an object. If Use Shutter Open/Close is selected, the Shutter Angle value is assumed to be 360, which essentially removes its influence.

The mental ray renderer also provides motion blur. To activate it, change the Motion Blur menu, found in the Quality tab of the Render Settings window, to No Deformation or Full (see Figure 6.24). No Deformation motion blur is equivalent to Maya Software 2D motion blur. Full motion blur is equivalent to Maya Software 3D motion blur.

Several attributes carry the same name as the Maya Software motion blur counterparts and function in a similar manner. These include Blur By Frame, Shutter Open, and Shutter Close. Other attributes are unique to mental ray. Time Samples determines the number of samples taken over time per shading sample. The higher the Time Samples values, the smoother the motion blur. Motion Steps determines the number of positions along a motion path or through a surface deformation that are used to calculate the motion blur trail. For example, spinning or rotating objects require higher Motion Steps attribute values to create appropriately curved blur trails.

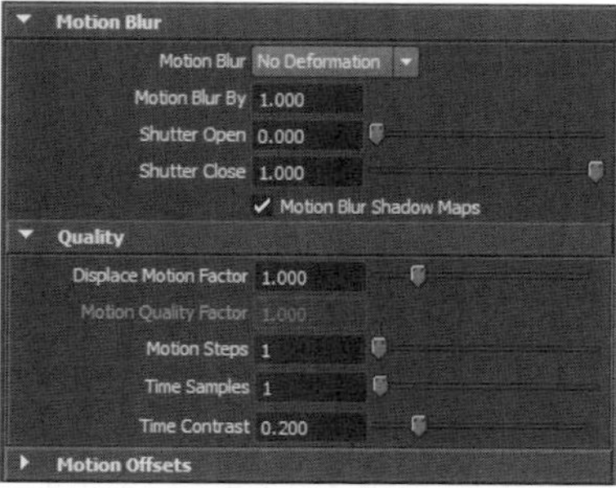

Figure 6.24
The Motion Blur section of the mental ray Quality tab in the Render Settings window

Figure 6.25

(Top) 3D motion blur. A sample file is included as `ambulance-step21.ma` **on the DVD. (Center) 2D motion blur. Note that the 2D motion blur produces a greater degree of vertical streaking on the fender at the left side of the screen as the ambulance body bounces up. In contrast, the 3D motion blur creates a greater degree of rotational blur on the tires, which is a more accurate representation of the motion. (Bottom) 3D motion blur with Blur By Frame set to 5.**

Project: Adding Motion Blur

Despite the movement of the camera and the ambulance, there is no motion blur within the scene. To activate motion blur, follow these steps:

1. Open the Render Settings window. In the Maya Software tab, expand the Motion Blur section and select the Motion Blur check box. Render a test.
2. By default, Maya Software uses the 3D motion blur style. You can activate 2D motion blur by selecting the 2D check box. 2D and 3D motion blur produce slightly different results (see Figure 6.25).

Note that different degrees of blur appear on various ambulance parts. Because the ambulance body is rocking and the wheels are spinning at different rates, the length of the blur trails for individual parts varies. In addition, the distance a part moves during one frame is relative to the camera. If a part is moving toward the camera, as opposed to moving across the camera, its blur trail will appear shorter.

The Render Layer Editor

When a shot is animated in a 3D program on a professional production, it is rarely rendered out as is. Instead, the shot is divided into layers and/or render passes. Dividing a shot into layers enables key elements—including characters, backgrounds, shadows, effects, and props—to be rendered separately. By dividing the shot into layers, you gain efficiency. Not only do the separate layers generally render faster than the complete shot, but revising the shot becomes easier because a specific layer can be re-rendered without affecting the other layers.

Render passes take the shot division further by breaking down each object into specific shading components, light contributions, or compositing encoders. Color, diffuse, ambient, specularity, and reflectivity are a few of the common shading components. The contributions of CG lights may be rendered separately or given unique colors in anticipation of additional processing. Compositing encoders, designed for specialized compositing tasks, include depth, ambient occlusion, reflection occlusion, surface normal, UV information, and motion vector renders.

One disadvantage of rendering separate layers or render passes is the necessity of recombining the renders in a compositing program. Although compositing programs such as Adobe After Effects or The Foundry's Nuke are often used, it's possible to undertake simple compositing steps through Maya's Render Layer Editor, which is part of the Layer Editor. In addition, the Render Layer Editor allows you to create and manage various render layers and render passes.

You can access the Layer Editor by clicking the Channel Box / Layer Editor tab along the right side of the program window. The Layer Editor is divided into three sections, which are represented by three tabs: Display (Display Layer Editor), Render (Render Layer Editor), and Anim (Animation Layer Editor).

Rendering Render Layers

To use the Render Layer Editor, click the Render tab. By default, a masterLayer is created and contains all the objects and lights within the scene. You can create a new layer and assign specific objects to it by selecting objects in a view panel and choosing Layers → Create Layer From Selected from the Render Layer Editor menu. The new layer appears at the top of the layer stack and is named layer*n* (see Figure 6.26).

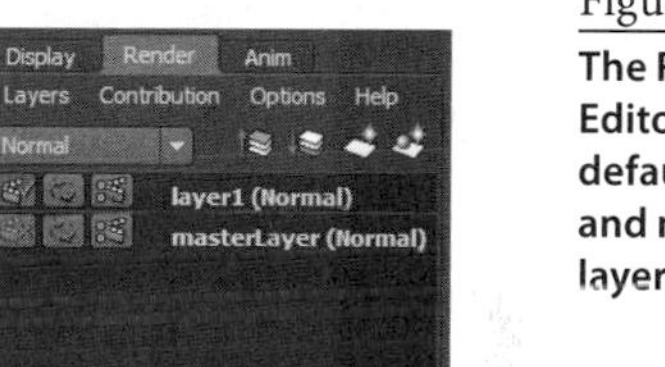

Figure 6.26

The Render Layer Editor with the default masterLayer and new layer, layer1, displayed

To look at the layer and its assigned objects, click the layer name; only objects assigned to the layer will appear in the view panels. To rename the layer, double-click the layer name and type into the name field. You can create additional render layers at any time. To delete a render layer, RMB+click the layer name and choose Delete Layer from the menu. To add an object to a render layer that already exists, select the masterLayer, select the object in a view panel, RMB+click the layer you wish to add to, and choose Add Selected Object from the Render Layer Editor menu.

When multiple render layers exist, Maya renders those with an activated Renderable button. The button appears in the leftmost column of the Render Layer Editor and features a small movie clapboard. If more than one render layer carries an activated Renderable button, Maya will ignore the lower-level layers *unless* the Render All Layers option is selected. You can select Render All Layers by choosing Options → Render All Layers through the Render Layer Editor menu. If Render All Layers is selected and more than one render layer has an activated Renderable button, Maya will composite the layers, composite and keep the layers, or keep the layers without compositing. The route Maya takes is determined by the Keep Image Mode radio buttons in the Render All Layers option window. You can also access the buttons by choosing Render → Render All Layers → ❐. Table 6.2 lists the render result for each of the Keep Image Mode options.

Table 6.2

Keep Image Mode options and the resulting render

KEEP IMAGE MODE OPTION	RENDER VIEW RESULT	BATCH RENDER RESULT
Composite Layers	Final composite is shown in the window.	Final composite is rendered to disk as a single image.
Composite And Keep Layers	Each layer is rendered. Lowest layers are rendered first. The composite frame is displayed at the end of the rendering process. Individual layers are accessible by dragging the scroll bar that appears at the bottom of the Render View window.	Each layer is rendered. Lowest layers are rendered first. Rendered layers are placed into folders bearing the layer name. If the Image Format is set to Layered PSD, the layers are arranged within a Photoshop PSD file.
Keep Layers	Each layer is rendered. Lowest layers are rendered first. At the end of the rendering process, the top layer is displayed in the window. Lower layers are accessible by dragging the scroll bar that appears at the bottom of the Render View window.	Each layer is rendered. Lowest layers are rendered first. Rendered layers are placed into folders bearing the layer name.

The way in which the layers are composited is determined by the Blend Mode menu carried by each render layer. If a render layer's Blend Mode is set to Normal, the layer obscures lower layers except where the layer contains no objects from the view of the camera. The remaining Blend Modes include Lighten, Darken, Screen, Multiply, and Overlay and are similar to the blending modes offered by Photoshop. The modes are discussed further in the section "Project: Breaking the Scene into Render Layers" later in this chapter.

Applying Member Overrides and Render Pass Options

By default, surfaces assigned to a render layer are illuminated only by the lights that have been assigned to the render layer as well. In addition, the surfaces cast shadows and receive shadows only if shadow-casting lights and shadow-casting objects are present on the render layer. You can change this behavior, however, by applying a layer override to the attributes of a surface's Render Stats section. For example, to prevent a surface from casting shadows on a particular layer, follow these steps:

1. Select a layer in the Render Layer Editor so that its assigned surfaces are visible in the view panels. Select a surface. Press Ctrl+A and switch to the surface's shape node tab in the Attribute Editor.
2. Expand the Render Stats section. Deselect the Casts Shadows radio button. The attribute name turns orange to indicate that there is layer override (see Figure 6.27). Render a test. The surface will no longer cast shadows.

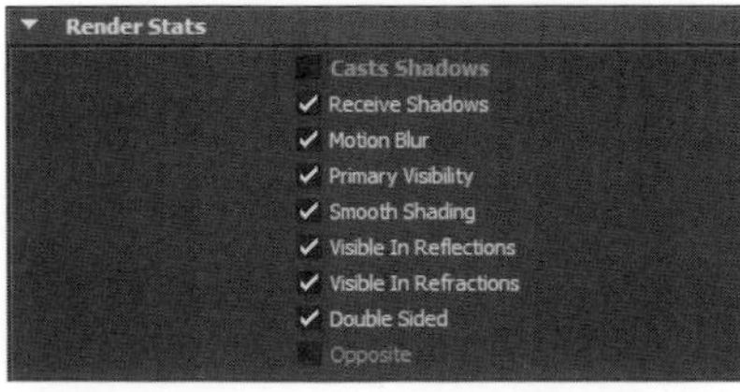

Figure 6.27

Render Stats section of the Attribute Editor tab for a surface's shape node. An override is applied to Casts Shadows, as indicated by orange lettering.

You can affect all the surfaces on a layer by accessing the Member Overrides section. To do so, RMB+click a layer in the Render Layer Editor and choose Attributes from the menu. The layer's Attribute Editor tab opens. The Member Overrides section features Use Scene, Override On, and

Override Off radio buttons for each of the attributes normally found in the Render Stats section of a surface's shape node (see Figure 6.28). For example, Casts Shadows is the first attribute listed in the Member Overrides section. If you select the Override On radio button, no surface assigned to the render layer will cast shadows. If you select the Override Off button, any override applied to the Render Stats section of a surface's shape node is ignored; in other words, all the Render Stats section check boxes are treated as if they are selected and on. The Use Scene radio button, which is selected by default, uses the Render Stats settings as they are applied to all the surface shape nodes on the masterLayer; that is, if you deselect Casts Shadows for a single surface on the masterLayer, Use Scene will honor that setting.

The layer's Attribute Editor tab also gives you access to the Render Pass Options section, which offers a quick way to create common render passes (see Figure 6.29). For example, if you select the Diffuse radio button, only the diffuse shading component of the render layer is rendered. The diffuse shading component includes the surface color and shading, but does not include specularity. In contrast, the Specular radio button causes the specular component to render without the diffuse component. The Shadow radio button causes shadows to render in the alpha channel while the RGB channel remains black. The Beauty button, which is selected by default, creates the standard render with all the shading components included. Unfortunately, the Render Pass Option section will no longer function for mental ray. However, mental ray supports the more advanced Contribution Map system, which is demonstrated in Chapter 8, "Texturing and Lighting an Environment, Part 2."

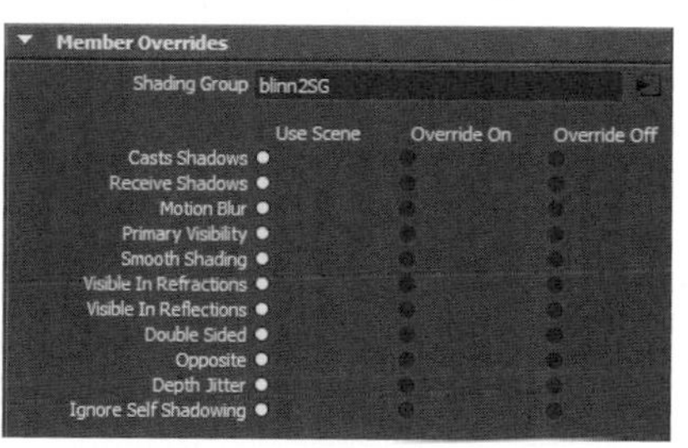

Figure 6.28
The Member Overrides section found in the Attribute Editor tab of a render layer

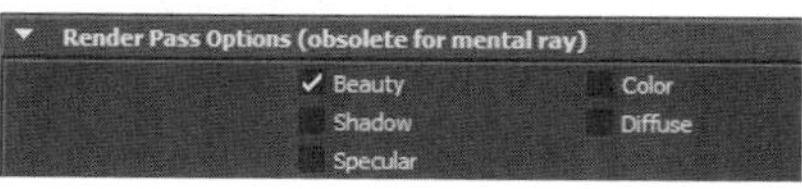

Figure 6.29
The Render Pass Options section found in the Attribute Editor tab of a render layer

Applying Material Overrides

By default, surfaces assigned to a render layer render with their assigned material intact. However, you can apply material overrides so that all the surfaces assigned to a layer are temporarily assigned to a single material. The assignment is nondestructive and does not affect the original material assignment on the masterLayer. To create a material override, follow these steps:

1. RMB+click a render layer and choose Overrides → Create New Material Override → *material name*. A new material is created and assigned to all surfaces within the render layer. The new material is accessible within the Hypershade and may be adjusted.
2. Alternatively, you can RMB+click a render layer and choose Override → Assign Existing Material Override → *material name*. In this case, you can choose any material that already exists. To remove an override, RMB+click and choose Remove Material Override.

Applying Render Setting Overrides

One advantage of using the Render Layer Editor is the ability to use different render settings for each layer. Initially, each layer you create takes the render settings from the masterLayer. To create a render settings override for a render layer (other than masterLayer), follow these steps:

1. Click the Controls icon for a render layer. The Controls icon is the rightmost button beside the layer name; it features a small film clapboard with two circles (see Figure 6.26 earlier in this chapter). The Render Settings window opens. The displayed settings, however, are specifically for the render layer. This is indicated by the updated Render Layer menu, which lists the layer name.
2. In the Render Settings window, RMB+click the attribute name and choose Create Layer Override from the menu. The attribute name turns orange to indicate that an override exists. Change the attribute value. The value change affects the current layer but does not affect any other layer. You can apply an override to any attribute that appears in any tab of the Render Settings window, including Render Using.
3. To remove an override, RMB+click the attribute name and choose Remove Layer Override. The attribute value is returned to a value established by the masterLayer.

You can change the attribute settings of the masterLayer at any time. Those changes are passed up to all the other layers except where an override has been applied.

Project: Breaking the Scene into Render Layers

Because professional productions often split their render into render layers and render passes, it pays to practice render layer setups. Although this book does not cover the compositing of render layers and passes in external compositing programs, this section will demonstrate how to create simple composites in the Render View by using the Blend Mode functions of the Render Layer Editor.

To break the ambulance scene into four new layers, three of which will become render passes, follow these steps:

1. Open the Render Layer Editor. In a view panel, select the Sky_Dome surface. Choose Layers → Create Layer From Selected. A new layer, layer1, is created. Select layer1 in the editor. Only the Sky_Dome surface appears in the view panels. Because the Sky_Dome surface is assigned to a Surface Shader material, it does not need lights on its layer. Rename layer1 **SkyDome**.
2. Return to the masterLayer. In a view panel, select all the geometry and lights. Choose Layers → Create Layer From Selected. A new layer is created; once again, the layer is named layer1. Rename the layer **Diffuse**. RMB+click the Diffuse layer and choose Attributes from the menu. The Attribute Editor tab for the layer opens. Scroll down to the Render Pass Options section. Deselect Beauty and select Diffuse. The layer will render only the diffuse shading component for all its assigned surfaces.

3. Close the Attribute Editor and return to the Render Layer Editor. Select the masterLayer. In a view panel, select all the geometry and lights (but do not select the Paint Effects strokes). Choose Layers → Create Layer From Selected. A new layer is created; once again, the layer is named layer1. Rename the layer **Shadow**. RMB+click over the Shadow layer and choose Attributes from the menu. The Attribute Editor tab for the layer opens. Scroll down to the Render Pass Options section. Deselect Beauty and select Shadow. The layer will render only the shadows for all its assigned surfaces. The shadow shapes will appear in the alpha channel, while the RGB channels will remain black. Close the Attribute Editor and return to the Render Layer Editor. Select the Shadow layer. Change its Blend Mode menu to Multiply. Multiply multiplies the pixel values of the layer by the corresponding pixel layers of all the lower layers. When Maya composites the render layers, this causes the shadows to appear over the lower layers without interfering with the nonshadow areas. Alternatively, you can set the Blend Mode menu to Darken, which utilizes the darkest corresponding pixel of all the layers.
4. Select the masterLayer. In a view panel, select all the geometry and lights (but do not select the Paint Effects strokes). Choose Layers → Create Layer From Selected. A new layer is created; once again, the layer is named layer1. Rename the layer **Specular**. RMB+click over the Specular layer and choose Attributes from the menu. The Attribute Editor tab for the layer opens. Scroll down to the Render Pass Options section. Deselect Beauty and select Specular. The layer will render only the specular shading component for all its assigned surfaces. Close the Attribute Editor and return to the Render Layer Editor. Select the Specular layer. Change its Blend Mode menu to Screen. Screen places the brightest area of the layer over the lower layers. When choosing the Specular render pass, the Screen mode is necessary to overcome the lack of alpha information. That is, the specular component is rendered with a completely opaque alpha channel. Alternatively, you can set the Blend Mode menu to Lighten, which utilizes the brightest corresponding pixel of all the layers. See Figure 6.30 for the final appearance of the layer stack.

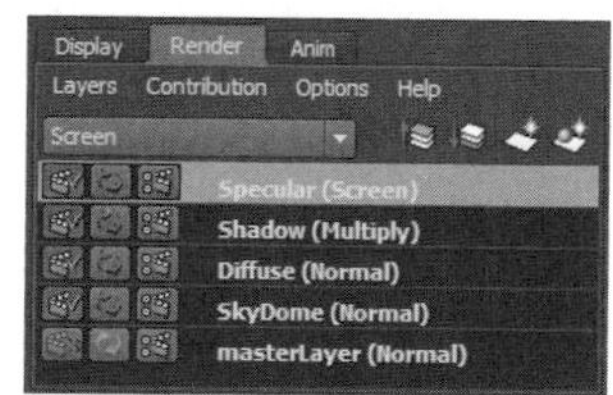

Figure 6.30
The final layer stack in the Render Layer Editor

5. Choose Options → Render All Layers from the Render Layer Editor menu so that Render All Layers receives a check mark at the left of the menu. Choose Options → Render All Layers → ❐. In the Render All Layers Options window, select the Composite And Keep Layers radio button and click the Apply And Close button.
6. Open the Attribute Editor tab for the Render camera. In the Environment section, return the Background Color to black. A nonblack Background Color will prevent the proper compositing of layers (in particular, semitransparent alpha edges will trap some of the nonblack color). Render a frame in the Render View. The layers render, one at a time, starting with the lowest layer (see Figure 6.31). The final composited frame appears last. To look at the layers individually, drag the scroll bar at the bot-

tom of the Render View window to the right. The Shadow layer appears black in RGB. To view the shadow shapes in the alpha channel, click the Display Alpha Channel button at the top of the window. To return to the RGB view, click the Display RGB Channels button. You can purge the image cache of the Render View window and remove the scroll bar by choosing File → Remove All Images From Render View from the Render View menu.

Note that the final composite varies somewhat from the beauty render created with no render layers. In particular, there is additional specularity on the tires and suspension parts that rest within the ambulance's shadow. This is due to the Specular render layer sitting at the top of the render stack. One disadvantage of using the Render Layer Editor is the difficulty with which surfaces and shading components are placed "on top of" or "behind" each other. One solution involves the use of render passes that employ mattes; however, this requires the use of an external compositing program such as After Effects to create the final composite. A second solution requires the adjustment of the materials. For example, you can reduce the Eccentricity and Specular Roll Off values of the materials assigned to the tires, suspension, and steering surfaces (see Figure 6.32).

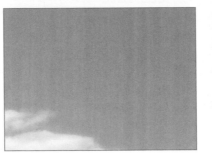

Figure 6.31

(Clockwise from Top Left) Final composite, Specular layer, Shadow layer, Diffuse layer, SkyDome layer

Project: Adding Reflectivity

Thus far, the ambulance has mimicked reflections through the use of the Reflected Color attribute. However, Reflected Color is unable to emulate the reflections of geometry in the scene, For example, the ambulance windows fail to reflect the spare tire mounted on the hood. Nevertheless, you can use the Reflected Color attribute in conjunction with raytracing. To do so, follow these steps:

1. In the Render Layer Editor, select the masterLayer. Open the Render Settings window. In the Raytracing Quality section of the Maya Software tab, select the Raytracing check box. To save render time, set Reflections to 2, Refractions to 0, and Shadows to 2. There are no surfaces in the scene that require refractions. Changes made to the masterLayer render settings are passed up the other layers. Alternatively, you can choose to activate raytracing on specific layers by creating render setting overrides (see the section "Applying Render Setting Overrides" earlier in this chapter).
2. Open the Hypershade window and examine the Reflectivity setting of each material. If a material is assigned to a surface that would not reflect in real life, set its Reflectivity to 0. Render a test. Continue to adjust the Reflectivity values of the materials.

The addition of reflectivity reduces the intense blue reflection found on the side mirrors, headlights, fog lights, and signal lights (see Figure 6.33). However, the windshield glass is relatively unaffected.

Figure 6.32

The Eccentricity and Specular Roll Off values are reduced for the materials assigned to the tires, steering, and suspension parts, thus improving the appearance of the shadowed areas. A sample file is included as `ambulance-step22.ma` **on the DVD.**

To add additional color variation to the windshield, map a Noise texture to the assigned material's Transparency and Specular Roll Off. Follow these steps:

1. Open the Attribute Editor tab of the material assigned to the Glass surface. Click the checkered Map button beside Reflectivity. In the Create Render Node window, click the Fractal icon. In the Attribute Editor tab for the new Fractal node, set Amplitude and Threshold to 0.4. This reduces the contrast in the noise pattern. Render a test.

The variation in reflectivity caused by the Fractal texture causes the window to appear dirty. However, the overall opacity of the window has decreased.

2. Click the checkered Map button beside Transparency. In the Create Render Node window, click the Noise icon. In the Attribute Editor tab for the new Noise node, set Amplitude to 0.4, Threshold to 0.4, and Noise Type to Perlin Noise to soften the noise pattern. Render a test. The window glass is further degraded, and the reflection no longer takes on a pure shade of blue (see Figure 6.34).

Figure 6.33
The addition of ray-traced reflectivity adds complexity to reflective parts such as the side mirrors, headlights, and ambulance body.

Figure 6.34
The addition of a Transparency map to the Glass material breaks up the reflectivity and makes the window appear dirty. A sample file is included as `ambulance-step23.ma` on the DVD.

Project: Creating the Final Render

In preparation for the final render, follow these guidelines:

- Set the Keep Image Mode option, in the Render All Layers window, to Composite. Unless you plan to take the individual render layers into an external compositing program, there's no need to keep them for a final render. Along those lines, render the render layers only if they offer you some advantage. If you prefer to produce a final image without the Render Layer Editor applying its own compositing, render out the masterLayer by itself. You can choose whether a render layer renders by toggling its Renderable button on or off.

- Reactivate the displacement mapping on the Hill surface. The displacement was deactivated at the beginning of this chapter to save render time. To reactivate the displacement, set the Alpha Gain of the File carrying the displacement bitmap to 0.35. In the example scene files, the file node is named file9 and is part of the Hill_material shading network.
- To fine-tune the displacement result, adjust the attributes found within the Displacement Map section of the Hill surface shape node's Attribute Editor tab. Of the available attributes, Initial Sample Rate, Extra Sample Rate, and Normal Threshold are the most useful. Initial Sample Rate sets the size of a sampling grid laid over the surface. The grid is used to determine whether a polygon triangle should be tessellated. Tessellation is deemed necessary if the contrast between neighboring pixels in the displacement map is sufficient. Extra Sample Rate, on the other hand, adds additional sampling. Higher Initial Sampling Rate and Extra Sampling Rate values make the displacement more accurate but can significantly affect the speed of the render. Normal Threshold controls the "softness" of the displacement. If the angle between two adjacent polygon triangles is less than the Normal Threshold value, the triangles are rendered smoothly; if not, the triangles are rendered with a sharp edge between them. For example, a Normal Threshold of 50 is used for the final sample scene file.

Batch render the animation to complete Part 2 of this project. For more information on batch rendering and Render Settings options, see Chapter 2, "Texturing and Lighting a Product, Part 2." Your rendered frames should appear similar to Figure 6.35.

Figure 6.35

Frame 1 and frame 48 from the final render. A sample file is included as `ambulance-final.ma` on the DVD. For a color version of this figure, see the color insert.

Texturing and Lighting an Environment, Part 1

In this chapter and Chapter 8, "Texturing and Lighting an Environment, Part 2," you will texture and light an interior room with skylights. The goal is to re-create the natural look of sunlight arriving from above. Several advanced techniques are discussed, including global illumination, mental ray portal lighting, and specialized Maya material and mental ray shader use. This chapter, which contains part 1 of the project, will guide you through the following steps:

- **Preparing the scene**
- **Assigning materials**
- **Setting up the skylights**
- **Adding textures**
- **Activating Global Illumination**

In addition, important lighting and texturing theory is included as follows:

- **mental ray shaders**
- **Physical Sun and Sky and portal lights**
- **Global Illumination**

Project: Preparing the Scene

Before starting the texturing process, review the scene file and its contents. Open the `room_start.ma` scene file from the `ProjectFiles/Project4` folder on the DVD.

The scene features an interior room. The room includes wall sconces, intricate molding, skylights, and minimal furniture. The Render camera is animated, moving forward slowly. The room was constructed by Nolan Miller at Graphite Digital (`www.graphite3d.com`) and has been adapted for use as a tutorial.

Note that the sample scene files included for this chapter and Chapter 8 assume that the bitmap textures are located within the `Textures` folder of the `ProjectFiles/Project4` project directory. Before opening a sample scene file, choose File → Project → Set and browse for the `Project4` folder, whether the folder remains at its original location on the DVD or is located on a drive after the DVD contents have been copied.

mental ray Shaders

By default, the mental ray renderer understands standard Maya materials. Nevertheless, a large number of mental ray shaders (materials) are provided with the program. You can access the shaders through the mental ray section of the Create tab in the Hypershade window. The shaders are also listed in the Create Render Node window (see Figure 7.1).

You can assign a shader to a surface by choosing Assign Material To Selection through the RMB marking menu in the Hypershade. However, to see the result in the render, you must switch to the mental ray renderer in the Render Settings window. If the mental ray shaders do not appear in the Hypershade, you must activate the `Mayatomr.mll` plug-in in the Plug-In Manager window.

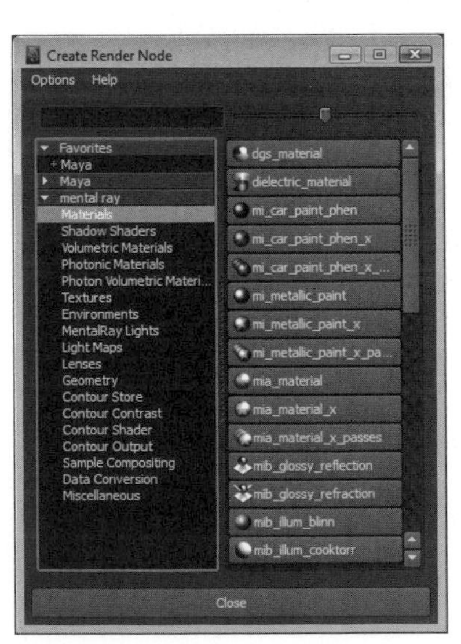

Figure 7.1

A small portion of the mental ray shaders provided by Maya, as seen in the Create Render Node window

Although a number of shaders have a functionality similar to Maya materials, many are specialized. Although it is beyond the scope of this book to cover all the shaders, the following four sections discuss a few important shaders and shader categories.

mib_ Shaders

Shaders carrying the mib_ (Mental Image Base library) prefix represent a common set of shading models. Several mib_shaders have direct correlations to Maya materials. mib_Illum_Lambert is equivalent to Lambert. mib_Illum_Blinn is equivalent to Blinn. mib_Illum_Phong is equivalent to Phong. Some of the material and shader attribute names differ, however. In addition, mental ray offers attributes that Maya materials do not carry. Descriptions of common mental ray shader attributes follow:

Diffuse Diffuse sets its namesake quality. High Diffuse values produce a bright surface. The color of a mib_ shader must be set through the Diffuse attribute.

Ambient and Ambience Ambient is a constant color offset and is equivalent to Ambient Color. It represents the net diffuse reflections arriving from all other surfaces and participating media in the scene. In contrast, Ambience is a multiplier for Ambient. If Ambience is left black, Ambient has no effect on the shader.

Specular Specular determines the color of specular highlights and is equivalent to Specular Color.

Roughness and Exponent Roughness, which is carried by the mib_Illum_Blinn shader, controls the width of the specular highlight and is equivalent to Eccentricity. Exponent, which is carried by the mib_Illum_Phong shader, also controls the specular width. Note that the mib_Illum_Blinn shader produces a diffuse specular highlight. To create a more intense highlight, use mib_Illum_Phong.

Ior Ior determines an assigned surface's index of refraction. In the real world, a *refractive index* is a number that indicates the change in the speed of light when a light ray crosses the boundary between two materials. Although refractions are commonly seen through semitransparent materials such as water or glass, all real-world materials possess a specific index. For example, titanium dioxide has a refractive index of 2.7. Ultimately, changes to the Ior value produce subtle variations in the diffuse quality of opaque surfaces—that is, the way in which the surface scatters light and is seen as light or dark varies. Note that the mib_ shaders discussed in this section do not carry a Transparency attribute.

Other mib_ shaders provide basic texturing functionality such as UV tiling. Several of these are demonstrated in the "Texturing the Poster" section later in the chapter.

dgs_material

The dgs_material shader provides a physically accurate shading model by offering Diffuse, Glossy, and Specular attributes. Diffuse represents the diffuse component and determines the base color of the surface. Glossy and Specular control the look of reflections and refractions when raytracing; you can use the attributes individually or in conjunction.

If Glossy is set to black, Specular controls the brightness of raytraced reflections and refractions. (The Specular attribute does not create an artificial specular highlight.) If Specular is set to black, Glossy controls the brightness of reflections, refractions, and specular highlights. In addition, Glossy provides distance-based degradation of reflections and refractions. The degradation is controlled by the Shiny attribute. Low Shiny values cause the reflections and refractions to degrade, or become less coherent, over distance (see Figure 7.2).

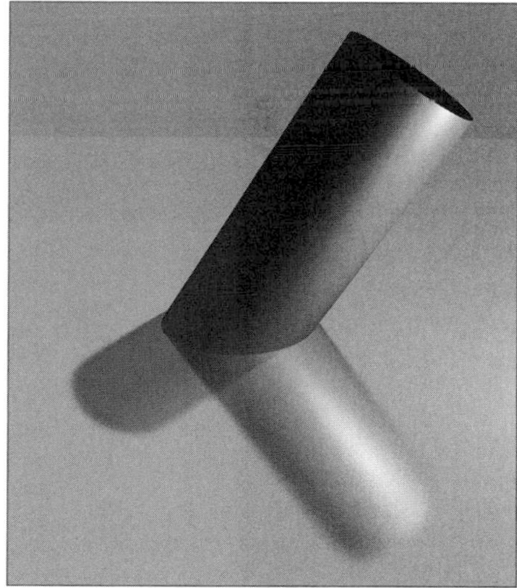

Figure 7.2

A dgs_material shader is assigned to a plane. The reflection and refraction of the cylinder degrade over distance. A sample scene file is included as `dgs_material.ma` **in the** `ProjectFiles/Project4/Reference` **folder on the DVD.**

dielectric_material

The dielectric_material shader replicates the interactions of light waves and material boundaries. Based on the angles of incidence of the arriving light waves and the refractive indices of the involved materials, the light wave will either transmit (refract) through the second material or reflect internally through the first material. For example, a boundary exists between air and the wall of a glass object. If a light ray reflects off the object, the light is sent back through the air. If the light wave transmits, it passes through the glass wall.

Figure 7.3

A dielectric_material shader is assigned to a cylinder and plane. The refraction and reflection are automatically provided by the shader. A sample scene file is included as `dielectric_material.ma` in the `ProjectFiles/Project4/Reference` folder on the DVD.

Because the light wave passes through a different material with a different atomic structure, its speed changes. The change in speed is perceived as a refractive distortion. In this example, the glass is considered the "inside" material and the air is considered the "outside" material. The dielectric_material shader allows you to set the index of refraction for the "inside" material through the Index Of Refraction attribute, and the "outside" material through the Outside Index Of Refraction attribute.

The Col attribute, on the other hand, controls how rapidly light is absorbed by the "inside" material; higher values create a darker refraction. Out Color determines how rapidly light diminishes when reflecting back into the "outside" material; an Out Color value of 1 is analogous to air, which has a refractive index close to 1.0.

When re-creating glass or other transparent surfaces, the dielectric_material shader creates a fairly realistic result with minimal adjustment (see Figure 7.3).

mia_material

The mia_material shader is specifically designed for architectural and product rendering. It utilizes a physically based shading model that employs diffuse, glossy, and specular components, as well as dielectric qualities. The mia_material shader is *monolithic*—that is, it presents a wide array of mental ray basic shader functions under a single node interface. The shader attributes are divided into sections (see Figure 7.4).

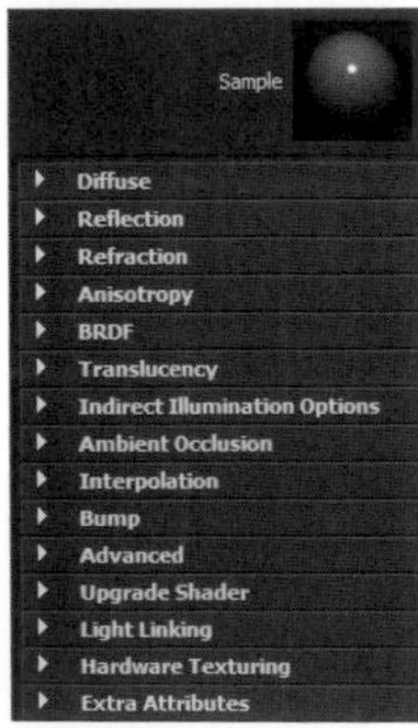

Figure 7.4

Attribute sections provided by the mia_material shader

The following are the most critical sections:

Diffuse The Diffuse section carries the Color, Weight, and Roughness attributes. Weight is equivalent to the Diffuse attribute of standard Maya materials in that it controls how much light the surface reflects (how bright or dark it is). Roughness, on the other hand, controls the degree to which the surface creates diffuse reflections. High Roughness values cause the surface to appear matte-like, or powdery. Low Roughness values cause the surface to appear shiny.

Reflection The Reflection section includes the Color, Reflectivity, and Glossiness attributes. The Color attribute sets the color of the reflections and is equivalent to the Specular Color attribute of standard Maya materials. Whereas a Blinn, Phong, or Anisotropic material fabricates a specular highlight from an idealized point light, the mia_material shader creates an actual reflection of the environment. In other words, mia_material creates a specular highlight that is derived from its surroundings. In contrast, the Glossiness attribute determines the degree to which reflections are coherent. The reflections can be perfect and mirror-like, or extremely diffuse and incoherent.

Anisotropy The Anisotropy section allows you to create anisotropic reflections (or specular highlights). Real-world anisotropic reflections are stretched in a direction perpendicular to grooves, channels, or undulations of the reflecting surface.

BRDF *BRDF* stands for Bidirectional Reflectance Distribution Function. The function is used to determine the reflective quality of opaque surfaces. Ultimately, the strength of a reflection is based on the viewing angle (the incident angle between the viewer and the surface normal) and the inherent properties of the surface. For example, many metals are uniformly reflective at every viewing angle, whereas layered materials (such as lacquered wood) create reflections that vary as the viewing angle changes. The BRDF section offers controls to customize the reflection strength based on the viewing angle. This is demonstrated in Chapter 8.

Indirect Illumination Options This section provides a means to fine-tune Final Gathering and Global Illumination qualities on a case-by-case basis for each mia_material.

Ambient Occlusion The mia_material has a built-in ambient occlusion shader that can add soft shadow detail to intricate geometry or areas where surfaces are in close proximity. Ambient occlusion is demonstrated in Chapter 8.

Advanced The Advanced section offers a means to employ a bump map. However, a custom shading network is required. This is demonstrated in the section "Texturing the Floor" later in this chapter.

Project: Assigning Materials

Of all surfaces in the scene, only the poster requires a specific bitmap texture. All the other parts—including the floor, walls, ceiling, molding, pillars, sconces, and chairs—will be assigned to generic textures that do not require specific UV alignment.

Because the render is designed for architectural visualization, you will render the objects as if the surfaces are pristine and clean. Hence, it's not necessary to introduce surface wear or variation. (In contrast, the Project 3 ambulance was given a heavy dose of rust and dirt.) As such, similar surfaces should appear identical. For example, each pillar should appear as if it was constructed and painted in the same manner. Ultimately, this allows you to assign similar surfaces to the same material.

The most suitable shader for architectural visualization is the mia_material. As discussed in the prior section, this shader offers the advantage of advanced reflection controls, additional indirect illumination options, and built-in ambient occlusion. To assign mia_material to the surfaces in the room, follow these steps:

1. Open the Hypershade window. In the Create tab, scroll down to the mental ray section. Click the word *Materials*. In the shader column, click the mia_material icon. Select one surface through the Hypergraph: Hierarchy or Outliner window. In the Hypershade, RMB+click the new mia_material and choose Assign Material To Selection.
2. Create a new mia_material and assign it to the next surface. Repeat the process until all the surfaces are assigned. As mentioned earlier in this section, you can assign many surfaces to a single shader. Table 7.1 suggests a minimum number of shaders, the shaders' new names, the surfaces they are assigned to, and the real-world materials they will try to emulate.
3. After all the surfaces are assigned, open the Render Settings window and change the Render Using menu to mental ray. Switch to the Quality tab. In the Anti-Aliasing Quality section, change Sampling Mode to Custom Sampling. Change Min Sample Level to –1 and Max Sample Level to 1 (this is a medium-level anti-aliasing quality). Render a test in the Render view. The surfaces reflect automatically (see Figure 7.5).

Table 7.1
Minimum shader list

SHADER NAME	REAL-WORLD MATERIAL	ASSIGNED SURFACES
Tile	White tile	Floor
Wallpaper	Red wallpaper	WallsHigh
		Ceiling
Wood	Painted wood	WallsLow
		CeilingBeams
		MoldingHigh
		MoldingLow
		WallSquares
		Pillar1, and so on
Glass	Clear glass	Skylight
Leather	Black leather	Chair1, and so on
Poster	Printed paper	Frame
Pewter	Gray metal	Sconce1, and so on

Physical Sun and Sky and Portal Lights

The Physical Sun and Sky system is designed to emulate an outdoor environment, complete with a simulated sun, atmospheric haze, and virtual ground plane. Although the system needs a set of mental ray utilities connected in a custom fashion, the Environment section of the Indirect Lighting tab of the Render settings window provides a Create button for the system. The Physical Sun and Sky system requires mental ray to function, as well as Final Gathering to produce bounced light. You can use the system in conjunction with Global Illumination.

Figure 7.5
mia_material shaders are assigned to all the surfaces in the scene. A sample scene file is included as `room_step1.ma` on the DVD.

The Physical Sun and Sky system is not designed for interior spaces. For example, using the system to light an interior through a window or doorway produces poor, and often inefficient, results. However, you can use the system in conjunction with mental ray portal lights. Portal lights are designed to extract lighting information from a global lighting system, such as Physical Sun and Sky, and pass it to the interior of a model that would otherwise be blocked from the light source. If portal lights are used with Global Illumination, they can produce their own set of photons. To create a portal light, a Maya area light must be converted to a mental ray area light, and several mental ray utilities must be connected to the light node. This is demonstrated in the next two sections.

Project: Setting Up the Skylights

The main light source for the room will be the large, square skylights. To create the sense that sunlight is entering the skylights and bouncing through the room, you can use mental ray's Physical Sun and Sky system, portal lights, Final Gathering, and Global Illumination.

Before activating the Physical Sun and Sky system, adjust the Color, Reflectivity, and Transparency of the mia_material shaders. You can find Reflectivity in the Reflection section, and Transparency in the Refraction section. Assign the Skylights surface a Transparency value of 1.0. Change the color of the walls to red, the chairs to black, and the pillars, ceiling beams, and molding to off-white.

To activate the Physical Sun and Sky system, follow these steps:

1. Open the Render Settings window. In the Render Options section of the Common tab, deselect the Enable Default Light check box. Switch to the Indirect Lighting tab. Click the Create button beside the Physical Sun And Sky attribute. Four nodes are automatically created: a directional light node named sunDirection, a mia_physicalsun node, a mia_physicalsky node, and a mia_exposure_simple node. The nodes are connected and immediately provide light to the scene. When you click the Create button, the Final Gathering check box, in the Final Gathering section, is selected automatically. However, you can isolate the Physical Sun And Sky's direct illumination by deselecting Final Gathering.
2. Render a test. The scene is lit solely by the Physical Sun and Sky system (see Figure 7.6). This creates an illuminated pattern on the floor, where the sunlight has passed through the transparent Skylights surface. In addition, the system creates the blue sky color. The direction from which the light arrives is determined by the directional light. You can rotate the light icon to change the position of the virtual sun. If the icon is too small to manipulate, feel free to scale it up.

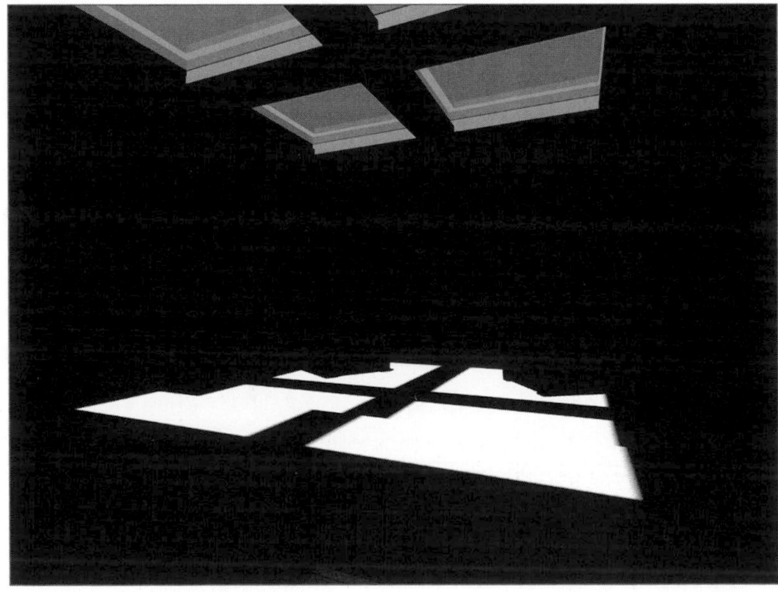

Figure 7.6
The Physical Sun and Sky system lights the room. Final Gathering is turned off. A sample scene file is included as `room_step2.ma` on the DVD.

3. You can change the light color by opening the mia_physicalsky node's Attribute Editor tab and changing the Red/Blue shift value. Higher values shift the sky color toward red. A value of 0 is an accurate blue for a mid-day sun. You can alter the overall light intensity by adjusting the Multiplier value. You can find the mia_physicalsky and mia_physicalsun nodes in the Utilities tab of the Hypershade. Note that many of the mia_physicalsky and

mia_physicalsun node attributes are identical. When you use the Create button to set up the system, the attributes are automatically connected.

Adding Portal Lights

At this stage, there is no bounced light. The majority of the room remains unlit. One method of adding bounced light to an interior room requires the use of mental ray portal lights with Final Gathering. To add a portal light, follow these steps:

1. Create an area light. Scale the light to 230, 230, 230 in X, Y, Z. Rotate the light –90 degrees in X so that its pointer points downward. Position the light so that it fits the four skylight niches and is below the Skylights surface. The light may intersect the ceiling beams.
2. Open the light's Attribute Editor tab. Expand the mental ray section and Area Light subsection and select the Use Light Shape check box. The Maya area light is converted into a mental ray area light. Expand the Custom Shaders section and click the checkered Map button beside Light Shader. In the Create Render Node window, expand the mental ray section of the left column. Click on the phrase *MentalRay Lights*. Click the mia_portal_light shader icon.
3. Although the portal light is now functional, it requires one additional connection to make it function fully when Global Illumination is activated in a later step. Open the Hypershade. Switch to the Utilities tab. MMB+drag the mia_portal_light1 node into the work area. With the node selected, click the Input And Output Connections button. A connection to the area light's shape node is revealed. MMB+drag the mia_portal_light1 node and drop it on the area light node. The Connect Input Of menu opens. Choose Other from the menu. In the Connection Editor, choose Display Left → Show Hidden and then Display Right → Show Hidden. In the left column, click the word *Message*. In the right column, scroll to the bottom, expand the + beside MentalRayControls, and click the word *miPhotonEmitter*. The mia_portal_light1 is now used as a light shader and as a photon emitter.
4. In the Indirect Illumination tab of the Render Settings window, select the Final Gathering check box in the Final Gathering section. Render a test. Bounced light reaches the corners of the rooms (see Figure 7.7). Initially, the mental ray area light renders with a grainy pattern. You can remove the grain by raising the area light's High Samples value. We will raise the High Samples value at several points during this project.

Adjusting Final Gathering

The illumination provided by the portal light is considered direct illumination by the Final Gathering system. Therefore, Final Gathering bounces the light one time. This additional bounce adds realism and produces additional soft shadows and variations in light intensity across the model. Nevertheless, you can improve the Final Gathering result by adjusting various attributes in the Render Settings window. Follow these steps:

1. With Final Gathering, the lighting calculation becomes more accurate. The dark shadows along the ceiling corners go away. In addition, the wall sconces produce subtle up-pointing shadows. However, Final Gathering produces its own form of noise, and the walls and molding become splotchy. To improve the quality, raise the Point Interpolation value in the Final Gathering section of the Render Settings window. Point Interpolation determines how many individual Final Gather points are averaged to render any given pixel. Although the default maximum value of 50 does not affect the render time, it's better to incrementally raise the value until the render is sufficiently improved. (Unnecessarily high values create a less accurate render of the indirect illumination.) With the project, a value of 50 does produce the best results, but other values, such as 10, 20, 30, and 40, were tested (see Figure 7.8).
2. You can increase the realism of the lighting even further by raising the Secondary Diffuse Bounces value in the Final Gathering section. For example, if you set Secondary Diffuse Bounces to 1, the light produced by the portal light is allowed to bounce off two surfaces. That is, the initial bounce is courtesy of Final Gathering in its default state, and a second bounce is provided by the Secondary Diffuse Bounces attribute. You can raise the Secondary Diffuse Bounces value above 1, but the changes will be subtle. For example, in Figure 7.9, Secondary Diffuse Bounces is set to 2, causing the tops of the pillars and walls to gain small degree of brightness.

For now, set Secondary Diffuse Bounces to 1. You'll raise the value again in Chapter 8.

Figure 7.7

Bounced light is provided by a portal light placed in the skylight niches. The directional light has been rotated to throw the light against the right wall. A sample file is included as `room_step3.ma` on the DVD.

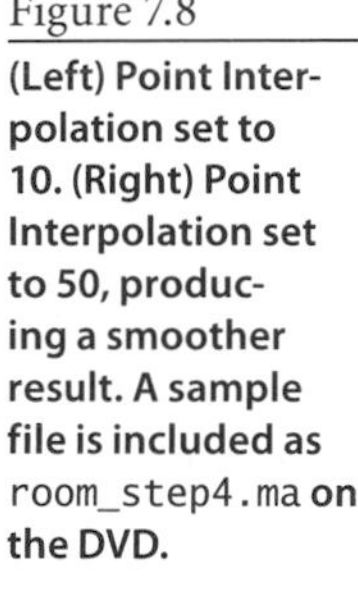

Figure 7.8

(Left) Point Interpolation set to 10. (Right) Point Interpolation set to 50, producing a smoother result. A sample file is included as `room_step4.ma` on the DVD.

Figure 7.9

(Left) Secondary Diffuse Bounces set to 0. (Right) Secondary Diffuse Bounces set to 2, which allows each light ray produced by the portal light to bounce two additional times. This results in a brightening of the upper pillars and walls. A sample file is included as `room_step5.ma` on the DVD.

Project: Adding Textures

For this project, you can create relatively pristine textures. Variation in textures created by wear and tear is not necessary. Therefore, you can use Maya's procedural textures to create many of the required texture patterns.

Note that the mia_material shader is inherently more accurate than any of the standard Maya materials. Because the shader is physically based, it interacts correctly with indirect illumination systems such as Physical Sun and Sky, portal lights, and Final Gathering.

Texturing the Floor

To add a white tile pattern to the floor, you can add a bump map. Whereas Maya offers a simple means to add a bump map to a material, a custom network must be built for the mia_material shader. As such, you can use the misss_set_normal utility to bridge between mental ray and Maya nodes. Follow these steps:

1. Open the Attribute Editor tab for the material assigned to the Floor surface. Scroll down and expand the Advanced section. Click the checkered Map button beside mental ray

Bump. In the mental ray section of the Create Render Node window, click the word *Materials*. Click the misss_set_normal shader icon. Although misss_set_normal is designed for subsurface scattering (a more realistic form of translucence), it can pass information from a Maya Bump 2d node to the mia_material shader.

2. In the misss_set_normal node's Attribute Editor tab, click the checkered Map button beside Normal Vector. In the Maya section of the Create Render Node window, click the word *Utilities*. Click the Bump 2d icon. In the Bump 2d node's Attribute Editor tab, click the checkered Map button beside Bump Value. In the Create Render Node window, click the Grid texture icon.
3. In the Grid node's Attribute Editor tab, change Fill Color to 0.5, 0.5, 0.5 gray, and Line Color to black. Set U Width and V Width to 0.5 to narrow the grid lines. In the Effects section, set Filter Offset to 0.05. Filter Offset adds additional blur to the texture before it is applied to the shading network; this will soften the tile seams slightly. Switch the place2dTexture node connected to the Grid node. Set Repeat UV to 13, 25. Render a test on a region of the floor. The bump appears. To reduce its intensity, reduce the Bump Depth value carried by the Bump 2d node. For example, the render illustrated by Figure 7.10 has a Bump Depth setting of 0.05.
4. Open the mia_material node's Attribute Editor tab. In the Diffuse section, change Color to an off-white. In the Reflection section, set the Reflectivity to 0.5. Set Glossiness to 0.5. A high Glossiness value creates a sharp reflection. A low Glossiness value creates an incoherent reflection. A value of 0.5 causes the reflection to degrade (that is, the reflection becomes more and more incoherent over distance).

Figure 7.10

A bump map adds tile seams to the floor. A Glossiness value of 0.5 degrades the reflections of the pillars. A sample file is included as `room_step6.ma` on the DVD.

Texturing the Painted Wood

To create the illusion that the wood pillars, beams, and molding are constructed from wood painted with glossy paint, you can map the mia_material shader's Glossiness attribute. Follow these steps:

1. Open the Attribute Editor tab for the mia_material shader assigned to the pillars, molding, and beams. In the Reflection section, set the Reflectivity value to 0.3 and select the Highlight Only check box. Highlight Only prevents specific reflections of the surrounding environment from appearing on the surface but maintains the shape and intensity of the specular highlight. Click the checkered Map button beside Glossiness. In the Maya section of the Create Render Node window, click the Fractal texture icon.
2. Render a test. The wood pieces pick up a specular highlight with a subtle organic pattern (see Figure 7.11). Because the wood trim is intricate, it contains noise created by the area light calculation. To remove the noise, open the light's Attribute Editor tab and set High Samples to 50.

Figure 7.11
The Glossiness attribute of the material assigned to the wood pieces adds variation to the specular highlight. A sample file is included as `room_step7.ma` on the DVD.

Texturing the Walls

To make the walls appear as if they are covered with wallpaper that has a rough pattern or weave, you can adjust the Anisotropy section of the mia_material shader. The Anisotropy section allows for the creation of irregular or streaked reflections and associated specular highlights. Follow these steps:

1. Open the Attribute Editor for the mia_material shader assigned to the Walls surface. In the Diffuse section, change Roughness to 1.0. Roughness controls the degree to which the assigned surface is diffuse. High values make the surface more matte-like, or powdery. (In contrast, the Weight attribute is equivalent to the Diffuse attribute on standard Maya materials.)
2. In the Reflection section, change Color to pale pink. This attribute tints the reflection and any associated specular highlight. Set Reflectivity to 0.5, Glossiness to 0.5, and Glossy Samples to 12. Higher Glossy Samples values smooth the reflections and reduce the appearance of noise.
3. In the Anisotropy section, raise Anisotropy to 10. A value of 1 makes the surface isotropic and creates coherent, clear reflections. Values higher than 1 create anisotropic reflections, which are streaked. Set Rotate to 45. The Rotate attribute determines the angle at which the streaked reflections run. Select Highlights Only. Render a test. The walls take on a reflective sheen, but there is no distinct reflection (see Figure 7.12).

Figure 7.12
Anisotropic reflections give the walls a specular sheen without a distinct reflection. A sample file is included as `room_step8.ma` on the DVD. For a color version of this figure, see the color insert.

Texturing the Chairs

Although the chair color has been set to black, you can give the chairs better definition by adjusting the attributes in the Diffuse and Reflection sections of the shader. Follow these steps:

1. Open the Attribute Editor for the mia_material shader assigned to the Chair surfaces. In the Diffuse section, change Color to 0, 0, 0 black, Weight to 0.4, and Roughness to 0.1.
2. In the Reflection section, change Color to dark gray, Reflectivity to 0.2, and Glossiness to 0.2. Render a test. The chairs remain dark but have their shapes defined by their diffuse reflections of the floor and surrounding walls (see Figure 7.13).

Figure 7.13
The adjustment of various Diffuse and Reflection attributes help define the shape of the chairs. A sample file is included as `room_step9.ma` on the DVD.

Texturing the Sconces

Although the light sconces are a minor part of the room scene, they can benefit from an adjustment of common color and reflectivity attributes. To make the surfaces appear as if they are made from a gray alloy (such as pewter) that creates bright, incoherent reflections, follow these steps:

1. Open the Attribute Editor for the mia_material shader assigned to the Sconce surfaces. In the Diffuse section, change Color to dark gray (0.3, 0.3, 0.3 in RGB), Weight to 0.5, and Roughness to 0.5.
2. In the Reflection section, change Reflectivity to 0.35, Glossiness to 0.5, and Glossy Samples to 64. A high Glossy Samples value prevents noise from appearing in the reflection of objects that take up a relatively small part of the screen space. Select the Metal Material check box, which forces mental ray to derive the reflection color from the Color attribute found within the Diffuse section. Deriving the reflection color from a material's diffuse color is a more accurate rendering method than choosing an arbitrary specular color. Note that the terms *reflection color* and *specular color* refer to the color of the same shading quality—specular reflection. However, the mia_material shader bases its specular reflection on the actual reflected environment, whereas Maya's standard materials, such as Blinn, base their specular reflections on an idealized point light.
3. Click the color swatch beside Color in the Reflection section. In the Color Chooser window, set the color to 10, 10, 10 in RGB. Raising the value above the default threshold of 1.0 increases the specular reflection intensity. Render a test. The sconces gain a metallic look (see Figure 7.14).

Figure 7.14
The light sconces are given a metallic look by raising the Reflection section's Color attribute above 1.0. A sample file is included as `room_step10.ma` on the DVD.

Texturing the Poster

The Frame surface requires a bitmap texture of a printed piece of art. The narrow frame of the poster sits along the four edges of the UV texture space and should be included as part of the bitmap. For example, in Figure 7.15, a render from a previous chapter is converted into an appropriate bitmap.

Applying a texture bitmap to a mia_material shader (and many other mental ray shaders) requires the construction of a custom network. The network must include separate nodes to import the bitmap texture, generate texture coordinates, and transfer the coordinates to the surface. To create the network, follow these steps:

1. Open the Attribute Editor for the mia_material shader assigned to the Frame surface. In the Reflection section, change Glossiness to 0.75. In the Diffuse section, click the checkered Map button beside Color. In the mental ray section of the Create Render Node window, click the word *Textures*. In the shader column, click the mib_texture_lookup icon. In the Attribute Editor tab for the new mib_texture_lookup node, click the checkered Map button beside Coord. In the Create Render Node window, click the mib_texture_remap icon.

2. In the Attribute Editor tab for the new mib_texture_remap node, click the checkered Map button beside Input. In the Create Render Node window, click the mib_texture_vector icon. In the Attribute Editor tab for the new mib_texture_vector node, change the Project menu to UV. The mib_texture_vector shader projects the texture space onto the assigned surface. When Project is set to UV, the texture space is mapped directly to the surface by identifying vertex locations of the surface. The mib_texture_remap shader serves as a tiling tool and functions in a similar manner to a Maya place2dTexture node. The mib_texture_lookup shader maps the bitmap (after it's loaded) to the UV texture space. Refer to Figure 7.16 for the final shading network.
3. Open the Attribute Editor tab of the new mib_texture_lookup node. Click the checkered Map button beside Tex. In the Create Render Node window, click the mentalrayTexture icon. In the Attribute Editor tab for the new mentalrayTexture node, click the file Browse button and retrieve the bitmap that will serve as a texture. Render a test. The bitmap appears across the surface (see Figure 7.17).

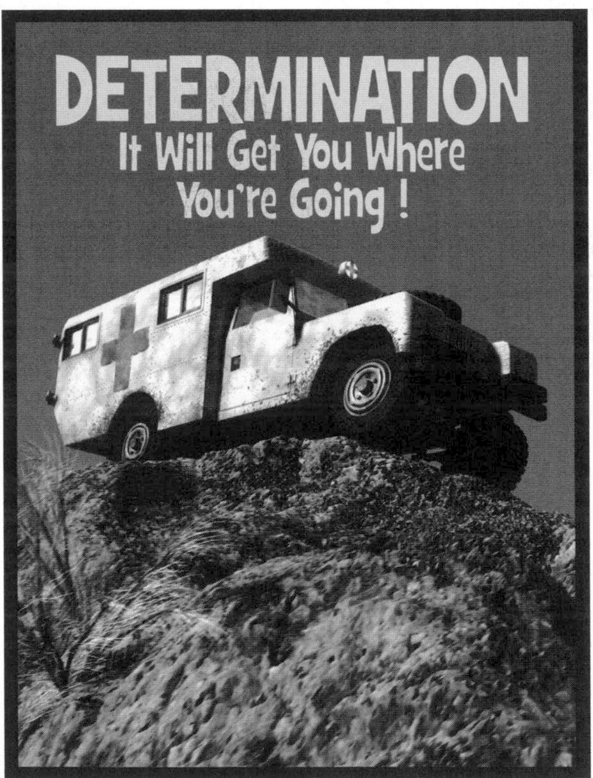

Figure 7.15

A render from a previous chapter is converted to a texture bitmap for the Frame surface. A sample file is included as `Poster_Color.tga` in the `ProjectFiles/Project4/Textures` folder on the DVD.

Global Illumination

To use Global Illumination, you must use the mental ray renderer. In addition, you must employ virtual photons. In Maya, spot, point, area, and directional lights generate photons when the light's Emit Photons attribute is selected.

When a scene is rendered, photons are traced from each photon-emitting light to surfaces in the scene. If a photon "hits" a surface, that photon is absorbed, reflected,

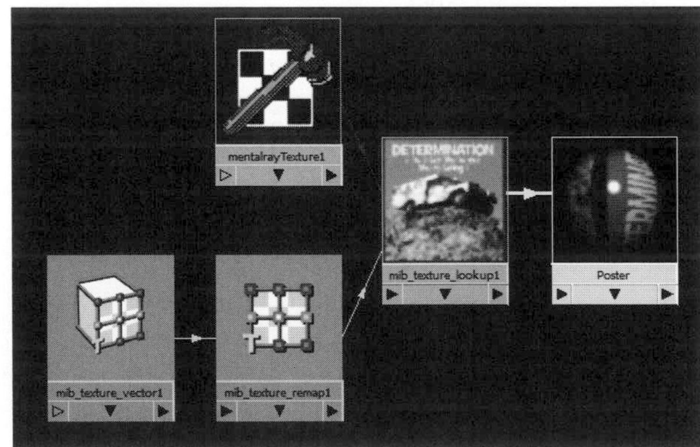

Figure 7.16

The final shading network necessary to map a bitmap to a surface via a mia_material shader.

or transmitted (refracted) based on the qualities of the material assigned to the surface. If a photon is reflected or transmitted, it survives with only a portion of its original energy. The amount of energy is determined by the reflection coefficient, which is established by the reflectivity attribute of the assigned material. The photon is affected by other material attributes as well. Attributes that establish the surface's diffuse, color, and various specular highlight qualities have an equal impact. If a photon survives a hit and is reflected or transmitted, it continues through the scene until it hits another surface. Once again, the photon is absorbed, reflected, or transmitted. This process continues until the surviving photons are stopped by the Max Photon Depth attribute, which defines the number of hits permitted per photon. (Max Photon depth is located in the Photon Tracing section of the Indirect Lighting tab in the Render Settings window.)

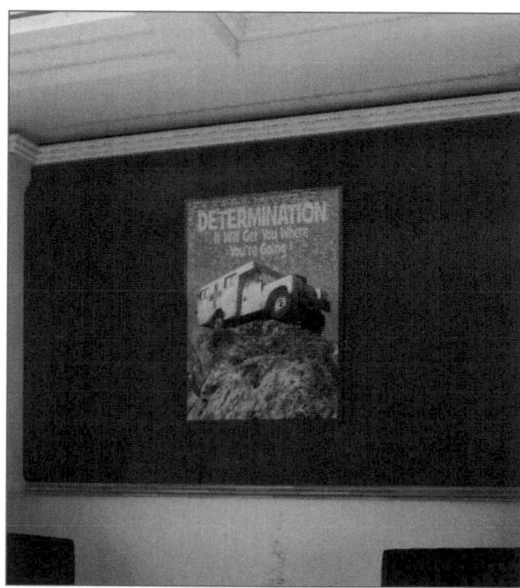

Figure 7.17

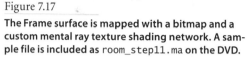

The Frame surface is mapped with a bitmap and a custom mental ray texture shading network. A sample file is included as `room_step11.ma` on the DVD.

To simplify the photon-tracing process, many global illumination systems, including the one employed by mental ray, randomly cull photons in a process known as *Russian Roulette.* Photons that survive a surface hit through reflection or refraction are given an increased energy that is proportional to the potential energy of all the photons generated by the light source. The photons that are culled and thereby absorbed by the surface have their position, incident direction, and energy stored in a special photon map.

Ultimately, the information stored in the photon map is combined with the direct illumination model, which in turn determines the color and intensity of each rendered pixel. The number of photons generated by a given light is set by the light's Global Illum Photons attribute. You can lower or raise the default value of 10,000 to decrease or increase quality. In addition, you can change the qualities of photons generated by a light with the following attributes (all of which are found in the Caustic And Global Illumination subsection of the mental ray section in the light's Attribute Editor tab):

Photon Color Photon Color represents the red, green, and blue components of a photon's energy. Photon Color is a "dummy" attribute. The RGB values of its color swatch are multiplied by the Photon Intensity attribute to produce Energy R, Energy G, and Energy B attributes.

Photon Intensity Photon Intensity is a scaling factor used to determine the intensity of photons produced by a light. A value of 0 will turn off photon tracing for the light.

Exponent Exponent simulates light falloff over distance. The default value of 2 replicates natural, quadratic decay. A value of 1 effectively prevents falloff from occurring. Values higher than 2 create a more rapid falloff by artificially decreasing photon energy with distance.

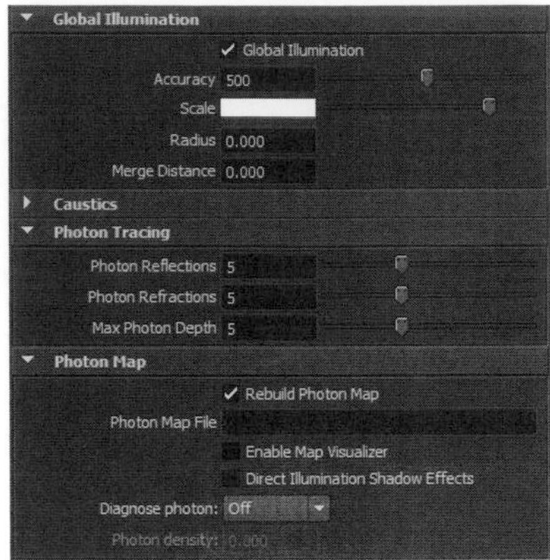

Figure 7.18
The Global Illumination section in the Indirect Lighting tab of the Render Settings window

Global Illumination attributes are contained within the Global Illumination section of the Indirect Lighting tab in the Render Settings window (see Figure 7.18).

The following are the most critical Global Illumination attributes:

Radius Radius controls the maximum distance from a surface point that the renderer will seek out photon hits to determine the color of the point in question. If photons hits are within the search region, their energies are averaged. The search regions render as colored discs when the Radius is inappropriately small for a scene or there are an insufficient number of photons present. The default value of 0 allows Maya to automatically pick a Radius based on the scene size.

Accuracy Accuracy sets the maximum number of neighboring photon hits included in the color estimate of a single rendered point. The search for neighboring photon hits is limited to the region established by the Radius attribute. In general, the higher the Accuracy value, the smoother the result. However, Accuracy affects only photon hits that are in close proximity. That is, if the photon count is low or the Radius value is small so that the photon hits are not discovered in the search region, the Accuracy attribute will have no effect on the render.

Scale Scale serves as a multiplier for the Photon Intensity attribute of all lights in the scene. If the slider is set to 50 percent gray, all the photons in the scene will be at half intensity.

Rebuild Photon Map Found within the Photon Map section, Rebuild Photon Map determines whether photon maps are rebuilt for each render. This attribute should be left selected unless the lighting is finalized and there is no object motion in the scene. If unselected, this attribute will look for the photon map listed in the Photon Map File attribute field.

Photon Reflections and Photon Refractions Found within the Photon Tracing section, Photon Reflections defines the maximum number of times a photon will reflect in a scene. This attribute is overridden by the Max Photon Depth attribute. The first surface encountered is not included in the count. Photon Refractions functions in the same manner but affects the maximum number of photon refractions.

Project: Activating Global Illumination

Follow these steps to activate Global Illumination:

1. Switch to the Indirect Illumination tab of the Render Settings window. In the Global Illumination section, select the Global Illumination check box. In the Final Gathering section, temporarily deselect Final Gathering. Temporarily disabling Final Gathering will speed up the render as you adjust the various Global Illumination settings.

2. Open the Attribute Editor tab for the area light. In the Caustic And Global Illumination section, select Emit Photons. Render a test. Large, splotchy dots appear across the scene. Each dot represents a photon hit. The dot indicates the area of influence the photon has when combining the photon's indirect illumination information with the direct illumination calculation. The dots are colored, indicating that their energy has been influenced by a surface they have bounced off. For example, the red dots indicate a bounce off a nearby red wall. Hence, a major advantage of Global Illumination is the ability to produce color bleed. Although Final Gathering is also used to produce bleed, it is generally more subtle.
3. At this point, the photon hits are not fully blended with the direct illumination provided by the portal light. To correct this, adjust the Radius attribute, found in the Global Illumination section of the Render Settings window. By default, Radius is set to 0, which means that Maya automatically selects a Radius value based on the scene size. Depending on the scene, this either can work perfectly or can produce photon hits whose influence is too large or too small. Change Radius to 1 and render a test on a region of the scene. A value of 1 produces small photon hits that are too small to blend together (see Figure 7.19). Change Radius to 20. Render a test. The photon hits begin to overlap, particularly along the ceiling beams. However, the hits are not blending together. Change Radius to 50 and then render a test. The render becomes smoother.
4. If the Radius value is too large, there is a danger that the indirect illumination provided by the photons will become inaccurate. In such a case, a single photon's influence might extend too far across the geometry. Therefore, it's important to adjust the total number of photons in the scene at the same time. To do so, adjust the Global Illum Photons value in the Caustic And Global Illumination section of the light's Attribute Editor tab. For example, increasing Global Illum Photons to 30,000 while leaving Radius set to 50 produces a cleaner result. When raising the Global Illum Photons value, do so incrementally. The more photons that are being traced, the longer the render will take.
5. Reactivate Final Gathering by selecting the Final Gathering check box. Final Gathering provides additional smoothing to the Global Illumination indirect illumination and helps hide unblended photon hits. The scene becomes brighter, and there is a greater degree of color bleed (see Figure 7.20). In particular, the red from the walls can be seen along the ceiling beams and molding.

The activation of Global Illumination concludes this portion of Project 4. In Chapter 8, you will refine the direct illumination provided by the portal light, as well as adjust the indirect illumination provided by Final Gathering and Global Illumination. In addition, you'll activate ambient occlusion, build a stereoscopic camera, and set up advanced render passes.

Figure 7.19

(Top) Scene is rendered with Global Illumination. Final Gathering is disabled. Initially, Radius is set to 0, producing large splotches. (Bottom) Radius is set to 1, producing small photon hits. A sample file is included as `room_step12.ma` **on the DVD.**

Figure 7.20

The final render for part 1 of the room project. A sample file is included as `room_step13.ma` **on the DVD. For a color version of this figure, see the color insert.**

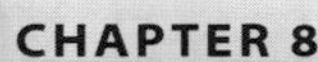

Texturing and Lighting an Environment, Part 2

In Chapter 7, "Texturing and Lighting an Environment, Part 1," you textured and lit an interior room with skylights. In this chapter, part 2 of the project will guide you through the following steps:

- **Preparing the scene**
- **Adding occlusion**
- **Creating multirender passes**
- **Fine-tuning the render**
- **Setting up a stereoscopic camera**

In addition, important lighting and texturing theory is included as follows:

- **Ambient occlusion**
- **Multirender passes**
- **Stereoscopic 3D**

Project: Preparing the Scene

To begin this phase of the tutorial, open the scene file you created for the last step of Chapter 7. A completed sample file is saved as `room_step13.ma` in the `ProjectFiles/Project4` folder on the DVD.

Note that the sample scene files included for Chapter 7 and this chapter assume that the bitmap textures are located within the `Textures` folder of the `ProjectFiles/Project4` project directory. Before opening a sample scene file, choose File → Project → Set and browse for the `Project4` folder, whether the folder remains at its original location on the DVD or is located on a drive after the DVD contents have been copied.

Ambient Occlusion

Ambient occlusion refers to the absorption or misdirection of indirect light as it bounces off surface convolutions or surfaces in close proximity. In such a situation, the indirect light is blocked and certain surface points appear darker. The darkened points are commonly seen within cracks, crevices, or pits, or where one surface sits close to another. Maya renderers, such as Maya Software or mental ray, do not produce the occlusion effects in their default state. However, mental ray is capable of producing ambient occlusion through several shaders and the contribution pass system. The mia_material shader carries an Ambient Occlusion section.

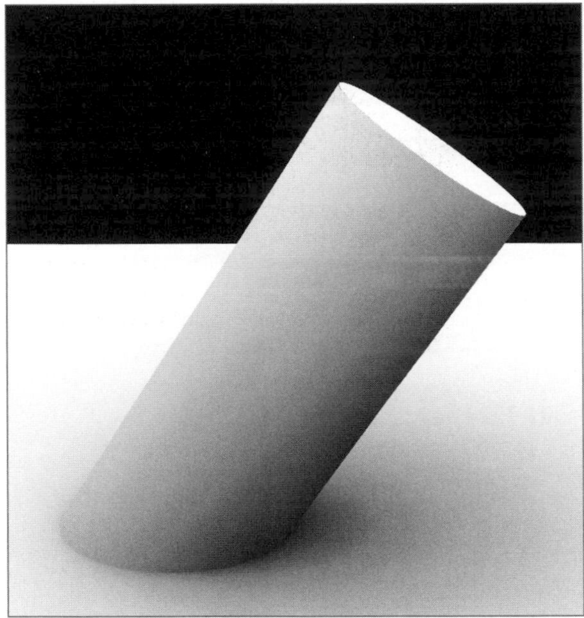

Figure 8.1

An ambient occlusion render. A sample scene file is included as `amb_occlusion.ma` in the `ProjectFiles/Project4/Reference` folder on the DVD.

An ambient occlusion shader ignores common material qualities such as color. Instead, the shader calculates whether a surface point is blocked by nearby surfaces, which potentially reduce the amount of light the surface point receives. If ambient occlusion is rendered as its own render pass, the render produces soft shadows over a white surface color (see Figure 8.1). Additional compositing is required to utilize such a render. Generally, an external compositing program is used; however, it is also possible to combine the render with other passes through Maya's Render Layer Editor. The mia_material shader, on the other hand, is able to combine the ambient occlusion shading component with the direct and indirect lighting information.

Project: Adding Occlusion

The effect of ambient occlusion can often appear extremely subtle. Therefore, it often pays to test the result on a piece of primitive geometry. To do so, follow these steps:

1. Create a primitive sphere. Translate and scale the sphere so it sits on the floor near the chairs. Assign the sphere to the same material that's assigned to the Floor surface.

2. To save test renders in the Render View buffer, choose Render → Render All Layers → ❒ and then select the Keep All Layers radio button. Render the region of the frame that contains the sphere. Note the quality of the shadow below the sphere.
3. Open the Attribute Editor for the material assigned to the Floor surface. Expand the Ambient Occlusion section and select the Use Ambient Occlusion check box. Render a test. Compare the result with the previous render. You can display previous renders by moving the Render View scroll bar to the right. The Ambient Occlusion attribute adds additional darkness to the part of the floor that is closest to the sphere (see Figure 8.2). To darken the result of the ambient occlusion contribution, lower the Ambient Shadow Color, in the Ambient Occlusion section, to black. Ambient Shadow Color sets the darkness of the occlusion contribution where total occlusion occurs (light is trapped within a surface convolution or is blocked by a neighboring surface).

Figure 8.2

(Left) A primitive sphere is added to the room and rendered without ambient occlusion. (Right) The same render with the Ambient Occlusion attribute activated. Note the darkening of the shadow where the sphere is in close proximity. A sample file is included as `room_step14.ma` on the DVD.

You can control the accuracy and quality of the ambient occlusion calculation by adjusting the Samples and Distance attributes, which are found in the Ambient Occlusion section (see Figure 8.3). Samples sets the number of probe rays sent out to determine occlusion. The higher the Samples value, the smoother the result. Distance determines the range within which geometry is probed. If Distance is set to 0, the entire scene is examined. If Distance is set to a non-0 value, only surfaces found within the range will be considered occluding surfaces.

The ability of the mia_material shader to combine ambient occlusion with the indirect lighting calculation is controlled by the Use Detail Distance attribute. If this attribute is deselected, the occlusion contribution does not affect the indirect lighting component of a render (although occlusion shadows are still added). For stylistic effect, you can tint the ambient occlusion contribution by changing the Ambient Light Color value.

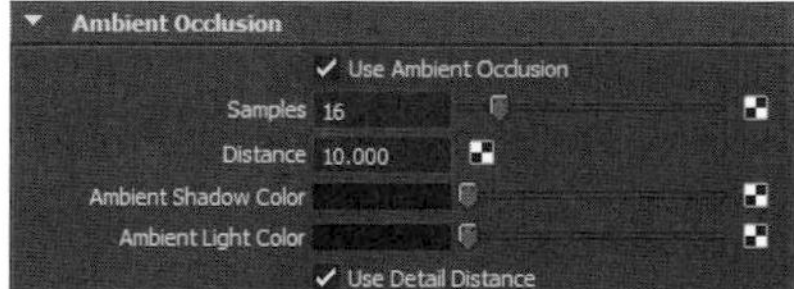

Figure 8.3

The Ambient Occlusion section of the mia_material shader

After you have tested the ambient occlusion settings, hide the sphere and render other regions of the frame. For a surface to be affected by the occlusion, its assigned material must have the Use Ambient Occlusion check box selected.

Note that mental ray provides the mib_amb_occlusion texture, which can be used to create an ambient occlusion render pass without the use of the mia_material shader.

Multirender Passes

You can use several methods to create render passes in Maya. As discussed in Chapter 6, "Texturing and Lighting a Vehicle, Part 2," you can create a few basic render passes through the Render Pass Options section of a render layer's Attribute Editor tab. In addition, you can create specialized passes by assigning a material override to a particular layer. However, these methods are somewhat limited. When using the mental ray renderer, however, you have access to a wide array of render passes through the multirender pass system.

Although the multirender pass system is applied through the Render Layer Editor, it's designed to reduce the need for numerous render layers. With the system, you can create an unlimited number of render passes and group them into sets called *pass contribution maps*. Hence, a single layer can host multiple render passes, which involve any desired combination of surfaces, lights, and render pass materials or shaders. This allows for the creation of a wide variety of render passes with a minimal number of layers and layer preparation.

As previously discussed, render passes break a scene into shading components (diffuse, ambient, specular, and so on) or into specialized compositing passes (ambient occlusion, motion vector, object normal, and so on). Render passes allow for a greater degree of control during the compositing process. For example, you can adjust the color, brightness, and sharpness of a specular highlight independent of all other surface qualities.

The Render Layer Editor is able to serve as a simple compositor by combining various render layers through the Render View. The way in which the layers are combined is controlled by each layer's blending mode settings. This system, however, does not function with contribution maps. Hence, you must use an external compositing program to combine contribution map render passes.

Although there are numerous render pass types, a handful of passes are commonly used in the animation industry. Brief descriptions of each follow, and several of these passes are illustrated in the next section of this chapter:

Diffuse Color information without specularity (see Figure 8.4). There are several variations, some of which exclude cast shadows and contributions of lights in the scene.

Specular The specular component by itself (see Figure 8.4).

Figure 8.4

(Left) A diffuse render pass. Shadows and specularity are excluded. (Right) A specular render pass. The hill surface is assigned to a Lambert material and thereby creates no specularity.

Shadow The shadow by itself. The shadow may appear in the alpha channel while the RGB channels remain black. If the shadow pass is created through a mental ray render pass, the shadow area will be cut out in the RGB channels (see Figure 8.5).

Motion Vector Encodes the motion of an object into an image's color channels (see Figure 8.5). With a motion vector pass and a nonblurred beauty pass, you can create and fine-tune motion blur in the composite.

Figure 8.5

(Left) A Shadow render pass created with mental ray. Shadow areas are rendered with the surfaces' material color. Nonshadowed areas are left black. (Right) 3D motion vector. Horizontal and vertical motion is encoded in the red and green channels. A sample scene file that includes the passes illustrated in this section is included as `ambulance_passes.ma` in the `ProjectFiles/Project3` folder on the DVD.

Occlusion As discussed in the previous section, an ambient occlusion pass renders additional soft shadows inside surface convolutions and at locations where surfaces are in close proximity. Ambient occlusion passes are used to darken areas of a beauty pass that are otherwise too bright and unrealistic. Reflection occlusion passes, on the other hand, record the strength of reflections, which are also affected by surface convolutions and surface proximity. Reflection occlusion passes are used to vary the intensity of reflection render passes. Ambient occlusion and reflection occlusion passes create soft shadows over an otherwise white environment.

Reflection Reflections by themselves. Objects that appear in reflections are not included in the render. It's also possible to render the refractions of semitransparent objects by themselves.

Depth (Z-Buffer) Encodes the distance from the camera to a surface point through a grayscale (scalar) image. You can use a depth map render to apply effects that vary along the z-axis of the camera. For example, you can simulate depth of field in the composite.

Matte Matte passes take on many forms, but are always used to cut or block a part of another render pass. For example, a matte pass might be created to cut out the sky of a beauty pass. Matte passes often take the form of a grayscale render in which the portion of the image to be cut is rendered as black. Matte passes are often converted to alpha channels within the composite. For an example render, see the next section.

Normal Normal passes encode surface normal direction as colors within RGB. The normal information may be relative to the camera, a particular light, or the surface itself in object or world space. Normal passes are used for specialized compositing tasks in which the relationship of the surface to the camera, lights, or other objects is critical. For example, a normal pass may be used to create a compositing effect that appears only on edges of a surface that *do not face* the camera. For an example render, see the next section.

Project: Creating Multirender Passes

To create a multirender pass, you must render with mental ray and create layers and pass contribution maps through the Render Layer Editor. You can follow these steps to create passes for the room scene:

1. Select all the surfaces and lights in the scene. From the Render Layer Editor menu, choose Layers → Create Layer From Selected. Open the Render Settings window and switch to the Passes tab (mental ray must be the renderer of choice).
2. Click the Create New Render Pass button. This button is the topmost button to the right of the Scene Passes section. The Create Render Passes window opens. A list of standard mental ray render passes is listed (see Figure 8.6). Highlight one or more pass names and click the Create And Close button. The new render passes are created and listed in the Scene Passes section.
3. To associate a new render pass with a layer, you must create a pass contribution map. To do so, select the pass name in the Scene Passes section and click the Associate Selected Passes With Current Render Layer button (at the bottom of the Scene Passes section). The pass is listed in the Associated Passes section (see Figure 8.7).

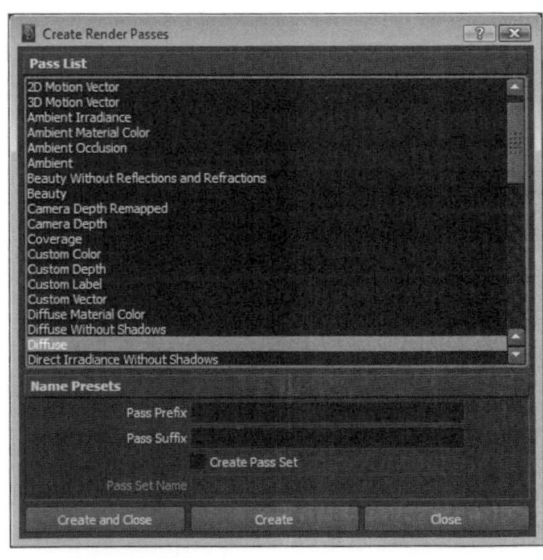

Figure 8.6

The Create Render Passes window with a small section of available mental ray render passes

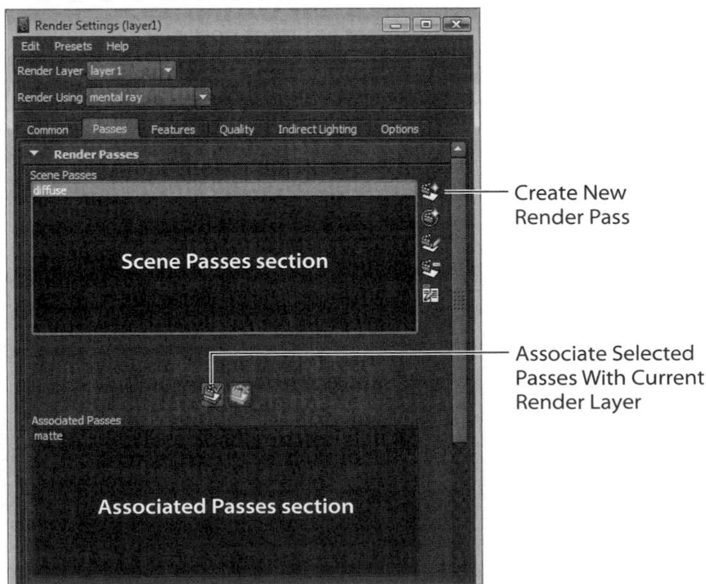

Figure 8.7

Top section of the Passes tab of the Render Settings window. A single render pass, diffuse, is listed in the Scene Passes section. A single pass, matte, is listed in the Associated Passes section.

4. Click the Create New Contribution Pass And Associate With Current Layer button (the topmost button beside the Passes Used By Contribution Map section). A new map is created and is listed under the layer name in the Render Layer Editor. In the Passes Used By Contribution Map section of the Passes tab, change the Associated Pass Contribution Map menu to the new map name. Highlight the pass name in the Associated Passes section and click the Associate Selected Passes With Current Pass Contribution Map button (at the top of the Passes Used By Contribution Map section, as shown in Figure 8.8). The pass appears in the Passes Used By Contribution Map section.

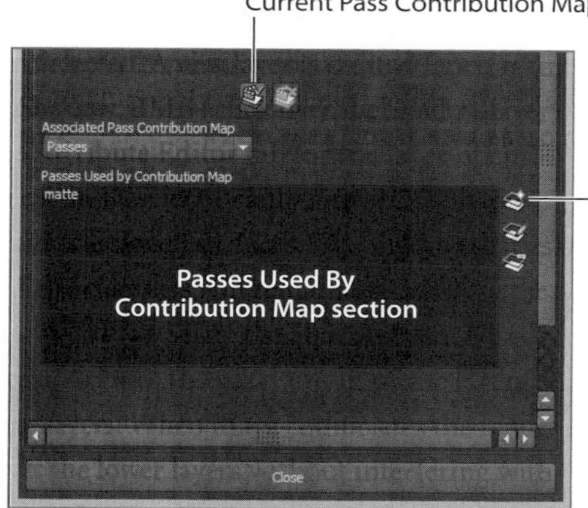

Figure 8.8

Bottom section of the Passes tab of the Render Settings window. A single render pass, matte, is listed in the Passes Used By Contribution Map section.

5. Launch a batch render (Render → Batch Render). Render a single frame. Each pass associated with a contribution map is rendered separately and placed within folders located in the default project directory. For example, an ambient occlusion pass will be placed within an AO folder, which in turned is located within a folder named after the rendered layer, such as *layer1*. A beauty pass is supplied automatically and is named MasterBeauty.

Figure 8.9 illustrates the application of contribution maps to the room scene.

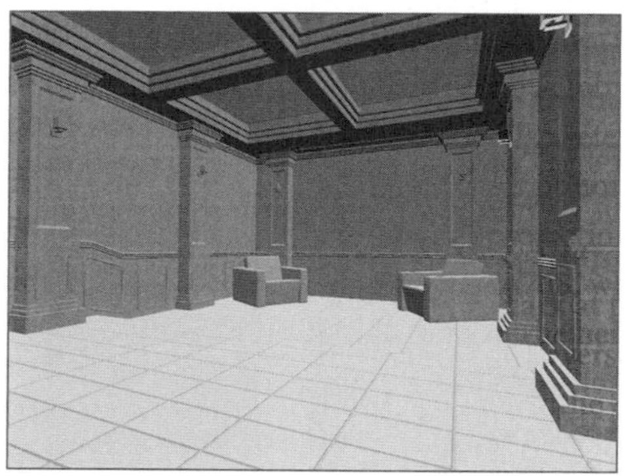

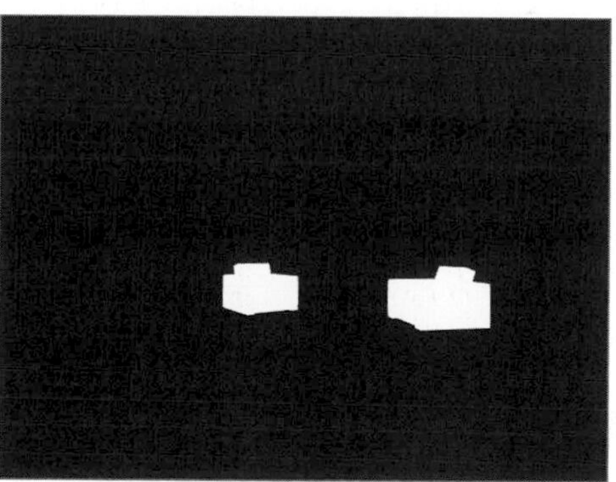

Figure 8.9

(Top) normalWorld pass. (Bottom) Matte pass

In this example, one render layer and two contribution maps are created. The first contribution map, named Map_All_Objects, has the normalWorld render pass assigned to it. The normalWorld pass reads the surface normals in world space and encodes the normal vectors as RGB colors. The second contribution map, named Map_Chairs_Only, has the chair surfaces assigned to it, but no other objects in the scene. The matte pass creates a black-and-white matte for the chairs. In a compositing program, you can interpret the white areas as opaque alpha and the black areas as transparent alpha.

The image format is set to Layered PSD, which creates a single Photoshop PSD file with both render passes, as well as a beauty pass, arranged as layers. (The background layer is provided for Photoshop and is solid black.) A sample PSD file is included as `Render_Passes.psd` in the `ProjectFiles/Project4/Reference` folder on the DVD. A sample Maya scene file is included as `room_step15.ma`.

Contribution Map Tips

Here are a few additional tips for working with render passes and contribution maps:

- For a contribution map and its associated render passes to be rendered, the parent layer must have its Renderable button activated. If a layer has more than one contribution map, all the maps' render passes are placed within subfolders located within a master folder named after the layer.
- If you choose Layered PSD as an image format, the individual render passes are arranged as layers in a single Photoshop file; the individual render pass files are destroyed. If you choose OpenEXR, the passes are carried by a single EXR file. You will need an advanced compositing program, such as The Foundry's Nuke, to extract the various passes.
- When you create a contribution map with Create New Contribution Pass And Associate With Current Layer button in the Render settings window, all the objects assigned to the layer are assigned to the map. However, you can remove objects from a map at any time by choosing Contribution → Remove Selected Objects From Selected Pass Contribution Maps from the Render Layer Editor menu. You can add objects by choosing Contribution → Add Selected Objects To Selected Pass Contribution Maps. Ultimately, a contribution map does not have to carry the same objects and lights as its parent layer.
- You can create a new contribution map through the Render Layer Editor by RMB+clicking a layer name and choosing Pass Contribution Map → Create Empty Pass Contribution Map or Pass Contribution Map → Create Pass Contribution Map And Add Selected.
- You can delete or empty a contribution map by RMB+clicking the map name in the Render Layer Editor and choosing the associated menu item. You can add a new render pass to a map at any time by RMB+clicking the map name in the Render Layer Editor and choosing Add New Render Pass → *pass name*.
- You cannot render passes associated with a contribution map in the Render View window. However, you can view rendered passes by choosing File → Load Render Pass → *pass name*.
- To rename a contribution pass, double-click the pass name in the Render Layer Editor layer stack. The name cell becomes active and allows a new name to be typed in its slot.

- Although you can create render passes for a contribution map, you cannot assign a Render Settings override, render flag override, or material override to a map. Overrides are an option exclusive to layers. In other words, a layer can have any number of contribution maps assigned to it, but an override can be activated only for the layer as a whole. For more information on overrides, see Chapter 6.
- You can fine-tune the way in which a render pass is created. To do so, double-click the pass name anywhere it appears in the Passes tab of the Render Settings window. A tab is opened in the Attribute Editor and displays any options associated with the pass.

Because a wide array of render passes are available through contribution maps, it may be difficult to decide which passes to use. As a rule of thumb, you should create a render layer and a contribution map only if it gives you additional flexibility as part of the compositing process. However, the flexibility must be weighed against any additional render time that multiple render layers and contribution maps might require.

Project: Fine-Tuning the Render

The final step of this project requires the creation of a stereoscopic camera. However, before moving onto that step, it's best to finalize a beauty render of the room. Although the texturing and lighting is in place, you can spend additional time fine-tuning material, indirect lighting, and render settings. While testing settings, you can deactivate any new render layers by disabling the layers' Renderable button. Recommendations for the fine-tuning follow:

mental ray Area Light The mental ray area light is prone to create fine noise, particularly where the light is in close proximity to geometry. To improve the quality, incrementally raise the High Samples value in the Area Light subsection of the area light's Attribute Editor tab. High Samples sets the number of shadow rays employed by the area light, as measured in the X and Y direction of the light's icon. Note that the High Sample Limit and Low Samples attributes control the number of times a shadow ray is allowed to reflect or refract in a scene. High Sample Limit determines the number of reflections and refractions. After the High Sample Limit is met by the shadow ray, the ray is limited by the Low Samples value.

mia_material If you are using the ambient occlusion feature of a mia_material shader, you can increase the quality of the occlusion contribution by raising the Samples value (in the Ambient Occlusion section). The mia_material shader also carries per-material Final Gathering and Global Illumination settings in the Indirect Illumination Options section. You can increase or decrease the indirect lighting intensity for Final Gathering and/or Global Illumination by raising or lowering the FG / GI Multiplier value. The FG / GI Multiplier value is multiplied by the Primary Diffuse Scale value, which is found in the Final Gathering section of the Rendering Settings window. To increase or decrease the number of Final Gather rays used for a Final Gather point, adjust the Final Gather Quality value. The Final Gather Quality value is multiplied by the Accuracy value, which is found in the Final Gathering section of the Rendering Settings window.

Final Gathering To increase the accuracy of the Final Gathering calculation, increase the Accuracy value. Accuracy determines the number of Final Gather rays used to calculate each Final Gather point. To add secondary diffuse bounces to the scene, and thereby make the indirect illumination calculation more accurate in places where objects are in close proximity, raise the Secondary Diffuse Bounces value. Accuracy and Secondary Diffuse Bounces are located in the Final Gathering section of the Indirect Illumination tab of the Render Settings window. Occasionally, Final Gathering will create noise in the form of gray dots or larger bright discs (see Chapter 2, "Texturing and Lighting a Product, Part 2," for examples of the discs). To remove the noise, raise the Filter value. Filter is found in the Final Gathering Quality subsection.

Global Illumination As discussed in Chapter 7, the Global Illumination quality is dependent on the number of photons generated by each light and the Radius value, which is used to blend photon hits into cohesive indirect illumination. In addition, you can adjust the Accuracy value (found in the Global Illumination section), which controls the smoothness with which the photon hits are blended together.

Anti-Aliasing Settings Throughout Chapter 7 and this chapter, the anti-aliasing option has been left at medium quality. To increase the quality and thus force the renderer to examine more subpixels, raise the Min Sample Level and Max Sample Level.

As an example of fine-tuning, the following settings produce the render illustrated by Figure 8.10:

- Area light High Samples: 256
- mia_material ambient occlusion Samples (Walls, Wood, and Floor materials only): 32
- Final Gathering Accuracy: 512
- Final Gathering Secondary Diffuse Bounces: 2
- Global Illumination Accuracy: 1000
- Anti-aliasing Min Sample Level: 0
- Anti-aliasing Max Sample Level: 2

Stereoscopic 3D

Stereoscopy is any technique that creates the illusion of depth through the capture of two slightly different views that replicate human binocular vision. Because left and right human eyes are separated by a distinct distance, each eye perceives a unique view. Objects at different distances from the viewer appear to have different horizontal positions in each view.

For example, objects close to the viewer will have significantly different horizontal positions in each view, while objects far from the viewer will have almost identical horizontal positions. The difference between each view is known as *binocular or horizontal disparity.* The horizontal disparity is measurable as an angle between two lines of sight, and the angle is defined as *parallax*. The human mind uses the horizontal disparity as a depth cue. When the cue is combined with monocular cues such as size estimation, the world is successfully perceived as three-dimensional. The process of yielding a depth cue from horizontal disparity is known as *stereopsis*.

Figure 8.10

The final beauty render of the room. For a color version of this figure, see the color insert. The sample file is included as `room_step16.ma` on the DVD.

The stereoscopic process was applied to motion pictures in the late 1890s. The peak of commercial stereoscopic filmmaking occurred in the early 1950s, with dozens of feature films released. By this point, the term *3D* referred to stereoscopic filmmaking. While pre-2000 3D theatrical motion pictures generally relied on anaglyph methods to create the depth illusion, post-2000 theatrical motion pictures usually employ polarization. In both cases, the viewer must wear glasses with unique lenses.

3D projects designed for television viewing, on the other hand, may employ anaglyph, polarization, checkerboard wobulation, or horizontal interlacing methods. That said, recent developments in technology allow specialized stereoscopic televisions to be viewed without glasses.

In all these cases, the subject must be shot with paired cameras. One camera captures the left eye, and one camera captures the right eye. The cameras must be arranged in such a manner (through physical placement, specialized optics, or beam splitters) that the distance between the lenses emulates the average distance between human eyes.

Anaglyphs carry left and right eye views; however, each view is printed or processed with chromatically opposite colors. The views are overlapped into a single image. Each lens of the viewer's glasses matches one of the two colors. For example, the left view is red, and the right view is cyan. The left lens of the viewer's glasses is therefore tinted cyan, allowing only the red left view to be seen by the left eye. The right lens of the viewer's glasses is tinted red, allowing only the cyan right view to be seen by the right eye.

In contrast, *polarization* relies on an unseen quality of light energy. Light consists of oscillating electrical fields, which are commonly represented by a waveform with a specific wavelength. When the light oscillation is oriented in a particular direction, it is polarized. Linear polarization traps the waveform in a plane. Circular polarization causes the waveform to corkscrew. When light is reflected from a nonmetallic surface, it's naturally polarized; that is, the light energy is emitted from the surface in a specific direction. Sky light, which is sunlight scattered through the Earth's atmosphere, is naturally polarized. Polarized filters take advantage of this phenomenon and are able to block light with specific polarization. For example, polarized sunglasses block light that is horizontally polarized (roughly parallel to the ground), thus reducing the intensity of specular reflections (which form glare). Professional photographic polarized filters can be rotated to target different polarizations. Stereoscopic 3D systems apply polarized filters to the projected left and right views as well as to each lens of the viewer's glasses. The polarization allows each view to be alternately hidden from sight.

The *checkerboard wobulation* method alternates pixels from the left camera and right camera views, forming a checkerboard pattern. The *horizontal interlacing* method alternates between rows of pixels from left camera and right camera views; this method is often employed by polarized LCD monitors.

Project: Setting Up a Stereoscopic Camera

To create a stereoscopic camera in Maya, follow these steps:

1. Choose Create → Cameras → Stereo Camera. A new stereo camera is created. The stereo camera consists of three camera icons, which represent the left eye, right eye, and averaged center view (see Figure 8.11). If the stereo camera icon is too small, scale the camera through the Channel Box.

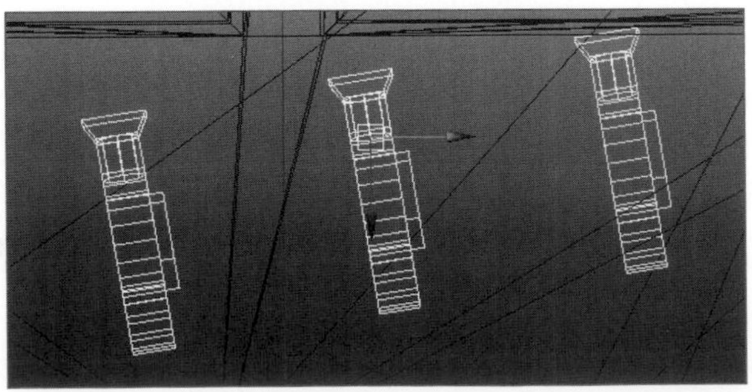

Figure 8.11

A stereo camera with left, right, and center views represented by camera icons

2. Translate and rotate the new camera so that it sits inside the room. To see the camera view, choose Panel → Stereo → stereoCamera. (The camera is named stereoCamera by default.) Initially, the view appears similar to any other nonstereo camera. To see the stereo result, choose Stereo → *stereo mode* from the panel menu. The view changes to reflect the menu choice. For example, if you choose Anaglyph, the view appears doubled with one "eye" tinted red and the second "eye" tinted cyan (see Figure 8.12). To take advantage of the stereo view, you must wear a special set of glasses. Anaglyph requires glasses with red and cyan lenses. Other stereo modes, such checkerboard or horizontal interlace, require their own specialized glasses; these modes are discussed in the previous section.

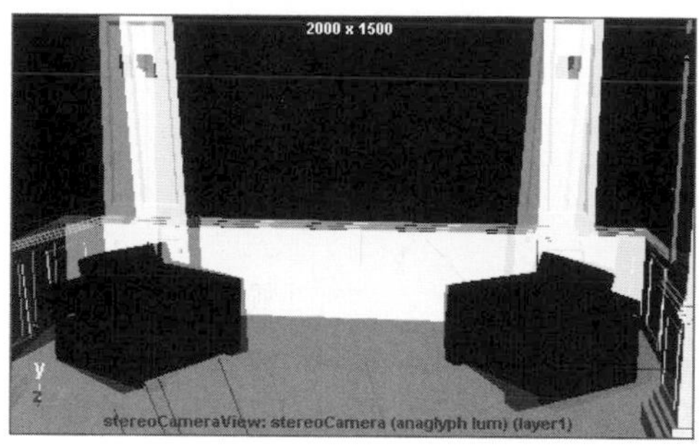

Figure 8.12

The Anaglyph mode, as seen in a panel view. For a color version of this figure, see the color insert. The sample file is included as `room_final.ma` on the DVD.

3. Two of the available modes require no glasses: Freeview (Parallel) and Freeview (Crossed). These modes place the left and right views side by side. Freeview (Parallel) places the left view on the left, and the right view on the right, and is useful for examining the views without any overlapping. With the Freeview (Crossed) mode, you can see the three-dimensional effect by softly crossing your eyes; the three-dimensional view appears in the center as a third view. Freeview (Crossed) places the left view on the right, and the right view on the left.

When rendering, the Render View applies the stereo mode to the rendered result. You also have the option of rendering the left view or right view by itself by choosing Render → Render → stereoCamera Rig → *view*. When batch rendering, you have the option to render the stereo mode as single frame, in which the left and right views are combined. You can also render the left and right views as separate images or render out one view by itself. To do so, set the Renderable Camera menu, in the Common tab of the Render Settings window, to the appropriate option. If you set the menu to stereoCamera, the left and right views will be combined into a single frame.

After you've switched to a stereo camera, it may be necessary to adjust the camera's options to make the three-dimensional effect visible and comfortable to view. Interaxial Separation and Zero Parallax, found in the Stereo section of the camera's Attribute Editor tab, are the most critical settings. Interaxial Separation controls the distance that separates the left and right view cameras in world space. An optimum value matches the distance between the viewer's real-world eyes. In contrast, Zero Parallax determines the distance from the camera that causes objects to create zero parallax. Objects that create zero parallax appear as if they are on the surface of the screen. Objects with positive parallax appear to float in front of the screen. Objects with negative parallax appear to be behind the screen.

The addition of a stereoscopic camera concludes step 2 of this project. I encourage you to revisit the early projects in this book and apply some of the techniques discussed in the later chapters.

About the Companion DVD

- **What you'll find on the DVD**
- **System requirements**
- **Using the DVD**
- **Troubleshooting**

This appendix summarizes the content you'll find on the DVD. If you need help with copying the items provided on the DVD, refer to the installation instructions in thc "Using the DVD" section of this appendix.

What You'll Find on the DVD

You will find all the files for completing the tutorials and understanding concepts in this book in the `ProjectFiles` directory on the DVD. In addition, color versions of the chapter figures are located in the `ColorFigures` folder.

The project files are located in the following directory structure:

`ProjectFiles\Projectn\`: Maya scene files

`ProjectFiles\Projectn\Textures\`: Bitmap textures

`ProjectFiles\Projectn\Reference\`: Maya scene files and bitmap textures that serve as reference but are not mandatory for the success of each tutorial

When opening sample Maya scene files, you can avoid missing bitmap textures by first choosing File → Project → Set and browsing for the `ProjectFiles/Projectn` folder, where *n* is the project number. Follow this step whether the folder remains at its original location on the DVD or is located on a drive after the DVD contents have been copied. You can also reload missing bitmap textures through the Hypershade window; techniques for accomplishing this are discussed in Chapter 1.

Working with files directly from the DVD is not encouraged because Maya scenes link to external files such as texture maps and dynamic caches. Copy the entire project for each chapter to your local drive, including the empty folders, to ensure that the example scenes function properly.

Please check the book's website at `www.sybex.com/go/msptexturelight`, where we'll post updates that supplement this book should the need arise.

System Requirements

You will need to be running Maya 2011 or 2012 to fully use all the files on the DVD (the software is not included on the DVD). Make sure your computer meets the minimum system requirements shown in the following list. If your computer doesn't match up to these requirements, you may have problems using the files on the companion DVD. For the latest information, please refer to the `ReadMe` file located at the root of the DVD-ROM.

- A computer running Microsoft Windows 7, Windows XP (SP2 or newer), Windows Vista, or Apple OS X 10.5.2 or newer
- An Internet connection
- A DVD-ROM drive
- Apple QuickTime 7 or later (Download the latest version from `www.quicktime.com`.)

For the latest information on the system requirements for Maya, go to `www.autodesk.com/maya`. Although you can find specific hardware recommendations there, you can also see some general information that will help you determine whether you're already set up to run

Maya: You need a fast processor, a minimum 2 GB of RAM, and a "workstation graphics card" for the best compatibility (rather than a consumer-grade gaming video card).

This DVD does not include the Maya software. You will need to have Maya 2011 or 2012 installed on your computer to complete the exercises in the book.

Using the DVD

For best results, you'll want to copy the files from your DVD to your computer. To copy the items from the DVD to your hard drive, follow these steps:

1. Insert the DVD into your computer's DVD-ROM drive. The license agreement appears.

Windows users: The interface won't launch if Autorun is disabled. In that case, choose Start → Run (for Windows Vista and Windows 7, choose Start → All Programs → Accessories → Run). In the dialog box that appears, type `D:\Start.exe`. (Replace D with the proper letter if your DVD drive uses a different letter. If you don't know the letter, see how your DVD drive is listed under My Computer.) Click OK.

2. Read through the license agreement, and then click the Accept button if you want to use the DVD.

The DVD interface appears. The interface allows you to access the content with just one or two clicks. Alternately, you can access the files at the root directory of your hard drive.

Mac users: The DVD icon will appear on your desktop; double-click the icon to open the DVD, and then navigate to the files you want.

Troubleshooting

Wiley has attempted to provide programs that work on most computers with the minimum system requirements. Alas, your computer may differ, and some programs may not work properly for some reason.

The two likeliest problems are that you don't have enough memory (RAM) for the programs you want to use or that you have other programs running that are affecting the installation or running of a program. If you get an error message such as "Not enough memory" or "Setup cannot continue," try one or more of the following suggestions and then try using the software again:

Turn off any antivirus software running on your computer. Installation programs sometimes mimic virus activity and may make your computer incorrectly believe that it's being infected by a virus.

Close all running programs. The more programs you have running, the less memory is available to other programs. Installation programs typically update files and programs; so if you keep other programs running, installation may not work properly.

Add more RAM to your computer. This is, admittedly, a drastic and somewhat expensive step. However, adding more memory can really help the speed of your computer and allow more programs to run at the same time.

Customer Care

If you have trouble with the book's companion DVD, please call the Wiley Product Technical Support phone number at (800) 762-2974. Outside the United States, call +1 (317) 572-3994. You can also contact Wiley Product Technical Support at `http://sybex.custhelp.com`. John Wiley & Sons will provide technical support only for installation and other general quality control items. For technical support on the applications themselves, consult the program's vendor or author.

To place additional orders or to request information about other Wiley products, please call (877) 762-2974.

Index

Note to the Reader: Throughout this index **boldfaced** page numbers indicate primary discussions of a topic. *Italicized* page numbers indicate illustrations.

S

T

Wiley Publishing, Inc. End-User License Agreement

READ THIS. You should carefully read these terms and conditions before opening the software packet(s) included with this book "Book". This is a license agreement "Agreement" between you and Wiley Publishing, Inc. "WPI". By opening the accompanying software packet(s), you acknowledge that you have read and accept the following terms and conditions. If you do not agree and do not want to be bound by such terms and conditions, promptly return the Book and the unopened software packet(s) to the place you obtained them for a full refund.

1. License Grant. WPI grants to you (either an individual or entity) a nonexclusive license to use one copy of the enclosed software program(s) (collectively, the "Software," solely for your own personal or business purposes on a single computer (whether a standard computer or a workstation component of a multi-user network). The Software is in use on a computer when it is loaded into temporary memory (RAM) or installed into permanent memory (hard disk, CD-ROM, or other storage device). WPI reserves all rights not expressly granted herein.

2. Ownership. WPI is the owner of all right, title, and interest, including copyright, in and to the compilation of the Software recorded on the physical packet included with this Book "Software Media". Copyright to the individual programs recorded on the Software Media is owned by the author or other authorized copyright owner of each program. Ownership of the Software and all proprietary rights relating thereto remain with WPI and its licensers.

3. Restrictions On Use and Transfer. (a) You may only (i) make one copy of the Software for backup or archival purposes, or (ii) transfer the Software to a single hard disk, provided that you keep the original for backup or archival purposes. You may not (i) rent or lease the Software, (ii) copy or reproduce the Software through a LAN or other network system or through any computer subscriber system or bulletin-board system, or (iii) modify, adapt, or create derivative works based on the Software. (b) You may not reverse engineer, decompile, or disassemble the Software. You may transfer the Software and user documentation on a permanent basis, provided that the transferee agrees to accept the terms and conditions of this Agreement and you retain no copies. If the Software is an update or has been updated, any transfer must include the most recent update and all prior versions.

4. Restrictions on Use of Individual Programs. You must follow the individual requirements and restrictions detailed for each individual program in the About the CD-ROM appendix of this Book or on the Software Media. These limitations are also contained in the individual license agreements recorded on the Software Media. These limitations may include a requirement that after using the program for a specified period of time, the user must pay a registration fee or discontinue use. By opening the Software packet(s), you will be agreeing to abide by the licenses and restrictions for these individual programs that are detailed in the About the CD-ROM appendix and/or on the Software Media. None of the material on this Software Media or listed in this Book may ever be redistributed, in original or modified form, for commercial purposes.

5. Limited Warranty. (a) WPI warrants that the Software and Software Media are free from defects in materials and workmanship under normal use for a period of sixty (60) days from the date of purchase of this Book. If WPI receives notification within the warranty period of defects in materials or workmanship, WPI will replace the defective Software Media. (b) WPI AND THE AUTHOR(S) OF THE BOOK DISCLAIM ALL OTHER WARRANTIES, EXPRESS OR IMPLIED, INCLUDING WITHOUT LIMITATION IMPLIED WARRANTIES OF MERCHANTABILITY AND FITNESS FOR A PARTICULAR PURPOSE, WITH RESPECT TO THE SOFTWARE, THE PROGRAMS, THE SOURCE CODE CONTAINED THEREIN, AND/OR THE TECHNIQUES DESCRIBED IN THIS BOOK. WPI DOES NOT WARRANT THAT THE FUNCTIONS CONTAINED IN THE SOFTWARE WILL MEET YOUR REQUIREMENTS OR THAT THE OPERATION OF THE SOFTWARE WILL BE ERROR FREE. (c) This limited warranty gives you specific legal rights, and you may have other rights that vary from jurisdiction to jurisdiction.

6. Remedies. (a) WPI's entire liability and your exclusive remedy for defects in materials and workmanship shall be limited to replacement of the Software Media, which may be returned to WPI with a copy of your receipt at the following address: Software Media Fulfillment Department, Attn.: *Maya Studio Projects: Texturing and Lighting*, Wiley Publishing, Inc., 10475 Crosspoint Blvd., Indianapolis, IN 46256, or call 1-800-762-2974. Please allow four to six weeks for delivery. This Limited Warranty is void if failure of the Software Media has resulted from accident, abuse, or misapplication. Any replacement Software Media will be warranted for the remainder of the original warranty period or thirty (30) days, whichever is longer. (b) In no event shall WPI or the author be liable for any damages whatsoever (including without limitation damages for loss of business profits, business interruption, loss of business information, or any other pecuniary loss) arising from the use of or inability to use the Book or the Software, even if WPI has been advised of the possibility of such damages. (c) Because some jurisdictions do not allow the exclusion or limitation of liability for consequential or incidental damages, the above limitation or exclusion may not apply to you.

7. U.S. Government Restricted Rights. Use, duplication, or disclosure of the Software for or on behalf of the United States of America, its agencies and/or instrumentalities "U.S. Government" is subject to restrictions as stated in paragraph (c)(1)(ii) of the Rights in Technical Data and Computer Software clause of DFARS 252.227-7013, or subparagraphs (c) (1) and (2) of the Commercial Computer Software - Restricted Rights clause at FAR 52.227-19, and in similar clauses in the NASA FAR supplement, as applicable.

8. General. This Agreement constitutes the entire understanding of the parties and revokes and supersedes all prior agreements, oral or written, between them and may not be modified or amended except in a writing signed by both parties hereto that specifically refers to this Agreement. This Agreement shall take precedence over any other documents that may be in conflict herewith. If any one or more provisions contained in this Agreement are held by any court or tribunal to be invalid, illegal, or otherwise unenforceable, each and every other provision shall remain in full force and effect.